WOMEN
WRITE

Also by Susan Cahill

~ NONFICTION ~

The Smiles of Rome

For the Love of Ireland
A Literary Companion for Readers and Travelers

Desiring Italy
Women Writers Celebrate a Country

A Literary Guide to Ireland
(with Thomas Cahill)

~ FICTION ~

Earth Angels

~ ANTHOLOGIES ~

QPB Anthology of Women's Writing
From the 14th Century to the Present

Wise Women
2,000 Years of Spiritual Writing by Women

Writing Women's Lives
*Autobiographical Narratives by
20th-Century American Women Writers*

Growing Up Female
Stories from the American Mosaic

Women and Fiction
Short Stories by and about Women

The Urban Reader
(with Michele F. Cooper)

WOMEN WRITE

A MOSAIC OF WOMEN'S VOICES IN FICTION, POETRY, MEMOIR, AND ESSAY

Edited and with an Introduction by
Susan Cahill, PhD

NAL BOOKS

NEW AMERICAN LIBRARY

New American Library
Published by New American Library, a division of
Penguin Group (USA) Inc., 375 Hudson Street,
New York, New York 10014, U.S.A.
Penguin Books Ltd, 80 Strand,
London WC2R 0RL, England
Penguin Books Australia Ltd, 250 Camberwell Road,
Camberwell, Victoria 3124, Australia
Penguin Books Canada Ltd, 10 Alcorn Avenue,
Toronto, Ontario, Canada M4V 3B2
Penguin Books (N.Z.) Ltd, Cnr Rosedale and Airborne Roads,
Albany, Auckland 1310, New Zealand

Penguin Books Ltd, Registered Offices:
80 Strand, London WC2R 0RL, England

First published by New American Library,
a division of Penguin Group (USA) Inc.

First Printing, April 2004
10 9 8 7 6 5 4 3 2 1

(Author copyrights and permissions can be found on pages 311–314.)

⊛ REGISTERED TRADEMARK—MARCA REGISTRADA

Library of Congress Cataloging-in-Publication Data:

Women write : a mosaic of women's voices in fiction, poetry, memoir, and essay / edited and with
an introduction by Susan Cahill.
    p. cm.
   ISBN 0-451-21121-9
  1. English literature—Women authors. 2. American literature—Women authors. 3.
Women—Literary collections. 4. Women—Biography. 5. Women. I. Cahill, Susan Neunzig.
PR 1110.W6W658 2004
820.8'09287—dc22   2004040200

Set in Galliard

Printed in the United States of America

for Catherine de Vinck
poet,
friend

CONTENTS

INTRODUCTION

The stories, poems, memoirs, and essays in this book represent a sampling of the best writing in English by women on both sides of the Atlantic since the mid-seventeenth century. That's when Anne Bradstreet, a pioneer everywoman up against an alien wilderness, became colonial America's first poet to make it into print.

In *Women Write*'s selected legacy, published writing spanning five centuries, you hear a distinctive voice. Readers will describe it differently, pick up on different modulations and dynamics. But through all the themes and variations, the voice carries, the effect of a writer's pitch-perfect ear. Through five centuries, out of an American, British, and Irish cultural mosaic, what comes across is each writer's contemplation of her particular world and how people live in it, making choices—or not—for better and worse. Some writers challenge the reader to change her life, or at least to rethink its assumptions, not to get stuck. Subversive points of view, though never soothing, are always invigorating, the voice strong.

Vladimir Nabokov said a good reader was someone who writes in the margins, folds down pages, underlines, has a conversation, or an argument, with the author, rather than just sitting back and having the story happen to her. The writers in this short book have the power to stir the willing reader to full, sometimes uneasy consciousness. We catch moments of insight, experience a glimpse of something new on the moral horizon.

For literature sees things the way they are, sounding the wide and deep and mysteriously paradoxical dimensions of human experience; it swings between the polarities of love and hate; hope and despair; life and death. Arriving at the dark places of women's lives, seeing the wastelands and dead ends, we wonder: Is there a more tragic story in American literature than Willa Cather's "A Wagner Matinée"? When a particular work is conceived in a generous or visionary imagination, it throws some light on the hard landscape—without denying the dark—as in the poetry of Mary Oliver, or in Mary Lavin's story "Happiness." Lorrie Moore's fiction is a quickening art, as indefinable as music. There's social comedy in Edith Wharton and a rebel wit in Aphra Behn and Angela Carter, a lovely sensuality of tone and image in the poetry of June Jordan, Sharon Olds. In the work of Tillie Olsen, Nadine Gordimer, and Denise Levertov—to name only a few—there's a bold resistance to the social and political forces that crush people.

Writing that is produced as a simultaneous act of resistance and of a determined self-affirmation is not just a modern phenomenon. Since the beginning of women's recorded literary history—the medieval English mystic Julian of Norwich was the first to be published—it has been spiritual experience, despite the patriarchal structures of religious institutions, that has often acted as a catalyst in liberating women's consciousness and creativity, awakening the courage to confront all that diminishes us as persons. You can feel the reverberations of this experience particularly in the work of African-American women writers of the last two centuries. What novelist A. S. Byatt says of Toni Morrison, that the religious imagination of the community empowers her writing, is also true of Maya Angelou (and Lucille Clifton and Rita Dove) and the earlier voices of Harriet Jacobs and Frances Harper who protest slavery, daring their narratives of freedom before the Civil War.

We, Nabokov's active readers, are the partners of these writers. As they imagine their understandings concerning identity and selfhood and our common humanity and also show the frightening costs of these—Alice Munro, Sandra Cisneros—we make the effort to follow them, across old boundaries, through the many layers of time and place and traditional roles to be found in this book's contents. We feel their recognitions and revelations. In their laments and dissonant protests and major key celebrations—*Women Write* sustains a spirited polyphony—you might not discern your own exact experience. What you will find in this lively selection is a kind of prophecy, a concrete circumstantial wisdom showing the possibility—or impossibility—of freedom, of a deeper consciousness; we hear the writers urging us, artfully, to join them as they reread and revise the cultural scripts that sap the spirit. The prize for cooperating with this intensely moral endeavor is a charge of new life. A few writers—Cynthia Ozick, Alice Walker—declare the importance of reading to the making of free women. But all of them invite us to desire more generous alternatives to some of the closed and cruel worlds we were born into.

In her poem "In Distrust of Merits," Marianne Moore had World War II in mind:

> Hate-hardened heart, O heart of iron,
> Iron is iron until it is rust.
> There never was a war that was
> not inward

The fifty or so writers gathered here, women of imagination, spark our sympathy, moving us toward what—and who—is beyond the self. Eudora Welty, in her character Old Phoenix, Grace Paley as her young self—all these women show us our affiliations, that we are joined to others, and are more like them than different from them. Flexible, funny, and smart, these artists *know*: We should cut one another some slack. Their writings help to make us human, to feel what those words might mean.

As an editor working the centuries-old territory of writing by women, I haven't traveled solo. Sifting this vast and varied treasure, I've welcomed the suggestions of friends, other editors, critics, readers, and the students with whom I've read much of this work in college classrooms of New York City. All of us respect certain writings as classics, certain writers as "among the best." They're included here. Emily Dickinson, Toni Morrison, Alice Munro. In a book even as short as this one, some names are simply *musts*.

I've left out many writers who are widely anthologized (Elizabeth Barrett Browning, Charlotte Perkins Gilman, Shirley Jackson). Writers who are primarily novelists—Jane Austen, the Brontës, George Eliot, Doris Lessing, Elizabeth Bowen, Mary McCarthy, Margaret Atwood, Jeannette Winterson, Margaret Drabble, Hannah Green, Hilary Mantel, to name a few—are enjoyed most in their novels.

This book is no doorstop; it was never meant to duplicate the *Norton Anthology of Literature by Women*. A shorter version of my *QPB Anthology of Women's Writing, Women Write* offers a modest but rich taste of highlights, some favorites of passionate readers.

—Susan Neunzig Cahill, PhD
New York City, 2003

WOMEN WRITE

ANNE BRADSTREET
(1612–72)

Leaving behind a leisured life and a good library in Lincolnshire, Anne Brad-street followed her father and husband into the Puritan wilderness of the Massachusetts Bay Colony. While bearing and raising eight children in this strange new world of sickness, savage weather, and fire, which destroyed life and homes on a regular basis, she wrote poetry. When her brother-in-law made a trip back to London, he brought along her manuscripts, which were published as *The Tenth Muse, Lately Sprung Up in America* (1650), making Bradstreet the author of the first book of original poems produced in America.

---

from
The Vanity of All Worldly Things

There is a path no vulture's eye hath seen,
Where lion fierce, nor lion's whelps have been,
Which leads unto that living crystal fount,
Who drinks thereof, the world doth nought account.
The depth and sea have said "'tis not in me,"
With pearl and gold it shall not valued be.
For sapphire, onyx, topaz who would change;
It's hid from eyes of men, they count it strange.
Death and destruction the fame hath heard,
But where and what it is, from heaven's declared;
It brings to honour which shall ne'er decay,
It stores with wealth which time can't wear away.
It yieldeth pleasures far beyond conceit,
And truly beautifies without deceit.
Nor strength, nor wisdom, nor fresh youth shall fade,
Nor death shall see, but are immortal made.
This pearl of price, this tree of life, this spring,
Who is possessed of shall reign a king.
Nor change of state nor cares shall ever see,
But wear his crown unto eternity.
This satiates the soul, this stays the mind,
And all the rest, but vanity we find.

The Prologue

I am obnoxious to each carping tongue
Who says my hand a needle better fits,
A poet's pen all scorn I should thus wrong,
For such despite they cast on female wits:
If what I do prove well, it won't advance,
They'll say it's stol'n, or else it was by chance.

But sure the antique Greeks were far more mild
Else of our sex, why feigned they those nine
And poesy made Calliope's own child;
So 'mongst the rest they placed the arts divine:
But this weak knot they will full soon untie,
The Greeks did nought, but play the fools and lie.

Let Greeks be Greeks, and women what they are
Men have precedency and still excel,
It is but vain unjustly to wage war;
Men can do best, and women know it well.
Preeminence in all and each is yours;
Yet grant some small acknowledgement of ours.

And oh ye high flown quills that soar the skies,
And ever with your prey still catch your praise,
If e'er you deign these lowly lines your eyes,
Give thyme or parsley wreath, I ask no bays;
This mean and unrefined ore of mine
Will make your glist'ring gold but ore to shine.

MARGARET CAVENDISH,
DUCHESS OF NEWCASTLE
(1623–74)

"Mad Margaret" was scorned as a child for the shyness that kept her tongue-tied and as a woman for her unconventional outfits, hairdos, and having the nerve to write books. In his diary Pepys called her husband, who encouraged her writing, an "ass" for "suffering" his wife's habit. She produced at a furious rate: letters, poems, plays, a biography of the beloved husband, philosophical studies in which she denounced the trivialization of women's lives. Virginia Woolf praised Mad Margaret's wit and ridiculed her dull-minded critics.

Mirth and Melancholy

Melancholy

Her voice is low and gives a hollow sound;
She hates the light and is in darkness found
Or sits with blinking lamps, or tapers small,
Which various shadows make against the wall.
She loves nought else but noise which discord makes;
As croaking frogs whose dwelling is in lakes;
The raven's hoarse, the mandrake's hollow groan
And shrieking owls which fly i' the night alone;
The tolling bell, which for the dead rings out;
A mill, where rushing waters run about;
The roaring winds, which shake the cedars tall,
Plough up the seas, and beat the rocks withal.
She loves to walk in the still moonshine night,
And in a thick dark grove she takes delight;
In hollow caves, thatched houses, and low cells
She loves to live, and there alone she dwells.

Mirth

I dwell in groves that gilt are with the sun;
Sit on the banks by which clear waters run;
In summers hot down in a shade I lie,
My music is the buzzing of a fly;

I walk in meadows where grows fresh green grass;
In fields where corn is high I often pass;
Walk up the hills, where round I prospects see,
Some bushy woods, and some all champaigns be;
Returning back, I in fresh pastures go,
To hear how sheep do bleat, and cows do low;
In winter cold, when nipping frosts come on,
Then do I live in a small house alone.

APHRA BEHN
(1640–89)

A widow, Mrs. Behn supported herself by writing and working for the government. A staunch supporter of the Stuarts, she was a spy for Charles II in Antwerp, did time in debtor's prison, and in the annals of literary history is considered England's first professional woman writer. One "novel," *Oroonoko*, is a passionate protest against the institution of slavery, which she observed firsthand on a visit to the West Indies. Her poems and plays were frankly erotic, provoking lampoons—she was "that lewd harlot" who deserved her poverty and illness. But when she died, she was honored with burial in Westminster Abbey under the name of Astrea Behn.

The Willing Mistress
This is a song from Behn's play *The Dutch Lover*

Amyntas led me to a grove,
    Where all the trees did shade us;
The sun itself, though it had strove,
    It could not have betrayed us.
The place secured from human eyes
    No other fear allows
But when the winds that gently rise
    Do kiss the yielding boughs.

Down there we sat upon the moss,
    And did begin to play
A thousand amorous tricks, to pass
    The heat of all the day.
A many kisses did he give
    And I returned the same,
Which made me willing to receive
    That which I dare not name.

His charming eyes no aid required
    To tell their softening tale;
On her that was already fired,
    'Twas easy to prevail.

> He did but kiss and clasp me round,
> Whilst those his thoughts expressed:
> And laid me gently on the ground;
> Ah who can guess the rest?

The Adventure of the Black Lady

About the beginning of last June (as near as I can remember) Bellamora came to town from Hampshire, and was obliged to lodge the first night at the same inn where the stage coach set up. The next day she took coach for Covent Garden, where she thought to find Madam Brightly, a relation of hers, with whom she designed to continue for about half a year undiscovered, if possible, by her friends in the country; and ordered therefore her trunk, with her clothes, and most of her money and jewels, to be brought after her to Madam Brightly's by a strange porter, whom she spoke to in the street as she was taking coach, being utterly unacquainted with the neat practices of this fine city. When she came to Bridges Street, where indeed her cousin had lodged near three or four years since, she was strangely surprised that she could not learn anything of her; no, nor so much as meet with anyone that had ever heard of her cousin's name; till, at last, describing Madam Brightly to one of the housekeepers in that place, he told her, that there was such a kind of lady, whom he had sometimes seen there about a year and a half ago, but that he believed she was married and removed towards Soho. In this perplexity she quite forgot her trunk and money, etc, and wandered in her hackney coach all over St Anne's parish, inquiring for Madam Brightly, still describing her person, but in vain, for no soul could give her any tale or tidings of such a lady. After she had thus fruitlessly rambled, till she, the coachman, and the very horses were even tired, by good fortune for her, she happened on a private house where lived a good, discreet, ancient gentlewoman, who was fallen to decay, and forced to let lodgings for the best part of her livelihood; from whom she understood, that there was such a kind of lady, who had lain there somewhat more than a twelvemonth, being near three months after she was married; but that she was now gone abroad with the gentleman her husband, either to the play, or to take the fresh air; and she believed would not return till night. This discourse of the good gentlewoman's so elevated Bellamora's drooping spirits that after she had begged the liberty of staying there till they came home, she discharged the coachman in all haste, still forgetting her trunk, and the more valuable furniture of it.

When they were alone, Bellamora desired she might be permitted the freedom to send for a pint of sack, which, with some little difficulty, was at last allowed her. They began then to chat for a matter of half an hour of things indifferent; and at length the ancient gentlewoman asked the fair innocent (I must not say foolish) one, of what country, and what her name was: to both which she answered directly and truly, though it might have proved not discreetly. She then enquired of Bellamora if her parents were living, and the occasion of her coming to town. The fair unthinking creature replied, that her father and mother were both dead, and that she had escaped from her uncle, under the pretence of making a visit to a young lady, her cousin, who was lately married, and lived above twenty miles from her uncle's, in the road to London, and that the cause of her quitting the country was to avoid the hated importunities of a gentleman, whose pretended love to her she feared had been her eternal ruin. At which she wept and sighed most extravagantly. The discreet gentlewoman endeavoured to comfort her by all the softest and most powerful arguments in her capacity, promising her all the friendly assistance that she could expect from her, during Bellamora's stay in town; which she did with so much earnestness, and visible integrity, that the pretty innocent creature was going to make her a full and real discovery of her imaginary insupportable misfortunes; and (doubtless) had done it, had she not been prevented by the return of the lady, whom she hoped to have found her cousin Brightly. The gentleman, her husband, just saw her within doors, and ordered the coach to drive to some of his bottle companions, which gave the women the better opportunity of entertaining one another, which happened to be with some surprise on all sides. As the lady was going up into her apartment, the gentlewoman of the house told her there was a young lady in the parlour, who came out of the country that very day on purpose to visit her; the lady stepped immediately to see who it was, and Bellamora approaching to receive her hoped-for cousin, stopped on the sudden just as she came to her, and sighed out aloud, "Ah, madam! I am lost—it is not your ladyship I seek." "No, madam," returned the other, "I am apt to think you did not intend me this honour. But you are as welcome to me, as you could be to the dearest of your acquaintance. Have you forgot me, Madam Bellamora?" continued she. That name startled the other. However, it was with a kind of joy. "Alas! Madam," replied the young one, "I now remember that I have been so happy to have seen you, but where and when, my memory can't tell me." " 'Tis indeed some years since," return'd the lady, "but of that another time. Meanwhile, if you are unprovided of a lodging, I dare undertake, you shall be welcome to this gentlewoman." The unfortunate returned her thanks; and whilst a chamber was preparing for her, the lady entertained her in her own. About ten o'clock they parted, Bellamora being conducted to her lodging by the mistress of the house, who then left her to take what rest she could amidst her so many misfortunes, returning to the other lady, who desired her to search into the cause of Bellamora's retreat to town.

The next morning the good gentlewoman of the house, coming up to her, found Bellamora almost drowned in tears, which by many kind and sweet words she at last stopped; and, asking whence so great signs of sorrow should proceed, vowed a most profound secrecy if she would discover to her their occasion; which, after some little reluctancy, she did, in this manner.

"I was courted," said she, "above three years ago, when my mother was yet living, by one Mr Fondlove, a gentleman of good estate, and true worth; and one who, I dare believe, did then really love me. He continued his passion for me, with all the earnest and honest solicitations imaginable, till some months before my mother's death, who, at that time, was most desirous to see me disposed of in marriage to another gentleman, of much better estate than Mr Fondlove, but one whose person and humour did by no means hit with my inclinations; and this gave Fondlove the unhappy advantage over me. For, finding me one day all alone in my chamber, and lying on my bed, in as mournful and wretched a condition to my then foolish apprehension, as now I am, he urged his passion with such violence and accursed success for me, with reiterated promises of marriage whensoever I pleased to challenge them, which he bound with the most sacred oaths, and most dreadful execrations that, partly with my aversion to the other, and partly with my inclinations to pity him, I ruined myself." Here she relapsed into a greater extravagance of grief than before, which was so extreme that it did not continue long. When therefore she was pretty well come to herself, the ancient gentlewoman asked her, why she imagined herself ruined. To which she answered, "I am great with child by him, madam, and wonder you did not perceive it last night. Alas! I have not a month to go. I am ashamed, ruined, and damned, I fear, for ever lost." "Oh! fie, madam, think not so," said the other, "for the gentleman may yet prove true, and marry you." "Ay, madam," replied Bellamora, "I doubt not that he would marry me; for soon after my mother's death, when I came to be at my own disposal, which happened about two months after, he offered, nay most earnestly solicited me to it, which still he perseveres to do." "This is strange!" returned the other, "and it appears to me to be your own fault that you are yet miserable. Why did you not or why will you not consent to your own happiness?" "Alas!" cried Bellamora, "'tis the only thing I dread in this world. For, I am certain, he can never love me after. Besides, ever since I have abhorred the sight of him, and this is the only cause that obliges me to forsake my uncle, and all my friends and relations in the country, hoping in this populous and public place to be most private, especially, madam, in your house, and in your fidelity and discretion." "Of the last you may assure yourself, madam," said the other, "but what provision have you made for the reception of the young stranger that you carry about you?" "Ah, madam!" cried Bellamora, "you have brought to my mind another misfortune." Then she acquainted her with the supposed loss of her money and jewels, telling her withal, that she had but three guineas and some silver left, and the rings she wore, in her present possession. The good gentlewoman of the house told her she would send to enquire at the inn where she lay the first night she came to town; for, haply, they might give some account of the porter to whom she had entrusted her trunk; and withal repeated her promise of all the help in her power, and for that time left her much more composed than she found her. The good gentlewoman went directly to the other lady, her lodger, to whom she recounted Bellamora's mournful confession; at which the lady appeared mightily concerned: and at last she told her landlady, that she would take care that Bellamora should lie in according to her quality. "For," added she, "the child, it seems, is my own brother's."

As soon as she had dined, she went to the Exchange, and brought childbed linen, but desired that Bellamora might not have the least notice of it. And at her return dispatched a letter to her brother Fondlove in Hampshire, with an account of every particular; which soon brought him up to town, without satisfying any of his or her friends with the reason of his sudden departure. Meanwhile, the good gentlewoman of the house had sent to the Star Inn on Fish Street Hill, to demand the trunk, which she rightly supposed to have been carried back thither. For, by good luck, it was a fellow that plied thereabouts who brought it to Bellamora's lodgings that very night, but unknown to her. Fondlove no sooner got to London, but he posts to his sister's lodgings, where he was advised not to be seen of Bellamora till they had worked farther upon her, which the landlady began in this manner. She told her that her things were miscarried and, she feared, lost; that she had but a little money herself, and if the overseers of the poor (justly so called from their over-looking them) should have the least suspicion of a stranger and unmarried person who was entertained in her house big with child, and so near her time as Bellamora was, she should be troubled, if they could not give security to the parish of twenty or thirty pounds that they should not suffer by her, which she could not; or otherwise she must be sent to the house of correction, and her child to a parish nurse. This discourse, one may imagine, was very dreadful to a person of her youth, beauty, education, family and estate. However, she resolutely protested that she had rather undergo all this than be exposed to the scorn of her friends and relations in the country. The other told her then that she must write down to her uncle a farewell letter, as if she were just going aboard the packet-boat for Holland, that he might not send to enquire for her in town, when he should understand she was not at her new-married cousin's in the country; which accordingly she did, keeping herself close prisoner to her chamber, where she was daily visited by Fondlove's sister and the landlady, but by no soul else, the first dissembling the knowledge she had of her misfortunes.

Thus she continued for above three weeks, not a servant being suffered to enter her chamber, so much as to make her bed, lest they should take notice of her great belly; but for all this caution, the secret had taken wind, by the means of an attendant of the other lady below, who had overheard her speaking of it to her husband. This soon got out of doors, and spread abroad, till it reached the long ears of the wolves of the parish, who, next day, designed to pay her a visit. But

Fondlove, by good providence, prevented it; who, the night before, was ushered in Bellamora's chamber by his sister, his brother-in-law, and the landlady. At the sight of him she had like to have swooned away, but he, taking her in his arms, began again, as he was wont to do, with tears in his eyes, to beg that she would marry him ere she was delivered; if not for his, nor her own, yet for the child's sake, which she hourly expected, that it might not be born out of wedlock, and so be made uncapable of inheriting either of their estates; with a great many more pressing arguments on all sides, to which at last she consented; and an honest officious gentleman, whom they had before provided, was called up, who made an end of the dispute. So to bed they went together that night; next day to the Exchange, for several pretty businesses that ladies in her condition want. Whilst they were abroad, came the vermin of the parish (I mean, the overseers of the poor, who eat the bread from them) to search for a young blackhaired lady (for so was Bellamora) who was either brought to bed, or just ready to lie down. The landlady showed them all the rooms in her house, but no such lady could be found. At last she bethought herself, and led them into her parlour, where she opened a little closet door, and showed them a black cat that had just kittened, assuring them that she should never trouble the parish as long as she had rats or mice in the house; and so dismissed them like loggerheads as they came.

LADY MARY WORTLEY MONTAGU
(1689–1762)

Essayist, dramatist, and journalist, Lady Mary declared at twenty, "I believe more follies are committed out of complaisance to the world than in following our own inclinations. I am amazed to see that people of good sense in other things can make their happiness consist in the opinion of others." Impulsively, she eloped with Mr. Montagu; the marriage was unhappy. After her death, her daughter, Lady Bute, who was not cut from the same bold cloth, burned her mother's journal. Lady Mary's letters—which fill three volumes—were thought superior to Madame de Sévigné's by Voltaire; Smollett, Dr. Johnson, and Byron praised their brilliance. "Her wit," said Lytton Strachey, "has that quality which is the best of all preservatives against dullness—it goes straight to the point."

---

from
The Letters of Lady Mary Wortley Montagu
To Mr. Wortley Montagu

[Indorsed "24th November," 1714.]

I have taken up and laid down my pen several times, very much unresolved in what stile I ought to write to you: for once I suffer my inclination to get the better of my reason. I have not oft opportunities of indulging myself, and I will do it in this one letter. I know very well that nobody was ever teized into a liking: and 'tis perhaps harder to revive a past one, than to overcome an aversion; but I cannot forbear any longer telling you, I think you use me very unkindly. I don't say so much of your absence, as I should do if you was in the country and I in London; because I would not have you believe I am impatient to be in town, when I say I am impatient to be with you; but I am very sensible I parted with you in July and 'tis now the middle of November. As if this was not hardship enough, you do not tell me you are sorry for it. You write seldom, and with so much indifference as shews you hardly think of me at all. I complain of ill health, and you only say you hope 'tis not so bad as I make it. You never enquire after your child. I would fain flatter myself you have more kindness for me and him than you express; but I reflect with grief a man that is ashamed of

11

passions that are natural and reasonable, is generally proud of those that [are] shameful and silly.

You should consider solitude, and spleen the consequence of solitude, is apt to give the most melancholy ideas, and there needs at least tender letters and kind expressions to hinder uneasinesses almost inseparable from absence. I am very sensible, how far I ought to be contented when your affairs oblige you to be without me. I would not have you do them any prejudice; but a little kindness will cost you nothing. I do not bid you lose any thing by hasting to see me, but I would have you think it a misfortune when we are asunder. Instead of that, you seem perfectly pleased with our separation, and indifferent how long it continues. When I reflect on all your behaviour, I am ashamed of my own: I think I am playing the part of my Lady Winchester. At least be as generous as my lord; and as he made her an early confession of his aversion, own to me your inconstancy, and upon my word I will give you no more trouble about it. I have concealed as long as I can, the uneasiness the nothingness of your letters has given me, under an affected indifference; but dissimulation always sits awkwardly upon me; I am weary of it; and must beg you to write to me no more, if you cannot bring yourself to write otherwise. Multiplicity of business or diversions may have engaged you, but all people find time to do what they have a mind to. If your inclination is gone, I had rather never receive a letter from you, than one which, in lieu of comfort for your absence, gives me a pain even beyond it. For my part, as 'tis my first, this is my last complaint, and your next of the kind shall go back enclosed to you in blank paper.

To Lady Bute*

Gottolengo, January 1750

MY DEAR CHILD,

I am extremely concerned to hear you complain of ill health at a time of life when you ought to be in the flower of your strength. I hope I need not recommend to you the care of it. The tenderness you have for your children is sufficient to enforce you to the utmost regard for the preservation of a life so necessary to their well-being. I do not doubt your prudence in their education; neither can I say anything particular relating to it at this distance, different tempers requiring

*Lady Mary's daughter

different management. In general, never attempt to govern them (as most people do) by deceit. If they find themselves cheated (even in trifles) it will so far lessen the authority of their instructor as to make them neglect all their future admonitions. And (if possible) breed them free from prejudices; those contracted in the nursery often influence the whole life after, of which I have seen many melancholy examples.

I shall say no more of this subject, nor would have said this little if you had not asked my advice. 'Tis much easier to give rules than to practise them. I am sensible my own natural temper is too indulgent. I think it the least dangerous error, yet still it is an error. I can only say with truth that I do not know in my whole life having ever endeavoured to impose on you or give a false colour to anything that I represented to you. If your daughters are inclined to love reading, do not check their inclination by hindering them of the diverting part of it. It is as necessary for the amusement of women as the reputation of men; but teach them not to expect or desire any applause from it. Let their brothers shine, and let them content themselves with making their lives easier by it, which I experimentally know is more effectually done by study than any other way. Ignorance is as much the fountain of vice as idleness, and indeed generally produces it. People that do not read or work for a livelihood have many hours they know not how to employ, especially women, who commonly fall into vapours or something worse. I am afraid you'll think this letter very tedious. Forgive it as coming from your most affectionate mother,

M.W.

My compliments to Lord Bute and blessing to my grandchildren.

To Lady Bute

Gottolengo, 28 January 1753

DEAR CHILD,

You have given me a great deal of satisfaction by your account of your eldest daughter. I am particularly pleased to hear she is a good arithmetician; it is the best proof of understanding. The knowledge of numbers is one of the chief distinctions between us and brutes. If there is anything in blood you may reasonably expect your children should be endowed with an uncommon share of good sense. Mr

Wortley's family and mine have both produced some of the greatest men that have been born in England. I mean Admiral Sandwich, and my great-grandfather who was distinguished by the name of Wise William. I have heard Lord Bute's father mentioned as an extraordinary genius (though he had not many opportunities of showing it), and his uncle the present Duke of Argyle has one of the best heads I ever knew.

I will therefore speak to you as supposing Lady Mary not only capable but desirous of learning. In that case, by all means let her be indulged in it. You will tell me, I did not make it a part of your education. Your prospect was very different from hers, as you had no defect either in mind or person to hinder, and much in your circumstances to attract, the highest offers. It seemed your business to learn how to live in the world, as it is hers to know how to be easy out of it. It is the common error of builders and parents to follow some plan they think beautiful (and perhaps is so) without considering that nothing is beautiful that is misplaced. Hence we see so many edifices raised that the raisers can never inhabit, being too large for their fortunes. Vistas are laid open over barren heaths, and apartments contrived for a coolness very agreeable in Italy but killing in the north of Britain. Thus every woman endeavours to breed her daughter a fine lady, qualifying her for a station in which she will never appear, and at the same time incapacitating her for that retirement to which she is destined. Learning (if she has a real taste for it) will not only make her contented but happy in it. No entertainment is so cheap as reading, nor any pleasure so lasting. She will not want new fashions nor regret the loss of expensive diversions or variety of company if she can be amused with an author in her closet. To render this amusement extensive, she should be permitted to learn the languages. I have heard it lamented that boys lose so many years in mere learning of words. This is no objection to a girl, whose time is not so precious. She cannot advance herself in any profession, and has therefore more hours to spare; and as you say her memory is good she will be very agreeably employed this way.

There are two cautions to be given on this subject: first, not to think herself learned when she can read Latin or even Greek. Languages are more properly to be called vehicles of learning than learning itself, as may be observed in many schoolmasters, who though perhaps critics in grammar are the most ignorant fellows upon earth. True knowledge consists in knowing things, not words. I would wish her no further a linguist than to enable her to read books in their originals, that are often corrupted and always injured by translations. Two hours application every morning will bring this about much sooner than you can imagine, and she will have leisure enough beside to run over the English poetry, which is a more important part of a woman's education than it is generally supposed. Many a young damsel has been ruined by a fine copy of verses, which she would have laughed at if she had known it had been stolen from Mr Waller. I remember when I was a girl I saved one of my companions from destruction, who communicated to me an epistle she was quite charmed with. As she had a natural good taste she observed the lines were not so smooth as Prior's or Pope's, but had more thought and spirit than any of theirs. She was wonderfully delighted with such a demonstration of her lover's sense and passion, and not a little pleased with her own charms, that had force enough to inspire such elegancies. In the midst of this triumph I showed her they were taken from Randolph's *Poems*, and the unfortunate transcriber was dismissed with the scorn he deserved. To say truth, the poor plagiary was very unlucky to fall into my hands; that author, being no longer in fashion, would have escaped anyone of less universal reading than myself. You should encourage your daughter to talk over with you what she reads, and as you are very capable of distinguishing, take care she does not mistake pert folly for wit and humour, or rhyme for poetry, which are the common errors of young people, and have a train of ill consequences.

The second caution to be given her (and which is most absolutely necessary) is to conceal whatever learning she attains, with as much solicitude as she would hide crookedness or lameness. The parade of it can only serve to draw on her the envy, and consequently the most inveterate hatred of all he and she fools, which will certainly be at least three parts in four of all her acquaintance. The use of knowledge in our sex (beside the amusement of solitude) is to moderate the passions and learn to be contented with a small expense, which are the certain effects of a studious life and, it may be, preferable even to that fame which men have engrossed to themselves and will not suffer us to share. You will tell me I have not observed this rule myself, but you are mistaken; it is only inevitable accident that has given me any reputation that way. I have always carefully avoided it, and ever thought it a misfortune. . . .

I am afraid you will think this a very long and insignificant letter. I hope the kindness of the design will excuse it, being willing to give you every proof in my power that I am your most affectionate mother,

M. Wortley

To Lady Bute

Gottolengo, 6 March 1753

I cannot help writing a sort of apology for my last letter, foreseeing that you will think it wrong, or at least Lord Bute will be extremely shocked at the proposal of a learned education for daughters, which the generality of men believe as great a profanation as the clergy would do if the laity should presume to exercise the functions of the priesthood. I desire you would take notice I would not have learning enjoined them as a task, but permitted as a pleasure if their genius leads them naturally to it. I look upon my granddaughters as a sort of lay nuns. Destiny may have laid up other things for them, but they have no reason to expect to pass their time otherwise than their aunts do at present, and I know by experience it is in the power of study not only to make solitude tolerable but agreeable. I have now lived almost seven years in a stricter retirement than yours in the Isle of Bute, and can assure you I have never had half an hour heavy on my hands for want of something to do.

Whoever will cultivate their own mind will find full employment. Every virtue does not only require great care in the planting, but as much daily solicitude in cherishing as exotic fruits and flowers; the vices and passions (which I am afraid are the natural product of the soil) demand perpetual weeding. Add to this the search after knowledge (every branch of which is entertaining), and the longest life is too short for the pursuit of it, which, though in some regards confined to very strait limits, leaves still a vast variety of amusements to those capable of tasting them, which is utterly impossible for those that are blinded by prejudices, which are the certain effect of an ignorant education. My own was one of the worst in the world, being exactly the same as Clarissa Harlowe's, her pious Mrs Norton so perfectly resembling my governess (who had been nurse to my mother) I could almost fancy the author was acquainted with her. She took so much pains from my infancy to fill my head with superstitious tales and false notions, it was none of her fault I am not at this day afraid of witches and hobgoblins, or turned Methodist.

Almost all girls are bred after this manner. I believe you are the only woman (perhaps I might say person) that never was either frighted or cheated into anything by your parents. I can truly affirm I never deceived anybody in my life excepting (which I confess has often happened undesignedly) by speaking plainly. As Earl Stanhope used to say (during his ministry), he always imposed on the foreign ministers by telling them the naked truth, which, as they thought impossible to come from the mouth of a statesman, they never failed to write informations to their respective courts directly contrary to the assurances he gave them, most people confounding the ideas of sense and cunning, though there are really no two things in nature more opposite. It is in part from this false reasoning, the unjust custom prevails of debarring our sex from the advantages of learning, the men fancying the improvement of our understandings would only furnish us with more art to deceive them, which is directly contrary to the truth. Fools are always enterprising, not seeing the difficulties of deceit or the ill consequences of detection. I could give many examples of ladies whose ill conduct has been very notorious, which has been owing to that ignorance which has exposed them to idleness, which is justly called the mother of mischief. . . .

If you follow my advice in relation to Lady Mary, my correspondence may be of use to her, and I shall very willingly give her those instructions that may be necessary in the pursuit of her studies. Before her age I was in the most regular commerce with my grandmother, though the difference of our time of life was much greater, she being past forty-five when she married my grandfather. She died at ninety-six, retaining to the last the vivacity and clearness of her understanding, which was very uncommon. You cannot remember her, being then in your nurse's arms. I conclude with repeating to you, I only recommend but am far from commanding, which I think I have no right to do. I tell you my sentiments because you desired to know them, and hope you will receive them with some partiality as coming from your most affectionate mother,

M. Wortley

MARY WOLLSTONECRAFT
(1759–97)

A Vindication of the Rights of Woman created a furor when it was published in 1792, its voice considered the voice of revolution. Wollstonecraft's feminism was bred in the bone. She spent her childhood protecting her submissive mother from an alcoholic and violent father. Leaving home at seventeen, she supported herself as a maid, a governess, a teacher, and finally as a writer who argued for a new order of equality between men and women. She died after giving birth to Mary Wollstonecraft Godwin Shelley, who in her youth read her mother's books while sitting next to her grave (see pages 21–22).

---

from
A Vindication of the Rights of Woman

Women are, therefore, to be considered either as moral beings, or so weak that they must be entirely subjected to the superior faculties of men.

Let us examine this question. Rousseau declares, that a woman should never, for a moment feel herself independent, that she should be governed by fear to exercise her *natural* cunning, and made a coquetish slave in order to render her a more alluring object of desire, a *sweeter* companion to man, whenever he chooses to relax himself. He carries the arguments, which he pretends to draw from the indications of nature, still further, and insinuates that truth and fortitude the corner stones of all human virtue, shall be cultivated with certain restrictions, because with respect to the female character, obedience is the grand lesson which ought to be impressed with unrelenting rigour.

What nonsense! when will a great man arise with sufficient strength of mind to puff away the fumes which pride and sensuality have thus spread over the subject! If women are by nature inferior to men, their virtues must be the same in quality, if not in degree, or virtue is a relative idea; consequently, their conduct should be founded on the same principles and have the same aim.

Connected with man as daughters, wives, and mothers, their moral character may be estimated by their manner of fulfilling those simple duties; but the end, the grand end of their exertions should be to unfold their own faculties, and acquire the dignity of conscious virtue. They may try to render their road pleasant; but ought never to forget, in common with man, that life yields not the felicity which can satisfy an immortal soul. I do not mean to insinuate, that either sex should be so lost, in abstract reflections or distant views, as to forget the affections and duties that lie before them, and are in truth, the means appointed to produce the fruit of life; on the contrary, I would warmly recommend them, even while I assert, that they afford most satisfaction when they are considered in their true subordinate light.

Probably the prevailing opinion, that woman was created for man, may have taken its rise from Moses's poetical story; yet, as very few it is presumed, who have bestowed any serious thought on the subject, ever supposed that Eve was, literally speaking, one of Adam's ribs, the deduction must be allowed to fall to the ground; or only be so far admitted as it proves that man, from the remotest antiquity, found it convenient to exert his strength to subjugate his companion, and his invention to show that she ought to have her neck bent under the yoke; because she as well as the brute creation, was created to do his pleasure.

Let it not be concluded, that I wish to invert the order of things; I have already granted, that, from the constitution of their bodies, men seem to be designed by Providence to attain a greater degree of virtue. I speak collectively of the whole sex; but I see not the shadow of a reason to conclude that their virtues should differ in respect to their nature. In fact, how can they, if virtue has only one eternal standard? I must, therefore, if I reason consequentially, as strenuously maintain, that they have the same simple direction, as that there is a God.

It follows then, that cunning should not be opposed to wisdom, little cares to great exertions, nor insipid softness, varnished over with the name of gentleness, to that fortitude which grand views alone can inspire.

I shall be told, that woman would then lose many of her peculiar graces, and the opinion of a well known poet might be quoted to refute my unqualified assertions. For Pope has said, in the name of the whole male sex,

> "Yet ne'er so sure our passions to create,
> As when she touch'd the brink of all we hate."

In what light this sally places men and women, I shall leave to the judicious to determine; meanwhile I shall content myself with observing, that I cannot discover why, unless they are mortal, females should always be degraded by being made subservient to love or lust.

To speak disrespectfully of love is, I know, high treason against sentiment and fine feelings; but I wish to speak the simple language of truth, and rather to address the head than the heart. To endeavour to reason love out of the world, would be to out Quixote Cervantes, and equally offend against common sense; but an endeavour to restrain this tumultuous passion, and to prove that it should not be allowed to dethrone superior powers, or to usurp the sceptre which the understanding should ever coolly wield, appears less wild.

Youth is the season for love in both sexes; but in those days of thoughtless enjoyment, provision should be made for the more important years of life, when reflection takes place of sensation. But Rousseau, and most of the male writers who have followed his steps, have warmly inculcated that the whole tendency of female education ought to be directed to one point to render them pleasing.

Let me reason with the supporters of this opinion, who have any knowledge of human nature, do they imagine that marriage can eradicate the habitude of life? The woman who has only been taught to please, will soon find that her charms are oblique sun-beams, and that they cannot have much effect on her husband's heart when they are seen every day, when the summer is past and gone. Will she then have sufficient native energy to look into herself for comfort and cultivate her dormant faculties? or, is it not more rational to expect, that she will try to please other men; and, in the emotions raised by the expectation of new conquests, endeavour to forget the mortification her love or pride has received? When the husband ceases to be a lover—and the time will inevitably come, her desire of pleasing will then grow languid, or become a spring of bitterness; and love, perhaps, the most evanescent of all passions, gives place to jealousy or vanity.

I now speak of women who are restrained by principle or prejudice; such women though they would shrink from an intrigue with real abhorrence, yet, nevertheless, wish to be convinced by the homage of gallantry, that they are cruelly neglected by their husbands; or, days and weeks are spent in dreaming of the happiness enjoyed by congenial souls, till the health is undermined and the spirits broken by discontent. How then can the great art of pleasing be such a necessary study? it is only useful to a mistress; the chaste wife, and serious mother, should only consider her power to please as the polish of her virtues, and the affection of her husband as one of the comforts that render her task less difficult, and her life happier. But, whether she be loved or neglected, her first wish should be to make herself respectable, and not rely for all her happiness on a being subject to like infirmities with herself.

MARY SHELLEY
(1797–1851)

The journal of Mary Shelley records a seemingly endless cycle of suffering and loss in the voice of a woman determined to survive her own despair. The daughter of Mary Wollstonecraft (see pages 18–20) and philosopher William Godwin, Mary Shelley ran away with the poet Percy Bysshe Shelley when she was seventeen, bore four children, only one of whom lived, wrote *Frankenstein*—the most famous work of science fiction in the English language—when she was nineteen, and after Shelley drowned off the coast of Italy in 1821, came back to England alone and poor, having herself and her child to support. ("I have my lovely Boy, without him I could not live.") Muriel Spark's biography recounts the nastiness Mary was dealt in her widowhood by literary London and by Shelley's father, who made the single mother pay for her irresponsible youth. She continued to publish her writing but was always in need of money and often depressed. In the 1840s, she returned to Italy and wrote a well-received travel book, *Rambles in Germany and Italy*.

---

from
The Journal of Mary Shelley

Albaro, Italy, 1822

Oct. 2.—On the 8th of July I finished my journal. This is a curious co-incidence. The date still remains—the fatal 8th—a monument to show that all ended then. And I begin again? Oh, never! But several motives induce me, when the day has gone down, and all is silent around me, steeped in sleep, to pen as occasion wills, my reflections and feelings. First, I have no friend. For eight years I communicated, with unlimited freedom, with one whose genius, far transcending mine, awakened and guided my thoughts. I conversed with him; rectified my errors of judgment; obtained new lights from him; and my mind was satisfied. Now I am alone—oh, how alone! The stars may behold my tears, and the winds drink my sighs; but my thoughts are a sealed treasure, which I can confide to none. But can I express all I feel? Can I give words to thoughts and feelings that, as a tempest, hurry me along? Is this the sand that the ever-flowing sea of thought would impress indelibly? Alas! I am alone. No eye answers mine; my voice can

21

with none assume its natural modulation. What a change! O my beloved Shelley! how often during those happy days—happy, though chequered—I thought how superiorly gifted I had been in being united to one to whom I could unveil myself, and who could understand me! Well, then, now I am reduced to these white pages, which I am to blot with dark imagery. As I write, let me think what he would have said if, speaking thus to him, he could have answered me. Yes, my own heart, I would fain know what to think of my desolate state; what you think I ought to do, what to think. I guess you would answer thus:—"Seek to know your own heart, and, learning what it best loves, try to enjoy that." Well, I cast my eyes around, and look forward to the bounded prospect in view; I ask myself what pleases me there? My child;—so many feelings arise when I think of him, that I turn aside to think no more. Those I most loved are gone for ever; those who held the second rank are absent; and among those near me as yet, I trust to the disinterested kindness of one alone. Beneath all this, my imagination never flags. Literary labours, the improvement of my mind, and the enlargement of my ideas, are the only occupations that elevate me from my lethargy; all events seem to lead me to that one point, and the courses of destiny having dragged me to that single resting-place, have left me. Father, mother, friend, husband, children—all made, as it were, the team that conducted me here; and now all, except you, my poor boy (and you are necessary to the continuance of my life), all are gone, and I am left to fulfil my task. So be it. . . .

MARGARET FULLER
(1810–50)

The best move Fuller ever made was to leave behind the New England Over-soul and its patronizing Concord fathers and go to work as a reporter for the *New York Tribune*, becoming the first self-supporting woman journalist in America. The *Tribune* sent her to Italy, where she covered the War for the Roman Republic. In Europe she found herself admired as the author of the widely read *Woman in the Nineteenth Century*. The articles she sent back to America, collected under the title *These Sad But Glorious Days: Dispatches from Europe 1846–1850*, are now considered the best writing she ever did.* She said Italy brought her back to life. "Once I was almost all intellect; now I am almost all feeling," she wrote in her journal. "Nature vindicates her rights, and I feel all Italy glowing beneath the Saxon crust." She had a baby with her Italian lover, Giovanni Angelo Ossoli, with whom she returned to America; the three of them drowned in a shipwreck a mile off the coast of Fire Island. Neither her body nor the manuscript she carried, her story of the short-lived Roman Republic, was ever found.

------

from
Woman in the Nineteenth Century

Male and female represent the two sides of the great radical dualism. But, in fact, they are perpetually passing into one another. Fluid hardens to solid, solid rushes to fluid. There is no wholly masculine man, no purely feminine woman. . . .

Let us be wise, and not impede the soul. Let her work as she will. Let us have one creative energy, one incessant revelation. Let it take what form it will, and let us not bind it by the past to man or woman, black or white. . . .

Women must leave off asking [men] and being influenced by them, but retire within themselves, and explore the ground-work of life till they find their peculiar secret. Then, when they come forth again, renovated and baptized, they will know how to turn all dross to gold, and will be rich and free though they live in a hut, tranquil if in a crowd. Then their sweet singing shall not be from passionate impulse, but the lyrical overflow of a divine rapture, and a new music shall be evolved from this many-chorded world.

*See *Desiring Italy: Women Writers Celebrate a Culture*, ed. Susan Cahill.

Grant her, then, for a while, the armor and the javelin. Let her put from her the press of other minds, and meditate in virgin loneliness. . . .

I have urged on Woman independence of Man, not that I do not think the sexes mutually needed by one another, but because in Woman this fact has led to an excessive devotion, which has cooled love, degraded marriage, and prevented either sex from being what it should be to itself or the other.

I wish Woman to live, *first* for God's sake. Then she will not make an imperfect man her god, and thus sink to idolatry. Then she will not take what is not fit for her from a sense of weakness and poverty. Then, if she finds what she needs in Man embodied, she will know how to love, and be worthy of being loved.

By being more a soul, she will not be less Woman, for nature is perfected through spirit.

Now there is no woman, only an overgrown child.

That her hand may be given with dignity, she must be able to stand alone. I wish to see men and women capable of such relations as are depicted by Landor in his Pericles and Aspasia, where grace is the natural garb of strength, and the affections are calm, because deep. The softness is that of a firm tissue, as when

> The gods approve
> The depth, but not the tumult of the soul,
> A fervent, not ungovernable love.

A profound thinker has said, "No married woman can represent the female world, for she belongs to her husband. The idea of Woman must be represented by a virgin."

But that is the very fault of marriage, and of the present relation between the sexes, that the woman *does* belong to the man, instead of forming a whole with him. Were it otherwise, there would be no such limitation to the thought.

Woman, self-centred, would never be absorbed by any relation; it would be only an experience to her as to man. It is a vulgar error that love, *a* love, to Woman is her whole existence; she also is born for Truth and Love in their universal energy. Would she but assume her inheritance, Mary would not be the only virgin mother. Not Manzoni alone would celebrate in his wife the virgin mind with the maternal wisdom and conjugal affections. The soul is ever young, ever virgin.

HARRIET A. JACOBS

(1813–97)

The most-read African-American woman of the nineteenth century, Harriet Jacobs was born a slave in North Carolina and became a fugitive in the 1830s. As she wrote to a friend, "God . . . gave me a soul that burned for freedom and a heart nerved with determination to suffer even unto death in pursuit of . . . liberty." In 1861, under the pseudonym Linda Brent, Jacobs published *Incidents in the Life of a Slave Girl*, the story of her family's enslavement and her own long run to freedom. She describes the sexual oppression she knew as a young slave in the home of her sanctimonious master, Dr. Flint, as well as the people who helped her on her dangerous flight to the north, before and after the Fugitive Slave Law of 1850. Most vivid is her indomitable grandmother, who hid her in an attic for seven years.

---

from
Incidents in the Life of a Slave Girl

→ I ←

Childhood

I was born a slave; but I never knew it till six years of happy childhood had passed away. My father was a carpenter, and considered so intelligent and skilful in his trade, that, when buildings out of the common line were to be erected, he was sent for from long distances, to be head workman. On condition of paying his mistress two hundred dollars a year, and supporting himself, he was allowed to work at his trade, and manage his own affairs. His strongest wish was to purchase his children; but, though he several times offered his hard earnings for that purpose, he never succeeded. In complexion my parents were a light shade of brownish yellow, and were termed mulattoes. They lived together in a comfortable home; and, though we were all slaves, I was so fondly shielded that I never dreamed I was a piece of merchandise, trusted to them for safe keeping, and liable to be demanded of them at any moment. I had one brother, William, who was two years younger than myself—a bright, affectionate child. I had also a great treasure in my maternal grandmother, who was a remarkable woman in many respects. She was the daughter of a planter in South Carolina, who, at his death, left her mother and his three children free, with money to go to St. Augustine, where they had relatives. It was during the Revolutionary War; and they were captured on their passage, carried back, and sold to different purchasers. Such was the story my grandmother used to tell me; but I do not remember all the particulars. She was a little girl when she was captured and sold to the keeper of a large hotel. I have often heard her tell how hard she fared during childhood. But as she grew older she evinced so much intelligence, and was so faithful, that her master and mistress could not help seeing it was for their interest to take care of such a valuable piece of property.

She became an indispensable personage in the household, officiating in all capacities, from cook and wet nurse to seamstress. She was much praised for her cooking; and her nice crackers became so famous in the neighborhood that many people were desirous of obtaining them. In consequence of numerous requests of this kind, she asked permission of her mistress to bake crackers at night, after all the household work was done; and she obtained leave to do it, provided she would clothe herself and her children from the profits. Upon these terms, after working hard all day for her mistress, she began her midnight bakings, assisted by her two oldest children. The business proved profitable; and each year she laid by a little, which was saved for a fund to purchase her children. Her master died, and the property was divided among his heirs. The widow had her dower in the hotel, which she continued to keep open. My grandmother remained in her service as a slave; but her children were divided among her master's children. As she had five, Benjamin, the youngest one, was sold, in order that each heir might have an equal portion of dollars and cents. There was so little difference in our ages that he seemed more like my brother than my uncle. He was a bright, handsome lad, nearly white; for he inherited the complexion my grandmother had derived from Anglo-Saxon ancestors. Though only ten years old, seven hundred and twenty dollars were paid for him. His sale was a terrible blow to my grandmother, but she was naturally hopeful, and she went to work with renewed energy, trusting in time to be able to purchase some of her children. She had laid up three hundred dollars, which her mistress one day begged as a loan, promising to pay her soon. The reader probably knows that no promise or writing given to a slave is legally binding; for, according to Southern laws, a slave, *being* property, can *hold* no property. When my grandmother lent her hard earnings to her mistress, she trusted solely to her honor. The honor of a slaveholder to a slave!

To this good grandmother I was indebted for many comforts. My brother Willie and I often received portions of the crackers, cakes, and preserves, she made to sell; and after we ceased to be children we were indebted to her for many more important services.

Such were the unusually fortunate circumstances of my early childhood. When I was six years old, my mother died; and then, for the first time, I learned, by the talk around me, that I was a slave. My mother's mistress was the daughter of my grandmother's mistress. She was the foster sister of my mother; they were both nourished at my grandmother's breast. In fact, my mother had been weaned at three months old, that the babe of the mistress might obtain sufficient food. They played together as children; and, when they became women, my mother was a most faithful servant to her whiter foster sister. On her death-bed her mistress promised that her children should never suffer for any thing; and during her lifetime she kept her word. They all spoke kindly of my dead mother, who had been a slave merely in name, but in nature was noble and womanly. I grieved for her, and my young mind was troubled with the thought who would now take care of me and my little brother. I was told that my home was now to be with her mistress; and I found it a happy one. No toilsome or disagreeable duties were imposed upon me. My mistress was so kind to me that I was always glad to do her bidding, and proud to labor for her as much as my young years would permit. I would sit by her side for hours, sewing diligently, with a heart as free from care as that of any free-born white child. When she thought I was tired, she would send me out to run and jump; and away I bounded, to gather berries or flowers to decorate her room. Those were happy days—too happy to last. The slave child had no thought for the morrow; but there came that blight, which too surely waits on every human being born to be a chattel.

When I was nearly twelve years old, my kind mistress sickened and died. As I saw the cheek grow paler, and the eye more glassy, how earnestly I prayed in my heart that she might live! I loved her; for she had been almost like a mother to me. My prayers were not answered. She died, and they buried her in the little churchyard, where, day after day, my tears fell upon her grave.

I was sent to spend a week with my grandmother. I was now old enough to begin to think of the future; and again and again I asked myself what they would do with me. I felt sure I should never find another mistress so kind as the one who was gone. She had promised my dying mother that her children should never suffer for any thing; and when I remembered that, and recalled her many proofs of attachment to me, I could not help having some hopes that she had left me free. My friends were almost certain it would be so. They thought she would be sure to do it, on account of my mother's love and faithful service. But, alas! we all know that the memory of a faithful slave does not avail much to save her children from the auction block.

After a brief period of suspense, the will of my mistress was read, and we learned that she had bequeathed me to her sister's daughter, a child of five years old. So vanished our hopes. My mistress had taught me the precepts of God's Word: "Thou shalt love thy neighbor as thyself." "Whatsoever ye would that men should do unto you, do ye even so unto them." But I was her slave, and I suppose she did not recognize me as her neighbor. I would give much to blot out from my memory that one great wrong. As a child, I loved my mistress; and, looking back on the happy days I spent with her, I try to think with less bitterness of this act of injustice. While I was with her, she taught me to read and spell; and for this privilege, which so rarely falls to the lot of a slave, I bless her memory.

She possessed but few slaves; and at her death those were all distributed among her relatives. Five of them were my grandmother's children, and had shared the same milk that nourished her mother's children. Notwithstanding my grandmother's long and faithful service to her owners, not one of her children escaped the auction block. These God-breathing machines are no more, in the sight of their masters, than the cotton they plant, or the horses they tend.

⤜ II ⤛

The New Master and Mistress

Dr. Flint, a physician in the neighborhood, had married the sister of my mistress, and I was now the property of their little daughter. It was not without murmuring that I prepared for my new home; and what added to my unhappiness, was the fact that my brother William was purchased by the same family. My father, by his nature, as well as by the habit of transacting business as a skilful mechanic, had more of the feelings of a freeman than is common among slaves. My brother was a spirited boy; and being brought up under such influences, he early detested the name of master and mistress. One day, when his father and his mistress had happened to call him at the same time, he hesitated between the two; being perplexed to know which had the strongest claim upon his obedience. He finally concluded to go to his mistress. When my father reproved him for it, he said, "You both called me, and I didn't know which I ought to go to first."

"You are *my* child," replied our father, "and when I call you, you should come immediately, if you have to pass through fire and water."

Poor Willie! He was now to learn his first lesson of obedience to a master. Grandmother tried to cheer us with hopeful words, and they found an echo in the credulous hearts of youth.

When we entered our new home we encountered cold looks, cold words, and cold treatment. We were glad when the night came. On my narrow bed I moaned and wept, I felt so desolate and alone.

I had been there nearly a year, when a dear little friend of mine was buried. I heard her mother sob, as the clods fell on the coffin of her only child, and I turned away from the grave, feeling thankful that I still had something left to love. I met my grandmother, who said, "Come with me, Linda;" and from her tone I knew that something sad had happened. She led me apart from the people, and then said, "My child, your father is dead." Dead! How could I believe it? He had died so suddenly I had not even heard that he was sick. I went home with my grand-mother. My heart rebelled against God, who had taken from me mother, father, mistress, and friend. The good grandmother tried to comfort me. "Who knows the ways of God?" said she. "Perhaps they have been kindly taken from the evil days to come." Years afterwards I often thought of this. She promised to be a mother to her grandchildren, so far as she might be permitted to do so; and strengthened by her love, I returned to my master's. I thought I should be al-lowed to go to my father's house the next morning; but I was ordered to go for flowers, that my mistress's house might be decorated for an evening party. I spent the day gathering flowers and weaving them into festoons, while the dead body of my father was lying within a mile of me. What cared my owners for that? he was merely a piece of property. Moreover, they thought he had spoiled his chil-dren, by teaching them to feel that they were human beings. This was blasphe-mous doctrine for a slave to teach; presumptuous in him, and dangerous to the masters.

The next day I followed his remains to a humble grave beside that of my dear mother. There were those who knew my father's worth, and respected his memory.

My home now seemed more dreary than ever. The laugh of the little slave-children sounded harsh and cruel. It was selfish to feel so about the joy of others. My brother moved about with a very grave face. I tried to comfort him, by say-ing, "Take courage, Willie; brighter days will come by and by."

"You don't know any thing about it, Linda," he replied. "We shall have to stay here all our days; we shall never be free."

I argued that we were growing older and stronger, and that perhaps we might, before long, be allowed to hire our own time, and then we could earn money to buy our freedom. William declared this was much easier to say than to do; more-over, he did not intend to *buy* his freedom. We held daily controversies upon this subject.

Little attention was paid to the slaves' meals in Dr. Flint's house. If they could catch a bit of food while it was going, well and good. I gave myself no trouble on that score, for on my various errands I passed my grandmother's house, where there was always something to spare for me. I was frequently threatened with punishment if I stopped there; and my grandmother, to avoid detaining me, of-ten stood at the gate with something for my breakfast or dinner. I was indebted to *her* for all my comforts, spiritual or temporal. It was *her* labor that supplied my scanty wardrobe. I have a vivid recollection of the linsey-woolsey dress given me every winter by Mrs. Flint. How I hated it! It was one of the badges of slavery.

While my grandmother was thus helping to support me from her hard earn-ings, the three hundred dollars she had lent her mistress were never repaid. When her mistress died, her son-in-law, Dr. Flint, was appointed executor. When grandmother applied to him for payment, he said the estate was insolvent, and the law prohibited payment. It did not, however, prohibit him from retaining the silver candelabra, which had been purchased with that money. I presume they will be handed down in the family, from generation to generation.

My grandmother's mistress had always promised her that, at her death, she should be free; and it was said that in her will she made good the promise. But when the estate was settled, Dr. Flint told the faithful old servant that, under existing circumstances, it was necessary she should be sold.

On the appointed day, the customary advertisement was posted up, proclaiming that there would be a "public sale of negroes, horses, &c." Dr. Flint called to tell my grandmother that he was unwilling to wound her feelings by putting her up at auction, and that he would prefer to dispose of her at private sale. My grandmother saw through his hypocrisy; she understood very well that he was ashamed of the job. She was a very spirited woman, and if he was base enough to sell her, when her mistress intended she should be free, she was determined the public should know it. She had for a long time supplied many families with crackers and preserves; consequently, "Aunt Marthy," as she was called, was generally known, and every body who knew her respected her intelligence and good character. Her long and faithful service in the family was also well known, and the intention of her mistress to leave her free. When the day of sale came, she took her place among the chattels, and at the first call she sprang upon the auction-block. Many voices called out, "Shame! Shame! Who is going to sell *you*, aunt Marthy? Don't stand there! That is no place for *you*." Without saying a word, she quietly awaited her fate. No one bid for her. At last, a feeble voice said, "Fifty dollars." It came from a maiden lady, seventy years old, the sister of my grandmother's deceased mistress. She had lived forty years under the same roof with my grandmother; she knew how faithfully she had served her owners, and how cruelly she had been defrauded of her rights; and she resolved to protect her. The auctioneer waited for a higher bid; but her wishes were respected; no one bid above her. She could neither read nor write; and when the bill of sale was made out, she signed it with a cross. But what consequence was that, when she had a big heart overflowing with human kindness? She gave the old servant her freedom.

At that time, my grandmother was just fifty years old. Laborious years had passed since then; and now my brother and I were slaves to the man who had defrauded her of her money, and tried to defraud her of her freedom. One of my mother's sisters, called Aunt Nancy, was also a slave in his family. She was a kind, good aunt to me; and supplied the place of both housekeeper and waiting maid to her mistress. She was, in fact, at the beginning and end of every thing.

Mrs. Flint, like many southern women, was totally deficient in energy. She had not strength to superintend her household affairs; but her nerves were so strong, that she could sit in her easy chair and see a woman whipped, till the blood trickled from every stroke of the lash. She was a member of the church; but partaking of the Lord's supper did not seem to put her in a Christian frame of mind. If dinner was not served at the exact time on that particular Sunday, she would station herself in the kitchen, and wait till it was dished, and then spit in all the kettles and pans that had been used for cooking. She did this to prevent the cook and her children from eking out their meagre fare with the remains of the gravy and other scrapings. The slaves could get nothing to eat except what she chose to give them. Provisions were weighed out by the pound and ounce, three times a day. I can assure you she gave them no chance to eat wheat bread from her flour barrel. She knew how many biscuits a quart of flour would make, and exactly what size they ought to be.

Dr. Flint was an epicure. The cook never sent a dinner to his table without fear and trembling; for if there happened to be a dish not to his liking, he would either order her to be whipped, or compel her to eat every mouthful of it in his presence. The poor, hungry creature might not have objected to eating it; but she did object to having her master cram it down her throat till she choked.

They had a pet dog, that was a nuisance in the house. The cook was ordered to make some Indian mush for him. He refused to eat, and when his head was held over it, the froth flowed from his mouth into the basin. He died a few minutes after. When Dr. Flint came in, he said the mush had not been well cooked, and that was the reason the animal would not eat it. He sent for the cook, and compelled her to eat it. He thought that the woman's stomach was stronger than the dog's; but her sufferings afterwards proved that he was mistaken. This poor woman endured many cruelties from her master and mistress; sometimes she was locked up, away from her nursing baby, for a whole day and night.

When I had been in the family a few weeks, one of the plantation slaves was brought to town, by order of his master. It was near night when he arrived, and Dr. Flint ordered him to be taken to the work house, and tied up to the joist, so that his feet would just escape the ground. In that situation he was to wait till the doctor had taken his tea. I shall never forget that night. Never before, in my life, had I heard hundreds of blows fall, in succession, on a human being. His piteous groans, and his "O, pray don't, massa," rang in my ear for months afterwards. There were many conjectures as to the cause of this terrible punishment. Some said master accused him of stealing corn; others said the slave had quarrelled with his wife, in presence of the overseer, and had accused his master of being the father of her child. They were both black, and the child was very fair.

I went into the work house next morning, and saw the cowhide still wet with blood, and the boards all covered with gore. The poor man lived, and continued to quarrel with his wife. A few months afterwards Dr. Flint handed them both over to a slavetrader. The guilty man put their value into his pocket, and had the satisfaction of knowing that they were out of sight and hearing. When the mother was delivered into the trader's hands, she said, "You *promised* to treat me well." To which he replied, "You have let your tongue run too far; damn you!" She had forgotten that it was a crime for a slave to tell who was the father of her child.

From others than the master persecution also comes in such cases. I once saw a young slave girl dying soon after the birth of a child nearly white. In her agony she cried out, "O Lord, come and take me!" Her mistress stood by, and mocked at her like an incarnate fiend. "You suffer, do you?" she exclaimed. "I am glad of it. You deserve it all, and more too."

The girl's mother said, "The baby is dead, thank God; and I hope my poor child will soon be in heaven, too."

FRANCES E. W. HARPER

(1825–1911)

F.E.W. Harper was born to free parents in Maryland, then a slave state. She received a good education at an uncle's school and became a teacher herself, but quit to work in the antislavery movement. During the 1850s she broke the Fugitive Slave Law by accompanying runaway slaves along the Underground Railroad. Over a long career she published novels, essays, poetry, stories, letters—writing that is now seen to have initiated the tradition of African-American protest literature. A widow after 1864, she supported four children by returning to the lecture circuit, where she'd worked as an abolitionist before the war. Politically active on many contentious fronts—including the campaigns for suffrage for black men and white women—she often acted as mediator in those early battles of identity politics, reminding the antagonists: "We are all bound up together in one great bundle of humanity."

The Slave Mother

Heard you that shriek? It rose
    So wildly on the air,
It seemed as if a burden'd heart
    Was breaking in despair.

Saw you those hands so sadly clasped—
    The bowed and feeble head—
The shuddering of that fragile form—
    That look of grief and dread?

Saw you the sad, imploring eye?
    Its every glance was pain,
As if a storm of agony
    Were sweeping through the brain.

She is a mother, pale with fear,
    Her boy clings to her side,
And in her kirtle vainly tries
    His trembling form to hide.

He is not hers, although she bore
 For him a mother's pains;
He is not hers, although her blood
 Is coursing through his veins!

He is not hers, for cruel hands
 May rudely tear apart
The only wreath of household love
 That binds her breaking heart.

His love has been a joyous light
 That o'er her pathway smiled,
A fountain gushing ever new,
 Amid life's desert wild.

His lightest word has been a tone
 Of music round her heart,
Their lives a streamlet blent in one—
 Oh, Father! must they part?

They tear him from her circling arms,
 Her last and fond embrace.
Oh! never more may her sad eyes
 Gaze on his mournful face.

No marvel, then, these bitter shrieks
 Disturb the listening air:
She is a mother, and her heart
 Is breaking in despair.

EMILY DICKINSON
(1830–86)

O nly eight of Dickinson's poems were published in her lifetime; after her
death, 1,776 others were found in her bedroom in Amherst, Massachusetts, where she lived an increasingly reclusive life as she grew older. Her with-
drawal from society is a subject of controversy. Did she insist on solitude as the
only access to the ecstasies of art? Was her behavior a manifestation of agorapho-
bia, a fear of public places? Did it start with a traumatic event, perhaps a hopeless
love affair? Many poems carry the tensions of ecstasy and terror, eroticism and re-
nunciation, many voice the presence of divinity in nature and the emptiness of
social forms. A rebel against orthodoxies, she was a mystical poet who conceived
of her writing as a sacred calling, a countercultural liturgy of language in a theo-
phanous universe. She read widely, loved in particular Charlotte Brontë's *Jane
Eyre*, Emily Brontë's *Wuthering Heights*, George Eliot's *Middlemarch*, and Elizabeth Barrett Browning's *Aurora Leigh*.

303

The Soul selects her own Society –
Then – shuts the Door –
To her divine Majority –
Present no more –

Unmoved – she notes the Chariots – pausing –
At her low Gate –
Unmoved – an Emperor be kneeling
Upon her Mat –

I've known her – from an ample nation –
Choose One –
Then – close the Valves of her attention –
Like Stone –

324

Some keep the Sabbath going to Church –
I keep it, staying at Home –
With a Bobolink for a Chorister –
And an Orchard, for a Dome –

Some keep the Sabbath in Surplice –
I just wear my Wings –
And instead of tolling the Bell, for Church,
Our little Sexton — sings.

God preaches, a noted Clergyman –
And the sermon is never long,

So instead of getting to Heaven, at last –
I'm going, all along.

479

She dealt her pretty words like Blades –
How glittering they shone –
And every One unbared a Nerve
Or wantoned with a Bone –

She never deemed – she hurt –
That – is not Steel's Affair –
A vulgar grimace in the Flesh –
How ill the Creatures bear –

To Ache is human – not polite –
The Film upon the eye
Mortality's old Custom –
Just locking up – to Die.

508

I'm ceded – I've stopped being Theirs –
The name They dropped upon my face
With water, in the country church

Is finished using, now,
And They can put it with my Dolls,
My childhood, and the string of spools,
I've finished threading – too –

Baptized, before, without the choice,
But this time, consciously, of Grace –
Unto supremest name –
Called to my Full – The Crescent dropped –
Existence's whole Arc, filled up,
With one small Diadem.

My second Rank – too small the first –
Crowned – Crowing – on my Father's breast –
A half unconscious Queen –
But this time – Adequate – Erect,
With Will to choose, or to reject,
And I choose, just a Crown –

829

Ample make this Bed –
Make this Bed with Awe –
In it wait till Judgment break
Excellent and Fair.

Be its Mattress straight –
Be its Pillow round –
Let no Sunrise' yellow noise
Interrupt this Ground –

917

Love – is anterior to Life –
Posterior – to Death –
Initial of Creation, and
The Exponent of Earth –

1075

The Sky is low – the Clouds are mean.
A Travelling Flake of Snow
Across a Barn or through a Rut
Debates if it will go –

A Narrow Wind complains all Day
How some one treated him
Nature, like Us is sometimes caught
Without her Diadem.

1718

Drowning is not so pitiful
As the attempt to rise.
Three times, 'tis said, a sinking man
Comes up to face the skies,
And then declines forever
To that abhorred abode,
Where hope and he part company –
For he is grasped of God.
The Maker's cordial visage,
However good to see,
Is shunned, we must admit it,
Like an adversity.

SARAH ORNE JEWETT

(1849–1909)

In her lifetime, Jewett's fiction—*Deephaven* (1877), *A White Heron* (1886), and *The Country of the Pointed Firs* (1896)—won her a reputation as a great regional colorist of her native south Maine coast. Henry James praised her; James Russell Lowell admired her use of dialect, "for flavor, but not so oppressively as to suggest garlic." Willa Cather, to whom Jewett was an important mentor, dedicated *O Pioneers!* to her. In recent years more attention has been paid to Jewett's biography and its reverberations in her fiction. She had as her own mentor Annie Adams Fields (1834–1915), wife of the publisher and editor James T. Fields. After the deaths of Fields' husband and Jewett's father, the two women became companions, their "Boston marriage" lasting until Jewett's death. Critic Josephine Donovan's reading of Jewett's fictional world as a community of matriarchal Christianity inspired by women's values reflects the centrality of same-sex friendships in Jewett's life.

Martha's Lady

One day, many years ago, the old Judge Pyne house wore an unwonted look of gayety and youthfulness. The high-fenced green garden was bright with June flowers. Under the elms in the large shady front yard you might see some chairs placed near together, as they often used to be when the family were all at home and life was going on gayly with eager talk and pleasure-making; when the elder judge, the grandfather, used to quote that great author, Dr. Johnson, and say to his girls, "Be brisk, be splendid, and be public."

One of the chairs had a crimson silk shawl thrown carelessly over its straight back, and a passer-by, who looked in through the latticed gate between the tall gate-posts with their white urns, might think that this piece of shining East Indian color was a huge red lily that had suddenly bloomed against the syringa bush. There were certain windows thrown wide open that were usually shut, and their curtains were blowing free in the light wind of a summer afternoon; it looked as if a large household had returned to the old house to fill the prim best rooms and find them full of cheer.

It was evident to every one in town that Miss Harriet Pyne, to use the village phrase, had company. She was the last of her family, and was by no means old; but being the last, and wonted to live with people much older than herself, she had formed all the habits of a serious elderly person. Ladies of her age, something past thirty, often wore discreet caps in those days, especially if they were married,

but being single, Miss Harriet clung to youth in this respect, making the one con-
cession of keeping her waving chestnut hair as smooth and stiffly arranged as possible. She had been the dutiful companion of her father and mother in their latest
years, all her elder brothers and sisters having married and gone, or died and
gone, out of the old house. Now that she was left alone it seemed quite the best
thing frankly to accept the fact of age, and to turn more resolutely than ever to
the companionship of duty and serious books. She was more serious and given to
routine than her elders themselves, as sometimes happened when the daughters
of New England gentlefolks were brought up wholly in the society of their elders. At thirty-five she had more reluctance than her mother to face an unforeseen
occasion, certainly more than her grandmother, who had preserved some cheerful
inheritance of gayety and worldliness from colonial times.

There was something about the look of the crimson silk shawl in the front yard
to make one suspect that the sober customs of the best house in a quiet New England village were all being set at defiance, and once when the mistress of the
house came to stand in her own doorway, she wore the pleased but somewhat apprehensive look of a guest. In these days New England life held the necessity of
much dignity and discretion of behavior; there was the truest hospitality and
good cheer in all occasional festivities, but it was sometimes a self-conscious hospitality, followed by an inexorable return to asceticism both of diet and of behavior. Miss Harriet Pyne belonged to the very dullest days of New England, those
which perhaps held the most priggishness for the learned professions, the most
limited interpretation of the word "evangelical," and the pettiest indifference to
large things. The outbreak of a desire for larger religious freedom caused at first a
most determined reaction toward formalism, especially in small and quiet villages
like Ashford, intently busy with their own concerns. It was high time for a little
leaven to begin its work, in this moment when the great impulses of the war for
liberty had died away and those of the coming war for patriotism and a new freedom had hardly yet begun.

The dull interior, the changed life of the old house, whose former activities seemed
to have fallen sound asleep, really typified these larger conditions, and a little leaven
had made its easily recognized appearance in the shape of a light-hearted girl. She
was Miss Harriet's young Boston cousin, Helena Vernon, who, half-amused and
half-impatient at the unnecessary sober-mindedness of her hostess and of Ashford
in general, had set herself to the difficult task of gayety. Cousin Harriet looked on
at a succession of ingenious and, on the whole, innocent attempts at pleasure, as she
might have looked on at the frolics of a kitten who easily substitutes a ball of yarn
for the uncertainties of a bird or a wind-blown leaf, and who may at any moment
ravel the fringe of a sacred curtain-tassle in preference to either.

Helena, with her mischievous appealing eyes, with her enchanting old songs and her guitar, seemed the more delightful and even reasonable because she was so kind to everybody, and because she was a beauty. She had the gift of most charming manners. There was all the unconscious lovely ease and grace that had come with the good breeding of her city home, where many pleasant people came and went; she had no fear, one had almost said no respect, of the individual, and she did not need to think of herself. Cousin Harriet turned cold with apprehension when she saw the minister coming in at the front gate, and wondered in agony if Martha were properly attired to go to the door, and would by any chance hear the knocker; it was Helena who, delighted to have anything happen, ran to the door to welcome the Reverend Mr. Crofton as if he were a congenial friend of her own age. She could behave with more or less propriety during the stately first visit, and even contrive to lighten it with modest mirth, and to extort the confession that the guest had a tenor voice, though sadly out of practice; but when the minister departed a little flattered, and hoping that he had not expressed himself too strongly for a pastor upon the poems of Emerson, and feeling the unusual stir of gallantry in his proper heart, it was Helena who caught the honored hat of the late Judge Pyne from its last resting-place in the hall, and holding it securely in both hands, mimicked the minister's self-conscious entrance. She copied his pompous and anxious expression in the dim parlor in such delicious fashion that Miss Harriet, who could not always extinguish a ready spark of the original sin of humor, laughed aloud.

"My dear!" she exclaimed severely the next moment, "I am ashamed of your being so disrespectful!" and then laughed again, and took the affecting old hat and carried it back to its place.

"I would not have had anyone else see you for the world," she said sorrowfully as she returned, feeling quite self-possessed again, to the parlor doorway; but Helena still sat in the minister's chair, with her small feet placed as his stiff boots had been, and a copy of his solemn expression before they came to speaking of Emerson and of the guitar. "I wish I had asked him if he would be so kind as to climb the cherry-tree," said Helena, unbending a little at the discovery that her cousin would consent to laugh no more. "There are all those ripe cherries on the top branches. I can climb as high as he, but I can't reach far enough from the last branch that will bear me. The minister is so long and thin—"

"I don't know what Mr. Crofton would have thought of you; he is a very serious young man," said cousin Harriet, still ashamed of her laughter. "Martha will get the cherries for you, or one of the men. I should not like to have Mr. Crofton think you were frivolous, a young lady of your opportunities"—but Helena had escaped through the hall and out at the garden door at the mention of Martha's name. Miss Harriet Pyne sighed anxiously, and then smiled, in spite of her deep convictions, as she shut the blinds and tried to make the house look solemn again.

The front door might be shut, but the garden door at the other end of the broad hall was wide open upon the large sunshiny garden, where the last of the red and white peonies and the golden lilies, and the first of the tall blue larkspurs lent their colors in generous fashion. The straight box borders were all in fresh and shining green of their new leaves, and there was a fragrance of the old garden's inmost life and soul blowing from the honeysuckle blossoms on a long trellis. It was now late in the afternoon, and the sun was low behind great apple-trees at the garden's end, which threw their shadows over the short turf of the bleaching-green. The cherry-trees stood at one side in full sunshine, and Miss Harriet, who presently came to the garden steps to watch like a hen at the water's edge, saw her cousin's pretty figure in its white dress of India muslin hurrying across the grass. She was accompanied by the tall, ungainly shape of Martha the new maid, who, dull and indifferent to everyone else, showed a surprising willingness and allegiance to the young guest.

"Martha ought to be in the dining-room, already, slow as she is; it wants but half an hour of tea-time," said Miss Harriet, as she turned and went into the shaded house. It was Martha's duty to wait at table, and there had been many trying scenes and defeated efforts toward her education. Martha was certainly very clumsy, and she seemed the clumsier because she had replaced her aunt, a most skillful person, who had but lately married a thriving farm and its prosperous owner. It must be confessed that Miss Harriet was a most bewildering instructor, and that her pupil's brain was easily confused and prone to blunders. The coming of Helena had been somewhat dreaded by reason of this incompetent service, but the guest took no notice of frowns or futile gestures at the first tea-table, except to establish friendly relations with Martha on her own account by a reassuring smile. They were about the same age, and next morning, before cousin Harriet came down, Helena showed by a word and a quick touch the right way to do something that had gone wrong and been impossible to understand the night before. A moment later the anxious mistress came in without suspicion, but Martha's eyes were as affectionate as a dog's, and there was a new look of hopefulness on her face; this dreaded guest was a friend after all, and not a foe come from proud Boston to confound her ignorance and patient efforts.

The two young creatures, mistress and maid, were hurrying across the bleaching-green.

"I can't reach the ripest cherries," explained Helena politely, "and I think Miss Pyne ought to send some to the minister. He has just made us a call. Why, Martha, you haven't been crying again!"

"Yes'm," said Martha sadly. "Miss Pyne always loves to send something to the minister," she acknowledged with interest, as if she did not wish to be asked to explain these latest tears.

"We'll arrange some of the best cherries in a pretty dish. I'll show you how, and you shall carry them over to the parsonage after tea," said Helena cheerfully, and Martha accepted the embassy with pleasure. Life was beginning to hold moments of something like delight in the last few days.

"You'll spoil your pretty dress, Miss Helena," Martha gave shy warning, and Miss Helena stood back and held up her skirts with unusual care while the country girl, in her heavy blue checked gingham, began to climb the cherry-tree like a boy.

Down came the scarlet fruit like bright rain into the green grass.

"Break some nice twigs with the cherries and leaves together; oh, you're a duck, Martha!" and Martha, flushed with delight, and looking far more like a thin and solemn blue heron, came rustling down to earth again, and gathered the spoils into her clean apron.

That night at tea, during her handmaiden's temporary absence, Miss Harriet announced, as if by way of apology, that she thought Martha was beginning to understand something about her work. "Her aunt was a treasure, she never had to be told anything twice; but Martha has been as clumsy as a calf," said the precise mistress of the house. "I have been afraid sometimes that I never could teach her anything. I was quite ashamed to have you come just now, and find me so unprepared to entertain a visitor."

"Oh, Martha will learn fast enough because she cares so much," said the visitor eagerly. "I think she is a dear good girl. I do hope that she will never go away. I think she does things better every day, cousin Harriet," added Helena pleadingly, with all her kind young heart. The china-closet door was open a little way, and Martha heard every word. From that moment, she not only knew what love was like, but she knew love's dear ambitions. To have come from a stony hill-farm and a bare small wooden house, was like a cave-dweller's coming to make a permanent home in an art museum, such had seemed the elaborateness and elegance of Miss Pyne's fashion of life; and Martha's simple brain was slow enough in its processes and recognitions. But with this sympathetic ally and defender, this exquisite Miss Helena who believed in her, all difficulties appeared to vanish.

Later that evening, no longer homesick or hopeless, Martha returned from her polite errand to the minister, and stood with a sort of triumph before the two ladies, who were sitting in the front doorway, as if they were waiting for visitors, Helena still in her white muslin and red ribbons, and Miss Harriet in a thin black silk. Being happily self-forgetful in the greatness of the moment, Martha's manners were perfect, and she looked for once almost pretty and quite as young as she was.

"The minister came to the door himself, and returned his thanks. He said that cherries were always his favorite fruit, and he was much obliged to both Miss Pyne and Miss Vernon. He kept me waiting a few minutes, while he got this book ready to send to you, Miss Helena."

"What are you saying, Martha? I have sent him nothing!" exclaimed Miss Pyne, much astonished. "What does she mean, Helena?"

"Only a few cherries," explained Helena. "I thought Mr. Crofton would like them after his afternoon of parish calls. Martha and I arranged them before tea, and I sent them with our compliments."

"Oh, I am very glad you did," said Miss Harriet, wondering, but much relieved. "I was afraid—"

"No, it was none of my mischief," answered Helena daringly. "I did not think that Martha would be ready to go so soon. I should have shown you how pretty they looked among their green leaves. We put them in one of your best white dishes with the openwork edge. Martha shall show you to-morrow; mamma always likes to have them so." Helena's fingers were busy with the hard knot of a parcel.

"See this, cousin Harriet!" she announced proudly, as Martha disappeared round the corner of the house, beaming with the pleasures of adventure and success. "Look! the minister has sent me a book: Sermons on *what*? Sermons—it is so dark that I can't quite see."

"It must be his 'Sermons on the Seriousness of Life'; they are the only ones he has printed, I believe," said Miss Harriet, with much pleasure. "They are considered very fine discourses. He pays you a great compliment, my dear. I feared that he noticed your girlish levity."

"I behaved beautifully while he stayed," insisted Helena. "Ministers are only men," but she blushed with pleasure. It was certainly something to receive a book from its author, and such a tribute made her of more value to the whole reverent household. The minister was not only a man, but a bachelor, and Helena was at the age that best loves conquest; it was at any rate comfortable to be reinstated in cousin Harriet's good graces.

"Do ask the kind gentleman to tea! He needs a little cheering up," begged the siren in India muslin, as she laid the shiny black volume of sermons on the stone doorstep with an air of approval, but as if they had quite finished their mission.

"Perhaps I shall, if Martha improves as much as she has within the last day or two," Miss Harriet promised hopefully. "It is something I always dread a little when I am all alone, but I think Mr. Crofton likes to come. He converses so elegantly."

These were the days of long visits, before affectionate friends thought it quite worth while to take a hundred miles' journey merely to dine or to pass a night in one another's houses. Helena lingered through the pleasant weeks of early summer, and departed unwillingly at last to join her family at the White Hills, where they had gone, like other households of high social station, to pass the month of

August out of town. The happy-hearted young guest left many lamenting friends behind her, and promised each that she would come back again next year. She left the minister a rejected lover, as well as the preceptor of the academy, but with their pride unwounded, and it may have been with wider outlooks upon the world and a less narrow sympathy both for their own work in life and for their neighbors' work and hindrances. Even Miss Harriet Pyne herself had lost some of the unnecessary provincialism and prejudice which had begun to harden a naturally good and open mind and affectionate heart. She was conscious of feeling younger and more free, and not so lonely. Nobody had ever been so gay, so fascinating, or so kind as Helena, so full of social resource, so simple and undemanding in her friendliness. The light of her young life cast no shadow on either young or old companions, her pretty clothes never seemed to make other girls look dull or out of fashion. When she went away up the street in Miss Harriet's carriage to take the slow train toward Boston and the gayeties of the new Profile House, where her mother waited impatiently with a group of Southern friends, it seemed as if there would never be any more picnics or parties in Ashford, and as if society had nothing left to do but to grow old and get ready for winter.

Martha came into Miss Helena's bedroom that last morning, and it was easy to see that she had been crying; she looked just as she did in that first sad week of homesickness and despair. All for love's sake she had been learning to do many things, and to do them exactly right; her eyes had grown quick to see the smallest chance for personal service. Nobody could be more humble and devoted; she looked years older than Helena, and wore already a touching air of caretaking.

"You spoil me, you dear Martha!" said Helena from the bed. "I don't know what they will say at home, I am so spoiled."

Martha went on opening the blinds to let in the brightness of the summer morning, but she did not speak.

"You are getting on splendidly, aren't you?" continued the little mistress. "You have tried so hard that you make me ashamed of myself. At first you crammed all the flowers together, and now you make them look beautiful. Last night cousin Harriet was so pleased when the table was so charming, and I told her that you did everything yourself, every bit. Won't you keep the flowers fresh and pretty in the house until I come back? It's so much pleasanter for Miss Pyne, and you'll feed my little sparrows, won't you? They're growing so tame."

"Oh, yes, Miss Helena!" and Martha looked almost angry for a moment, then she burst into tears and covered her face with her apron. "I couldn't understand a single thing when I first came. I never had been anywhere to see anything, and Miss Pyne frightened me when she talked. It was you made me think I could ever learn. I wanted to keep the place, 'count of mother and the little boys; we're dreadful hard pushed. Hepsy has been good in the kitchen; she said she ought to have patience with me, for she was awkward herself when she first came."

Helena laughed; she looked so pretty under the tasseled white curtains.

"I dare say Hepsy tells the truth," she said. "I wish you had told me about your mother. When I come again, some day we'll drive up country, as you call it, to see her. Martha I wish you would think of me sometimes after I go away. Won't you promise?" and the bright young face suddenly grew grave. "I have hard times myself; I don't always learn things that I ought to learn, I don't always put things straight. I wish you wouldn't forget me ever, and would just believe in me. I think it does help more than anything."

"I won't forget," said Martha slowly. "I shall think of you every day." She spoke almost with indifference, as if she had been asked to dust a room, but she turned aside quickly and pulled the little mat under the hot water jug quite out of its former straightness; then she hastened away down the long white entry, weeping as she went.

To lose out of sight the friend whom one has loved and lived to please is to lose joy out of life. But if love is true, there comes presently a higher joy of pleasing the ideal, that is to say, the perfect friend. The same old happiness is lifted to a higher level. As for Martha, the girl who stayed behind in Ashford, nobody's life could seem duller to those who could not understand; she was slow of step, and her eyes were almost always downcast as if intent upon incessant toil; but they startled you when she looked up, with their shining light. She was capable of the happiness of holding fast to a great sentiment, the ineffable satisfaction of trying to please one whom she truly loved. She never thought of trying to make other people pleased with herself; all she lived for was to do the best she could for others, and to conform to an ideal, which grew at last to be like a saint's vision, a heavenly figure painted upon the sky.

On Sunday afternoons in summer, Martha sat by the window of her chamber, a low-storied little room, which looked into the side yard and the great branches of an elm-tree. She never sat in the old wooden rocking-chair except on Sundays like this; it belonged to the day of rest and to the happy meditation. She wore her plain black dress and a clean white apron, and held in her lap a little wooden box, with a brass ring on top for a handle. She was past sixty years of age and looked even older, but there was the same look on her face that it had sometimes worn in girlhood. She was the same Martha; her hands were old-looking and work-worn, but her face still shone. It seemed like yesterday that Helena Vernon had gone away, and it was more than forty years.

War and peace had brought their changes and great anxieties, the face of the earth was furrowed by floods and fire, the faces of mistress and maid were furrowed by smiles and tears, and in the sky the stars shone on as if nothing had happened. The village of Ashford added a few pages to its unexciting history, the minister preached, the people listened; now and then a funeral crept along the street, and now and then the bright face of a little child rose above the horizon of a family pew. Miss Harriet Pyne lived on in the large white house, which gained more and more distinction because it suffered no changes, save successive repaintings and a new railing about its stately roof. Miss Harriet herself had moved far beyond the uncertainties of an anxious youth. She had long ago made all her decisions, and settled all necessary questions; her scheme of life was as faultless as the miniature landscape of a Japanese garden, and as easily kept in order. The only important change she would ever be capable of making was the final change to another and a better world; and for that nature itself would gently provide, and her own innocent life.

Hardly any great social event had ruffled the easy current of life since Helena Vernon's marriage. To this Miss Pyne had gone, stately in appearance and carrying gifts of some old family silver which bore the Vernon crest, but not without some protest in her heart against the uncertainties of married life. Helena was so equal to a happy independence and even to the assistance of other lives grown strangely dependent upon her quick sympathies and instinctive decisions, that it was hard to let her sink her personality in the affairs of another. Yet a brilliant English match was not without its attractions to an old-fashioned gentlewoman like Miss Pyne, and Helena herself was amazingly happy; one day there had come a letter to Ashford, in which her very heart seemed to beat with love and self-forgetfulness, to tell cousin Harriet of such new happiness and high hope. "Tell Martha all that I say about my dear Jack," wrote the eager girl; "please show my letter to Martha, and tell her that I shall come home next summer and bring the handsomest and best man in the world to Ashford. I have told him all about the dear house and the dear garden; there never was such a lad to reach for cherries with his six-foot-two." Miss Pyne, wondering a little, gave the letter to Martha, who took it deliberately and as if she wondered too, and went away to read it slowly by herself. Martha cried over it, and felt a strange sense of loss and pain; it hurt her heart a little to read about the cherry-picking. Her idol seemed to be less her own since she had become the idol of a stranger. She never had taken such a letter in her hands before, but love at last prevailed, since Miss Helena was happy, and she kissed the last page where her name was written, feeling overbold, and laid the envelope on Miss Pyne's secretary without a word.

The most generous love cannot but long for reassurance, and Martha had the joy of being remembered. She was not forgotten when the day of the wedding drew near, but she never knew that Miss Helena had asked if cousin Harriet would not bring Martha to town; she should like to have Martha there to see her married. "She would help about the flowers," wrote the happy girl; "I know she will like to come, and I'll ask mamma to plan to have someone take her all about Boston and make her have a pleasant time after the hurry of the great day is over."

Cousin Harriet thought it was very kind and exactly like Helena, but Martha would be out of her element; it was most imprudent and girlish to have thought of such a thing. Helena's mother would be far from wishing for any unnecessary guest just then, in the busiest part of her household, and it was best not to speak of the invitation. Some day Martha should go to Boston if she did well, but not now. Helena did not forget to ask if Martha had come, and was astonished by the indifference of the answer. It was the first thing which reminded her that she was not a fairy princess having everything her own way in that last day before the wedding. She knew that Martha would have loved to be near, for she could not help understanding in that moment of her own happiness the love that was hidden in another heart. Next day this happy young princess, the bride, cut a piece of a great cake and put it into a pretty box that had held one of her wedding presents. With eager voices calling her, and all her friends about her, and her mother's face growing more and more wistful at the thought of parting, she still lingered and ran to take one or two trifles from her dressing-table, a little mirror and some tiny scissors that Martha would remember, and one of the pretty handkerchiefs marked with her maiden name. These she put in the box too; it was half a girlish freak and fancy, but she could not help trying to share her happiness, and Martha's life was so plain and dull. She whispered a message, and put the little package into cousin Harriet's hand for Martha as she said good-by. She was very fond of cousin Harriet. She smiled with a gleam of her old fun; Martha's puzzled look and tall awkward figure seemed to stand suddenly before her eyes, as she promised to come again to Ashford. Impatient voices called to Helena, her lover was at the door, and she hurried away, leaving her old home and her girlhood gladly. If she had only known it, as she kissed cousin Harriet good-by, they were never going to see each other again until they were old women. The first step that she took out of her father's house that day, married, and full of hope and joy, was a step that led her away from the green elms of Boston Common and away from her own country and those she loved best, to a brilliant, much-varied foreign life, and to nearly all the sorrows and nearly all the joys that the heart of one woman could hold or know.

On Sunday afternoons Martha used to sit by the window in Ashford and hold the wooden box which a favorite young brother, who afterward died at sea, had made for her, and she used to take out of it the pretty little box with a gilded cover that had held the piece of wedding-cake, and the small scissors, and the blurred bit of a mirror in its silver case; as for the handkerchief with the narrow lace edge, once in two or three years she sprinkled it as if it were a flower, and spread it out in the sun on the old bleaching-green, and sat near by in the shrubbery to watch lest some bold robin or cherry-bird should seize it and fly away.

* * *

Miss Harriet Pyne was often congratulated upon the good fortune of having such a helper and friend as Martha. As time went on this tall, gaunt woman, always thin, always slow, gained a dignity of behavior and simple affectionateness of look which suited the charm and dignity of the ancient house. She was unconsciously beautiful like a saint, like the picturesqueness of a lonely tree which lives to shelter unnumbered lives and to stand quietly in its place. There was such rustic homeliness and constancy belonging to her, such beautiful powers of apprehension, such reticence, such gentleness for those who were troubled or sick; all these gifts and graces Martha hid in her heart. She never joined the church because she thought she was not good enough, but life was such a passion and happiness of service that it was impossible not to be devout, and she was always in her humble place on Sundays, in the back pew next to the door. She had been educated by a remembrance; Helena's young eyes forever looked at her reassuringly from a gay girlish face. Helena's sweet patience in teaching her own awkwardness could never be forgotten.

"I owe everything to Miss Helena," said Martha, half aloud, as she sat alone by the window; she had said it to herself a thousand times. When she looked in the little keepsake mirror she always hoped to see some faint reflection of Helena Vernon, but there was only her own brown old New England face to look back at her wonderingly.

Miss Pyne went less and less often to pay visits to her friends in Boston; there were very few friends left to come to Ashford and make long visits in the summer, and life grew more and more monotonous. Now and then there came news from across the sea and messages of remembrance, letters that were closely written on thin sheets of paper, and that spoke of lords and ladies, of great journeys, of the death of little children and the proud successes of boys at school, of the wedding of Helena Dysart's only daughter; but even that had happened years ago. These things seemed far away and vague, as if they belonged to a story and not to life itself; the true links with the past were quite different. There was the unvarying flock of ground-sparrows that Helena had begun to feed; every morning Martha scattered crumbs for them from the side doorsteps while Miss Pyne watched from the dining-room window, and they were counted and cherished year by year.

Miss Pyne herself had many fixed habits, but little ideality or imagination, and so at last it was Martha who took thought for her mistress, and gave freedom to her own good taste. After a while, without anyone's observing the change, the every-day ways of doing things in the house came to be the stately ways that had once belonged only to the entertainment of guests. Happily both mistress and maid seized all possible chances for hospitality, yet Miss Harriet nearly always sat alone at her exquisitely served table with its fresh flowers, and the beautiful old china which Martha handled so lovingly that there was no good excuse for keeping it hidden on closet shelves. Every year when the old cherry-trees were in fruit, Martha carried the round white old English dish with a fretwork edge, full of pointed green leaves and scarlet cherries, to the minister, and his wife never quite understood why every year he blushed and looked so conscious of the pleasure, and thanked Martha as if he had received a very particular attention. There was no pretty suggestion toward the pursuit of the fine art of housekeeping in Martha's limited acquaintance with newspapers that she did not adopt; there was no refined old custom of the Pyne housekeeping that she consented to let go. And every day, as she had promised, she thought of Miss Helena,—oh, many times in every day: whether this thing would please her, or that be likely to fall in with her fancy or ideas of fitness. As far as was possible the rare news that reached Ashford through an occasional letter or the talk of guests was made part of Martha's own life, the history of her own heart. A worn old geography often stood open at the map of Europe on the lightstand in her room, and a little old-fashioned gilt button, set with a bit of glass like a ruby, that had broken and fallen from the trimming of one of Helena's dresses, was used to mark the city of her dwelling-place. In the changes of a diplomatic life Martha followed her lady all about the map. Sometimes the button was at Paris, and sometimes at Madrid; once, to her great anxiety, it remained long at St. Petersburg. For such a slow scholar Martha was not unlearned at last, since everything about life in these foreign towns was of interest to her faithful heart. She satisfied her own mind as she threw crumbs to the tame sparrows; it was all part of the same thing and for the same affectionate reasons.

One Sunday afternoon in early summer Miss Harriet Pyne came hurrying along the entry that led to Martha's room and called two or three times before its inhabitant could reach the door. Miss Harriet looked unusually cheerful and excited, and she held something in her hand. "Where are you, Martha?" she called again. "Come quick, I have something to tell you!"

"Here I am, Miss Pyne," said Martha, who had only stopped to put her precious box in the drawer, and to shut the geography.

"Who do you think is coming this very night at half-past six? We must have everything as nice as we can; I must see Hannah at once. Do you remember my cousin Helena who has lived abroad so long? Miss Helena Vernon,—the Honorable Mrs. Dysart, she is now."

"Yes, I remember her," answered Martha, turning a little pale.

"I knew that she was in this country, and I had written to ask her to come for a long visit," continued Miss Harriet, who did not often explain things, even to Martha, though she was always conscientious about the kind messages that were sent back by grateful guests. "She telegraphs that she means to anticipate her visit by a few days and come to me at once. The heat is beginning in town, I suppose. I daresay, having been a foreigner so long, she does not mind traveling on Sunday. Do you think Hannah will be prepared? We must have tea a little later."

"Yes, Miss Harriet," said Martha. She wondered that she could speak as usual, there was such a ringing in her ears. "I shall have time to pick some fresh strawberries; Miss Helena is so fond of our strawberries."

"Why, I had forgotten," said Miss Pyne, a little puzzled by something quite unusual in Martha's face. "We must expect to find Mrs. Dysart a good deal changed, Martha; it is a great many years since she was here; I have not seen her since her wedding, and she has had a great deal of trouble, poor girl. You had better open the parlor chamber, and make it ready before you go down."

"It is all ready," said Martha. "I can carry some of those little sweet-brier roses upstairs before she comes."

"Yes, you are always thoughtful," said Miss Pyne, with unwonted feeling.

Martha did not answer. She glanced at the telegram wistfully. She had never really suspected before that Miss Pyne knew nothing of the love that had been in her heart all these years; it was half a pain and half a golden joy to keep such a secret; she could hardly bear this moment of surprise.

Presently the news gave wings to her willing feet. When Hannah, the cook, who never had known Miss Helena, went to the parlor an hour later on some errand to her old mistress, she discovered that this stranger guest must be a very important person. She had never seen the tea-table look exactly as it did that night, and in the parlor itself there were fresh blossoming boughs in the old East India jars, and lilies in the paneled hall, and flowers everywhere, as if there were some high festivity.

Miss Pyne sat by the window watching, in her best dress, looking stately and calm; she seldom went out now, and it was almost time for the carriage. Martha was just coming in from the garden with the strawberries, and with more flowers in her apron. It was a bright cool evening in June, the golden robins sang in the elms, and the sun was going down behind the apple-trees at the foot of the garden. The beautiful old house stood wide open to the long-expected guest.

"I think that I shall go down to the gate," said Miss Pyne, looking at Martha for approval, and Martha nodded and they went together slowly down the broad front walk.

There was a sound of horses and wheels on the roadside turf: Martha could not see at first; she stood back inside the gate behind the white lilac-bushes as the carriage came. Miss Pyne was there; she was holding out both arms and taking a tired, bent little figure in black to her heart. "Oh, my Miss Helena is an old woman like me!" and Martha gave a pitiful sob; she had never dreamed it would be like this; this was the one thing she could not bear.

"Where are you, Martha?" called Miss Pyne. "Martha will bring these in; you have not forgotten my good Martha, Helena?" Then Mrs. Dysart looked up and smiled just as she used to smile in the old days. The young eyes were there still in the changed face, and Miss Helena had come.

That night Martha waited in her lady's room just as she used to, humble and silent, and went through with the old unforgotten loving services. The long years seemed like days. At last she lingered a moment trying to think of something else that might be done, then she was going silently away, but Helena called her back. She suddenly knew the whole story and could hardly speak.

"Oh, my dear Martha!" she cried, "won't you kiss me good-night? Oh, Martha, have you remembered like this, all these long years!"

EDITH WHARTON
(1862–1937)

Edith Wharton led a double life. A child of cold, snobbish parents, she knew how to play her part in cold and snobbish New York society. As a woman and an artist, she also imagined and lived alternatives. She fled to Europe from what she called the ignorance and crassness of late-nineteenth-century America, and wrote fiction (*The House of Mirth* [1905], *Ethan Frome* [1911], *The Age of Innocence* [1920]) exposing the myths of class—predominantly, the suffocating consequences for women—all the while cultivating and enjoying the world of money and privilege she knew from the cradle and dramatized as a moral wasteland in her novels and stories. She married a dunce (Henry James referred to Edward Wharton as the "cerebrally compromised Teddy"), and after trying to make the absurd marriage work for twelve years, she suffered a nervous breakdown. She resurrected herself as a committed, professional writer (who would publish fifty volumes of fiction and nonfiction), eventually finding the nerve to divorce Teddy, engage in a love affair, and in numerous plots and characters dramatize the power of sexual desire and the hypocrisy of the rich and respectable.

Souls Belated

I

Their railway carriage had been full when the train left Bologna; but at the first station beyond Milan their only remaining companion—a courtly person who ate garlic out of a carpetbag—had left his crumb-strewn seat with a bow.

Lydia's eye regretfully followed the shiny broadcloth of his retreating back till it lost itself in the cloud of touts and cab drivers hanging about the station; then she glanced across at Gannett and caught the same regret in his look. They were both sorry to be alone.

"*Par-ten-za!*" shouted the guard. The train vibrated to a sudden slamming of doors; a waiter ran along the platform with a tray of fossilized sandwiches; a belated porter flung a bundle of shawls and bandboxes into a third-class carriage; the guard snapped out a brief *Partenza!* which indicated the purely ornamental nature of his first shout; and the train swung out of the station.

The direction of the road had changed, and a shaft of sunlight struck across the dusty red-velvet seats into Lydia's corner. Gannett did not notice it. He had returned to his *Revue de Paris*, and she had to raise and lower the shade of the farther window. Against the vast horizon of their leisure such incidents stood out sharply.

Having lowered the shade, Lydia sat down, leaving the length of the carriage between herself and Gannett. At length he missed her and looked up.

"I moved out of the sun," she hastily explained.

He looked at her curiously: the sun was beating on her through the shade.

"Very well," he said pleasantly; adding, "You don't mind?" as he drew a cigarette case from his pocket.

It was a refreshing touch, relieving the tension of her spirit with the suggestion that, after all, if he could *smoke*—! The relief was only momentary. Her experience of smokers was limited (her husband had disapproved of the use of tobacco) but she knew from hearsay that men sometimes smoked to get away from things; that a cigar might be the masculine equivalent of darkened windows and a headache. Gannett, after a puff or two, returned to his review.

It was just as she had foreseen; he feared to speak as much as she did. It was one of the misfortunes of their situation that they were never busy enough to necessitate, or even to justify, the postponement of unpleasant discussions. If they avoided a question it was obviously, unconcealably because the question was disagreeable. They had unlimited leisure and an accumulation of mental energy to devote to any subject that presented itself; new topics were in fact at a premium. Lydia sometimes had premonitions of a famine-stricken period when there would be nothing left to talk about, and she had already caught herself doling out piecemeal what, in the first prodigality of their confidences, she would have flung to him in a breath. Their silence therefore might simply mean that they had nothing to say; but it was another disadvantage of their position that it allowed infinite opportunity for the classification of minute differences. Lydia had learned to distinguish between real and factitious silences; and under Gannett's she now detected a hum of speech to which her own thoughts made breathless answer.

How could it be otherwise, with that thing between them? She glanced up at the rack overhead. The *thing* was there, in her dressing bag, symbolically suspended over her head and his. He was thinking of it now, just as she was; they had been thinking of it in unison ever since they had entered the train. While the carriage had held other travelers they had screened her from his thoughts; but now that he and she were alone she knew exactly what was passing through his mind; she could almost hear him asking himself what he should say to her.

The thing had come that morning, brought up to her in an innocent-looking envelope with the rest of their letters, as they were leaving the hotel at Bologna. As she tore it open, she and Gannett were laughing over some ineptitude of the local guidebook—they had been driven, of late, to make the most of such incidental humors of travel. Even when she had unfolded the document she took it for some unimportant business paper sent abroad for her signature, and her eye traveled inattentively over the curly *Whereases* of the preamble until a word arrested her: Divorce. There it stood, an impassable barrier, between her husband's name and hers.

She had been prepared for it, of course, as healthy people are said to be prepared for death, in the sense of knowing it must come without in the least expecting that it will. She had known from the first that Tillotson meant to divorce her—but what did it matter? Nothing mattered, in those first days of supreme deliverance, but the fact that she was free; and not so much (she had begun to be aware) that freedom had released her from Tillotson as that it had given her to Gannett. This discovery had not been agreeable to her self-esteem. She had preferred to think that Tillotson had himself embodied all her reasons for leaving him; and those he represented had seemed cogent enough to stand in no need of reinforcement. Yet she had not left him till she met Gannett. It was her love for Gannett that had made life with Tillotson so poor and incomplete a business. If she had never, from the first, regarded her marriage as a full canceling of her claims upon life, she had at least, for a number of years, accepted it as a provisional compensation,—she had made it "do." Existence in the commodious Tillotson mansion in Fifth Avenue—with Mrs. Tillotson senior commanding the approaches from the second-story front windows—had been reduced to a series of purely automatic acts. The moral atmosphere of the Tillotson interior was as carefully screened and curtained as the house itself: Mrs. Tillotson senior dreaded ideas as much as a draft in her back. Prudent people liked an even temperature; and to do anything unexpected was as foolish as going out in the rain. One of the chief advantages of being rich was that one need not be exposed to unforeseen contingencies: by the use of ordinary firmness and common sense one could make sure of doing exactly the same thing every day at the same hour. These doctrines, reverentially imbibed with his mother's milk, Tillotson (a model son who had never given his parents an hour's anxiety) complacently expounded to his wife, testifying to his sense of their importance by the regularity with which he wore galoshes on damp days, his punctuality at meals, and his elaborate precautions against burglars and contagious diseases. Lydia, coming from a smaller town, and entering New York life through the portals of the Tillotson mansion, had mechanically accepted this point of view as inseparable from having a front pew in church and a parterre box at the opera. All the people who came to the house revolved in the same small circle of prejudices. It was the kind of society in which, after dinner, the ladies compared the exorbitant charges of their children's teachers, and agreed that, even with the new duties on French clothes, it was cheaper in the end to get everything from Worth; while the husbands, over their cigars, lamented municipal corruption, and decided that the men to start a reform were those who had no private interests at stake.

To Lydia this view of life had become a matter of course, just as lumbering about in her mother-in-law's landau had come to seem the only possible means of locomotion, and listening every Sunday to a fashionable Presbyterian divine the inevitable atonement for having thought oneself bored on the other six days of the week. Before she met Gannett her life had seemed merely dull; his coming made it appear like one of those dismal Cruikshank prints in which the people are all ugly and all engaged in occupations that are either vulgar or stupid.

It was natural that Tillotson should be the chief sufferer from this readjustment of focus. Gannett's nearness had made her husband ridiculous, and a part of the ridicule had been reflected on herself. Her tolerance laid her open to a suspicion of obtuseness from which she must, at all costs, clear herself in Gannett's eyes.

She did not understand this until afterwards. At the time she fancied that she had merely reached the limits of endurance. In so large a charter of liberties as the mere act of leaving Tillotson seemed to confer, the small question of divorce or no divorce did not count. It was when she saw that she had left her husband only to be with Gannett that she perceived the significance of anything affecting their relations. Her husband, in casting her off, had virtually flung her at Gannett: it was thus that the world viewed it. The measure of alacrity with which Gannett would receive her would be the subject of curious speculation over afternoon tea tables and in club corners. She knew what would be said—she had heard it so often of others! The recollection bathed her in misery. The men would probably back Gannett to "do the decent thing"; but the ladies' eyebrows would emphasize the worthlessness of such enforced fidelity; and after all, they would be right. She had put herself in a position where Gannett "owed" her something; where, as a gentleman, he was bound to "stand the damage." The idea of accepting such compensation had never crossed her mind; the so-called rehabilitation of such a marriage had always seemed to her the only real disgrace. What she dreaded was the necessity of having to explain herself; of having to combat his arguments; of calculating, in spite of herself, the exact measure of insistence with which he pressed them. She knew not whether she most shrank from his insisting too much or too little. In such a case the nicest sense of proportion might be at fault; and how easily to fall into the error of taking her resistance for a test of his sincerity! Whichever way she turned, an ironical implication confronted her: she had the exasperated sense of having walked into the trap of some stupid practical joke.

Beneath all these preoccupations lurked the dread of what he was thinking. Sooner or later, of course, he would have to speak; but that, in the meantime, he should think, even for a moment, that there was any use in speaking, seemed to her simply unendurable. Her sensitiveness on this point was aggravated by another fear, as yet barely on the level of consciousness; the fear of unwillingly involving Gannett in the trammels of her dependence. To look upon him as the instrument of her liberation; to resist in herself the least tendency to a wifely taking possession of his future; had seemed to Lydia the one way of maintaining the dignity of their relation. Her view had not changed, but she was aware of a growing inability to keep her thoughts fixed on the essential point—the point of parting with Gannett. It was easy to face as long as she kept it sufficiently far off: but what was this act of mental postponement but a gradual encroachment on his future? What was needful was the courage to recognize the moment when, by some word or look, their voluntary fellowship should be transformed into a bondage the more wearing that it was based on none of those common obligations which make the most imperfect marriage in some sort a center of gravity.

When the porter, at the next station, threw the door open, Lydia drew back, making way for the hoped-for intruder; but none came, and the train took up its leisurely progress through the spring wheat fields and budding copses. She now began to hope that Gannett would speak before the next station. She watched him furtively, half-disposed to return to the seat opposite his, but there was an artificiality about his absorption that restrained her. She had never before seen him read with so conspicuous an air of warding off interruption. What could he be thinking of? Why should he be afraid to speak? Or was it her answer that he dreaded?

The train paused for the passing of an express, and he put down his book and leaned out of the window. Presently he turned to her with a smile.

"There's a jolly old villa out here," he said.

His easy tone relieved her, and she smiled back at him as she crossed over to his corner.

Beyond the embankment, through the opening in a mossy wall, she caught sight of the villa, with its broken balustrades, its stagnant fountains, and the stone satyr closing the perspective of a dusky grass walk.

"How should you like to live there?" he asked as the train moved on.

"There?"

"In some such place, I mean. One might do worse, don't you think so? There must be at least two centuries of solitude under those yew trees. Shouldn't you like it?"

"I—I don't know," she faltered. She knew now that he meant to speak.

He lit another cigarette. "We shall have to live somewhere, you know," he said as he bent above the match.

Lydia tried to speak carelessly. *"Je n'en vois pas la nécessité!* Why not live everywhere, as we have been doing?"

"But we can't travel forever, can we?"

"Oh, forever's a long word," she objected, picking up the review he had thrown aside.

"For the rest of our lives then," he said, moving nearer.

She made a slight gesture which caused his hand to slip from hers.

"Why should we make plans? I thought you agreed with me that it's pleasanter to drift."

He looked at her hesitatingly. "It's been pleasant, certainly; but I suppose I shall have to get at my work again some day. You know I haven't written a line since—all this time," he hastily amended.

She flamed with sympathy and self-reproach. "Oh, if you mean *that*—if you want to write—of course we must settle down. How stupid of me not to have thought of it sooner! Where shall we go? Where do you think you could work best? We oughtn't to lose any more time."

He hesitated again. "I had thought of a villa in these parts. It's quiet; we shouldn't be bothered. Should you like it?"

"Of course I should like it." She paused and looked away. "But I thought—I remember your telling me once that your best work had been done in a crowd—in big cities. Why should you shut yourself up in a desert?"

Gannett, for a moment, made no reply. At length he said, avoiding her eye as carefully as she avoided his: "It might be different now; I can't tell, of course, till I try. A writer ought not to be dependent on his *milieu*; it's a mistake to humor oneself in that way; and I thought that just at first you might prefer to be—"

She faced him. "To be what?"

"Well—quiet. I mean—"

"What do you mean by 'at first'?" she interrupted.

He paused again. "I mean after we are married."

She thrust up her chin and turned toward the window. "Thank you!" she tossed back at him.

"Lydia!" he exclaimed blankly; and she felt in every fiber of her averted person that he had made the inconceivable, the unpardonable mistake of anticipating her acquiescence.

The train rattled on and he groped for a third cigarette. Lydia remained silent.

"I haven't offended you?" he ventured at length, in the tone of a man who feels his way.

She shook her head with a sigh. "I thought you understood," she moaned. Their eyes met and she moved back to his side.

"Do you want to know how not to offend me? By taking it for granted, once for all, that you've said your say on the odious question and that I've said mine, and that we stand just where we did this morning before that—that hateful paper came to spoil everything between us!"

"To spoil everything between us? What on earth do you mean? Aren't you glad to be free?"

"I was free before."

"Not to marry me," he suggested.

"But I don't *want* to marry you!" she cried.

She saw that he turned pale. "I'm obtuse, I suppose," he said slowly. "I confess I don't see what you're driving at. Are you tired of the whole business? Or was I simply a—an excuse for getting away? Perhaps you didn't care to travel alone? Was that it? And now you want to chuck me?" His voice had grown harsh. "You owe me a straight answer, you know; don't be tenderhearted!"

Her eyes swam as she leaned to him. "Don't you see it's because I care—because I care so much? Oh, Ralph! Can't you see how it would humiliate me? Try to feel it as a woman would! Don't you see the misery of being made your wife in this way? If I'd known you as a girl—that would have been a real marriage! But now—this vulgar fraud upon society—and upon a society we despised and laughed at—this sneaking back into a position that we've voluntarily forfeited: don't you see what a cheap compromise it is? We neither of us believe in the abstract 'sacredness' of marriage; we both know that no ceremony is needed to consecrate our love for each other; what object can we have in marrying, except the secret fear of each that the other may escape, or the secret longing to work our way back gradually—oh, very gradually—into the esteem of the people whose conventional morality we have always ridiculed and hated? And the very fact that, after a decent interval, these same people would come and dine with us—the women who talk about the indissolubility of marriage, and who would let me die in a gutter today because I am 'leading a life of sin'—doesn't that disgust you more than their turning their backs on us now? I can stand being cut by them, but I couldn't stand their coming to call and asking what I meant to do about visiting that unfortunate Mrs. So-and-so!"

She paused, and Gannett maintained a perplexed silence.

"You judge things too theoretically," he said at length, slowly. "Life is made up of compromises."

"The life we ran away from—yes! If we had been willing to accept them"—she flushed—"we might have gone on meeting each other at Mrs. Tillotson's dinners."

He smiled slightly. "I didn't know that we ran away to found a new system of ethics. I supposed it was because we loved each other."

"Life is complex, of course; isn't it the very recognition of that fact that separates us from the people who see it *tout d'une pièce*? If *they* are right—if marriage is sacred in itself and the individual must always be sacrificed to the family—then there can be no real marriage between us, since our—our being together is a protest against the sacrifice of the individual to the family." She interrupted herself with a laugh. "You'll say now that I'm giving you a lecture on sociology! Of course one acts as one can—as one must, perhaps—pulled by all sorts of invisible threads; but at least one needn't pretend, for social advantages, to subscribe to a creed that ignores the complexity of human motives—that classifies people by arbitrary signs, and puts it in everybody's reach to be on Mrs. Tillotson's visiting list. It may be necessary that the world should be ruled by conventions—but if we believed in them, why did we break through them? And if we don't believe in them, is it honest to take advantage of the protection they afford?"

Gannett hesitated. "One may believe in them or not; but as long as they do rule the world it is only by taking advantage of their protection that one can find a *modus vivendi*."

"Do outlaws need a *modus vivendi?*"

He looked at her hopelessly. Nothing is more perplexing to man than the mental process of a woman who reasons her emotions.

She thought she had scored a point and followed it up passionately. "You do understand, don't you? You see how the very thought of the thing humiliates me! We are together today because we choose to be—don't let us look any farther than that!" She caught his hands. "*Promise* me you'll never speak of it again; promise me you'll never *think* of it even," she implored, with a tearful prodigality of italics.

Through what followed—his protests, his arguments, his final unconvinced submission to her wishes—she had a sense of his but half-discerning all that, for her, had made the moment so tumultuous. They had reached that memorable point in every heart history when, for the first time, the man seems obtuse and the woman irrational. It was the abundance of his intentions that consoled her, on reflection, for what they lacked in quality. After all, it would have been worse, incalculably worse, to have detected any overreadiness to understand her.

II

When the train at nightfall brought them to their journey's end at the edge of one of the lakes, Lydia was glad that they were not, as usual, to pass from one solitude to another. Their wanderings during the year had indeed been like the flight of the outlaws: through Sicily, Dalmatia, Transylvania and Southern Italy they had persisted in their tacit avoidance of their kind. Isolation, at first, had deepened the flavor of their happiness, as night intensifies the scent of certain flowers; but in the new phase on which they were entering, Lydia's chief wish was that they should be less abnormally exposed to the action of each other's thoughts.

She shrank, nevertheless, as the brightly-looming bulk of the fashionable Anglo-American hotel on the water's brink began to radiate toward their advancing boat its vivid suggestion of social order, visitors' lists, Church services, and the bland inquisition of the *table d'hôte*. The mere fact that in a moment or two she must take her place on the hotel register as Mrs. Gannett seemed to weaken the springs of her resistance.

They had meant to stay for a night only, on their way to a lofty village among the glaciers of Monte Rosa; but after the first plunge into publicity, when they entered the dining room, Lydia felt the relief of being lost in a crowd, of ceasing for a moment to be the center of Gannett's scrutiny; and in his face she caught the reflection of her feeling. After dinner, when she went upstairs, he strolled into the smoking room, and an hour or two later, sitting in the darkness of her window, she heard his voice below and saw him walking up and down the terrace with a companion cigar at his side. When he came he told her he had been talking to the hotel chaplain—a very good sort of fellow.

"Queer little microcosms, these hotels! Most of these people live here all summer and then migrate to Italy or the Riviera. The English are the only people who can lead that kind of life with dignity—those soft-voiced old ladies in Shetland shawls somehow carry the British Empire under their caps. *Civis Romanus sum*. It's a curious study—there might be some good things to work up here."

He stood before her with the vivid preoccupied stare of the novelist on the trail of a "subject." With a relief that was half painful she noticed that, for the first time since they had been together, he was hardly aware of her presence.

"Do you think you could write here?"

"Here? I don't know." His stare dropped. "After being out of things so long one's first impressions are bound to be tremendously vivid, you know. I see a dozen threads already that one might follow—"

He broke off with a touch of embarrassment.

"Then follow them. We'll stay," she said with sudden decision.

"Stay here?" He glanced at her in surprise, and then, walking to the window, looked out upon the dusky slumber of the garden.

"Why not?" she said at length, in a tone of veiled irritation.

"The place is full of old cats in caps who gossip with the chaplain. Shall you like—I mean, it would be different if —"

She flamed up.

"Do you suppose I care? It's none of their business."

"Of course not; but you won't get them to think so."

"They may think what they please."

He looked at her doubtfully.

"It's for you to decide."

"We'll stay," she repeated.

Gannett, before they met, had made himself known as a successful writer of short stories and of a novel which had achieved the distinction of being widely discussed. The reviewers called him "promising," and Lydia now accused herself of having too long interfered with the fulfilment of his promise. There was a special irony in the fact, since his passionate assurances that only the stimulus of her companionship could bring out his latent faculty had almost given the dignity of a "vocation" to her course: there had been moments when she had felt unable to assume, before posterity, the responsibility of thwarting his career. And, after all, he had not written a line since they had been together: his first desire to write had come from renewed contact with the world! Was it all a mistake then? Must the most intelligent choice work more disastrously than the blundering combinations of chance? Or was there a still more humiliating answer to her perplexities? His sudden impulse of activity so exactly coincided with her own wish to withdraw, for a time, from the range of his observation, that she wondered if he too were not seeking sanctuary from intolerable problems.

"You must begin tomorrow!" she cried, hiding a tremor under the laugh with which she added, "I wonder if there's any ink in the inkstand?"

Whatever else they had at the Hotel Bellosguardo, they had, as Miss Pinsent said, "a certain tone." It was to Lady Susan Condit that they owed this inestimable benefit; an advantage ranking in Miss Pinsent's opinion above even the lawn tennis courts and the resident chaplain. It was the fact of Lady Susan's annual visit that made the hotel what it was. Miss Pinsent was certainly the last to underrate such a privilege: "It's so important, my dear, forming as we do a little family, that there should be someone to give *the tone*; and no one could do it better than Lady Susan—an earl's daughter and a person of such determination. Dear Mrs. Ainger now—who really *ought*, you know, when Lady Susan's away—absolutely refuses to assert herself." Miss Pinsent sniffed derisively. "A bishop's niece!—my dear, I saw her once actually give in to some South Americans—and before us all. She gave up her seat at table to oblige them—such a lack of dignity! Lady Susan spoke to her very plainly about it afterwards."

Miss Pinsent glanced across the lake and adjusted her auburn front.

"But of course I don't deny that the stand Lady Susan takes is not always easy to live up to—for the rest of us, I mean. Monsieur Grossart, our good proprietor, finds it trying at times, I know—he has said as much, privately, to Mrs. Ainger and me. After all, the poor man is not to blame for wanting to fill his hotel, is he? And Lady Susan is so difficult—so very difficult—about new people. One might almost say that she disapproves of them beforehand, on principle. And yet she's had warnings—she very nearly made a dreadful mistake once with the Duchess of Levens, who dyed her hair and—well, swore and smoked. One would have thought that might have been a lesson to Lady Susan." Miss Pinsent resumed her knitting with a sigh. "There are exceptions, of course. She took at once to you and Mr. Gannett—it was quite remarkable, really. Oh, I don't mean that either—of course not! It was perfectly natural—we *all* thought you so charming and interesting from the first day—we knew at once that Mr. Gannett was intellectual, by the magazines you took in; but you know what I mean. Lady Susan is so very—well, I won't say prejudiced, as Mrs. Ainger does—but so prepared *not* to like new people, that her taking to you in that way was a surprise to us all, I confess."

Miss Pinsent sent a significant glance down the long laurustinus alley from the other end of which two people—a lady and a gentleman—were strolling toward them through the smiling neglect of the garden.

"In this case, of course, it's very different; that I'm willing to admit. Their looks are against them; but, as Mrs. Ainger says, one can't exactly tell them so."

"She's very handsome," Lydia ventured, with her eyes on the lady, who showed, under the dome of a vivid sunshade, the hourglass figure and superlative coloring of a Christmas chromo.

"That's the worst of it. She's too handsome."

"Well, after all, she can't help that."

"Other people manage to," said Miss Pinsent skeptically.

"But isn't it rather unfair of Lady Susan—considering that nothing is known about them?"

"But, my dear, that's the very thing that's against them. It's infinitely worse than any actual knowledge."

Lydia mentally agreed that, in the case of Mrs. Linton, it possibly might be.

"I wonder why they came here?" she mused.

"That's against them too. It's always a bad sign when loud people come to a quiet place. And they've brought van loads of boxes—her maid told Mrs. Ainger's that they meant to stop indefinitely."

"And Lady Susan actually turned her back on her in the salon?"

"My dear, she said it was for our sakes: that makes it so unanswerable! But poor Grossart *is* in a way! The Lintons have taken his most expensive suite, you know—the yellow damask drawing room above the portico—and they have champagne with every meal!"

They were silent as Mr. and Mrs. Linton sauntered by; the lady with tempestuous brows and challenging chin; the gentleman, a blond stripling, trailing after her, head downward, like a reluctant child dragged by his nurse.

"What does your husband think of them, my dear?" Miss Pinsent whispered as they passed out of earshot.

Lydia stooped to pick a violet in the border.

"He hasn't told me."

"Of your speaking to them, I mean. Would he approve of that? I know how very particular nice Americans are. I think your action might make a difference; it would certainly carry weight with Lady Susan."

"Dear Miss Pinsent, you flatter me!"

Lydia rose and gathered up her book and sunshade.

"Well, if you're asked for an opinion—if Lady Susan asks you for one—I think you ought to be prepared," Miss Pinsent admonished her as she moved away.

III

Lady Susan held her own. She ignored the Lintons, and her little family, as Miss Pinsent phrased it, followed suit. Even Mrs. Ainger agreed that it was obligatory. If Lady Susan owed it to the others not to speak to the Lintons, the others clearly owed it to Lady Susan to back her up. It was generally found expedient, at the Hotel Bellosguardo, to adopt this form of reasoning.

Whatever effect this combined action may have had upon the Lintons, it did not at least have that of driving them away. Monsieur Grossart, after a few days of suspense, had the satisfaction of seeing them settle down in his yellow damask *premier* with what looked like a permanent installation of palm trees and silk cushions, and a gratifying continuance in the consumption of champagne. Mrs. Linton trailed her Doucet draperies up and down the garden with the same challenging air, while her husband, smoking innumerable cigarettes, dragged himself dejectedly in her wake; but neither of them, after the first encounter with Lady Susan, made any attempt to extend their acquaintance. They simply ignored their ignorers. As Miss Pinsent resentfully observed, they behaved exactly as though the hotel were empty.

It was therefore a matter of surprise, as well as of displeasure, to Lydia, to find, on glancing up one day from her seat in the garden, that the shadow which had fallen across her book was that of the enigmatic Mrs. Linton.

"I want to speak to you," that lady said, in a rich hard voice that seemed the audible expression of her gown and her complexion.

Lydia started. She certainly did not want to speak to Mrs. Linton.

"Shall I sit down here?" the latter continued, fixing her intensely-shaded eyes on Lydia's face, "or are you afraid of being seen with me?"

"Afraid?" Lydia colored. "Sit down, please. What is it that you wish to say?"

Mrs. Linton, with a smile, drew up a garden chair and crossed one openwork ankle above the other.

"I want you to tell me what my husband said to your husband last night."

Lydia turned pale.

"My husband—to yours?" she faltered, staring at the other.

"Didn't you know they were closeted together for hours in the smoking room after you went upstairs? My man didn't get to bed until nearly two o'clock and when he did I couldn't get a word out of him. When he wants to be aggravating I'll back him against anybody living!" Her teeth and eyes flashed persuasively upon Lydia. "But you'll tell me what they were talking about, won't you? I know I can trust you—you look so awfully kind. And it's for his own good. He's such a precious donkey and I'm so afraid he's got into some beastly scrape or other. If he'd only trust his own old woman! But they're always writing to him and setting him against me. And I've got nobody to turn to." She laid her hand on Lydia's with a rattle of bracelets. "You'll help me, won't you?"

Lydia drew back from the smiling fierceness of her brows.

"I'm sorry—but I don't think I understand. My husband has said nothing to me of—of yours."

The great black crescents above Mrs. Linton's eyes met angrily.

"I say—is that true?" she demanded.

Lydia rose from her seat.

"Oh, look here, I didn't mean that, you know—you mustn't take one up so! Can't you see how rattled I am?"

Lydia saw that, in fact, her beautiful mouth was quivering beneath softened eyes.

"I'm beside myself!" the splendid creature wailed, dropping into her seat.

"I'm so sorry," Lydia repeated, forcing herself to speak kindly; "but how can I help you?"

Mrs. Linton raised her head sharply.

"By finding out—there's a darling!"

"Finding what out?"

"What Trevenna told him."

"Trevenna—?" Lydia echoed in bewilderment.

Mrs. Linton clapped her hand to her mouth.

"Oh, Lord—there, it's out! What a fool I am! But I supposed of course you knew; I supposed everybody knew." She dried her eyes and bridled. "Didn't you know that he's Lord Trevenna? I'm Mrs. Cope."

Lydia recognized the names. They had figured in a flamboyant elopement which had thrilled fashionable London some six months earlier.

"Now you see how it is—you understand, don't you?" Mrs. Cope continued on a note of appeal. "I knew you would—that's the reason I came to you. I suppose *he* felt the same thing about your husband; he's not spoken to another soul in the place." Her face grew anxious again. "He's awfully sensitive, generally—he feels our position, he says—as if it wasn't *my* place to feel that! But when he does get talking there's no knowing what he'll say. I know he's been brooding over something lately, and I *must* find out what it is—it's to his interest that I should. I always tell him that I think only of his interest; if he'd only trust me! But he's been so odd lately—I can't think what he's plotting. You will help me, dear?"

Lydia, who had remained standing, looked away uncomfortably.

"If you mean by finding out what Lord Trevenna has told my husband, I'm afraid it's impossible."

"Why impossible?"

"Because I infer that it was told in confidence."

Mrs. Cope stared incredulously.

"Well, what of that? Your husband looks such a dear—anyone can see he's awfully gone on you. What's to prevent your getting it out of him?"

Lydia flushed.

"I'm not a spy!" she exclaimed.

"A spy—a spy? How dare you?" Mrs. Cope flamed out. "Oh, I don't mean that either! Don't be angry with me—I'm so miserable." She essayed a softer note. "Do you call that spying—for one woman to help out another? I do need help so dreadfully! I'm at my wits' end with Trevenna, I am indeed. He's such a boy—a mere baby, you know; he's only two-and-twenty." She dropped her orbed lids. "He's younger than me—only fancy, a few months younger. I tell him he ought to listen to me as if I was his mother; oughtn't he now? But he won't, he won't! All his people are at him, you see—oh, I know *their* little game! Trying to get him away from me before I can get my divorce—that's what they're up to. At first he wouldn't listen to them; he used to toss their letters over to me to read; but now he reads them himself, and answers 'em too, I fancy; he's always shut up in his room, writing. If I only knew what his plan is I could stop him fast enough—he's such a simpleton. But he's dreadfully deep too—at times I can't make him out. But I know he's told your husband everything—I knew that last night the minute I laid eyes on him. And I *must* find out—you must help me—I've got no one else to turn to!"

She caught Lydia's fingers in a stormy pressure.

"Say you'll help me—you and your husband."

Lydia tried to free herself.

"What you ask is impossible; you must see that it is. No one could interfere in—in the way you ask."

Mrs. Cope's clutch tightened.

"You won't, then? You won't?"

"Certainly not. Let me go, please."

Mrs. Cope released her with a laugh.

"Oh, go by all means—pray don't let me detain you! Shall you go and tell Lady Susan Condit that there's a pair of us—or shall I save you the trouble of enlightening her?"

Lydia stood still in the middle of the path, seeing her antagonist through a mist of terror. Mrs. Cope was still laughing.

"Oh, I'm not spiteful by nature, my dear; but you're a little more than flesh and blood can stand! It's impossible, is it? Let you go, indeed! You're too good to be mixed up in my affairs, are you? Why, you little fool, the first day I laid eyes on you I saw that you and I were both in the same box—that's the reason I spoke to you."

She stepped nearer, her smile dilating on Lydia like a lamp through a fog.

"You can take your choice, you know; I always play fair. If you'll tell I'll promise not to. Now then, which is it to be?"

Lydia, involuntarily, had begun to move away from the pelting storm of words; but at this she turned and sat down again.

"You may go," she said simply. "I shall stay here."

IV

She stayed there for a long time, in the hypnotized contemplation, not of Mrs. Cope's present, but of her own past. Gannett, early that morning, had gone off on a long walk—he had fallen into the habit of taking these mountain tramps with various fellow lodgers; but even had he been within reach she could not have gone to him just then. She had to deal with herself first. She was surprised to find how, in the last months, she had lost the habit of introspection. Since their coming to the Hotel Bellosguardo she and Gannett had tacitly avoided themselves and each other.

She was aroused by the whistle of the three o'clock steamboat as it neared the landing just beyond the hotel gates. Three o'clock! Then Gannett would soon be back—he had told her to expect him before four. She rose hurriedly, her face averted from the inquisitorial façade of the hotel. She could not see him just yet; she could not go indoors. She slipped through one of the overgrown garden alleys and climbed a steep path to the hills.

It was dark when she opened their sitting-room door. Gannett was sitting on the window ledge smoking a cigarette. Cigarettes were now his chief resource: he had not written a line during the two months they had spent at the Hotel Bellosguardo. In that respect, it had turned out not to be the right *milieu* after all.

He started up at Lydia's entrance.

"Where have you been? I was getting anxious."

She sat down in a chair near the door.

"Up the mountain," she said wearily.

"Alone?"

"Yes."

Gannett threw away his cigarette: the sound of her voice made him want to see her face.

"Shall we have a little light?" he suggested.

She made no answer and he lifted the globe from the lamp and put a match to the wick. Then he looked at her.

"Anything wrong? You look done up."

She sat glancing vaguely about the little sitting room, dimly lit by the pallidglobed lamp, which left in twilight the outlines of the furniture, of his writing table heaped with books and papers, of the tea roses and jasmine drooping on the mantelpiece. How like home it had all grown—how like home!

"Lydia, what is wrong?" he repeated.

She moved away from him, feeling for her hatpins and turning to lay her hat and sunshade on the table.

Suddenly she said: "That woman has been talking to me."

Gannett stared.

"That woman? What woman?"

"Mrs. Linton—Mrs. Cope."

He gave a start of annoyance, still, as she perceived, not grasping the full import of her words.

"The deuce! She told you—?"

"She told me everything."

Gannett looked at her anxiously.

"What impudence! I'm so sorry that you should have been exposed to this, dear."

"Exposed!" Lydia laughed.

Gannett's brow clouded and they looked away from each other.

"Do you know *why* she told me? She had the best of reasons. The first time she laid eyes on me she saw that we were both in the same box."

"Lydia!"

"So it was natural, of course, that she should turn to me in a difficulty."

"What difficulty?"

"It seems she has reason to think that Lord Trevenna's people are trying to get him away from her before she gets her divorce—"

"Well?"

"And she fancied he had been consulting with you last night as to—as to the best way of escaping from her."

Gannett stood up with an angry forehead.

"Well—what concern of yours was all this dirty business? Why should she go to you?"

"Don't you see? It's so simple. I was to wheedle his secret out of you."

"To oblige that woman?"

"Yes; or, if I was unwilling to oblige her, then to protect myself."

"To protect yourself? Against whom?"

"Against her telling everyone in the hotel that she and I are in the same box."

"She threatened that?"

"She left me the choice of telling it myself or of doing it for me."

"The beast!"

There was a long silence. Lydia had seated herself on the sofa, beyond the radius of the lamp, and he leaned against the window. His next question surprised her.

"When did this happen? At what time, I mean?"

She looked at him vaguely.

"I don't know—after luncheon, I think. Yes, I remember; it must have been at about three o'clock."

He stepped into the middle of the room and as he approached the light she saw that his brow had cleared.

"Why do you ask?" she said.

"Because when I came in, at about half-past three, the mail was just being distributed, and Mrs. Cope was waiting as usual to pounce on her letters; you know she was always watching for the postman. She was standing so close to me that I couldn't help seeing a big official-looking envelope that was handed to her. She tore it open, gave one look at the inside, and rushed off upstairs like a whirlwind, with the director shouting after her that she had left all her other letters behind. I don't believe she ever thought of you again after that paper was put into her hand."

"Why?"

"Because she was too busy. I was sitting in the window, watching for you, when the five o'clock boat left, and who should go on board, bag and baggage, valet and maid, dressing bags and poodle, but Mrs. Cope and Trevenna. Just an hour and a half to pack up in! And you should have seen her when they started. She was radiant—shaking hands with everybody—waving her handkerchief from the deck—distributing bows and smiles like an empress. If ever a woman got what she wanted just in the nick of time that woman did. She'll be Lady Trevenna within a week, I'll wager."

"You think she has her divorce?"

"I'm sure of it. And she must have got it just after her talk with you."

Lydia was silent.

At length she said, with a kind of reluctance, "She was horribly angry when she left me. It wouldn't have taken long to tell Lady Susan Condit."

"Lady Susan Condit has not been told."

"How do you know?"

"Because when I went downstairs half an hour ago I met Lady Susan on the way—"

He stopped, half smiling.

"Well?"

"And she stopped to ask if I thought you would act as patroness to a charity concert she is getting up."

In spite of themselves they both broke into a laugh. Lydia's ended in sobs and she sank down with her face hidden. Gannett bent over her, seeking her hands.

"That vile woman—I ought to have warned you to keep away from her; I can't forgive myself! But he spoke to me in confidence; and I never dreamed—well, it's all over now."

Lydia lifted her head.

"Not for me. It's only just beginning."

"What do you mean?"

She put him gently aside and moved in her turn to the window. Then she went on, with her face turned toward the shimmering blackness of the lake, "You see of course that it might happen again at any moment."

"What?"

"This—this risk of being found out. And we could hardly count again on such a lucky combination of chances, could we?"

He sat down with a groan.

Still keeping her face toward the darkness, she said, "I want you to go and tell Lady Susan—and the others."

Gannett, who had moved towards her, paused a few feet off.

"Why do you wish me to do this?" he said at length, with less surprise in his voice than she had been prepared for.

"Because I've behaved basely, abominably, since we came here: letting these people believe we were married—lying with every breath I drew—"

"Yes, I've felt that too," Gannett exclaimed with sudden energy.

The words shook her like a tempest: all her thoughts seemed to fall about her in ruins.

"You—you've felt so?"

"Of course I have." He spoke with low-voiced vehemence. "Do you suppose I like playing the sneak any better than you do? It's damnable."

He had dropped on the arm of a chair, and they stared at each other like blind people who suddenly see.

"But you have liked it here," she faltered.

"Oh, I've liked it—I've liked it." He moved impatiently. "Haven't you?"

"Yes," she burst out; "that's the worst of it—that's what I can't bear. I fancied it was for your sake that I insisted on staying—because you thought you could write here; and perhaps just at first that really was the reason. But afterwards I wanted to stay myself—I loved it." She broke into a laugh. "Oh, do you see the full derision of it? These people—the very prototypes of the bores you took me away from, with the same fenced-in view of life, the same keep-off-the-grass morality, the same little cautious virtues and the same little frightened vices—well, I've clung to them, I've delighted in them, I've done my best to please them. I've toadied Lady Susan, I've gossiped with Miss Pinsent, I've pretended to be shocked with Mrs. Ainger. Respectability! It was the one thing in life that I was sure I didn't care about, and it's grown so precious to me that I've stolen it because I couldn't get it in any other way."

She moved across the room and returned to his side with another laugh.

"I who used to fancy myself unconventional! I must have been born with a card-case in my hand. You should have seen me with that poor woman in the garden. She came to me for help, poor creature, because she fancied that, having 'sinned,' as they call it, I might feel some pity for others who had been tempted in the same way. Not I! She didn't know me. Lady Susan would have been kinder, because Lady Susan wouldn't have been afraid. I hated the woman—my one thought was not to be seen with her—I could have killed her for guessing my secret. The one thing that mattered to me at that moment was my standing with Lady Susan!"

Gannett did not speak.

"And you—you've felt it too!" she broke out accusingly. "You've enjoyed being with these people as much as I have; you've let the chaplain talk to you by the hour about The Reign of Law and Professor Drummond. When they asked you to hand the plate in church I was watching you—*you wanted to accept*."

She stepped close, laying her hand on his arm.

"Do you know, I begin to see what marriage is for. It's to keep people away from each other. Sometimes I think that two people who love each other can be saved from madness only by the things that come between them—children, duties, visits, bores, relations—the things that protect married people from each other. We've been too close together—that has been our sin. We've seen the nakedness of each other's souls."

She sank again on the sofa, hiding her face in her hands.

Gannett stood above her perplexedly: he felt as though she were being swept away by some implacable current while he stood helpless on its bank.

At length he said, "Lydia, don't think me a brute—but don't you see yourself that it won't do?"

"Yes, I see it won't do," she said without raising her head.

His face cleared.

"Then we'll go tomorrow."

"Go—where?"

"To Paris; to be married."

For a long time she made no answer; then she asked slowly, "Would they have us here if we were married?"

"Have us here?"

"I mean Lady Susan—and the others."

"Have us here? Of course they would."

"Not if they knew—at least, not unless they could pretend not to know."

He made an impatient gesture.

"We shouldn't come back here, of course; and other people needn't know—no one need know."

She sighed. "Then it's only another form of deception and a meaner one. Don't you see that?"

"I see that we're not accountable to any Lady Susans on earth!"

"Then why are you ashamed of what we are doing here?"

"Because I'm sick of pretending that you're my wife when you're not—when you won't be."

She looked at him sadly.

"If I were your wife you'd have to go on pretending. You'd have to pretend that I'd never been—anything else. And our friends would have to pretend that they believed what you pretended."

Gannett pulled off the sofa tassel and flung it away.

"You're impossible," he groaned.

"It's not I—it's our being together that's impossible. I only want you to see that marriage won't help it."

"What will help it then?"

She raised her head.

"My leaving you."

"Your leaving me?" He sat motionless, staring at the tassel which lay at the other end of the room. At length some impulse of retaliation for the pain she was inflicting made him say deliberately:

"And where would you go if you left me?"

"Oh!" she cried.

He was at her side in an instant.

"Lydia—Lydia—you know I didn't mean it; I couldn't mean it! But you've driven me out of my senses; I don't know what I'm saying. Can't you get out of this labyrinth of self-torture? It's destroying us both."

"That's why I must leave you."

"How easily you say it!" He drew her hands down and made her face him. "You're very scrupulous about yourself—and others. But have you thought of me? You have no right to leave me unless you've ceased to care—"

"It's because I care—"

"Then I have a right to be heard. If you love me you can't leave me."

Her eyes defied him.

"Why not?"

He dropped her hands and rose from her side.

"Can you?" he said sadly.

The hour was late and the lamp flickered and sank. She stood up with a shiver and turned toward the door of her room.

V

At daylight a sound in Lydia's room woke Gannett from a troubled sleep. He sat up and listened. She was moving about softly, as though fearful of disturbing him. He heard her push back one of the creaking shutters; then there was a moment's silence, which seemed to indicate that she was waiting to see if the noise had roused him.

Presently she began to move again. She had spent a sleepless night, probably, and was dressing to go down to the garden for a breath of air. Gannett rose also; but some undefinable instinct made his movements as cautious as hers. He stole to his window and looked out through the slats of the shutter.

It had rained in the night and the dawn was gray and lifeless. The cloud-muffled hills across the lake were reflected in its surface as in a tarnished mirror. In the garden, the birds were beginning to shake the drops from the motionless laurustinus boughs.

An immense pity for Lydia filled Gannett's soul. Her seeming intellectual independence had blinded him for a time to the feminine cast of her mind. He had never thought of her as a woman who wept and clung: there was a lucidity in her intuitions that made them appear to be the result of reasoning. Now he saw the cruelty he had committed in detaching her from the normal conditions of life; he felt, too, the insight with which she had hit upon the real cause of their suffering. Their life was "impossible," as she had said—and its worst penalty was that it had made any other life impossible for them. Even had his love lessened, he was bound to her now by a hundred ties of pity and self-reproach; and she, poor child, must turn back to him as Latude returned to his cell.

A new sound startled him: it was the stealthy closing of Lydia's door. He crept to his own and heard her footsteps passing down the corridor. Then he went back to the window and looked out.

A minute or two later he saw her go down the steps of the porch and enter the garden. From his post of observation her face was invisible, but something about her appearance struck him. She wore a long traveling cloak and under its folds he detected the outline of a bag or bundle. He drew a deep breath and stood watching her.

She walked quickly down the laurustinus alley toward the gate; there she paused a moment, glancing about the little shady square. The stone benches under the trees were empty, and she seemed to gather resolution from the solitude about her, for she crossed the square to the steamboat landing, and he saw her pause before the ticket office at the head of the wharf. Now she was buying her ticket. Gannett turned his head a moment to look at the clock: the boat was due in five minutes. He had time to jump into his clothes and overtake her—

He made no attempt to move; an obscure reluctance restrained him. If any thought emerged from the tumult of his sensations, it was that he must let her go if she wished it. He had spoken last night of his rights: what were they? At the last issue, he and she were two separate beings, not made one by the miracle of common forbearances, duties, abnegations, but bound together in a *noyade* of passion that left them resisting yet clinging as they went down.

After buying her ticket, Lydia had stood for a moment looking out across the lake; then he saw her seat herself on one of the benches near the landing. He and she, at that moment, were both listening for the same sound: the whistle of the boat as it rounded the nearest promontory. Gannett turned again to glance at the clock: the boat was due now.

Where would she go? What would her life be when she had left him? She had no near relations and few friends. There was money enough . . . but she asked so much of life, in ways so complex and immaterial. He thought of her as walking barefooted through a stony waste. No one would understand her—no one would pity her—and he, who did both, was powerless to come to her aid.

He saw that she had risen from the bench and walked toward the edge of the lake. She stood looking in the direction from which the steamboat was to come; then she turned to the ticket office, doubtless to ask the cause of the delay. After that she went back to the bench and sat down with bent head. What was she thinking of?

The whistle sounded; she started up, and Gannett involuntarily made a movement toward the door. But he turned back and continued to watch her. She stood motionless, her eyes on the trail of smoke that preceded the appearance of the boat. Then the little craft rounded the point, a dead white object on the leaden water: a minute later it was puffing and backing at the wharf.

The few passengers who were waiting—two or three peasants and a snuffy priest—were clustered near the ticket office. Lydia stood apart under the trees.

The boat lay alongside now; the gangplank was run out and the peasants went on board with their baskets of vegetables, followed by the priest. Still Lydia did not move. A bell began to ring querulously; there was a shriek of steam, and someone must have called to her that she would be late, for she started forward, as though in answer to a summons. She moved waveringly, and at the edge of the wharf she paused. Gannett saw a sailor beckon to her; the bell rang again and she stepped upon the gangplank.

Halfway down the short incline to the deck she stopped again; then she turned and ran back to the land. The gangplank was drawn in, the bell ceased to ring, and the boat backed out into the lake. Lydia, with slow steps, was walking toward the garden.

As she approached the hotel she looked up furtively and Gannett drew back into the room. He sat down beside a table; a Bradshaw* lay at his elbow, and mechanically, without knowing what he did, he began looking out the trains to Paris.

*a railway timetable

WILLA CATHER
(1873–1947)

Born of Anglo-Irish parents in the Shenandoah Valley of Virginia, Willa Cather was transplanted to Nebraska at the age of ten. She grew up riding the prairie and learning how to kill rattlesnakes in the company of new immigrants from Scandinavia, Germany, and Russia. While working her way through the University of Nebraska as a journalist, she discovered her love of music, a life-long passion that gives "A Wagner Matinée" its power. After earning her living as a journalist, editor, and teacher, she finally devoted herself to the full-time writing of fiction on the advice of her friend Sarah Orne Jewett (see pages 39–52). *The Song of the Lark* (1915), *My Ántonia* (1918), *The Professor's House* (1925), *Death Comes for the Archbishop* (1927), and *Lucy Gayheart* (1935), some of her best-known titles, are now classics of American literature. Wallace Stevens remarked in a letter, "We have nothing better than she is." ·

A Wagner Matinée

I received one morning a letter, written in pale ink on glassy, blue-lined note-paper, and bearing the postmark of a little Nebraska village. This communication, worn and rubbed, looking as if it had been carried for some days in a coat pocket that was none too clean, was from my uncle Howard, and informed me that his wife had been left a small legacy by a bachelor relative, and that it would be necessary for her to go to Boston to attend to the settling of the estate. He requested me to meet her at the station and render her whatever services might be necessary. On examining the date indicated as that of her arrival, I found it to be no later than tomorrow. He had characteristically delayed writing until, had I been away from home for a day, I must have missed my aunt altogether.

The name of my Aunt Georgiana opened before me a gulf of recollection so wide and deep that, as the letter dropped from my hand, I felt suddenly a stranger to all the present conditions of my existence, wholly ill at ease and out of place amid the familiar surroundings of my study. I became, in short, the gangling farmer-boy my aunt had known, scourged with chilblains and bashfulness, my hands cracked and sore from the corn husking. I sat again before her parlour organ, fumbling the scales with my stiff, red fingers, while she, beside me, made canvas mittens for the huskers.

The next morning, after preparing my landlady for a visitor, I set out for the station. When the train arrived I had some difficulty finding my aunt. She was the last of the passengers to alight, and it was not until I got her into the carriage that she seemed really to recognize me. She had come all the way in a day coach; her linen duster had become black with soot and her black bonnet grey with dust during her journey. When we arrived at my boarding-house the landlady put her to bed at once and I did not see her again until the next morning.

Whatever shock Mrs. Springer experienced at my aunt's appearance, she considerately concealed. As for myself, I saw my aunt's battered figure with that feeling of awe and respect with which we behold explorers who have left their ears and fingers north of Franz-Joseph-Land, or their health somewhere along the Upper Congo. My Aunt Georgiana had been a music teacher at the Boston Conservatory, somewhere back in the latter sixties. One summer, while visiting in the little village among the Green Mountains where her ancestors had dwelt for generations, she had kindled the callow fancy of my uncle, Howard Carpenter, then an idle, shiftless boy of twenty-one. When she returned to her duties in Boston, Howard followed her, and the upshot of this infatuation was that she eloped with him, eluding the reproaches of her family and the criticism of her friends by going with him to the Nebraska frontier. Carpenter, who, of course, had no money, took up a homestead in Red Willow County, fifty miles from the railroad. There they had measured off their land themselves, driving across the prairie in a wagon, to the wheel of which they had tied a red cotton handkerchief, and counting its revolutions. They built a dug-out in the red hillside, one of those cave dwellings whose inmates so often reverted to primitive conditions. Their water they got from the lagoons where the buffalo drank, and their slender stock of provisions was always at the mercy of bands of roving Indians. For thirty years my aunt had not been farther than fifty miles from the homestead.

I owed to this woman most of the good that ever came my way in my boyhood, and had a reverential affection for her. During the years when I was riding herd for my uncle, my aunt, after cooking the three meals—the first of which was ready at six o'clock in the morning—and putting the six children to bed, would often stand until midnight at her ironing-board, with me at the kitchen table beside her, hearing me recite Latin declensions and conjugations, gently shaking me when my drowsy head sank down over a page of irregular verbs. It was to her, at her ironing or mending, that I read my first Shakespeare, and her old textbook on mythology was the first that ever came into my empty hands. She taught me my scales and exercises on the little parlour organ which her husband had bought her after fifteen years during which she had not so much as seen a musical instrument. She would sit beside me by the hour, darning and counting, while I struggled with the "Joyous Farmer." She seldom talked to me about music, and I understood why. Once when I had been doggedly beating out some easy passages from an old score of *Euryanthe* I had found among her music books, she came up to me and, putting her hands over my eyes, gently drew my head back upon her shoulder, saying tremulously, "Don't love it so well, Clark, or it may be taken from you."

When my aunt appeared on the morning after her arrival in Boston, she was still in a semi-somnambulant state. She seemed not to realize that she was in the city where she had spent her youth, the place longed for hungrily half a lifetime. She had been so wretchedly trainsick throughout the journey that she had no recollection of anything but her discomfort, and, to all intents and purposes, there were but a few hours of nightmare between the farm in Red Willow County and my study on Newbury Street. I had planned a little pleasure for her that afternoon, to repay her for some of the glorious moments she had given me when we used to milk together in the straw-thatched cowshed and she, because I was more than usually tired, or because her husband had spoken sharply to me, would tell me of the splendid performance of the *Huguenots* she had seen in Paris, in her youth.

At two o'clock the Symphony Orchestra was to give a Wagner program, and I intended to take my aunt; though, as I conversed with her, I grew doubtful about her enjoyment of it. I suggested our visiting the Conservatory and the Common before lunch, but she seemed altogether too timid to wish to venture out. She questioned me absently about various changes in the city, but she was chiefly concerned that she had forgotten to leave instructions about feeding half-skimmed milk to a certain weakling calf, "old Maggie's calf, you know, Clark," she explained, evidently having forgotten how long I had been away. She was further troubled because she had neglected to tell her daughter about the freshly-opened kit of mackerel in the cellar, which would spoil if it were not used directly.

I asked her whether she had ever heard any of the Wagnerian operas, and found that she had not, though she was perfectly familiar with their respective situations, and had once possessed the piano score of *The Flying Dutchman*. I began to think it would be best to get her back to Red Willow County without waking her, and regretted having suggested the concert.

From the time we entered the concert hall, however, she was a trifle less passive and inert, and for the first time seemed to perceive her surroundings. I had felt some trepidation lest she might become aware of her queer, country clothes, or might experience some painful embarrassment at stepping suddenly into the world to which she had been dead for a quarter of a century. But, again, I found how superficially I had judged her. She sat looking about her with eyes as impersonal, almost as stony, as those with which the granite Rameses in a museum watches the froth and fret that ebbs and flows about his pedestal. I have seen this same aloofness in old miners who drift into the Brown hotel at Denver, their pockets full of bullion, their linen soiled, their haggard faces unshaven; standing in the thronged corridors as solitary as though they were still in a frozen camp on the Yukon.

The matinée audience was made up chiefly of women. One lost the contour of faces and figures, indeed any effect of line whatever, and there was only the colour of bodices past counting, the shimmer of fabrics soft and firm, silky and sheer; red, mauve, pink, blue, lilac, purple, écru, rose, yellow, cream, and white, all the colours that an impressionist finds in a sunlit landscape, with here and there the dead shadow of a frock coat. My Aunt Georgiana regarded them as though they had been so many daubs of tube-paint on a palette.

When the musicians came out and took their places, she gave a little stir of anticipation, and looked with quickening interest down over the rail at that invariable grouping, perhaps the first wholly familiar thing that had greeted her eye since she had left old Maggie and her weakling calf. I could feel how all those details sank into her soul, for I had not forgotten how they had sunk into mine when I came fresh from ploughing forever and forever between green aisles of corn, where, as in a treadmill, one might walk from daybreak to dusk without perceiving a shadow of change. The clean profiles of the musicians, the gloss of their linen, the dull black of their coats, the beloved shapes of the instruments, the patches of yellow light on the smooth, varnished bellies of the 'cellos and the bass viols in the rear, the restless, wind-tossed forest of fiddle necks and bows—I recalled how, in the first orchestra I ever heard, those long bow-strokes seemed to draw the heart out of me, as a conjurer's stick reels out yards of paper ribbon from a hat.

The first number was the *Tannhäuser* overture. When the horns drew out the first strain of the Pilgrim's chorus, Aunt Georgiana clutched my coat sleeve. Then it was I first realized that for her this broke a silence of thirty years. With the battle between the two motives, with the frenzy of the Venusberg theme and its ripping of strings, there came to me an overwhelming sense of the waste and wear we are so powerless to combat; and I saw again the tall, naked house on the prairie, black and grim as a wooden fortress; the black pond where I had learned to swim, its margin pitted with sun-dried cattle tracks; the rain-gullied clay banks about the naked house, the four dwarf-ash seedlings where the dish-cloths were always hung to dry before the kitchen door. The world there was the flat world of the ancients; to the east, a cornfield that stretched to daybreak; to the west, a corral that reached to sunset; between, the conquests of peace, dearer-bought than those of war.

The overture closed, my aunt released my coat sleeve, but she said nothing. She sat staring dully at the orchestra. What, I wondered, did she get from it? She had been a good pianist in her day, I knew, and her musical education had been broader than that of most music teachers of a quarter of a century ago. She had often told me of Mozart's operas and Meyerbeer's, and I could remember hearing her sing, years ago, certain melodies of Verdi. When I had fallen ill with a fever in her house she used to sit by my cot in the evening—when the cool, night wind blew in through the faded mosquito netting tacked over the window and I lay watching a certain bright star that burned red above the cornfield—and sing "Home to our mountains, O, let us return!" in a way fit to break the heart of a Vermont boy near dead of homesickness already.

I watched her closely through the prelude to *Tristan and Isolde*, trying vainly to conjecture what that seething turmoil of strings and winds might mean to her, but she sat mutely staring at the violin bows that drove obliquely downward, like the pelting streaks of rain in a summer shower. Had this music any message for her? Had she enough left to at all comprehend this power which had kindled the world since she had left it? I was in a fever of curiosity, but Aunt Georgiana sat silent upon her peak in Darien. She preserved this utter immobility throughout the number from *The Flying Dutchman*, though her fingers worked mechanically upon her black dress, as if, of themselves, they were recalling the piano score they had once played. Poor hands! They had been stretched and twisted into mere tentacles to hold and lift and knead with;—on one of them a thin, worn band that had once been a wedding ring. As I pressed and gently quieted one of those groping hands, I remembered with quivering eyelids their services for me in other days.

Soon after the tenor began the "Prize Song," I heard a quick drawn breath and turned to my aunt. Her eyes were closed, but the tears were glistening on her cheeks, and I think, in a moment more, they were in my eyes as well. It never really died, then—the soul which can suffer so excruciatingly and so interminably; it withers to the outward eye only; like that strange moss which can lie on a dusty shelf half a century and yet, if placed in water, grows green again. She wept so throughout the development and elaboration of the melody.

During the intermission before the second half, I questioned my aunt and found that the "Prize Song" was not new to her. Some years before there had drifted to the farm in Red Willow County a young German, a tramp cowpuncher, who had sung in the chorus at Bayreuth when he was a boy, along with the other peasant boys and girls. Of a Sunday morning he used to sit on his gingham-sheeted bed in the hands' bedroom which opened off the kitchen, cleaning the leather of his boots and saddle, singing the "Prize Song," while my aunt went about her work in the kitchen. She had hovered over him until she had prevailed upon him to join the country church, though his sole fitness for this step, in so far as I could gather, lay in his boyish face and his possession of this divine melody. Shortly afterward, he had gone to town on the Fourth of July, been drunk for several days, lost his money at a faro table, ridden a saddled Texas steer on a bet, and disappeared with a fractured collar-bone. All this my aunt told me huskily, wanderingly, as though she were talking in the weak lapses of illness.

"Well, we have come to better things than the old *Trovatore* at any rate, Aunt Georgie?" I queried, with a well-meant effort at jocularity.

Her lip quivered and she hastily put her handkerchief up to her mouth. From behind it she murmured, "And you have been hearing this ever since you left me, Clark?" Her question was the gentlest and saddest of reproaches.

The second half of the program consisted of four numbers from the *Ring*, and closed with Siegfried's funeral march. My aunt wept quietly, but almost continuously, as a shallow vessel overflows in a rain-storm. From time to time her dim eyes looked up at the lights, burning softly under their dull glass globes.

The deluge of sound poured on and on; I never knew what she found in the shining current of it; I never knew how far it bore her, or past what happy islands. From the trembling of her face I could well believe that before the last number she had been carried out where the myriad graves are, into the grey, nameless burying grounds of the sea; or into some world of death vaster yet, where, from the beginning of the world, hope has lain down with hope and dream with dream and, renouncing, slept.

The concert was over; the people filed out of the hall chattering and laughing, glad to relax and find the living level again, but my kinswoman made no effort to rise. The harpist slipped the green felt cover over his instrument; the flute-players shook the water from their mouthpieces; the men of the orchestra went out one by one, leaving the stage to the chairs and music stands, empty as a winter corn-field.

I spoke to my aunt. She burst into tears and sobbed pleadingly. "I don't want to go, Clark, I don't want to go!"

I understood. For her, just outside the concert hall, lay the black pond with the cattle-tracked bluffs; the tall, unpainted house, with weather-curled boards, naked as a tower; the crook-backed ash seedlings where the dish-cloths hung to dry; the gaunt, moulting turkeys picking up refuse about the kitchen door.

VIRGINIA WOOLF
(1882–1941)

As great a writer of fiction as Woolf is—*Mrs. Dalloway* (1925), *To the Lighthouse* (1927), and *Orlando* (1928) are among her best—it's possible that her nonfiction has made at least as influential a contribution to modern literary history. *A Room of One's Own* (1929), her essay on women and the writing of fiction, is already regarded as the first major contribution to feminist criticism in the English language. In her most radical piece of cultural commentary, *Three Guineas* (1938), the sequel to *A Room of One's Own* that was ridiculed in the press, her point about the connection between private and public politics belongs now to the common wisdom. As Kennedy Fraser puts it in "Ornament and Silence":

> . . . [Woolf] was harsh on patriarchs in general. She thought that the model of the patriarchal family, with men given license to bully and rant while women and children submitted and served, was unwholesome. She went further: such a model in private life, when it was mirrored in the public life of nations, led to Fascism. "The tyrannies and servilities of the one are the tyrannies and servilities of the other," she wrote.

Woolf had in mind Hitler's Nazis, who were holding mass parades for the Fatherland in the years she was writing *Three Guineas*. Oppression of the psychologically weak and helpless is the background dynamic in much of her fiction. Louise De Salvo's *Virginia Woolf: The Impact of Childhood Sexual Abuse on Her Life and Work* attributes her dark sense of the forces that destroy the self to her experience of sexual molestation by her stepbrothers, which started when she was six. The self-deprecating Mabel Waring in "The New Dress" embodies Woolf's intimate knowledge of an obsessive insecurity and alienation.

---

from
A Room of One's Own

And since a novel has this correspondence to real life, its values are to some extent those of real life. But it is obvious that the values of women differ very often from the values which have been made by the other sex; naturally, this is so. Yet it is the masculine values that prevail. Speaking crudely, football and sport are "important"; the worship of fashion, the buying of clothes "trivial." And these values are inevitably transferred from life to fiction. This is an important book, the critic assumes, because it deals with war. This is an insignificant book because it deals with the feelings of women in a drawing-room. A scene in a battlefield is more important than a scene in a shop—everywhere and much more subtly the difference of value persists. The whole structure, therefore, of the early nineteenth-century novel was raised, if one was a woman, by a mind which was slightly pulled from the straight, and made to alter its clear vision in deference to external authority. One has only to skim those old forgotten novels and listen to the tone of voice in which they are written to divine that the writer was meeting criticism; she was saying this by way of aggression, or that by way of conciliation. She was admitting that she was "only a woman," or protesting that she was "as good as a man". She met that criticism as her temperament dictated, with docility and diffidence, or with anger and emphasis. It does not matter which it was; she was thinking of something other than the thing itself. Down comes her book upon our heads. There was a flaw in the centre of it. And I thought of all the women's novels that lie scattered, like small pock-marked apples in an orchard, about the second-hand book shops of London. It was the flaw in the centre that had rotted them. She had altered her values in deference to the opinion of others.

But how impossible it must have been for them not to budge either to the right or to the left. What genius, what integrity it must have required in face of all that criticism, in the midst of that purely patriarchal society, to hold fast to the thing as they saw it without shrinking. Only Jane Austen did it and Emily Brontë. It is another feather, perhaps the finest, in their caps. They wrote as women write, not as men write. Of all the thousand women who wrote novels then, they alone entirely ignored the perpetual admonitions of the eternal pedagogue—write this, think that. They alone were deaf to that persistent voice, now grumbling, now patronizing, now domineering, now grieved, now shocked, now angry, now avuncular, that voice which cannot let women alone, but must be at them like some too-conscientious governess, adjuring them, like Sir Egerton Brydges, to be refined; dragging even into the criticism of poetry criticism of sex; admonishing them, if they would be good and win, as I suppose, some shiny prize, to keep within certain limits which the gentleman in question thinks suitable—". . . female novelists should only aspire to excellence by courageously acknowledging the limitations of their sex." That puts the matter in a nutshell, and when I tell you, rather to your surprise, that this sentence was written not in August 1828 but in August 1928, you will agree, I think, that however delightful it is to us now, it represents a vast body of opinion—I am not going to stir those old pools; I take only what chance has floated to my feet—that was far more vigorous and far more vocal a century ago. It would have needed a very stalwart young woman in 1828 to disregard all those snubs and chidings and promises of prizes. One must have been something of a firebrand to say to oneself, Oh, but they can't buy literature too. Literature is open to everybody. I refuse to allow you, Beadle though you are, to turn me off the grass. Lock up your libraries if you like; but there is no gate, no lock, no bolt that you can set upon the freedom of my mind.

But whatever effect discouragement and criticism had upon their writing—and I believe that they had a very great effect—that was unimportant compared with the other difficulty which faced them (I was still considering those early nineteenth-century novelists) when they came to set their thoughts on paper—that is that they had no tradition behind them, or one so short and partial that it was of little help. For we think back through our mothers if we are women. It is useless to go to the great men writers for help, however much one may go to them for pleasure. Lamb, Browne, Thackeray, Newman, Sterne, Dickens, De Quincey—whoever it may be—never helped a woman yet, though she may have learnt a few tricks of them and adapted them to her use. The weight, the pace, the stride of a man's mind are too unlike her own for her to lift anything substantial from him successfully. The ape is too distant to be sedulous. Perhaps the first thing she would find, setting pen to paper, was that there was no common sentence ready for her use. All the great novelists like Thackeray and Dickens and Balzac have written a natural prose, swift but not slovenly, expressive but not precious, taking their own tint without ceasing to be common property. They have based it on the sentence that was current at the time. The sentence that was current at the beginning of the nineteenth century ran something like this perhaps: "The grandeur of their works was an argument with them, not to stop short, but to proceed. They could have no higher excitement or satisfaction than in the exercise of their art and endless generations of truth and beauty. Success prompts to exertion; and habit facilitates success." That is a man's sentence; behind it one can see Johnson, Gibbon and the rest. It was a sentence that was unsuited for a woman's use. Charlotte Brontë, with all her splendid gift for prose, stumbled and fell with that clumsy weapon in her hands. George Eliot committed atrocities with it that beggar description. Jane Austen looked at it and laughed at it and devised a perfectly natural, shapely sentence proper for her own use and never departed from it. Thus, with less genius for writing than Charlotte Brontë, she got infinitely more said. Indeed, since freedom and fullness of expression are of the essence of the art, such a lack of tradition, such a scarcity and inadequacy of tools, must have told enormously upon the writing of women. Moreover, a book is not made of sentences laid end to end, but of sentences built, if an image helps, into arcades or domes. And this shape too has been made by men out of their own needs for their own uses. There is no reason to think that the form of the epic or of the poetic play suit a woman any more than the sentence suits her. But all the older forms of literature were hardened and set by the time she became a writer. The novel alone was young enough to be soft in her hands—another reason, perhaps, why she wrote novels. Yet who shall say that even now "the novel" (I give it inverted commas to mark my sense of the words' inadequacy), who shall say that even this most pliable of all forms is rightly shaped for her use? No doubt we shall find her knocking that into shape for herself when she has the free use of her limbs; and providing some new vehicle, not necessarily in verse, for the poetry in her. For it is the poetry that is still denied outlet. And I went on to ponder how a woman nowadays would write a poetic tragedy in five acts. Would she use verse?—would she not use prose rather?

But these are difficult questions which lie in the twilight of the future. I must leave them, if only because they stimulate me to wander from my subject into trackless forests where I shall be lost and, very likely, devoured by wild beasts. I do not want, and I am sure that you do not want me, to broach that very dismal subject, the future of fiction, so that I will only pause here one moment to draw your attention to the great part which must be played in that future so far as women are concerned by physical conditions. The book has somehow to be adapted to the body, and at a venture one would say that women's books should be shorter, more concentrated, than those of men, and framed so that they do not need long hours of steady and uninterrupted work. For interruptions there will always be. Again, the nerves that feed the brain would seem to differ in men and women, and if you are going to make them work their best and hardest, you must find out what treatment suits them—whether these hours of lectures, for instance, which the monks devised, presumably, hundreds of years ago, suit them—what alternations of work and rest they need, interpreting rest not as doing nothing but as doing something but something that is different; and what should that difference be? All this should be discussed and discovered; all this is part of the question of women and fiction. And yet, I continued, approaching the bookcase again, where shall I find that elaborate study of the psychology of women by a woman? If through their incapacity to play football women are not going to be allowed to practise medicine—

Happily my thoughts were now given another turn....

The New Dress

Mabel had her first serious suspicion that something was wrong as she took her cloak off and Mrs. Barnet, while handing her the mirror and touching the brushes and thus drawing her attention, perhaps rather markedly, to all the appliances for tidying and improving hair, complexion, clothes, which existed on the dressing table, confirmed the suspicion—that it was not right, not quite right, which growing stronger as she went upstairs and springing at her, with conviction as she greeted Clarissa Dalloway, she went straight to the far end of the room, to a shaded corner where a looking-glass hung and looked. No! It was not *right*. And at once the misery which she always tried to hide, the profound dissatisfaction—

the sense she had had, ever since she was a child, of being inferior to other people—set upon her, relentlessly, remorselessly, with an intensity which she could not beat off, as she would when she woke at night at home, by reading Borrow or Scott; for oh these men, oh these women, all were thinking—"What's Mabel wearing? What a fright she looks! What a hideous new dress!"—their eyelids flickering as they came up and then their lids shutting rather tight. It was her own appalling inadequacy; her cowardice; her mean, water-sprinkled blood that depressed her. And at once the whole of the room where, for ever so many hours, she had planned with the little dressmaker how it was to go, seemed sordid, repulsive; and her own drawing-room so shabby, and herself, going out, puffed up with vanity as she touched the letters on the hall table and said: "How dull!" to show off—all this now seemed unutterably silly, paltry, and provincial. All this had been absolutely destroyed, shown up, exploded, the moment she came into Mrs. Dalloway's drawing-room.

What she had thought that evening when, sitting over the teacups, Mrs. Dalloway's invitation came, was that, of course, she could not be fashionable. It was absurd to pretend it even—fashion meant cut, meant style, meant thirty guineas at least—but why not be original? Why not be herself, anyhow? And, getting up, she had taken that old fashion book of her mother's, a Paris fashion book of the time of the Empire, and had thought how much prettier, more dignified, and more womanly they were then, and so set herself—oh, it was foolish—trying to be like them, pluming herself in fact, upon being modest and old-fashioned, and very charming, giving herself up, no doubt about it, to an orgy of self-love, which deserved to be chastised, and so rigged herself out like this.

But she dared not look in the glass. She could not face the whole horror—the pale yellow, idiotically old-fashioned silk dress with its long skirt and its high sleeves and its waist and all the things that looked so charming in the fashion book, but not on her, not among all these ordinary people. She felt like a dressmaker's dummy standing there, for young people to stick pins into.

"But, my dear, it's perfectly charming!" Rose Shaw said, looking her up and down with that little satirical pucker of the lips which she expected—Rose herself being dressed in the height of fashion, precisely like everybody else, always.

We are all like flies trying to crawl over the edge of the saucer, Mabel thought, and repeated the phrase as if she were crossing herself, as if she were trying to find some spell to annul this pain, to make this agony endurable. Tags of Shakespeare, lines from books she had read ages ago, suddenly came to her when she was in agony, and she repeated them over and over again. "Flies trying to crawl," she repeated. If she could say that over often enough and make herself see the flies, she would become numb, chill, frozen, dumb. Now she could see flies crawling slowly out of a saucer of milk with their wings stuck together; and she strained and strained (standing in front of the looking-glass, listening to Rose Shaw) to make herself see Rose Shaw and all the other people as flies, trying to hoist themselves out of something, or into something, meagre, insignificant, toiling flies. But she could not see them like that, not other people. She saw herself like that— she was a fly, but the others were dragonflies, butterflies, beautiful insects, dancing, fluttering, skimming, while she alone dragged herself up out of the saucer. (Envy and spite, the most detestable of the vices, were her chief faults.)

"I feel like some dowdy, decrepit, horribly dingy old fly," she said, making Robert Haydon stop just to hear her say that, just to reassure herself by furbishing up a poor weak-kneed phrase and so showing how detached she was, how witty, that she did not feel in the least out of anything. And, of course, Robert Haydon answered something, quite polite, quite insincere, which she saw through instantly, and said to herself, directly he went (again from some book), "Lies, lies, lies!" For a party makes things either much more real, or much less real, she thought; she saw in a flash to the bottom of Robert Haydon's heart; she saw through everything. She saw the truth. *This* was true, this drawing-room, this self, and the other false. Miss Milan's little workroom was really terribly hot, stuffy, sordid. It smelt of clothes and cabbage cooking; and yet, when Miss Milan put the glass in her hand, and she looked at herself with the dress on, finished, an extraordinary bliss shot through her heart. Suffused with light, she sprang into existence. Rid of cares and wrinkles, what she had dreamed of herself was there— a beautiful woman. Just for a second (she had not dared look longer, Miss Milan wanted to know about the length of the skirt), there looked at her, framed in the scrolloping mahogany, a grey-white, mysteriously smiling, charming girl, the core of herself, the soul of herself; and it was not vanity only, not only self-love that made her think it good, tender, and true. Miss Milan said that the skirt could not well be longer; if anything the skirt, said Miss Milan, puckering her forehead, considering with all her wits about her, must be shorter; and she felt, suddenly, honestly, full of love for Miss Milan, much, much fonder of Miss Milan than of any one in the whole world, and could have cried for pity that she should be crawling on the floor with her mouth full of pins, and her face red and her eyes bulging—that one human being should be doing this for another, and she saw them all as human beings merely, and herself going off to her party, and Miss Milan pulling the cover over the canary's cage, or letting him pick a hempseed from between her lips, and the thought of it, of this side of human nature and its patience and its endurance and its being content with such miserable, scanty, sordid, little pleasures filled her eyes with tears.

And now the whole thing had vanished. The dress, the room, the love, the pity, the scrolloping looking-glass, and the canary's cage—all had vanished, and here she was in a corner of Mrs. Dalloway's drawing-room, suffering tortures, woken wide awake to reality.

But it was all so paltry, weak-blooded, and petty-minded to care so much at her age with two children, to be still so utterly dependent on people's opinions and not have principles or convictions, not to be able to say as other people did, "There's Shakespeare! There's death! We're all weevils in a captain's biscuit"—or whatever it was that people did say.

She faced herself straight in the glass; she pecked at her left shoulder; she issued out into the room, as if spears were thrown at her yellow dress from all sides. But instead of looking fierce or tragic, as Rose Shaw would have done—Rose would have looked like Boadicea—she looked foolish and self-conscious, and simpered like a schoolgirl and slouched across the room, positively slinking, as if she were a beaten mongrel, and looked at a picture, an engraving. As if one went to a party to look at a picture! Everybody knew why she did it—it was from shame, from humiliation.

"Now the fly's in the saucer," she said to herself, "right in the middle, and can't get out, and the milk," she thought, rigidly staring at the picture, "is sticking its wings together."

"It's so old-fashioned," she said to Charles Burt, making him stop (which by itself he hated) on his way to talk to some one else.

She meant, or she tried to make herself think that she meant, that it was the picture and not her dress, that was old-fashioned. And one word of praise, one word of affection from Charles would have made all the difference to her at the moment. If he had only said, "Mabel, you're looking charming tonight!" it would have changed her life. But then she ought to have been truthful and direct. Charles said nothing of the kind, of course. He was malice itself. He always saw through one, especially if one were feeling particularly mean, paltry, or feeble-minded.

"Mabel's got a new dress!" he said, and the poor fly was absolutely shoved into the middle of the saucer. Really, he would like her to drown, she believed. He had no heart, no fundamental kindness, only a veneer of friendliness. Miss Milan was much more real, much kinder. If only one could feel that and stick to it, always. "Why," she asked herself—replying to Charles much too pertly, letting him see that she was out of temper, or "ruffled" as he called it. ("Rather ruffled?" he said and went on to laugh at her with some woman over there)—"Why," she asked herself, "can't I feel one thing always, feel quite sure that Miss Milan is right, and Charles wrong and stick to it, feel sure about the canary and pity and love and not be whipped all round in a second by coming into a room full of people?" It was her odious, weak, vacillating character again, always giving at the critical moment and not being seriously interested in conchology, etymology, botany, archaeology, cutting up potatoes and watching them fructify like Mary Dennis, like Violet Searle.

Then Mrs. Holman, seeing her standing there, bore down upon her. Of course a thing like a dress was beneath Mrs. Holman's notice, with her family always tumbling downstairs or having the scarlet fever. Could Mabel tell her if Elmthorpe was ever let for August and September? Oh, it was a conversation that bored her unutterably!—it made her furious to be treated like a house agent or a messenger boy, to be made use of. Not to have value, that was it, she thought, trying to grasp something hard, something real, while she tried to answer sensibly about the bathroom and the south aspect and the hot water to the top of the house; and all the time she could see little bits of her yellow dress in the round looking-glass which made them all the size of boot-buttons or tadpoles; and it was amazing to think how much humiliation and agony and self-loathing and ef-fort and passionate ups and downs of feeling were contained in a thing the size of a threepenny bit. And what was still odder, this thing, this Mabel Waring, was separate, quite disconnected: and though Mrs. Holman (the black button) was leaning forward and telling her how her eldest boy had strained his heart running, she could see her, too, quite detached in the looking-glass, and it was impossible that the black dot, leaning forward, gesticulating, should make the yellow dot, sit-ting solitary, self-centred, feel what the black dot was feeling, yet they pretended.

"So impossible to keep boys quiet"—that was the kind of thing one said.

And Mrs. Holman, who could never get enough sympathy and snatched what little there was greedily, as if it were her right (but she deserved much more for, there was her little girl who had come down this morning with a swollen knee-joint), took this miserable offering and looked at it suspiciously, grudgingly, as if it were a half-penny when it ought to have been a pound and put it away in her purse, must put up with it, mean and miserly though it was, times being hard, so very hard; and on she went, creaking, injured Mrs. Holman, about the girl with the swollen joints. Ah, it was tragic, this greed, this clamour of human beings, like a row of cormorants, barking and flapping their wings for sympathy—it was tragic, could one have felt it and not merely pretended to feel it!

But in her yellow dress to-night she could not wring out one drop more; she wanted it all, all for herself. She knew (she kept on looking into the glass, dipping into that dreadfully showing-up blue pool) that she was condemned, despised, left like this in a backwater, because of her being like this a feeble, vacillating crea-ture; and it seemed to her that the yellow dress was a penance which she had de-served, and if she had been dressed like Rose Shaw, in lovely, clinging green with a ruffle of swansdown, she would have deserved that; and she thought that there was no escape for her—none whatever. But it was not her fault altogether, after all. It was being one of a family of ten; never having money enough, always skimping and paring; and her mother carrying great cans, and the linoleum worn on the stair edges, and one sordid little domestic tragedy after another—nothing catastrophic, the sheep farm failing, but not utterly; her eldest brother marrying beneath him but not very much—there was no romance, nothing extreme about them all. They petered out respectably in seaside resorts; every watering-place had one of her aunts even now asleep in some lodging with the front windows not quite facing the sea. That was so like them—they had to squint at things always. And she had done the same—she was just like her aunts. For all her dreams of living in India, married to some hero like Sir Henry Lawrence, some empire builder (still the sight of a native in a turban filled her with romance), she had failed utterly. She had married Hubert, with his safe, permanent underling's job in the Law Courts, and they managed tolerably in a smallish house, without proper maids, and hash when she was alone or just bread and butter, but now and then— Mrs. Holman was off, thinking her the most dried-up, unsympathetic twig she had ever met, absurdly dressed, too, and would tell every one about Mabel's fantastic appearance—now and then, thought Mabel Waring, left alone on the blue sofa, punching the cushion in order to look occupied, for she would not join Charles Burt and Rose Shaw, chattering like magpies and perhaps laughing at her by the fireplace—now and then, there did come to her delicious moments, reading the other night in bed, for instance, or down by the sea on the sand in the sun, at Easter—let her recall it—a great tuft of pale sand-grass standing all twisted like a shock of spears against the sky, which was blue like a smooth china egg, so firm, so hard, and then the melody of the waves—"Hush, hush," they said, and the children's shouts paddling—yes, it was a divine moment, and there she lay, she felt, in the hand of the Goddess who was the world; rather a hard-hearted, but very beautiful Goddess, a little lamb laid on the altar (one did think these silly things, and it didn't matter so long as one never said them). And also with Hubert sometimes she had quite unexpectedly—carving the mutton for Sunday lunch, for no reason, opening a letter, coming into a room—divine moments, when she said to herself (for she would never say this to anybody else), "This is it. This has happened. This is it!" And the other way about it was equally surprising—that is, when everything was arranged—music, weather, holidays, every reason for happiness was there—then nothing happened at all. One wasn't happy. It was flat, just flat, that was all.

Her wretched self again, no doubt! She had always been a fretful, weak, unsatisfactory mother, a wobbly wife, lolling about in a kind of twilight existence with nothing very clear or very bold, or more one thing than another, like all her brothers and sisters, except perhaps Herbert—they were all the same poor water-veined creatures who did nothing. Then in the midst of this creeping, crawling life, suddenly she was on the crest of a wave. That wretched fly—where had she read the story that kept coming into her mind about the fly and the saucer?— struggled out. Yes, she had those moments. But now that she was forty, they might come more and more seldom. By degrees she would cease to struggle any more. But that was deplorable! That was not to be endured! That made her feel ashamed of herself!

She would go to the London Library tomorrow. She would find some wonderful, helpful, astonishing book, quite by chance, a book by a clergyman, by an American no one had ever heard of; or she would walk down the Strand and drop, accidentally, into a hall where a miner was telling about the life in the pit, and suddenly she would become a new person. She would be absolutely trans-formed. She would wear a uniform; she would be called Sister Somebody; she would never give a thought to clothes again. And for ever after she would be per-fectly clear about Charles Burt and Miss Milan and this room and that room; and it would be always, day after day, as if she were lying in the sun or carving the mutton. It would be it!

So she got up from the blue sofa, and the yellow button in the looking-glass got up too, and she waved her hand to Charles and Rose to show them she did not depend on them one scrap, and the yellow button moved out of the looking-glass, and all the spears were gathered into her breast as she walked towards Mrs. Dalloway and said, "Good night."

"But it's too early to go," said Mrs. Dalloway, who was always so charming.

"I'm afraid I must," said Mabel Waring. "But," she added in her weak, wobbly voice which only sounded ridiculous when she tried to strengthen it, "I have en-joyed myself enormously."

"I have enjoyed myself," she said to Mr. Dalloway, whom she met on the stairs.

"Lies, lies, lies!" she said to herself, going downstairs, and "Right in the saucer!" she said to herself as she thanked Mrs. Barnet for helping her and wrapped herself, round and round and round, in the Chinese cloak she had worn these twenty years.

MARIANNE MOORE
(1887–1972)

M oore's *Collected Poems* (1951) won the Pulitzer Prize, the Bollingen Prize, and the National Book Award. Her poetry, which is not confessional or "personal"—"compression," she said, is "the first grace of style"—has received little attention from feminist critics. A modest and shy woman who lived with her mother in their native Missouri and after 1918 in New York City, she wrote in the voice of an elegant conversationalist. There's also a tough American pragmatism beneath the fastidious lines. "In Distrust of Merits," written during World War II, posits a moral responsibility rooted in her firm religious belief. A passionate baseball fan and Brooklynite who wore a tricorn hat and a black cape, she was asked one year to throw out the first ball of the Brooklyn Dodgers' baseball season.

Silence

My father used to say,
"Superior people never make long visits,
have to be shown Longfellow's grave
or the glass flowers at Harvard.
Self-reliant like the cat—
that takes its prey to privacy,
the mouse's limp tail hanging like a shoelace from its mouth—
they sometimes enjoy solitude,
and can be robbed of speech
by speech which has delighted them.
The deepest feeling always shows itself in silence;
not in silence, but restraint."
Nor was he insincere in saying, "Make my house your inn."
Inns are not residences.

In Distrust of Merits

Strengthened to live, strengthened to die for
    medals and positioned victories?
They're fighting, fighting, fighting the blind
    man who thinks he sees,—
who cannot see that the enslaver is

enslaved; the hater, harmed. O shining O
    firm star, O tumultuous
        ocean lashed till small things go
  as they will, the mountainous
      wave makes us who look, know

depth. Lost at sea before they fought! O
    star of David, star of Bethlehem,
O black imperial lion
    of the Lord—emblem
of a risen world—be joined at last, be
joined. There is hate's crown beneath which all is
      death; there's love's without which none
        is king; the blessed deeds bless
the halo. As contagion
    of sickness makes sickness,

contagion of trust can make trust. They're
    fighting in deserts and caves, one by
one, in battalions and squadrons;
    they're fighting that I
may yet recover from the disease, My
Self; some have it lightly; some will die. "Man's
    wolf to man" and we devour
      ourselves. The enemy could not
    have made a greater breach in our
      defenses. One pilot-

ing a blind man can escape him, but
    Job disheartened by false comfort knew
that nothing can be so defeating
    as a blind man who
can see. O alive who are dead, who are
proud not to see, O small dust of the earth
    that walks so arrogantly,
      trust begets power and faith is
an affectionate thing. We
      vow, we make this promise

to the fighting—it's a promise—"We'll
    never hate black, white, red, yellow, Jew,

Gentile, Untouchable." We are
    not competent to
make our vows. With set jaw they are fighting,
fighting, fighting,—some we love whom we know,
        some we love but know not—that
            hearts may feel and not be numb.
        It cures me; or am I what
            I can't believe in? Some

in snow, some on crags, some in quicksands,
    little by little, much by much, they
are fighting fighting fighting that where
    there was death there may
be life. "When a man is prey to anger,
he is moved by outside things; when he holds
        his ground in patience patience
            patience, that is action or
        beauty," the soldier's defense
            and hardest armor for

the fight. The world's an orphans' home. Shall
    we never have peace without sorrow?
without pleas of the dying for
    help that won't come? O
quiet form upon the dust, I cannot
look and yet I must. If these great patient
        dyings—all these agonies
            and wound bearings and bloodshed—
        can teach us how to live, these
            dyings were not wasted.

Hate-hardened heart, O heart of iron,
    iron is iron till it is rust.
There never was a war that was
    not inward; I must
fight till I have conquered in myself what
causes war, but I would not believe it.
        I inwardly did nothing.
            O Iscariot-like crime!
        Beauty is everlasting
            and dust is for a time.

KATHERINE MANSFIELD
(1888–1923)

Born Kathleen Beauchamp in New Zealand, Mansfield was always an outsider, a "colonial" in London, though she was befriended by Virginia Woolf (Mansfield's was "the only writing I have ever been jealous of," Woolf told her diary) and D. H. Lawrence, and married the critic John Middleton Murry, who edited her letters and journals after she died of tuberculosis at the age of thirty-four. The character of Gudrun in Lawrence's *Women in Love* is based on Mansfield, and Gudrun's lover, Gerald, is based on Murry; Lawrence and his wife, Frieda, and the Murrys lived as a ménage à quatre in Cornwall during part of World War I. Frequently compared with Chekhov, Mansfield set her best stories in New Zealand (where in later years she couldn't bear to return): "Prelude," "At the Bay," and "The Garden Party" are each a luminous memory of childhood.

The Garden Party

And after all the weather was ideal. They could not have had a more perfect day for a garden-party if they had ordered it. Windless, warm, the sky without a cloud. Only the blue was veiled with a haze of light gold, as it is sometimes in early summer. The gardener had been up since dawn, mowing the lawns and sweeping them, until the grass and the dark flat rosettes where the daisy plants had been seemed to shine. As for the roses, you could not help feeling they understood that roses are the only flowers that impress people at garden-parties; the only flowers that everybody is certain of knowing. Hundreds, yes, literally hundreds, had come out in a single night; the green bushes bowed down as though they had been visited by archangels.

Breakfast was not yet over before the men came to put up the marquee.

"Where do you want the marquee put, mother?"

"My dear child, it's no use asking me. I'm determined to leave everything to you children this year. Forget I am your mother. Treat me as an honoured guest."

But Meg could not possibly go and supervise the men. She had washed her hair before breakfast, and she sat drinking coffee in a green turban, with a dark wet curl stamped on each cheek. Jose, the butterfly, always came down in a silk petticoat and a kimono jacket.

"You'll have to go, Laura; you're the artistic one."

Away Laura flew, still holding her piece of bread-and-butter. It's so delicious to have an excuse for eating out of doors, and besides, she loved having to arrange things; she always felt she could do it so much better than anybody else.

Four men in their shirt-sleeves stood grouped together on the garden path. They carried staves covered with rolls of canvas, and they had big tool-bags slung on their backs. They looked impressive. Laura wished now that she had not got the bread-and-butter, but there was nowhere to put it, and she couldn't possibly throw it away. She blushed and tried to look severe and even a little bit short-sighted as she came up to them.

"Good morning," she said, copying her mother's voice. But that sounded so fearfully affected that she was ashamed, and stammered like a little girl, "Oh—er—have you come—is it about the marquee?"

"That's right, miss," said the tallest of the men, a lanky, freckled fellow, and he shifted his tool-bag, knocked back his straw hat and smiled down at her. "That's about it."

His smile was so easy, so friendly that Laura recovered. What nice eyes he had, small, but such a dark blue! And now she looked at the others, they were smiling too. "Cheer up, we won't bite," their smile seemed to say. How very nice workmen were! And what a beautiful morning! She mustn't mention the morning; she must be businesslike. The marquee.

"Well, what about the lily-lawn? Would that do?"

And she pointed to the lily-lawn with the hand that didn't hold the bread-and-butter. They turned, they stared in the direction. A little fat chap thrust out his under-lip, and the tall fellow frowned.

"I don't fancy it," said he. "Not conspicuous enough. You see, with a thing like a marquee," and he turned to Laura in his easy way, "you want to put it somewhere where it'll give you a bang slap in the eye, if you follow me."

Laura's upbringing made her wonder for a moment whether it was quite respectful of a workman to talk to her of bangs slap in the eye. But she did quite follow him.

"A corner of the tennis-court," she suggested. "But the band's going to be in one corner."

"H'm, going to have a band, are you?" said another of the workmen. He was pale. He had a haggard look as his dark eyes scanned the tennis-court. What was he thinking?

"Only a very small band," said Laura gently. Perhaps he wouldn't mind so much if the band was quite small. But the tall fellow interrupted.

"Look here, miss, that's the place. Against those trees, over there. That'll do fine."

Against the karakas. Then the karakas-trees would be hidden. And they were so lovely, with their broad, gleaming leaves, and their clusters of yellow fruit. They were like trees you imagined growing on a desert island, proud, solitary, lifting their leaves and fruits to the sun in a kind of silent splendour. Must they be hidden by a marquee?

They must. Already the men had shouldered their staves and were making for the place. Only the tall fellow was left. He bent down, pinched a sprig of lavender, put his thumb and forefinger to his nose and snuffed up the smell. When Laura saw that gesture she forgot all about the karakas in her wonder at him caring for things like that—caring for the smell of lavender. How many men that she knew would have done such a thing? Oh, how extraordinarily nice workmen were, she thought. Why couldn't she have workmen for friends rather than the silly boys she danced with and who came to Sunday night supper? She would get on much better with men like these.

It's all the fault, she decided, as the tall fellow drew something on the back of an envelope, something that was to be looped up or left to hang, of these absurd class distinctions. Well, for her part, she didn't feel them. Not a bit, not an atom. . . . And now there came the chock-chock of wooden hammers. Some one whistled, some one sang out, "Are you right there, matey?" "Matey!" The friendliness of it, the—the— Just to prove how happy she was, just to show the tall fellow how at home she felt, and how she despised stupid conventions, Laura took a big bite of her bread-and-butter as she stared at the little drawing. She felt just like a work-girl.

"Laura, Laura, where are you? Telephone, Laura!" a voice cried from the house.

"Coming!" Away she skimmed, over the lawn, up the path, up the steps, across the veranda, and into the porch. In the hall her father and Laurie were brushing their hats ready to go to the office.

"I say, Laura," said Laurie very fast, "you might just give a squiz at my coat before this afternoon. See if it wants pressing."

"I will," said she. Suddenly she couldn't stop herself. She ran at Laurie and gave him a small, quick squeeze. "Oh, I do love parties, don't you?" gasped Laura.

"Ra-ther," said Laurie's warm, boyish voice, and he squeezed his sister too, and gave her a gentle push. "Dash off to the telephone, old girl."

The telephone. "Yes, yes; oh yes. Kitty? Good morning, dear. Come to lunch? Do, dear. Delighted of course. It will only be a very scratch meal—just the sandwich crusts and broken meringue-shells and what's left over. Yes, isn't it a perfect morning? Your white? Oh, I certainly should. One moment—hold the line. Mother's calling." And Laura sat back. "What, mother? Can't hear."

Mrs. Sheridan's voice floated down the stairs. "Tell her to wear that sweet hat she had on last Sunday."

"Mother says you're to wear that *sweet* hat you had on last Sunday. Good. One o'clock. Bye-bye."

Laura put back the receiver, flung her arms over her head, took a deep breath, stretched and let them fall. "Huh," she sighed, and the moment after the sigh sat up quickly. She was still, listening. All the doors in the house seemed to be open. The house was alive with soft, quick steps and running voices. The green baize door that led to the kitchen regions swung open and shut with a muffled thud. And now there came a long, chuckling absurd sound. It was the heavy piano being moved on its stiff castors. But the air! If you stopped to notice, was the air always like this? Little faint winds were playing chase, in at the tops of the windows, out at the doors. And there were two tiny spots of sun, one on the inkpot, one on a silver photograph frame, playing too. Darling little spots. Especially the one on the inkpot lid. It was quite warm. A warm little silver star. She could have kissed it.

The front door bell pealed, and there sounded the rustle of Sadie's print skirt on the stairs. A man's voice murmured; Sadie answered, careless, "I'm sure I don't know. Wait. I'll ask Mrs. Sheridan."

"What is it, Sadie?" Laura came into the hall.

"It's the florist, Miss Laura."

It was, indeed. There, just inside the door, stood a wide, shallow tray full of pots of pink lilies. No other kind. Nothing but lilies—canna lilies, big pink flowers, wide open, radiant, almost frighteningly alive on bright crimson stems.

"O-oh, Sadie!" said Laura, and the sound was like a little moan. She crouched down as if to warm herself at that blaze of lilies; she felt they were in her fingers, on her lips, growing in her breast.

"It's some mistake," she said faintly. "Nobody ever ordered so many. Sadie, go and find mother."

But at that moment Mrs. Sheridan joined them.

"It's quite right," she said calmly. "Yes, I ordered them. Aren't they lovely?" She pressed Laura's arm. "I was passing the shop yesterday, and I saw them in the window. And I suddenly thought for once in my life I shall have enough canna lilies. The garden-party will be a good excuse."

"But I thought you said you didn't mean to interfere," said Laura. Sadie had gone. The florist's man was still outside at his van. She put her arm round her mother's neck and gently, very gently, she bit her mother's ear.

"My darling child, you wouldn't like a logical mother, would you? Don't do that. Here's the man."

He carried more lilies still, another whole tray.

"Bank them up, just inside the door, on both sides of the porch, please," said Mrs. Sheridan. "Don't you agree, Laura?"

"Oh, I *do*, mother."

In the drawing-room Meg, Jose and good little Hans had at last succeeded in moving the piano.

"Now, if we put this chesterfield against the wall and move everything out of the room except the chairs, don't you think?"

"Quite."

"Hans, move these tables into the smoking-room, and bring a sweeper to take these marks off the carpet and—one moment, Hans—" Jose loved giving orders to the servants, and they loved obeying her. She always made them feel they were taking part in some drama. "Tell mother and Miss Laura to come here at once."

"Very good, Miss Jose."

She turned to Meg. "I want to hear what the piano sounds like, just in case I'm asked to sing this afternoon. Let's try over 'This Life is Weary.'"

Pom! Ta-ta-ta *Tee*-ta! The piano burst out so passionately that Jose's face changed. She clasped her hands. She looked mournfully and enigmatically at her mother and Laura as they came in.

> This Life is *Wee*-ary,
> A Tear—A Sigh.
> A Love that *Chan-ges*,
>   This Life is *Wee*-ary,
> A Tear—a Sigh.
> A Love that *Chan*-ges,
> And then . . . Good-bye!

But at the word "Good-bye," and although the piano sounded more desperate than ever, her face broke into a brilliant, dreadfully unsympathetic smile.

"Aren't I in good voice, mummy?" she beamed.

> This Life is *Wee*-ary,
> Hope comes to Die.
> A Dream—a *Wa*-kening.

But now Sadie interrupted them. "What is it, Sadie?"

"If you please, m'm, cook says have you got the flags for the sandwiches?"

"The flags for the sandwiches, Sadie?" echoed Mrs. Sheridan dreamily. And the children knew by her face that she hadn't got them. "Let me see." And she said to Sadie firmly, "Tell cook I'll let her have them in ten minutes."

Sadie went.

"Now, Laura," said her mother quickly. "Come with me into the smoking-room. I've got the names somewhere on the back of an envelope. You'll have to write them out for me. Meg, go upstairs this minute and take that wet thing off your head. Jose, run and finish dressing this instant. Do you hear me, children, or shall I have to tell your father when he comes home to-night? And—and, Jose, pacify cook if you do go into the kitchen, will you? I'm terrified of her this morning."

The envelope was found at last behind the dining-room clock, though how it had got there Mrs. Sheridan could not imagine.

"One of you children must have stolen it out of my bag, because I remember vividly—cream cheese and lemon-curd. Have you done that?"

"Yes."

"Egg and—" Mrs. Sheridan held the envelope away from her. "It looks like mice. It can't be mice, can it?"

"Olive, pet," said Laura, looking over her shoulder.

"Yes, of course, olive. What a horrible combination it sounds. Egg and olive."

They were finished at last, and Laura took them off to the kitchen. She found Jose there pacifying the cook, who did not look at all terrifying.

"I have never seen such exquisite sandwiches," said Jose's rapturous voice. "How many kinds did you say there were, cook? Fifteen?"

"Fifteen, Miss Jose."

"Well, cook, I congratulate you."

Cook swept up crusts with the long sandwich knife, and smiled broadly.

"Godber's has come," announced Sadie, issuing out of the pantry. She had seen the man pass the window.

That meant the cream puffs had come. Godber's were famous for their cream puffs. Nobody ever thought of making them at home.

"Bring them in and put them on the table, my girl," ordered cook.

Sadie brought them in and went back to the door. Of course Laura and Jose were far too grown-up to really care about such things. All the same, they couldn't help agreeing that the puffs looked very attractive. Very. Cook began arranging them, shaking off the extra icing sugar.

"Don't they carry one back to all one's parties?" said Laura.

"I suppose they do," said practical Jose, who never liked to be carried back. "They look beautifully light and feathery, I must say."

"Have one each, my dears," said cook in her comfortable voice. "Yer ma won't know."

Oh, impossible. Fancy cream puffs so soon after breakfast. The very idea made one shudder. All the same, two minutes later Jose and Laura were licking their fingers with that absorbed inward look that only comes from whipped cream.

"Let's go into the garden, out by the back way," suggested Laura. "I want to see how the men are getting on with the marquee. They're such awfully nice men."

But the back door was blocked by cook, Sadie, Godber's man and Hans.

Something had happened.

"Tuk-tuk-tuk," clucked cook like an agitated hen. Sadie had her hand clapped to her cheek as though she had toothache. Hans's face was screwed up in the effort to understand. Only Godber's man seemed to be enjoying himself; it was his story.

"What's the matter? What's happened?"

"There's been a horrible accident," said cook. "A man killed."

"A man killed! Where? How? When?"

But Godber's man wasn't going to have his story snatched from under his very nose.

"Know those little cottages just below here, miss?" Know them? Of course, she knew them. "Well, there's a young chap living there, name of Scott, a carter. His horse shied at a traction-engine, corner of Hawke Street this morning, and he was thrown out on the back of his head. Killed."

"Dead!" Laura stared at Godber's man.

"Dead when they picked him up," said Godber's man with relish. "They were taking the body home as I come up here." And he said to the cook, "He's left a wife and five little ones."

"Jose, come here." Laura caught hold of her sister's sleeve and dragged her through the kitchen to the other side of the green baize door. There she paused and leaned against it. "Jose!" she said, horrified, "however are we going to stop everything?"

"Stop everything, Laura!" cried Jose in astonishment. "What do you mean?"

"Stop the garden-party, of course." Why did Jose pretend?

But Jose was still more amazed. "Stop the garden-party? My dear Laura, don't be so absurd. Of course we can't do anything of the kind. Nobody expects us to. Don't be so extravagant."

"But we can't possibly have a garden-party with a man dead just outside the front gate."

That really was extravagant, for the little cottages were in a lane to themselves at the very bottom of a steep rise that led up to the house. A broad road ran between. True, they were far too near. They were the greatest possible eyesore, and they had no right to be in that neighbourhood at all. They were little mean dwellings painted a chocolate brown. In the garden patches there was nothing but cabbage stalks, sick hens and tomato cans. The very smoke coming out of their chimneys was poverty-stricken. Little rags and shreds of smoke, so unlike the great silvery plumes that uncurled from the Sheridans' chimneys. Washer-women lived in the lane and sweeps and a cobbler, and a man whose house-front was studded all over with minute bird-cages. Children swarmed. When the Sheridans were little they were forbidden to set foot there because of the revolting language and of what they might catch. But since they were grown up, Laura and Laurie on their prowls sometimes walked through. It was disgusting and sordid. They came out with a shudder. But still one must go everywhere; one must see everything. So through they went.

"And just think of what the band would sound like to that poor woman," said Laura.

"Oh, Laura!" Jose began to be seriously annoyed. "If you're going to stop a band playing every time some one has an accident, you'll lead a very strenuous life. I'm every bit as sorry about it as you. I feel just as sympathetic." Her eyes hardened. She looked at her sister just as she used to when they were little and fighting together. "You won't bring a drunken workman back to life by being sentimental," she said softly.

"Drunk! Who said he was drunk?" Laura turned furiously on Jose. She said, just as they had used to say on those occasions, "I'm going straight up to tell mother."

"Do, dear," cooed Jose.

"Mother, can I come into your room?" Laura turned the big glass door-knob.

"Of course, child. Why, what's the matter? What's given you such a colour?" And Mrs. Sheridan turned round from her dressing-table. She was trying on a new hat.

"Mother, a man's been killed," began Laura.

"*Not* in the garden?" interrupted her mother.

"No, no!"

"Oh, what a fright you gave me!" Mrs. Sheridan sighed with relief, and took off the big hat and held it on her knees.

"But listen, mother," said Laura. Breathless, half-choking, she told the dreadful story. "Of course, we can't have our party, can we?" she pleaded. "The band and everybody arriving. They'd hear us, mother; they're nearly neighbours!"

To Laura's astonishment her mother behaved just like Jose; it was harder to bear because she seemed amused. She refused to take Laura seriously.

"But, my dear child, use your common sense. It's only by accident we've heard of it. If some one had died there normally—and I can't understand how they keep alive in those poky little holes—we should still be having our party, shouldn't we?"

Laura had to say "yes" to that, but she felt it was all wrong. She sat down on her mother's sofa and pinched the cushion frill.

"Mother, isn't it really terribly heartless of us?" she asked.

"Darling!" Mrs. Sheridan got up and came over to her, carrying the hat. Before Laura could stop her she had popped it on. "My child!" said her mother, "the hat is yours. It's made for you. It's much too young for me. I have never seen you look such a picture. Look at yourself!" And she held up her hand-mirror.

"But, mother," Laura began again. She couldn't look at herself; she turned aside.

This time Mrs. Sheridan lost patience just as Jose had done.

"You are being very absurd, Laura," she said coldly. "People like that don't expect sacrifices from us. And it's not very sympathetic to spoil everybody's enjoyment as you're doing now."

"I don't understand," said Laura, and she walked quickly out of the room into her own bedroom. There, quite by chance, the first thing she saw was this charming girl in the mirror, in her black hat trimmed with gold daisies, and a long black velvet ribbon. Never had she imagined she could look like that. Is mother right? she thought. And now she hoped her mother was right. Am I being extravagant? Perhaps it was extravagant. Just for a moment she had another glimpse of that poor woman and those little children, and the body being carried into the house. But it all seemed blurred, unreal, like a picture in the newspaper. I'll remember it again after the party's over, she decided. And somehow that seemed quite the best plan. . . .

Lunch was over by half-past one. By half-past two they were all ready for the fray. The green-coated band had arrived and was established in a corner of the tennis-court.

"My dear!" trilled Kitty Maitland, "aren't they too like frogs for words? You ought to have arranged them round the pond with the conductor in the middle on a leaf."

Laurie arrived and hailed them on his way to dress. At the sight of him Laura remembered the accident again. She wanted to tell him. If Laurie agreed with the others, then it was bound to be all right. And she followed him into the hall.

"Laurie!"

"Hallo!" He was half-way upstairs, but when he turned round and saw Laura he suddenly puffed out his cheeks and goggled his eyes at her. "My word, Laura! You do look stunning," said Laurie. "What an absolutely topping hat!"

Laura said faintly "Is it?" and smiled up at Laurie, and didn't tell him after all.

Soon after that people began coming in streams. The band struck up; the hired waiters ran from the house to the marquee. Wherever you looked there were couples strolling, bending to the flowers, greeting, moving on over the lawn. They were like bright birds that had alighted in the Sheridans' garden for this one afternoon, on their way to—where? Ah, what happiness it is to be with people who all are happy, to press hands, press cheeks, smile into eyes.

"Darling Laura, how well you look!"

"What a becoming hat, child!"

"Laura, you look quite Spanish. I've never seen you look so striking."

And Laura, glowing, answered softly, "Have you had tea? Won't you have an ice? The passion-fruit ices really are rather special." She ran to her father and begged him. "Daddy darling, can't the band have something to drink?"

And the perfect afternoon slowly ripened, slowly faded, slowly its petals closed.

"Never a more delightful garden-party . . . " "The greatest success . . . " "Quite the most . . . "

Laura helped her mother with the good-byes. They stood side by side in the porch till it was all over.

"All over, all over, thank heaven," said Mrs. Sheridan. "Round up the others, Laura. Let's go and have some fresh coffee. I'm exhausted. Yes, it's been very successful. But oh, these parties, these parties! Why will you children insist on giving parties!" And they all of them sat down in the deserted marquee.

"Have a sandwich, daddy dear. I wrote the flag."

"Thanks." Mr. Sheridan took a bite and the sandwich was gone. He took another. "I suppose you didn't hear of a beastly accident that happened to-day?" he said.

"My dear," said Mrs. Sheridan, holding up her hand, "we did. It nearly ruined the party. Laura insisted we should put it off."

"Oh, mother!" Laura didn't want to be teased about it.

"It was a horrible affair all the same," said Mr. Sheridan. "The chap was married too. Lived just below in the lane, and leaves a wife and half a dozen kiddies, so they say."

An awkward little silence fell. Mrs. Sheridan fidgeted with her cup. Really, it was very tactless of father . . .

Suddenly she looked up. There on the table were all those sandwiches, cakes, puffs, all uneaten, all going to be wasted. She had one of her brilliant ideas.

"I know," she said. "Let's make up a basket. Let's send that poor creature some of this perfectly good food. At any rate, it will be the greatest treat for the children. Don't you agree? And she's sure to have neighbours calling in and so on. What a point to have it all ready prepared. Laura!" She jumped up. "Get me the big basket out of the stairs cupboard."

"But, mother, do you really think it's a good idea?" said Laura.

Again, how curious, she seemed to be different from them all. To take scraps from their party. Would the poor woman really like that?

"Of course! What's the matter with you to-day? An hour or two ago you were insisting on us being sympathetic, and now—"

Oh, well! Laura ran for the basket. It was filled, it was heaped by her mother.

"Take it yourself, darling," said she. "Run down just as you are. No, wait, take the arum lilies too. People of that class are so impressed by arum lilies."

"The stems will ruin her lace frock," said practical Jose.

So they would. Just in time. "Only the basket, then. And, Laura!"—her mother followed her out of the marquee—"don't on any account—"

"What, mother?"

No, better not put such ideas into the child's head! "Nothing! Run along."

It was just growing dusky as Laura shut their garden gates. A big dog ran by like a shadow. The road gleamed white, and down below in the hollow the little cottages were in deep shade. How quiet it seemed after the afternoon. Here she was going down the hill to somewhere where a man lay dead, and she couldn't realize it. Why couldn't she? She stopped a minute. And it seemed to her that kisses, voices, tinkling spoons, laughter, the smell of crushed grass were somehow inside her. She had no room for anything else. How strange! She looked up at the pale sky, and all she thought was, "Yes, it was the most successful party."

Now the broad road was crossed. The lane began, smoky and dark. Women in shawls and men's tweed caps hurried by. Men hung over the palings; the children played in the doorways. A low hum came from the mean little cottages. In some of them there was a flicker of light, and a shadow, crab-like, moved across the window. Laura bent her head and hurried on. She wished now she had put on a coat. How her frock shone! And the big hat with the velvet streamer—if only it was another hat! Were the people looking at her? They must be. It was a mistake to have come; she knew all along it was a mistake. Should she go back even now?

No, too late. This was the house. It must be. A dark knot of people stood outside. Beside the gate an old, old woman with a crutch sat in a chair, watching. She had her feet on a newspaper. The voices stopped as Laura drew near. The group parted. It was as though she was expected, as though they had known she was coming here.

Laura was terribly nervous. Tossing the velvet ribbon over her shoulder, she said to a woman standing by, "Is this Mrs. Scott's house?" and the woman, smiling queerly, said, "It is, my lass."

Oh, to be away from this! She actually said, "Help me, God," as she walked up the tiny path and knocked. To be away from those staring eyes, or to be covered up in anything, one of those women's shawls even. I'll just leave the basket and go, she decided. I shan't even wait for it to be emptied.

Then the door opened. A little woman in black showed in the gloom.

Laura said, "Are you Mrs. Scott?" But to her horror the woman answered, "Walk in please, miss," and she was shut in the passage.

"No," said Laura, "I don't want to come in. I only want to leave this basket. Mother sent—"

The little woman in the gloomy passage seemed not to have heard her. "Step this way, please, miss," she said in an oily voice, and Laura followed her.

She found herself in a wretched little low kitchen, lighted by a smoky lamp. There was a woman sitting before the fire.

"Em," said the little creature who had let her in. "Em! It's a young lady." She turned to Laura. She said meaningly, "I'm 'er sister, miss. You'll excuse 'er, won't you?"

"Oh, but of course!" said Laura. "Please, please don't disturb her. I—I only want to leave—"

But at that moment the woman at the fire turned round. Her face, puffed up, red, with swollen eyes and swollen lips, looked terrible. She seemed as though she couldn't understand why Laura was there. What did it mean? Why was this stranger standing in the kitchen with a basket? What was it all about? And the poor face puckered up again.

"All right, my dear," said the other. "I'll thenk the young lady."

And again she began, "You'll excuse her, miss, I'm sure," and her face, swollen too, tried an oily smile.

Laura only wanted to get out, to get away. She was back in the passage. The door opened. She walked straight through into the bedroom, where the dead man was lying.

"You'd like a look at 'im, wouldn't you?" said Em's sister, and she brushed past Laura over to the bed. "Don't be afraid, my lass—" and now her voice sounded fond and sly, and fondly she drew down the sheet—"'e looks a picture. There's nothing to show. Come along, my dear."

Laura came.

There lay a young man, fast asleep—sleeping so soundly, so deeply, that he was far, far away from them both. Oh, so remote, so peaceful. He was dreaming. Never wake him up again. His head was sunk in the pillow, his eyes were closed; they were blind under the closed eyelids. He was given up to his dream. What did garden-parties and baskets and lace frocks matter to him? He was far from all those things. He was wonderful, beautiful. While they were laughing and while the band was playing, this marvel had come to the lane. Happy . . . happy. . . . All is well, said that sleeping face. This is just as it should be. I am content.

But all the same you had to cry, and she couldn't go out of the room without saying something to him. Laura gave a loud childish sob.

"Forgive my hat," she said.

And this time she didn't wait for Em's sister. She found her way out of the door, down the path, past all those dark people. At the corner of the lane she met Laurie.

He stepped out of the shadow. "Is that you, Laura?"

"Yes."

"Mother was getting anxious. Was it all right?"

"Yes, quite. Oh, Laurie!" She took his arm, she pressed up against him.

"I say, you're not crying, are you?" asked her brother.

Laura shook her head. She was.

Laurie put his arm round her shoulder. "Don't cry," he said in his warm, loving voice. "Was it awful?"

"No," sobbed Laura. "It was simply marvellous. But, Laurie—" She stopped, she looked at her brother. "Isn't life," she stammered, "isn't life—" But what life was she couldn't explain. No matter. He quite understood.

"*Isn't* it, darling?" said Laurie.

ZORA NEALE HURSTON
(1891–1960)

As a child in Florida, Hurston was told by her mother: "Jump at de sun—and you might at least catch holt to de moon." After her mother died, she left home to move north, graduated from Barnard, and became a professional folklorist and one of the great writers of the Harlem Literary Renaissance. She celebrated the expressive beauty and courage of African-American culture in more than one hundred manuscripts—short stories, novels, plays, essays, articles. Her masterpiece, the novel *Their Eyes Were Watching God* (1937), the story of Janie Crawford's rise above racism, sexism, and poverty to a triumphant wisdom, is now a favorite of African-American literature. *Dust Tracks on a Road* (1942) is one of the twentieth century's most popular autobiographies. Hurston died in poverty and obscurity in Florida. Her unmarked pauper's grave was discovered by Alice Walker during her crusade to reclaim Hurston's reputation, a literary revival published as *I Love Myself When I Am Laughing: A Zora Neale Hurston Reader* (1977). In Walker's words, Hurston inspires all African-American writers as a symbol of "racial health—a sense of black people as complete, complex, undiminished human beings."

How It Feels to Be Colored Me

I am colored but I offer nothing in the way of extenuating circumstances except the fact that I am the only Negro in the United States whose grandfather on the mother's side was *not* an Indian chief.

I remember the very day that I became colored. Up to my thirteenth year I lived in the little Negro town of Eatonville, Florida. It is exclusively a colored town. The only white people I knew passed through the town going to or coming from Orlando. The native whites rode dusty horses, the Northern tourists chugged down the sandy village road in automobiles. The town knew the Southerners and never stopped cane chewing when they passed. But the Northerners were something else again. They were peered at cautiously from behind curtains by the timid. The more venturesome would come out on the porch to watch them go past and got just as much pleasure out of the tourists as the tourists got out of the village.

The front porch might seem a daring place for the rest of the town, but it was a gallery seat for me. My favorite place was atop the gate-post. Proscenium box for a born first-nighter. Not only did I enjoy the show, but I didn't mind the actors knowing that I liked it. I usually spoke to them in passing. I'd wave at them and when they returned my salute, I would say something like this: "Howdy-do-well-I-thank-you-where-you-goin'?" Usually automobile or the horse paused at this, and after a queer exchange of compliments, I would probably "go a piece of the way" with them, as we say in farthest Florida. If one of my family happened to come to the front in time to see me, of course negotiations would be rudely broken off. But even so, it is clear that I was the first "welcome-to-our-state" Floridian, and I hope the Miami Chamber of Commerce will please take notice.

During this period, white people differed from colored to me only in that they rode through town and never lived there. They liked to hear me "speak pieces" and sing and wanted to see me dance the parse-me-la, and gave me generously of their small silver for doing these things, which seemed strange to me for I wanted to do them so much that I needed bribing to stop. Only they didn't know it. The colored people gave no dimes. They deplored any joyful tendencies in me, but I was their Zora nevertheless. I belonged to them, to the nearby hotels, to the county—everybody's Zora.

But changes came in the family when I was thirteen, and I was sent to school in Jacksonville. I left Eatonville, the town of the oleanders, as Zora. When I disembarked from the river-boat at Jacksonville, she was no more. It seemed that I had suffered a sea change. I was not Zora of Orange County any more, I was now a little colored girl. I found it out in certain ways. In my heart as well as in the mirror, I became a fast brown—warranted not to rub nor run.

But I am not tragically colored. There is no great sorrow dammed up in my soul, nor lurking behind my eyes. I do not mind at all. I do not belong to the sobbing school of Negrohood who hold that nature somehow has given them a low-down dirty deal and whose feelings are all hurt about it. Even in the helter-skelter skirmish that is my life, I have seen that the world is to the strong regardless of a little pigmentation more or less. No, I do not weep at the world—I am too busy sharpening my oyster knife.

Someone is always at my elbow reminding me that I am the granddaughter of slaves. It fails to register depression with me. Slavery is sixty years in the past. The operation was successful and the patient is doing well, thank you. The terrible struggle that made me an American out of a potential slave said "On the line!" The Reconstruction said "Get set!"; and the generation before said "Go!" I am off to a flying start and I must not halt in the stretch to look behind and weep. Slavery is the price I paid for civilization, and the choice was not with me. It is a bully adventure and worth all that I have paid through my ancestors for it. No one on earth ever had a greater chance for glory. The world to be won and nothing to be lost. It is thrilling to think—to know that for any act of mine, I shall get twice as much praise or twice as much blame. It is quite exciting to hold the center of the national stage, with the spectators not knowing whether to laugh or to weep.

The position of my white neighbor is much more difficult. No brown specter pulls up a chair beside me when I sit down to eat. No dark ghost thrusts its leg against mine in bed. The game of keeping what one has is never so exciting as the game of getting.

I do not always feel colored. Even now I often achieve the unconscious Zora of Eatonville before the Hegira. I feel most colored when I am thrown against a sharp white background.

For instance at Barnard. "Beside the waters of the Hudson" I feel my race. Among the thousand white persons, I am a dark rock surged upon, and over-swept, but through it all, I remain myself. When covered by the waters, I am; and the ebb but reveals me again.

Sometimes it is the other way around. A white person is set down in our midst, but the contrast is just as sharp for me. For instance, when I sit in the drafty base-ment that is The New World Cabaret with a white person, my color comes. We enter chatting about any little nothing that we have in common and are seated by the jazz waiters. In the abrupt way that jazz orchestras have, this one plunges into a number. It loses no time in circumlocutions, but gets right down to business. It constricts the thorax and splits the heart with its tempo and narcotic harmonies. This orchestra grows rambunctious, rears on its hind legs and attacks the tonal veil with primitive fury, rending it, clawing it until it breaks through to the jungle beyond. I follow those heathen—follow them exultingly. I dance wildly inside myself; I yell within, I whoop; I shake my assegai* above my head, I hurl it true to the mark *yeeeeooww!* I am in the jungle and living in the jungle way. My face is painted red and yellow and my body is painted blue. My pulse is throbbing like a war drum. I want to slaughter something—give pain, give death to what, I do not know. But the piece ends. The men of the orchestra wipe their lips and rest their fingers. I creep back slowly to the veneer we call civilization with the last tone and find the white friend sitting motionless in his seat, smoking calmly.

"Good music they have here," he remarks, drumming the table with his finger-tips.

Music. The great blobs of purple and red emotion have not touched him. He has only heard what I felt. He is far away and I see him but dimly across the ocean and the continent that have fallen between us. He is so pale with his whiteness then and I am *so* colored.

At certain times I have no race, I am *me*. When I set my hat at a certain angle and saunter down Seventh Avenue, Harlem City, feeling as snooty as the lions in front of the Forty-Second Street Library, for instance. So far as my feelings

*spear

are concerned, Peggy Hopkins Joyce on the Boule Mich with her gorgeous raiment, stately carriage, knees knocking together in a most aristocratic manner, has nothing on me. The cosmic Zora emerges. I belong to no race nor time. I am the eternal feminine with its string of beads.

I have no separate feeling about being an American citizen and colored. I am merely a fragment of the Great Soul that surges within the boundaries. My country, right or wrong.

Sometimes, I feel discriminated against, but it does not make me angry. It merely astonishes me. How *can* any deny themselves the pleasure of my company? It's beyond me.

But in the main, I feel like a brown bag of miscellany propped against a wall. Against a wall in company with other bags, white, red and yellow. Pour out the contents, and there is discovered a jumble of small things priceless and worthless. A first-water diamond, an empty spool, bits of broken glass, lengths of string, a key to a door long since crumbled away, a rusty knife-blade, old shoes saved for a road that never was and never will be, a nail bent under the weight of things too heavy for any nail, a dried flower or two still a little fragrant. In your hand is the brown bag. On the ground before you is the jumble it held—so much like the jumble in the bags, could they be emptied, that all might be dumped in a single heap and the bags refilled without altering the content of any greatly. A bit of colored glass more or less would not matter. Perhaps that is how the Great Stuffer of Bags filled them in the first place—who knows?

EDNA ST. VINCENT MILLAY
(1892–1950)

E dna St. Vincent Millay grew up in rural Maine, the eldest of three daughters whose father abandoned the family when she was twelve years old. A precocious child poet, she went to Vassar on a scholarship and after graduation moved to Greenwich Village, where, in the words of Dan Jacobson, "she lived like a modernist—sex, alcohol, drugs, feminism, nervous breakdowns, left-wing politics—but wrote like a late Victorian." Red-haired, reckless, beautiful, and gifted, she became the first woman to receive the Pulitzer Prize in poetry, for *The Harp-Weaver*. She wrote plays, essays, and poetry prolifically, publishing seventeen volumes of poetry. She was intensely involved in the unsuccessful fight to save the anarchists Sacco and Vanzetti from execution in 1928. Because of her use of traditional poetic forms, especially the sonnet, during an experimental age, her work went out of style in the thirties and forties; now, however, Millay's poetry, which voices the sexual and emotional freedom she extolled in her politics, is receiving attention again. There is a new edition of her early poems as well as two new biographies.

First Fig

My candle burns at both ends;
It will not last the night;
But ah, my foes, and oh, my friends—
It gives a lovely light!

What Lips My Lips Have Kissed, and Where, and Why

What lips my lips have kissed, and where, and why,
I have forgotten, and what arms have lain
Under my head till morning; but the rain
Is full of ghosts tonight, that tap and sigh
Upon the glass and listen for reply,
And in my heart there stirs a quiet pain
For unremembered lads that not again
Will turn to me at midnight with a cry.

Thus in the winter stands the lonely tree,
Nor knows what birds have vanished one by one,
Yet knows its boughs more silent than before:
I cannot say what loves have come and gone;
I only know that summer sang in me
A little while, that in me sings no more.

LOUISE BOGAN
(1897–1970)

Louise Bogan has been compared to Emily Dickinson, Blake, and Yeats; she influenced Sylvia Plath, and in her lifetime, other writers praised her work: Auden admired her wresting "beauty and truth out of dark places"; Theodore Roethke, her lover and friend, called her "one of the true inheritors of the great tradition. [Her] best work will stay in the language as long as the language survives." Bogan grew up poor in Maine, oppressed by the misery of her parents' marriage. "My father had his job. . . . My mother had nothing but her temperament, her fantasies, her despairs, her secrets, her subterfuges," Bogan wrote in *Journey Around My Room*, a "mosaic" of autobiographical fragments. After she moved to New York City, she began to publish her poems; she was the poetry editor at *The New Yorker* for thirty-eight years. Throughout her life, she suffered from depression, receiving treatment at the New York Neurological Institute of Columbia Presbyterian Hospital as well as in Europe for the periodic breakdowns she referred to as her "sabbatical six months." Her friends remember her sense of humor. "To be with her was to laugh with her." Her reaction to the many honors that came her way—the Bollingen Prize, membership in the National Institute of Arts and Letters and the Academy of American Poets, a Guggenheim fellowship, poetry consultant to the Library of Congress—was always modest: "Not bad," she'd say, "for an Irish girl from Camden, Maine."

Evening in the Sanitarium

The free evening fades, outside the windows fastened with decorative iron
    grilles.
The lamps are lighted; the shades drawn; the nurses are watching a little.
It is the hour of the complicated knitting on the safe bone needles; of the games
    of anagrams and bridge;
The deadly game of chess; the book held up like a mask.

The period of the wildest weeping, the fiercest delusion, is over.
The women rest their tired half-healed hearts; they are almost well.
Some of them will stay almost well always: the blunt-faced woman whose thinking
    dissolved
Under academic discipline; the manic-depressive girl

Now leveling off; one paranoiac afflicted with jealousy.
Another with persecution. Some alleviation has been possible.

O fortunate bride, who never again will become elated after childbirth!
O lucky older wife, who has been cured of feeling unwanted!
To the suburban railway station you will return, return,
To meet forever Jim home on the 5:35.
You will be again as normal and selfish and heartless as anybody else.

There is life left: the piano says it with its octave smile.
The soft carpets pad the thump and splinter of the suicide to be.
Everything will be splendid: the grandmother will not drink habitually.
The fruit salad will bloom on the plate like a bouquet
And the garden produce the blue-ribbon aquilegia.
The cats will be glad; the fathers feel justified; the mothers relieved.

The sons and husbands will no longer need to pay the bills.
Childhoods will be put away, the obscene nightmare abated.

At the ends of the corridors the baths are running.
Mrs. C. again feels the shadow of the obsessive idea.
Miss R. looks at the mantel-piece, which must mean something.

STEVIE SMITH
(1902–71)

Florence Margaret Smith spent most of her adult life working as a secretary and taking care of an elderly aunt in their home at Palmers Green, a suburb of North London. Yet throughout the humdrum years she published three novels—*Novel on Yellow Paper* (1936) is the best known—and more than ten volumes of poetry, which were admired for their mordant originality and humor as well as an utter absence of sentimentality. Robert Lowell expressed his admiration of Smith's "unique and cheerfully gruesome voice." In the sixties, her writing was rediscovered after a successful series of public readings, which created a large audience for Smith on both sides of the Atlantic. She was awarded the Queen's Gold Medal for Poetry in 1969.

How Cruel Is the Story of Eve

How cruel is the story of Eve
What responsibility
It has in history
For cruelty.

Touch, where the feeling is most vulnerable,
Unblameworthy—ah reckless—desiring children,
Touch there with a touch of pain?
Abominable.

Ah what cruelty,
In history
What misery.

Put up to barter
The tender feelings
Buy her a husband to rule her
Fool her to marry a master
She must or rue it
The Lord said it.

And man, poor man,
Is he fit to rule,
Pushed to it?
How can he carry it, the governance,
And not suffer for it
Insuffisance?
He must make woman lower then

So he can be higher then.
Oh what cruelty,
In history what misery.

Soon woman grows cunning
Masks her wisdom,
How otherwise will he
Bring food and shelter, kill enemies?
If he did not feel superior
It would be worse for her
And for the tender children
Worse for them.

Oh what cruelty,
In history what misery
Of falsity.

It is only a legend
You say? But what
Is the meaning of the legend
If not
To give blame to women most
And most punishment?
This is the meaning of a legend that colours
All human thought; it is not found among animals.

How cruel is the story of Eve,
What responsibility it has
In history
For misery.

Yet there is this to be said still:
Life would be over long ago

If men and women had not loved each other
Naturally, naturally,
Forgetting their mythology
They would have died of it else
Long ago, long ago,
And all would be emptiness now
And silence.

Oh dread Nature, for your purpose,
To have made them love so.

KATHLEEN RAINE

(1908–   )

Londoner Kathleen Raine sees her writing as the fruit of her Scottish ancestry—"my poetic roots were in wild Northumberland, where I lived as a child." She attributes her interest in specifically women's writing about women's lives to her reading of Virginia Woolf's *A Room of One's Own*. But her poetry—a dozen books were included in *The Collected Poems: 1935–1980*—is associated most of all with the antimaterialist, mystical Romantic tradition and with William Blake in particular. Educated at Cambridge in the natural sciences, she wrote four books about Blake as well as studies of Coleridge and William Butler Yeats, who was her friend.

Heirloom

She gave me childhood's flowers,
Heather and wild thyme,
Eyebright and tormentil,
Lichen's mealy cup
Dry on wind-scored stone,
The corbies on the rock,
The rowan by the burn.

Sea-marvels a child beheld
Out in the fisherman's boat,
Fringed pulsing violet
Medusa, sea-gooseberries,
Starfish on the sea-floor,
Cowries and rainbow-shells
From pools on a rocky shore.

Gave me her memories,
But kept her last treasure:
"When I was a lass," she said,
"Sitting among the heather,
"Suddenly I saw
"That all the moor was alive!
"I have told no one before."

That was my mother's tale.
Seventy years had gone
Since she saw the living skein
Of which the world is woven,
And having seen, knew all;
Through long indifferent years
Treasuring the priceless pearl.

EUDORA WELTY
(1909–2001)

"I have been told," Eudora Welty wrote in the preface to *The Collected Stories*, "both in approval and in accusation, that I seem to love all my characters. What I do in writing of any character is to try to enter into the mind, heart, and skin of a human being who is not myself. Whether this happens to be a man or a woman, old or young, with skin black or white, the primary challenge lies in making the jump itself. It is the act of a writer's imagination that I set most high." Among the most honored of American writers—every prize in the literary pantheon has gone to her—Welty was born in Jackson, Mississippi, where she lived all her life. Her memoir *One Writer's Beginnings* evokes the region she loves: "It's my source of knowledge. It tells me the important things." A storyteller of hidden inner lives (fiction must keep a private address, she wrote, "for life is lived in a private place; where it means anything is inside the mind and inside the heart"), she finds a similarity between herself and Chekhov: "He's one of us. . . . He loved the singularity in people, the individuality. . . . There's a great love and understanding that prevails . . . and a knowledge and acceptance of each other's idiosyncracies, a tolerance of them." The story that follows, her first published in a commercial magazine—*The Atlantic* took it in 1941 after her agent had sent it out for over a year, getting back rejection after rejection—has become a classic of American literature.

A Worn Path

It was December—a bright frozen day in the early morning. Far out in the country there was an old Negro woman with her head tied in a red rag, coming along a path through the pinewoods. Her name was Phoenix Jackson. She was very old and small and she walked slowly in the dark pine shadows, moving a little from side to side in her steps, with the balanced heaviness and lightness of a pendulum in a grandfather clock. She carried a thin, small cane made from an umbrella, and with this she kept tapping the frozen earth in front of her. This made a grave and persistent noise in the still air, that seemed meditative like the chirping of a solitary little bird.

She wore a dark striped dress reaching down to her shoe tops, and an equally long apron of bleached sugar sacks, with a full pocket: all neat and tidy, but every time she took a step she might have fallen over her shoelaces, which dragged from her unlaced shoes. She looked straight ahead. Her eyes were blue with age. Her skin had a pattern all its own of numberless branching wrinkles and as though a whole little tree stood in the middle of her forehead, but a golden color ran underneath, and the two knobs of her cheeks were illumined by a yellow burning under the dark. Under the red rag her hair came down on her neck in the frailest of ringlets, still black, and with an odor like copper.

Now and then there was a quivering in the thicket. Old Phoenix said, "Out of my way, all you foxes, owls, beetles, jack rabbits, coons and wild animals! . . . Keep out from under these feet, little bob-whites. . . . Keep the big wild hogs out of my path. Don't let none of those come running my direction. I got a long way." Under her small black-freckled hand her cane, limber as a buggy whip, would switch at the brush as if to rouse up any hiding things.

On she went. The woods were deep and still. The sun made the pine needles almost too bright to look at, up where the wind rocked. The cones dropped as light as feathers. Down in the hollow was the mourning dove—it was not too late for him.

The path ran up a hill. "Seem like there is chains about my feet, time I get this far," she said, in the voice of argument old people keep to use with themselves. "Something always take a hold of me on this hill—pleads I should stay."

After she got to the top she turned and gave a full, severe look behind her where she had come. "Up through pines," she said at length. "Now down through oaks."

Her eyes opened their widest, and she started down gently. But before she got to the bottom of the hill a bush caught her dress.

Her fingers were busy and intent, but her skirts were full and long, so that before she could pull them free in one place they were caught in another. It was not possible to allow the dress to tear. "I in the thorny bush," she said. "Thorns, you doing your appointed work. Never want to let folks pass, no sir. Old eyes thought you was a pretty little *green* bush."

Finally, trembling all over, she stood free, and after a moment dared to stoop for her cane.

"Sun so high!" she cried, leaning back and looking, while the thick tears went over her eyes. "The time getting all gone here."

At the foot of this hill was a place where a log was laid across the creek.

"Now comes the trial," said Phoenix.

Putting her right foot out, she mounted the log and shut her eyes. Lifting her skirt, leveling her cane fiercely before her, like a festival figure in some parade, she began to march across. Then she opened her eyes and she was safe on the other side.

"I wasn't as old as I thought," she said.

But she sat down to rest. She spread her skirts on the bank around her and folded her hands over her knees. Up above her was a tree in a pearly cloud of mistletoe. She did not dare to close her eyes, and when a little boy brought her a plate with a slice of marble-cake on it she spoke to him. "That would be acceptable," she said. But when she went to take it there was just her own hand in the air.

So she left that tree, and had to go through a barbed-wire fence. There she had to creep and crawl, spreading her knees and stretching her fingers like a baby trying to climb the steps. But she talked loudly to herself: she could not let her dress be torn now, so late in the day, and she could not pay for having her arm or her leg sawed off if she got caught fast where she was.

At last she was safe through the fence and risen up out in the clearing. Big dead trees, like black men with one arm, were standing in the purple stalks of the withered cotton field. There sat a buzzard.

"Who you watching?"

In the furrow she made her way along.

"Glad this not the season for bulls," she said, looking sideways, "and the good Lord made his snakes to curl up and sleep in the winter. A pleasure I don't see no two-headed snake coming around that tree, where it come once. It took a while to get by him, back in the summer."

She passed through the old cotton and went into a field of dead corn. It whispered and shook and was taller than her head. "Through the maze now," she said, for there was no path.

Then there was something tall, black, and skinny there, moving before her.

At first she took it for a man. It could have been a man dancing in the field. But she stood still and listened, and it did not make a sound. It was as silent as a ghost.

"Ghost," she said sharply, "who be you the ghost of? For I have heard of nary death close by."

But there was no answer—only the ragged dancing in the wind.

She shut her eyes, reached out her hand, and touched a sleeve. She found a coat and inside that an emptiness, cold as ice.

"You scarecrow," she said. Her face lighted. "I ought to be shut up for good," she said with laughter. "My senses is gone. I too old. I the oldest people I ever know. Dance, old scarecrow," she said, "while I dancing with you."

She kicked her foot over the furrow, and with mouth drawn down, shook her head once or twice in a little strutting way. Some husks blew down and whirled in streamers about her skirts.

Then she went on, parting her way from side to side with the cane, through the whispering field. At last she came to the end, to a wagon track where the silver grass blew between the red ruts. The quail were walking around like pullets, seeming all dainty and unseen.

"Walk pretty," she said. "This the easy place. This the easy going."

She followed the track, swaying through the quiet bare fields, through the little strings of trees silver in their dead leaves, past cabins silver from weather, with the doors and windows boarded shut, all like old women under a spell sitting there. "I walking in their sleep," she said, nodding her head vigorously.

In a ravine she went where a spring was silently flowing through a hollow log. Old Phoenix bent and drank. "Sweet-gum makes the water sweet," she said, and drank more. "Nobody know who made this well, for it was here when I was born."

The track crossed a swampy part where the moss hung as white as lace from every limb. "Sleep on, alligators, and blow your bubbles." Then the track went into the road.

Deep, deep the road went down between the high green-colored banks. Overhead the live-oaks met, and it was as dark as a cave.

A black dog with a lolling tongue came up out of the weeds by the ditch. She was meditating, and not ready, and when he came at her she only hit him a little with her cane. Over she went in the ditch, like a little puff of milkweed.

Down there, her senses drifted away. A dream visited her, and she reached her hand up, but nothing reached down and gave her a pull. So she lay there and presently went to talking. "Old woman," she said to herself, "that black dog come up out of the weeds to stall you off, and now there he sitting on his fine tail, smiling at you."

A white man finally came along and found her—a hunter, a young man, with his dog on a chain.

"Well, Granny!" he laughed. "What are you doing there?"

"Lying on my back like a June-bug waiting to be turned over, mister," she said, reaching up her hand.

He lifted her up, gave her a swing in the air, and set her down. "Anything broken, Granny?"

"No sir, them old dead weeds is springy enough," said Phoenix, when she had got her breath. "I thank you for your trouble."

"Where do you live, Granny?" he asked, while the two dogs were growling at each other.

"Away back yonder, sir, behind the ridge. You can't even see it from here."

"On your way home?"

"No sir, I going to town."

"Why, that's too far! That's as far as I walk when I come out myself, and I get something for my trouble." He patted the stuffed bag he carried, and there hung down a little closed claw. It was one of the bob-whites, with its beak hooked bitterly to show it was dead. "Now you go on home, Granny!"

"I bound to go to town, mister," said Phoenix. "The time come around."

He gave another laugh, filling the whole landscape. "I know you old colored people! Wouldn't miss going to town to see Santa Claus!"

But something held old Phoenix very still. The deep lines in her face went into a fierce and different radiation. Without warning, she had seen with her own eyes a flashing nickel fall out of the man's pocket onto the ground.

"How old are you, Granny?" he was saying.

"There is no telling, mister," she said, "no telling."

Then she gave a little cry and clapped her hands and said, "Git on away from here, dog! Look! Look at that dog!" She laughed as if in admiration. "He ain't scared of nobody. He a big black dog." She whispered, "Sic him!"

"Watch me get rid of that cur," said the man. "Sic him, Pete! Sic him!"

Phoenix heard the dogs fighting, and heard the man running and throwing sticks. She even heard a gunshot. But she was slowly bending forward by that time, further and further forward, the lids stretched down over her eyes, as if she were doing this in her sleep. Her chin was lowered almost to her knees. The yellow palm of her hand came out from the fold of her apron. Her fingers slid down and along the ground under the piece of money with the grace and care they would have in lifting an egg from under a setting hen. Then she slowly straightened up, she stood erect, and the nickel was in her apron pocket. A bird flew by. Her lips moved. "God watching me the whole time. I come to stealing."

The man came back, and his own dog panted about them. "Well, I scared him off that time," he said, and then he laughed and lifted his gun and pointed it at Phoenix.

She stood straight and faced him.

"Doesn't the gun scare you?" he said, still pointing it.

"No, sir, I seen plenty go off closer by, in my day, and for less than what I done," she said, holding utterly still.

He smiled, and shouldered the gun. "Well, Granny," he said, "you must be a hundred years old, and scared of nothing. I'd give you a dime if I had any money with me. But you take my advice and stay home, and nothing will happen to you."

"I bound to go on my way, mister," said Phoenix. She inclined her head in the red rag. Then they went in different directions, but she could hear the gun shooting again and again over the hill.

She walked on. The shadows hung from the oak trees to the road like curtains. Then she smelled wood-smoke, and smelled the river, and she saw a steeple and the cabins on their steep steps. Dozens of little black children whirled around her. There ahead was Natchez shining. Bells were ringing. She walked on.

In the paved city it was Christmas time. There were red and green electric lights strung and crisscrossed everywhere, and all turned on in the daytime. Old Phoenix would have been lost if she had not distrusted her eyesight and depended on her feet to know where to take her.

She paused quietly on the sidewalk where people were passing by. A lady came along in the crowd, carrying an armful of red-, green- and silver-wrapped presents; she gave off perfume like the red roses in hot summer, and Phoenix stopped her.

"Please, missy, will you lace up my shoe?" She held up her foot.

"What do you want, Grandma?"

"See my shoe," said Phoenix. "Do all right for out in the country, but wouldn't look right to go in a big building."

"Stand still then, Grandma," said the lady. She put her packages down on the sidewalk beside her and laced and tied both shoes tightly.

"Can't lace 'em with a cane," said Phoenix. "Thank you, missy. I doesn't mind asking a nice lady to tie up my shoe, when I gets out on the street."

Moving slowly and from side to side, she went into the big building, and into a tower of steps, where she walked up and around and around until her feet knew to stop.

She entered a door, and there she saw nailed up on the wall the document that had been stamped with the gold seal and framed in the gold frame, which matched the dream that was hung up in her head.

"Here I be," she said. There was a fixed and ceremonial stiffness over her body.

"A charity case, I suppose," said an attendant who sat at the desk before her.

But Phoenix only looked above her head. There was sweat on her face, the wrinkles in her skin shone like a bright net.

"Speak up, Grandma," the woman said. "What's your name? We must have your history, you know. Have you been here before? What seems to be the trouble with you?"

Old Phoenix only gave a twitch to her face as if a fly were bothering her.

"Are you deaf?" cried the attendant.

But then the nurse came in.

"Oh, that's just old Aunt Phoenix," she said. "She doesn't come for herself — she has a little grandson. She makes these trips just as regular as clockwork. She lives away back off the Old Natchez Trace." She bent down. "Well, Aunt Phoenix, why don't you just take a seat? We won't keep you standing after your long trip." She pointed.

The old woman sat down, bolt upright in the chair.

"Now, how is the boy?" asked the nurse.

Old Phoenix did not speak.

"I said, how is the boy?"

But Phoenix only waited and stared straight ahead, her face very solemn and withdrawn into rigidity.

"Is his throat any better?" asked the nurse. "Aunt Phoenix, don't you hear me? Is your grandson's throat any better since the last time you came for the medicine?"

With her hands on her knees, the old woman waited, silent, erect and motionless, just as if she were in armor.

"You mustn't take up our time this way, Aunt Phoenix," the nurse said. "Tell us quickly about your grandson, and get it over. He isn't dead, is he?"

At last there came a flicker and then a flame of comprehension across her face, and she spoke.

"My grandson. It was my memory had left me. There I sat and forgot why I made my long trip."

"Forgot?" The nurse frowned. "After you came so far?"

Then Phoenix was like an old woman begging a dignified forgiveness for waking up frightened in the night. "I never did go to school, I was too old at the Surrender," she said in a soft voice. "I'm an old woman without an education. It was my memory fail me. My little grandson, he is just the same, and I forgot it in the coming."

"Throat never heals, does it?" said the nurse, speaking in a loud, sure voice to old Phoenix. By now she had a card with something written on it, a little list. "Yes. Swallowed lye. When was it?—January—two, three years ago—"

Phoenix spoke unasked now. "No, missy, he not dead, he just the same. Every little while his throat begin to close up again, and he not able to swallow. He not get his breath. He not able to help himself. So the time come around, and I go on another trip for the soothing medicine."

"All right. The doctor said as long as you came to get it, you could have it," said the nurse. "But it's an obstinate case."

"My little grandson, he sit up there in the house all wrapped up, waiting by himself," Phoenix went on. "We is the only two left in the world. He suffer and it don't seem to put him back at all. He got a sweet look. He going to last. He wear a little patch quilt and peep out holding his mouth open like a little bird. I remembers so plain now. I not going to forget him again, no, the whole enduring time. I could tell him from all the others in creation."

"All right." The nurse was trying to hush her now. She brought her a bottle of medicine. "Charity," she said, making a check mark in a book.

Old Phoenix held the bottle close to her eyes, and then carefully put it into her pocket.

"I thank you," she said.

"It's Christmas time, Grandma," said the attendant. "Could I give you a few pennies out of my purse?"

"Five pennies is a nickel," said Phoenix stiffly.

"Here's a nickel," said the attendant.

Phoenix rose carefully and held out her hand. She received the nickel and then fished the other nickel out of her pocket and laid it beside the new one. She stared at her palm closely, with her head on one side.

Then she gave a tap with her cane on the floor.

"This is what come to me to do," she said. "I going to the store and buy my child a little windmill they sells, made out of paper. He going to find it hard to believe there such a thing in the world. I'll march myself back where he waiting, holding it straight up in this hand."

She lifted her free hand, gave a little nod, turned around, and walked out of the doctor's office. Then her slow step began on the stairs, going down.

MARY LAVIN
(1912–96)

Born in Massachusetts to Irish parents, Mary Lavin, at the age of ten, moved back to Ireland, where she became a prominent writer on modern Ireland's literary landscape, publishing twelve volumes of short stories (many originally in *The New Yorker*) and several prizewinning novels. After her husband died, she supported her three young daughters by writing and running a farm in County Meath. Well-known for her support of younger writers, including Irish-American novelist and short story writer Elizabeth Cullinan and Dublin memoirist Nuala O'Faolain, she has received generous tributes from many other writers. In the words of Alice Munro: "Mary Lavin's stories have always given me a feeling of wonder and security—security because of the way the view keeps opening up, with such ease and authority, and wonder because she is, after all, so intrepid, so original and astonishing."

Happiness

Mother had a lot to say. This does not mean she was always talking but that we children felt the wells she drew upon were deep, deep, deep. Her theme was happiness: what it was, what it was not; where we might find it, where not; and how, if found, it must be guarded. Never must we confound it with pleasure. Nor think sorrow its exact opposite.

"Take Father Hugh," Mother's eyes flashed as she looked at him. "According to him, sorrow is an ingredient of happiness—a *necessary* ingredient, if you please!" And when he tried to protest she put up her hand. "There may be a freakish truth in the theory—for some people. But not for me. And not, I hope, for my children." She looked severely at us three girls. We laughed. None of us had had much experience with sorrow. Bea and I were children and Linda only a year old when our father died suddenly after a short illness that had not at first seemed serious. "I've known people to make sorrow a *substitute* for happiness," Mother said.

Father Hugh protested again. "You're not putting me in that class, I hope?"

Father Hugh, ever since our father died, had been the closest of anyone to us as a family, without being close to any one of us in particular—even to Mother. He lived in a monastery near our farm in County Meath, and he had been one of the celebrants at the Requiem High Mass our father's political importance had demanded. He met us that day for the first time, but he took to dropping in to see us, with the idea of filling the crater of loneliness left at our centre. He did not know that there was a cavity in his own life, much less that we would fill it. He and Mother were both young in those days, and perhaps it gave scandal to some that he was so often in our house, staying till late into the night and, indeed, thinking nothing of stopping all night if there was any special reason, such as one of us being sick. He had even on occasion slept there if the night was too wet for tramping home across the fields.

When we girls were young, we were so used to having Father Hugh around that we never stood on ceremony with him but in his presence dried our hair and pared our nails and never minded what garments were strewn about. As for Mother—she thought nothing of running out of the bathroom in her slip, brushing her teeth or combing her hair, if she wanted to tell him something she might otherwise forget. And she brooked no criticism of her behaviour. "Celibacy was never meant to take all the warmth and homeliness out of their lives," she said.

On this point, too, Bea was adamant. Bea, the middle sister, was our oracle. "I'm so glad he *has* Mother," she said, "as well as her having him, because it must be awful the way most women treat them—priests, I mean—as if they were pariahs. Mother treats him like a human being—that's all!"

And when it came to Mother's ears that there had been gossip about her making free with Father Hugh, she opened her eyes wide in astonishment. "But he's only a priest!" she said.

Bea giggled. "It's a good job he didn't hear *that*," she said to me afterwards. "It would undo the good she's done him. You'd think he was a eunuch."

"Bea!" I said. "Do you think he's in love with her?"

"If so, he doesn't know it," Bea said firmly. "It's her soul he's after! Maybe he wants to make sure of her in the next world!"

But thoughts of the world to come never troubled Mother. "If anything ever happens to me, children," she said, "suddenly, I mean, or when you are not near me, or I cannot speak to you, I want you to promise you won't feel bad. There's no need! Just remember that I had a happy life—and that if I had to choose my kind of heaven I'd take it on this earth with you again, no matter how much you might annoy me!"

You see, annoyance and fatigue, according to Mother, and even illness and pain, could coexist with happiness. She had a habit of asking people if they were happy at times and in places that—to say the least of it—seemed to us inappropriate. "But are you happy?" she'd probe as one lay sick and bathed in sweat, or in the throes of a jumping toothache. And once in our presence she made the inquiry of an old friend as he lay upon his deathbed.

"Why not?" she said when we took her to task for it later. "Isn't it more important than ever to be happy when you're dying? Take my own father! You know what he said in his last moments? On his deathbed, he defied me to name a man who had enjoyed a better life. In spite of dreadful pain, his face *radiated* happiness!" Mother nodded her head comfortably. "Happiness drives out pain, as fire burns out fire."

Having no knowledge of our own to pit against hers, we thirstily drank in her rhetoric. Only Bea was sceptical. "Perhaps you *got* it from him, like spots, or fever," she said. "Or something that could at least be slipped from hand to hand."

"Do you think I'd have taken it if that were the case!" Mother cried. "Then, when he needed it most?"

"Not there and then!" Bea said stubbornly. "I meant as a sort of legacy."

"Don't you think in *that* case," Mother said, exasperated, "he would have felt obliged to leave it to your grandmother?"

Certainly we knew that in spite of his lavish heart our grandfather had failed to provide our grandmother with enduring happiness. He had passed that job on to Mother. And Mother had not made too good a fist of it, even when Father was living and she had him—and, later, us children—to help.

As for Father Hugh, he had given our grandmother up early in the game. "God Almighty couldn't make that woman happy," he said one day, seeing Mother's face, drawn and pale with fatigue, preparing for the nightly run over to her own mother's flat that would exhaust her utterly.

There were evenings after she came home from the library where she worked when we saw her stand with the car keys in her hand, trying to think which would be worse—to slog over there on foot, or take out the car again. And yet the distance was short. It was Mother's day that had been too long.

"Weren't you over to see her this morning?" Father Hugh demanded.

"No matter!" said Mother. She was no doubt thinking of the forlorn face our grandmother always put on when she was leaving. ("Don't say good night, Vera," Grandmother would plead. "It makes me feel too lonely. And you never can tell— you might slip over again before you go to bed!")

"Do you know the time?" Bea would say impatiently, if she happened to be with Mother. Not indeed that the lateness of the hour counted for anything, because in all likelihood Mother *would* go back, if only to pass by under the window and see that the lights were out, or stand and listen and make sure that as far as she could tell all was well.

"I wouldn't mind if she was happy," Mother said.

"And how do you know she's not?" we'd ask.

"When people are happy, I can feel it. Can't you?"

We were not sure. Most people thought our grandmother was a gay creature, a small birdy being who even at a great age laughed like a girl, and—more remarkably—sang like one, as she went about her day. But beak and claw were of steel. She'd think nothing of sending Mother back to a shop three times if her errands were not exactly right. "Not sugar like that—that's *too* fine; it's not castor sugar I want. But *not* as coarse as *that*, either. I want an in-between kind."

Provoked one day, my youngest sister, Linda, turned and gave battle. "You're mean!" she cried. "You love ordering people about!"

Grandmother preened, as if Linda had acclaimed an attribute. "I was always hard to please," she said. "As a girl, I used to be called Miss Imperious."

And Miss Imperious she remained as long as she lived, even when she was a great age. Her orders were then given a wry twist by the fact that as she advanced in age she took to calling her daughter Mother, as we did.

There was one great phrase with which our grandmother opened every sentence: "if only." "If only," she'd say, when we came to visit her—"if only you'd come earlier, before I was worn out expecting you!" Or if we were early, then if only it was later, after she'd had a rest and could enjoy us, be *able* for us. And if we brought her flowers, she'd sigh to think that if only we'd brought them the previous day she'd have had a visitor to appreciate them, or say it was a pity the stems weren't longer. If only we'd picked a few green leaves, or included some buds, because, she said disparagingly, the poor flowers we'd brought were already wilting. We might just as well not have brought them! As the years went on, Grandmother had a new bead to add to her rosary: if only her friends were not all dead! By their absence, they reduced to nil all *real* enjoyment in anything. Our own father—her son-in-law—was the one person who had ever gone close to pleasing her. But even here there had been a snag. "If only he was my real son!" she used to say, with a sigh.

Mother's mother lived on through our childhood and into our early maturity (though she outlived the money our grandfather left her), and in our minds she was a complicated mixture of valiance and defeat. Courageous and generous within the limits of her own life, her simplest demand was yet enormous in the larger frame of Mother's life, and so we never could see her with the same clarity of vision with which we saw our grandfather, or our own father. Them we saw only through Mother's eyes.

"Take your grandfather!" she'd cry, and instantly we'd see him, his eyes burning upon us—yes, upon *us*, although in his day only one of us had been born: me. At another time, Mother would cry, "Take your own father!" and instantly we'd see *him*—tall, handsome, young, and much more suited to marry one of us than poor bedraggled Mother.

Most fascinating of all were the times Mother would say "Take me!" By magic then, staring down the years, we'd see blazingly clear a small girl with black hair and buttoned boots, who, though plain and pouting, burned bright, like a star. "I was happy, you see," Mother said. And we'd strain hard to try and understand the mystery of the light that still radiated from her. "I used to lean along a tree that grew out over the river," she said, "and look down through the grey leaves at the water flowing past below, and I used to think it was not the stream that flowed but me, spread-eagled over it, who flew through the air! Like a bird! That I'd found the secret!" She made it seem there might *be* such a secret, just waiting to be found. Another time she'd dream that she'd be a great singer.

"We didn't know you sang, Mother!"

She had to laugh. "Like a crow," she said.

Sometimes she used to think she'd swim the Channel.

"Did you swim *that* well, Mother?"

"Oh, not really—just the breast stroke," she said. "And then only by the aid of two pig bladders blown up by my father and tied around my middle. But I used to throb—yes, throb—with happiness."

Behind Mother's back, Bea raised her eyebrows.

What was it, we used to ask ourselves—that quality that she, we felt sure, mis-named? Was it courage? Was it strength, health, or high spirits? Something you could not give or take—a conundrum? A game of catch-as-catch-can?

"I know," cried Bea. "A sham!"

Whatever it was, we knew that Mother would let no wind of violence from within or without tear it from her. Although, one evening when Father Hugh was with us, our astonished ears heard her proclaim that there might be a time when one had to slacken hold on it—let go—to catch at it again with a surer hand. In the way, we supposed, that the high-wire walker up among the painted stars of his canvas sky must wait to fling himself through the air until the bar he catches at has started to sway perversely from him. Oh no, no! That downward drag at our innards we could not bear, the belly swelling to the shape of a pear. Let happiness go by the board. "After all, lots of people seem to make out without it," Bea cried. It was too tricky a business. And might it not be that one had to be born with a flair for it?

"A flair would not be enough," Mother answered. "Take Father Hugh. He, if anyone, had a flair for it—a natural capacity! You've only to look at him when he's off guard, with you children, or helping me in the garden. But he rejects happi-ness! He casts it from him."

"That is simply not true, Vera," cried Father Hugh, overhearing her. "It's just that I don't place an inordinate value on it like you. I don't think it's enough to carry one all the way. To the end, I mean—and after."

"Oh, don't talk about the end when we're only in the middle," cried Mother. And, indeed, at that moment her own face shone with such happiness it was hard to believe that her earth was not her heaven. Certainly it was her constant contention that of happiness she had had a lion's share. This, however, we, in private, doubted. Perhaps there were times when she had had a surplus of it—when she was young, say, with her redoubtable father, whose love blazed circles around her, making win-ter into summer and ice into fire. Perhaps she did have a brimming measure in her early married years. By straining hard, we could find traces left in our minds from those days of milk and honey. Our father, while he lived, had cast a magic over everything, for us as well as for her. He held his love up over us like an umbrella and kept off the troubles that afterwards came down on us, pouring cats and dogs!

But if she did have more than the common lot of happiness in those early days, what use was that when we could remember so clearly how our father's death had ravaged her? And how could we forget the distress it brought on us when, afraid to let her out of our sight, Bea and I stumbled after her everywhere, through the woods and along the bank of the river, where, in the weeks that followed, she tried vainly to find peace.

The summer after Father died, we were invited to France to stay with friends, and when she went walking on the cliffs at Fécamp our fears for her grew frenzied, so that we hung on to her arm and dragged at her skirt, hoping that like leaded weights we'd pin her down if she went too near to the edge. But at night we had to abandon our watch, being forced to follow the conventions of a family still whole—a home still intact—and go to bed at the same time as the other children. It was at that hour, when the coast guard was gone from his rowing boat offshore and the sand was as cold and grey as the sea, that Mother liked to swim. And when she had washed, kissed, and left us, our hearts almost died inside us and we'd creep out of bed again to stand in our bare feet at the mansard and watch as she ran down the shingle, striking out when she reached the water where, far out, wave and sky and mist were one, and the greyness closed over her. If we took our eyes off her for an instant, it was impossible to find her again.

"Oh, make her turn back, God, please!" I prayed out loud one night.

Startled, Bea turned away from the window. "She'll *have* to turn back sometime, won't she? Unless . . . ?"

Locking our damp hands together, we stared out again. "She wouldn't!" I whispered. "It would be a sin!"

Secure in the deterring power of sin, we let out our breath. Then Bea's breath caught again. "What if she went out so far she used up all her strength? She couldn't swim back! It wouldn't be a sin then!"

"It's the intention that counts," I whispered.

A second later, we could see an arm lift heavily up and wearily cleave down, and at last Mother was in the shallows, wading back to shore.

"Don't let her see us!" cried Bea. As if our chattering teeth would not give us away when she looked in at us before she went to her own room on the other side of the corridor, where, later in the night, sometimes the sound of crying would reach us.

What was it worth—a happiness bought that dearly.

Mother had never questioned it. And once she told us, "On a wintry day, I brought my own mother a snowdrop. It was the first one of the year—a bleak bud that had come up stunted before its time—and I meant it for a sign. But do you know what your grandmother said? 'What good are snowdrops to me now?' Such a thing to say! What good is a snowdrop at all if it doesn't hold its value always, and never lose it! Isn't that the whole point of a snowdrop? And that is the whole point of happiness, too! What good would it be if it could be erased without trace? Take me and those daffodils!" Stooping, she buried her face in a bunch that lay on the table waiting to be put in vases. "If they didn't hold their beauty absolute and inviolable, do you think I could bear the sight of them after what happened when your father was in hospital?"

It was a fair question. When Father went to hospital, Mother went with him and stayed in a small hotel across the street so she could be with him all day from early to late. "Because it was so awful for him—being in Dublin!" she said. "You have no idea how he hated it."

That he was dying neither of them realised. How could they know, as it rushed through the sky, that their star was a falling star! But one evening when she'd left him asleep Mother came home for a few hours to see how we were faring, and it broke her heart to see the daffodils out all over the place—in the woods, under the trees, and along the sides of the avenue. There had never been so many, and she thought how awful it was that Father was missing them. "You sent up little bunches to him, you poor dears!" she said. "Sweet little bunches, too—squeezed tight as posies by your little fists! But stuffed into vases they couldn't really make up to him for not being able to see them growing!"

So on the way back to the hospital she stopped her car and pulled a great bunch—the full of her arms. "They took up the whole back seat," she said, "and I was so excited at the thought of walking into his room and dumping them on his bed—you know—just plomping them down so he could smell them, and feel them, and look and look! I didn't mean them to be put in vases, or anything ridiculous like that—it would have taken a rainwater barrel to hold them. Why, I could hardly see over them as I came up the steps; I kept tripping. But when I came into the hall, that nun—I told you about her—that nun came up to me, sprang out of nowhere it seemed, although I know now that she was waiting for me, knowing that somebody had to bring me to my senses. But the way she did it! Reached out and grabbed the flowers, letting lots of them fall—I remember them getting stood on. 'Where are you going with those foolish flowers, you foolish woman?' she said. 'Don't you know your husband is dying? Your prayers are all you can give him now!'

"She was right. I *was* foolish. But I wasn't cured. Afterwards, it was nothing but foolishness the way I dragged you children after me all over Europe. As if any one place was going to be different from another, any better, any less desolate. But there was great satisfaction in bringing you places your father and I had planned to bring you—although in fairness to him I must say that he would not perhaps have brought you so young. And he would not have had an ulterior motive. But above all, he would not have attempted those trips in such a dilapidated car."

Oh, that car! It was a battered and dilapidated red sports car, so depleted of accessories that when, eventually, we got a new car Mother still stuck out her hand on bends, and in wet weather jumped out to wipe the windscreen with her sleeve. And if fussed, she'd let down the window and shout at people, forgetting she now had a horn. How we had ever fitted into it with all our luggage was a miracle.

"You were never lumpish—any of you!" Mother said proudly. "But you were very healthy and very strong." She turned to me. "Think of how you got that car up the hill in Switzerland!"

"The Alps are not hills, Mother!" I pointed out coldly, as I had done at the time, when, as actually happened, the car failed to make it on one of the inclines. Mother let it run back until it wedged against the rock face, and I had to get out and push till she got going again in first gear. But when it got started it couldn't be stopped to pick me up until it got to the top, where they had to wait for me, and for a very long time.

"Ah, well," she said, sighing wistfully at the thought of those trips. "You got something out of them, I hope. All that travelling must have helped you with your geography and your history."

We looked at each other and smiled, and then Mother herself laughed. "Remember the time," she said, "when we were in Italy, and it was Easter, and all the shops were chock-full of food? The butchers' shops had poultry and game hanging up outside the doors, fully feathered, and with their poor heads dripping blood, and in the windows they had poor little lambs and suckling pigs and young goats, all skinned and hanging by their hindfeet." Mother shuddered. "They think so much about food. I found it revolting. I had to hurry past. But Linda, who must have been only four then, dragged at me and stared and stared. You know how children are at that age; they have a morbid fascination for what is cruel and bloody. Her face was flushed and her eyes were wide. I hurried her back to the hotel. But next morning she crept into my room. She crept up to me and pressed against me. 'Can't we go back, just once, and look again at that shop?' she whispered. 'The shop where they have the little children hanging up for Easter!' It was the young goats, of course, but I'd said 'kids,' I suppose. How we laughed." But her face was grave. "You were *so* good on those trips, all of you," she said. "You were really very good children in general. Otherwise I would never have put so much effort into rearing you, because I wasn't a bit maternal. You brought out the best in me! I put an unnatural effort into you, of course, because I was taking my standards from your father, forgetting that his might not have remained so inflexible if he had lived to middle age and was beset by life, like other parents."

"Well, the job is nearly over now, Vera," said Father Hugh. "And you didn't do so badly."

"That's right, Hugh," said Mother, and she straightened up, and put her hand to her back the way she sometimes did in the garden when she got up from her knees after weeding. "I didn't go over to the enemy anyway! We survived!" Then a flash of defiance came into her eyes. "And we were happy. That's the main thing!"

Father Hugh frowned. "There you go again!" he said.

Mother turned on him. "I don't think you realise the onslaughts that were made upon our happiness! The minute Robert died, they came down on me—cohorts of relatives, friends, even strangers, all draped in black, opening their arms like bats to let me pass into their company. 'Life is a vale of tears,' they said. 'You are privileged to find it out so young!' Ugh! After I staggered on to my feet and began to take hold of life once more, they fell back defeated. And the first day I gave a laugh—pouff, they were blown out like candles. They weren't living in a real world at all; they belonged to a ghostly world where life was easy: all one had to do was sit and weep. It takes effort to push back the stone from the mouth of the tomb and walk out."

Effort. Effort. Ah, but that strange-sounding word could invoke little sympathy from those who had not learned yet what it meant. Life must have been hardest for Mother in those years when we older ones were at college—no longer children, and still dependent on her. Indeed, we made more demands on her than ever then, having moved into new areas of activity and emotion. And our friends! Our friends came and went as freely as we did ourselves, so that the house was often like a café—and one where pets were not prohibited but took their places on our chairs and beds, as regardless as the people. And anyway it was hard to have sympathy for someone who got things into such a state as Mother. All over the house there was clutter. Her study was like the returned-letter department of a post-office, with stacks of paper everywhere, bills paid and unpaid, letters answered and unanswered, tax returns, pamphlets, leaflets. If by mistake we left the door open on a windy day, we came back to find papers flapping through the air like frightened birds. Efficient only in that she managed eventually to conclude every task she began, it never seemed possible to outsiders that by Mother's methods anything whatever could be accomplished. In an attempt to keep order elsewhere, she made her own room the clearing house into which the rest of us put everything: things to be given away, things to be mended, things to be stored, things to be treasured, things to be returned—even things to be thrown out! By the end of the year, the room resembled an obsolescence dump. And no one could help her; the chaos of her life was as personal as an act of creation—one might as well try to finish another person's poem.

As the years passed, Mother rushed around more hectically. And although Bea and I had married and were not at home any more, except at holiday time and for occasional weekends, Linda was noisier than the two of us put together had been, and for every follower we had brought home she brought twenty. The house was never still. Now that we were reduced to being visitors, we watched Mother's tension mount to vertigo, knowing that, like a spinning top, she could not rest till she fell. But now at the smallest pretext Father Hugh would call in the doctor and Mother would be put on the mail boat and dispatched for London. For it was essential that she get far enough away to make phoning home every night prohibitively costly.

Unfortunately, the thought of departure often drove a spur into her and she redoubled her effort to achieve order in her affairs. She would be up until the early hours ransacking her desk. To her, as always the shortest parting entailed a preparation as for death. And as if it were her end that was at hand, we would all be summoned, although she had no time to speak a word to us, because five minutes before departure she would still be attempting to reply to letters that were the acquisition of weeks and would have taken whole days to dispatch.

"Don't you know the taxi is at the door, Vera?" Father Hugh would say, running his hand through his grey hair and looking very dishevelled himself. She had him at times as distracted as herself. "You can't do any more. You'll have to leave the rest till you come back."

"I can't, I can't!" Mother would cry. "I'll have to cancel my plans."

One day, Father Hugh opened the lid of her case, which was strapped up in the hall, and with a swipe of his arm he cleared all the papers on the top of the desk pell-mell into the suitcase. "You can sort them on the boat," he said, "or the train to London!"

Thereafter, Mother's luggage always included an empty case to hold the unfinished papers on her desk. And years afterwards a steward on the Irish Mail told us she was a familiar figure, working away at letters and bills nearly all the way from Holyhead to Euston. "She gave it up about Rugby or Crewe," he said. "She'd get talking to someone in the compartment." He smiled. "There was one time coming down the train I was just in time to see her close up the window with a guilty look. I didn't say anything, but I think she'd emptied those papers of hers out the window!"

Quite likely. When we were children, even a few hours away from us gave her composure. And in two weeks or less, when she'd come home, the well of her spirit would be freshened. We'd hardly know her—her step so light, her eye so bright, and her love and patience once more freely flowing. But in no time at all the house would fill up once more with the noise and confusion of too many people and too many animals, and again we'd be fighting our corner with cats and dogs, bats, mice, bees and even wasps. "Don't kill it!" Mother would cry if we raised a hand to an angry wasp. "Just catch it, dear, and put it outside. Open the window and let it fly away!" But even this treatment could at times be deemed too harsh. "Wait a minute. Close the window!" she'd cry. "It's too cold outside. It will die. That's why it came in, I suppose! Oh dear, what will we do?" Life would be going full blast again.

There was only one place Mother found rest. When she was at breaking point and fit to fall, she'd go out into the garden—not to sit or stroll around but to dig, to drag up weeds, to move great clumps of corms or rhizomes, or indeed quite frequently to haul huge rocks from one place to another. She was always laying down a path, building a dry wall, or making compost heaps as high as hills. However jaded she might be going out, when dark forced her in at last her step had the spring of a daisy. So if she did not succeed in defining happiness to our understanding, we could see that whatever it was, she possessed it to the full when she was in her garden.

One of us said as much one Sunday when Bea and I had dropped round for the afternoon. Father Hugh was with us again. "It's an unthinking happiness, though," he cavilled. We were standing at the drawing-room window, looking out to where in the fading light we could see Mother on her knees weeding, in the long border that stretched from the house right down to the woods. "I wonder how she'd take it if she were stricken down and had to give up that heavy work!" he said. Was he perhaps a little jealous of how she could stoop and bend? He himself had begun to use a stick. I was often a little jealous of her myself, because although I was married and had children of my own, I had married young and felt the weight of living as heavy as a weight of years. "She doesn't take enough care of herself," Father Hugh said sadly. "Look at her out there with nothing under her knees to protect her from the damp ground." It was almost too dim for us to see her, but even in the drawing room it was chilly. "She should not be let stay out there after the sun goes down."

"Just you try to get her in then!" said Linda, who had come into the room in time to hear him. "Don't you know by now anyway that what would kill another person only seems to make Mother thrive?"

Father Hugh shook his head again. "You seem to forget it's not younger she's getting!" He fidgeted and fussed, and several times went to the window to stare out apprehensively. He was really getting quite elderly.

"Come and sit down, Father Hugh," Bea said, and to take his mind off Mother she turned on the light and blotted out the garden. Instead of seeing through the window, we saw into it as into a mirror, and there between the flower-laden tables and the lamps it was ourselves we saw moving vaguely. Like Father Hugh, we, too, were waiting for her to come in before we called an end to the day.

"Oh, this is ridiculous!" Father Hugh cried at last. "She'll have to listen to reason." And going back to the window he threw it open. "Vera!" he called. "Vera!"—sternly, so sternly that, more intimate than an endearment, his tone shocked us. "She didn't hear me," he said, turning back blinking at us in the lighted room.

"I'm going out to get her." And in a minute he was gone from the room. As he ran down the garden path, we stared at each other, astonished; his step, like his voice, was the step of a lover. "I'm coming, Vera!" he cried.

Although she was never stubborn except in things that mattered, Mother had not moved. In the whole-hearted way she did everything, she was bent down close to the ground. It wasn't the light only that was dimming; her eyesight also was failing, I thought, as instinctively I followed Father Hugh.

But halfway down the path I stopped. I had seen something he had not: Mother's hand that appeared to support itself in a forked branch of an old tree peony she had planted as a bride was not in fact gripping it but impaled upon it. And the hand that appeared to be grubbing in the clay in fact was sunk into the soft mould. "Mother!" I screamed, and I ran forward, but when I reached her I covered my face with my hands. "Oh Father Hugh!" I cried. "Is she dead?"

It was Bea who answered, hysterical. "She is! She is!" she cried, and she began to pound Father Hugh on the back with her fists, as if his pessimistic words had made this happen.

But Mother was not dead. And at first the doctor even offered hope of her pulling through. But from the moment Father Hugh lifted her up to carry her into the house we ourselves had no hope, seeing how effortlessly he, who was not strong, could carry her. When he put her down on her bed, her head hardly creased the pillow. Mother lived for four more hours.

Like the days of her life, those four hours that Mother lived were packed tight with concern and anxiety. Partly conscious, partly delirious, she seemed to think the counterpane was her desk, and she scrabbled her fingers upon it as if trying to sort out a muddle of bills and correspondence. No longer indifferent now, we listened, anguished, to the distracted cries that had for all our lifetime been so familiar to us. "Oh, where is it? Where is it? I had it a minute ago! Where on earth did I put it?"

"Vera, Vera, stop worrying," Father Hugh pleaded, but she waved him away and went on sifting through the sheets as if they were sheets of paper. "Oh, Vera!" he begged. "Listen to me. Do you not know—"

Bea pushed between them. "You're not to tell her!" she commanded. "Why frighten her?"

"But it ought not to frighten her," said Father Hugh. "This is what I was always afraid would happen—that she'd be frightened when it came to the end."

At that moment, as if to vindicate him, Mother's hands fell idle on the coverlet, palm upward and empty. And turning her head she stared at each of us in turn, beseechingly. "I cannot face it," she whispered. "I can't! I can't! I can't!"

"Oh, my God!" Bea said, and she started to cry.

"Vera. For God's sake listen to me," Father Hugh cried, and pressing his face to hers, as close as a kiss, he kept whispering to her, trying to cast into the dark tunnel before her the light of his own faith.

But it seemed to us that Mother must already be looking into God's exigent eyes. "I can't!" she cried. "I can't !"

Then her mind came back from the stark world of the spirit to the world where her body was still detained, but even that world was now a whirling kaleidoscope of things which only she could see. Suddenly her eyes focussed, and, catching at Father Hugh, she pulled herself up a little and pointed to something we could not see. "What will be done with them?" Her voice was anxious. "They ought to be put in water anyway," she said, and, leaning over the edge of the bed, she pointed to the floor. "Don't step on that one!" she said sharply. Then, more sharply still, she addressed us all. "Have them sent to the public ward," she said peremptorily. "Don't let that nun take them; she'll only put them on the altar. And God doesn't want them! He made them for *us*—not for Himself!"

It was the familiar rhetoric that all her life had characterised her utterances. For a moment we were mystified. Then Bea gasped. "The daffodils!" she cried. "The day Father died!" And over her face came the light that had so often blazed over Mother's. Leaning across the bed, she pushed Father Hugh aside. And, putting out her hands, she held Mother's face between her palms as tenderly as if it were the face of a child. "It's all right, Mother. You don't *have* to face it! It's over!" Then she who had so fiercely forbade Father Hugh to do so blurted out the truth. "You've finished with this world, Mother," she said, and, confident that her tidings were joyous, her voice was strong.

Mother made the last effort of her life and grasped at Bea's meaning. She let out a sigh, and, closing her eyes, she sank back, and this time her head sank so deep into the pillow that it would have been dented had it been a pillow of stone.

TILLIE OLSEN
(1913–   )

Readers and critics discovered Olsen in 1961, when the title story of the collection *Tell Me A Riddle* won the O. Henry Award as the best American story of the year. "When she wrote 'Tell Me A Riddle,'" said John Leonard, "Tillie Olsen, like William Blake, covered paper with words for the angels to read." Olsen's fiction, which has been translated into thirteen languages, is internationally renowned for the voice she has created for the world's voiceless. Human beings hobbled by the poverty she knew growing up as the child of Russian Jewish immigrants in Nebraska have been the focus of her life's work. A labor activist in Nebraska, Kansas City, and then in San Francisco, where she raised her four children (with Jack Olsen), she went to jail twice for public resistance of economic and political injustice. The founding godmother of the literary awakening of the 1960s women's movement, Olsen has influenced publishing programs and university English departments. She taught the first women in literature class at Stanford. In 1981, May 18 was proclaimed Tillie Olsen Day in San Francisco.

I Stand Here Ironing

I stand here ironing, and what you asked me moves tormented back and forth with the iron.

"I wish you would manage the time to come in and talk with me about your daughter. I'm sure you can help me understand her. She's a youngster who needs help and whom I'm deeply interested in helping."

"Who needs help." . . . Even if I came, what good would it do? You think because I am her mother I have a key, or that in some way you could use me as a key? She has lived for nineteen years. There is all that life that has happened outside of me, beyond me.

And when is there time to remember, to sift, to weigh, to estimate, to total? I will start and there will be an interruption and I will have to gather it all together again. Or I will become engulfed with all I did or did not do, with what should have been and what cannot be helped.

She was a beautiful baby. The first and only one of our five that was beautiful at birth. You do not guess how new and uneasy her tenancy in her now-loveliness. You did not know her all those years she was thought homely, or see her poring over her baby pictures, making me tell her over and over how beautiful she had been—and would be, I would tell her—and was now, to the seeing eye. But the seeing eyes were few or non-existent. Including mine.

I nursed her. They feel that's important nowadays. I nursed all the children, but with her, with all the fierce rigidity of first motherhood, I did like the books then said. Though her cries battered me to trembling and my breasts ached with swollenness, I waited till the clock decreed.

Why do I put that first? I do not even know if it matters, or if it explains anything.

She was a beautiful baby. She blew shining bubbles of sound. She loved motion, loved light, loved color and music and textures. She would lie on the floor in her blue overalls patting the surface so hard in ecstasy her hands and feet would blur. She was a miracle to me, but when she was eight months old I had to leave her daytimes with the woman downstairs to whom she was no miracle at all, for I worked or looked for work and for Emily's father, who "could no longer endure" (he wrote in his good-bye note) "sharing want with us."

I was nineteen. It was the pre-relief, pre-WPA world of the depression. I would start running as soon as I got off the streetcar, running up the stairs, the place smelling sour, and awake or asleep to startle awake, when she saw me she would break into clogged weeping that could not be comforted, a weeping I can hear yet.

After a while I found a job hashing at night so I could be with her days, and it was better. But it came to where I had to bring her to his family and leave her.

It took a long time to raise the money for her fare back. Then she got chicken pox and I had to wait longer. When she finally came, I hardly knew her, walking quick and nervous like her father, looking like her father, thin, and dressed in a shoddy red that yellowed her skin and glared at the pockmarks. All the baby loveliness gone.

She was two. Old enough for nursery school they said, and I did not know then what I know now—the fatigue of the long day, and the lacerations of group life in the kinds of nurseries that are only parking places for children.

Except that it would have made no difference if I had known. It was the only place there was. It was the only way we could be together, the only way I could hold a job.

And even without knowing, I knew. I knew the teacher that was evil because all these years it has curdled into my memory, the little boy hunched in the corner, her rasp, "why aren't you outside, because Alvin hits you? that's no reason, go out, scaredy." I knew Emily hated it even if she did not clutch and implore "don't go Mommy" like the other children, mornings.

She always had a reason why we should stay home. Momma, you look sick, Momma. I feel sick. Momma, the teachers aren't there today, they're sick.

Momma, we can't go, there was a fire there last night. Momma, it's a holiday today, no school, they told me.

But never a direct protest, never rebellion. I think of our others in their three-,
four-year-oldness—the explosions, the tempers, the denunciations, the demands—
and I feel suddenly ill. I put the iron down. What in me demanded that goodness in
her? And what was the cost, the cost to her of such goodness?

The old man living in the back once said in his gentle way: "You should smile
at Emily more when you look at her." What *was* in my face when I looked at her?
I loved her. There were all the acts of love.

It was only with the others I remembered what he said, and it was the face of
joy, and not of care or tightness or worry I turned to them—too late for Emily.
She does not smile easily, let alone almost always as her brothers and sisters do.
Her face is closed and sombre, but when she wants, how fluid. You must have
seen it in her pantomimes, you spoke of her rare gift for comedy on the stage that
rouses a laughter out of the audience so dear they applaud and applaud and do
not want to let her go.

Where does it come from, that comedy? There was none of it in her when she
came back to me that second time, after I had had to send her away again. She had
a new daddy now to learn to love, and I think perhaps it was a better time.

Except when we left her alone nights, telling ourselves she was old enough.

"Can't you go some other time, Mommy, like tomorrow?" she would ask.
"Will it be just a little while you'll be gone? Do you promise?"

The time we came back, the front door open, the clock on the floor in the hall.
She rigid awake. "It wasn't just a little while. I didn't cry. Three times I called you,
just three times, and then I ran downstairs to open the door so you could come
faster. The clock talked loud. I threw it away, it scared me what it talked."

She said the clock talked loud again that night I went to the hospital to have Susan. She was delirious with the fever that comes before red measles, but she was
fully conscious all the week I was gone and the week after we were home when she
could not come near the new baby or me.

She did not get well. She stayed skeleton thin, not wanting to eat, and night after night she had nightmares. She would call for me, and I would rouse from exhaustion to sleepily call back: "You're all right, darling, go to sleep, it's just a
dream," and if she still called, in a sterner voice, "now go to sleep, Emily, there's
nothing to hurt you." Twice, only twice, when I had to get up for Susan anyhow,
I went in to sit with her.

Now when it is too late (as if she would let me hold and comfort her like I do
the others) I get up and go to her at once at her moan or restless stirring. "Are you
awake, Emily? Can I get you something?" And the answer is always the same:
"No, I'm all right, go back to sleep, Mother."

They persuaded me at the clinic to send her away to a convalescent home in the country where "she can have the kind of food and care you can't manage for her, and you'll be free to concentrate on the new baby." They still send children to that place. I see pictures on the society page of sleek young women planning affairs to raise money for it, or dancing at the affairs, or decorating Easter eggs or filling Christmas stockings for the children.

They never have a picture of the children so I do not know if the girls still wear those gigantic red bows and the ravaged looks on the every other Sunday when parents can come to visit "unless otherwise notified"—as we were notified the first six weeks.

Oh it is a handsome place, green lawns and tall trees and fluted flower beds. High up on the balconies of each cottage the children stand, the girls in their red bows and white dresses, the boys in white suits and giant red ties. The parents stand below shrieking up to be heard and the children shriek down to be heard, and between them the invisible wall "Not To Be Contaminated by Parental Germs or Physical Affection."

There was a tiny girl who always stood hand in hand with Emily. Her parents never came. One visit she was gone. "They moved her to Rose Cottage" Emily shouted in explanation. "They don't like you to love anybody here."

She wrote once a week, the labored writing of a seven-year-old. "I am fine. How is the baby. If I write my leter nicly I will have a star. Love." There never was a star. We wrote every other day, letters she could never hold or keep but only hear read—once. "We simply do not have room for children to keep any personal possessions," they patiently explained when we pieced one Sunday's shrieking together to plead how much it would mean to Emily, who loved so to keep things, to be allowed to keep her letters and cards.

Each visit she looked frailer. "She isn't eating," they told us.

(They had runny eggs for breakfast or mush with lumps, Emily said later, I'd hold it in my mouth and not swallow. Nothing ever tasted good, just when they had chicken.)

It took us eight months to get her released home, and only the fact that she gained back so little of her seven lost pounds convinced the social worker.

I used to try to hold and love her after she came back, but her body would stay stiff, and after a while she'd push away. She ate little. Food sickened her, and I think much of life too. Oh she had physical lightness and brightness, twinkling by on skates, bouncing like a ball up and down up and down over the jump rope, skimming over the hill; but these were momentary.

She fretted about her appearance, thin and dark and foreign-looking at a time when every little girl was supposed to look or thought she should look a chubby blonde replica of Shirley Temple. The doorbell sometimes rang for her, but no one seemed to come and play in the house or be a best friend. Maybe because we moved so much.

There was a boy she loved painfully through two school semesters. Months later she told me how she had taken pennies from my purse to buy him candy. "Licorice was his favorite and I brought him some every day, but he still liked Jennifer better'n me. Why, Mommy?" The kind of question for which there is no answer.

School was a worry to her. She was not glib or quick in a world where glibness and quickness were easily confused with ability to learn. To her overworked and exasperated teachers she was an overconscientious "slow learner" who kept trying to catch up and was absent entirely too often.

I let her be absent, though sometimes the illness was imaginary. How different from my now-strictness about attendance with the others. I wasn't working. We had a new baby, I was home anyhow. Sometimes, after Susan grew old enough, I would keep her home from school, too, to have them all together.

Mostly Emily had asthma, and her breathing, harsh and labored, would fill the house with a curiously tranquil sound. I would bring the two old dresser mirrors and her boxes of collections to her bed. She would select beads and single earrings, bottle tops and shells, dried flowers and pebbles, old postcards and scraps, all sorts of oddments; then she and Susan would play Kingdom, setting up landscapes and furniture, peopling them with action.

Those were the only times of peaceful companionship between her and Susan. I have edged away from it, that poisonous feeling between them, that terrible balancing of hurts and needs I had to do between the two, and did so badly, those earlier years.

Oh there are conflicts between the others too, each one human, needing, demanding, hurting, taking—but only between Emily and Susan, no, Emily toward Susan, that corroding resentment. It seems so obvious on the surface, yet it is not obvious. Susan, the second child, Susan, golden- and curly-haired and chubby, quick and articulate and assured, everything in appearance and manner Emily was not; Susan, not able to resist Emily's precious things, losing or sometimes clumsily breaking them; Susan telling jokes and riddles to company for applause while Emily sat silent (to say to me later: that was *my* riddle, Mother, I told it to Susan); Susan, who for all the five years' difference in age was just a year behind Emily in developing physically.

I am glad for that slow physical development that widened the difference between her and her contemporaries, though she suffered over it. She was too vulnerable for that terrible world of youthful competition, of preening and parading, of constant measuring of yourself against every other, of envy, "If I had that copper hair," "If I had that skin. . . . " She tormented herself enough about not looking like the others, there was enough of the unsureness, the having to be conscious of words before you speak, the constant caring—what are they thinking of me? without having it all magnified by the merciless physical drives.

Ronnie is calling. He is wet and I change him. It is rare there is such a cry now.

That time of motherhood is almost behind me when the ear is not one's own but must always be racked and listening for the child cry, the child call. We sit for a while and I hold him, looking out over the city spread in charcoal with its soft aisles of light. *"Shoogily,"* he breathes and curls closer. I carry him back to bed, asleep. *Shoogily.* A funny word, a family word, inherited from Emily, invented by her to say: *comfort.*

In this and other ways she leaves her seal, I say aloud. And startle at my saying it. What do I mean? What did I start to gather together, to try and make coherent? I was at the terrible, growing years. War years. I do not remember them well. I was working, there were four smaller ones now, there was not time for her. She had to help be a mother, and housekeeper, and shopper. She had to set her seal. Mornings of crisis and near hysteria trying to get lunches packed, hair combed, coats and shoes found, everyone to school or Child Care on time, the baby ready for transportation. And always the paper scribbled on by a smaller one, the book looked at by Susan then mislaid, the homework not done. Running out to that huge school where she was one, she was lost, she was a drop; suffering over the unpreparedness, stammering and unsure in her classes.

There was so little time left at night after the kids were bedded down. She would struggle over books, always eating (it was in those years she developed her enormous appetite that is legendary in our family) and I would be ironing, or preparing food for the next day, or writing V-mail to Bill, or tending the baby. Sometimes, to make me laugh, or out of her despair, she would imitate happenings or types at school.

I think I said once: "Why don't you do something like this in the school amateur show?" One morning she phoned me at work, hardly understandable through the weeping: "Mother, I did it. I won, I won; they gave me first prize; they clapped and clapped and wouldn't let me go."

Now suddenly she was Somebody, and as imprisoned in her difference as she had been in anonymity.

She began to be asked to perform at other high schools, even in colleges, then at city and statewide affairs. The first one we went to, I only recognized her that first moment when thin, shy, she almost drowned herself into the curtains. Then: Was this Emily? The control, the command, the convulsing and deadly clowning, the spell, then the roaring, stamping audience, unwilling to let this rare and precious laughter out of their lives.

Afterwards: You ought to do something about her with a gift like that—but without money or knowing how, what does one do? We have left it all to her, and the gift has as often eddied inside, clogged and clotted, as been used and growing.

She is coming. She runs up the stairs two at a time with her light graceful step, and I know she is happy tonight. Whatever it was that occasioned your call did not happen today.

"Aren't you ever going to finish the ironing, Mother? Whistler painted his mother in a rocker. I'd have to paint mine standing over an ironing board." This is one of her communicative nights and she tells me everything and nothing as she fixes herself a plate of food out of the icebox.

She is so lovely. Why did you want me to come in at all? Why were you concerned? She will find her way.

She starts up the stairs to bed. "Don't get me up with the rest in the morning." "But I thought you were having midterms." "Oh, those," she comes back in, kisses me, and says quite lightly, "in a couple of years when we'll all be atom-dead they won't matter a bit."

She has said it before. She *believes* it. But because I have been dredging the past, and all that compounds a human being is so heavy and meaningful in me, I cannot endure it tonight.

I will never total it all. I will never come in to say: She was a child seldom smiled at. Her father left me before she was a year old. I had to work her first six years when there was work, or I sent her home and to his relatives. There were years she had care she hated. She was dark and thin and foreign-looking in a world where the prestige went to blondeness and curly hair and dimples, she was slow where glibness was prized. She was a child of anxious, not proud, love. We were poor and could not afford for her the soil of easy growth. I was a young mother, I was a distracted mother. There were the other children pushing up, demanding. Her younger sister seemed all that she was not. There were years she did not want me to touch her. She kept too much in herself, her life was such she had to keep too much in herself. My wisdom came too late. She has much to her and probably little will come of it. She is a child of her age, of depression, of war, of fear.

Let her be. So all that is in her will not bloom—but in how many does it? There is still enough left to live by. Only help her to know— help make it so there is cause for her to know—that she is more than this dress on the ironing board, helpless before the iron.

MURIEL SPARK
(1918–   )

Born into an Italian-Jewish family in Edinburgh—the setting of her best-known novel, *The Prime of Miss Jean Brodie* (1961)—Muriel Spark lived for a number of years in Rhodesia (now Zimbabwe). A prolific novelist, she's lived most of her adult life in Rome. In the fifties, she wrote biographies of Mary Shelley and the Brontës; after editing the letters of John Henry Cardinal Newman, she converted to Catholicism. A powerful satirist, she called, in an address to the American Academy of Arts and Letters in 1970, for a literature of savage ridicule as "the only honorable weapon we have left."

The First Year of My Life

I was born on the first day of the second month of the last year of the First World War, a Friday. Testimony abounds that during the first year of my life I never smiled. I was known as the baby whom nothing and no one could make smile. Everyone who knew me then has told me so. They tried very hard, singing and bouncing me up and down, jumping around, pulling faces. Many times I was told this later by my family and their friends; but, anyway, I knew it at the time.

You will shortly be hearing of that new school of psychology, or maybe you have heard of it already, which, after long and far-adventuring research and experiment, has established that all of the young of the human species are born omniscient. Babies, in their waking hours, know everything that is going on everywhere in the world; they can tune in to any conversation they choose, switch on to any scene. We have all experienced this power. It is only after the first year that it was brainwashed out of us; for it is demanded of us by our immediate environment that we grow to be of use to it in a practical way. Gradually, our know-all brain-cells are blacked out, although traces remain in some individuals in the form of E.S.P., and in the adults of some primitive tribes.

It is not a new theory. Poets and philosophers, as usual, have been there first. But scientific proof is now ready and to hand. Perhaps the final touches are being put to the new manifesto in some cell at Harvard University. Any day now it will be given to the world, and the world will be convinced.

Let me therefore get my word in first, because I feel pretty sure, now, about the authenticity of my remembrance of things past. My autobiography, as I very well perceive at the time, started in the very worst year that the world had ever seen so far. Apart from being born bedridden and toothless, unable to raise my-

147

self on the pillow or utter anything but farmyard squawks or police-siren wails, my bladder and my bowels totally out of control, I was further depressed by the curious behavior of the two-legged mammals around me. There were those black-dressed people, females of the species to which I appeared to belong, saying they had lost their sons. I slept a great deal. Let them go and find their sons. It was like the special pin for my nappies which my mother or some other hoverer dedicated to my care was always losing. These careless women in black lost their husbands and their brothers. Then they came to visit my mother and clucked and crowed over my cradle. I was not amused.

"Babies never really smile till they're three months old," said my mother. "They're not *supposed* to smile till they're three months old."

My brother, aged six, marched up and down with a toy rifle over his shoulder.

> The grand old Duke of York
> He had ten thousand men;
> He marched them up to the top of the hill
> And he marched them down again.
>
> And when they were up, they were up.
> And when they were down, they were down.
> And when they were neither down nor up
> They were neither up nor down.

"Just listen to him!"
"Look at him with his rifle!"
I was about ten days old when Russia stopped fighting. I tuned in to the Czar, a prisoner, with the rest of his family, since evidently the country had put him off his throne and there had been a revolution not long before I was born. Everyone was talking about it. I tuned in to the Czar. "Nothing would ever induce me to sign the treaty of Brest-Litovsk," he said to his wife. Anyway, nobody had asked him to.

At this point I was sleeping twenty hours a day to get my strength up. And from what I discerned in the other four hours of the day I knew I was going to need it. The Western Front on my frequency was sheer blood, mud, dismembered bodies, blistering crashes, hectic flashes of light in the night skies, explosions, total terror. Since it was plain I had been born into a bad moment in the history of the world, the future bothered me, unable as I was to raise my head from the pillow and as yet only twenty inches long. "I truly wish I were a fox or a bird," D. H. Lawrence was writing to somebody. Dreary old creeping Jesus. I fell asleep.

Red sheets of flame shot across the sky. It was 21 March, the fiftieth day of my life, and the German Spring Offensive had started before my morning feed. Infinite slaughter. I scowled at the scene, and made an effort to kick out. But the attempt was feeble. Furious, and impatient for some strength, I wailed for my feed. After which I stopped wailing but continued to scowl.

> The grand old Duke of York
> He had ten thousand men. . . .

They rocked the cradle. I never heard a sillier song. Over in Berlin and Vienna the people were starving, freezing, striking, rioting and yelling in the streets. In London everyone was bustling to work and muttering that it was time the whole damn business was over.

The big people around me bared their teeth; that meant a smile, it meant they were pleased or amused. They spoke of ration cards for meat and sugar and butter.

"Where will it all end?"

I went to sleep. I woke and tuned in to Bernard Shaw who was telling someone to shut up. I switched over to Joseph Conrad who, strangely enough, was saying precisely the same thing. I still didn't think it worth a smile, although it was expected of me any day now. I got on to Turkey. Women draped in black huddled and chattered in their harems; yak-yak-yak. This was boring, so I came back to home base.

In and out came and went the women in British black. My mother's brother, dressed in his uniform, came coughing. He had been poison-gassed in the trenches. *"Tout le monde à la bataille!"* declaimed Marshal Foch the old swine. He was now Commander-in-Chief of the Allied Forces. My uncle coughed from deep within his lungs, never to recover but destined to return to the Front. His brass buttons gleamed in the firelight. I weighed twelve pounds by now; I stretched and kicked for exercise, seeing that I had a lifetime before me, coping with this crowd. I took six feeds a day and kept most of them down by the time the *Vindictive* was sunk in Ostend harbour, on which day I kicked with special vigour in my bath.

In France the conscripted soldiers leapfrogged over the dead on the advance and littered the fields with limbs and hands, or drowned in the mud. The strongest men on all fronts were dead before I was born. Now the sentries used bodies for barricades and the fighting men were unhealthy from the start. I checked my toes and my fingers, knowing I was going to need them. *The Playboy of the Western World* was playing at the Court Theatre in London, but occasionally I beamed over to the House of Commons which made me drop off gently to sleep. Generally, I preferred the Western Front where one got the true state of affairs. It was essential to know the worst, blood and explosions and all, for one had to be prepared, as the boy scouts said. Virginia Woolf yawned and reached for her diary. Really, I preferred the Western Front.

In the fifth month of my life I could raise my head from my pillow and hold it up. I could grasp the objects that were held out to me. Some of these things rattled and squawked. I gnawed on them to get my teeth started. "She hasn't smiled yet?" said the dreary old aunties. My mother, on the defensive, said I was probably one of those late smilers. On my wavelength Pablo Picasso was getting married and early in that month of July the Silver Wedding of King George V and Queen Mary was celebrated in joyous pomp at St Paul's Cathedral. They drove through the streets of London with their children. Twenty-five years of domestic happiness. A lot of fuss and ceremonial handing over of swords went on at the Guildhall where the King and Queen received a cheque for £53,000 to dispose of for charity as they thought fit. *Tout le monde à la bataille!* Income tax in England had reached six shillings in the pound. Everyone was talking about the Silver Wedding; yak-yak-yak, and ten days later the Czar and his family, now in Siberia, were invited to descend to a little room in the basement. Crack, crack, went the guns; screams and blood all over the place, and that was the end of the Romanoffs. I flexed my muscles. "A fine healthy baby," said the doctor; which gave me much satisfaction.

Tout le monde à la bataille! That included my gassed uncle. My health had improved to the point where I was able to crawl in my playpen. Bertrand Russell was still cheerily in prison for writing something seditious about pacifism. Tuning in as usual to the Front Lines it looked as if the Germans were winning all the battles yet losing the war. And so it was. The upper-income people were upset about the income tax at six shillings to the pound. But all women over thirty got the vote. "It seems a long time to wait," said one of my drab old aunts, aged twenty-two. The speeches in the House of Commons always sent me to sleep which was why I missed, at the actual time, a certain oration by Mr. Asquith following the armistice on 11 November. Mr. Asquith was a greatly esteemed former prime minister later to be an Earl, and had been ousted by Mr. Lloyd George. I clearly heard Asquith, in private, refer to Lloyd George as "that damned Welsh goat."

The armistice was signed and I was awake for that. I pulled myself on to my feet with the aid of the bars of my cot. My teeth were coming through very nicely in my opinion, and well worth all the trouble I was put to in bringing them forth. I weighed twenty pounds. On all the world's fighting fronts the men killed in action or dead of wounds numbered 8,538,315 and the warriors wounded and maimed were 21,219,452. With these figures in my mind I sat up in my high chair and banged my spoon on the table. One of my mother's black-draped friends recited:

> I have a rendezvous with Death
> At some disputed barricade,
> When spring comes back with rustling shade
> And apple blossoms fill the air—
> I have a rendezvous with Death.

Most of the poets, they said, had been killed. The poetry made them dab their eyes with clean white handkerchiefs.

Next February on my first birthday, there was a birthday-cake with one candle. Lots of children and their elders. The war had been over two months and twenty-one days. "Why doesn't she smile?" My brother was to blow out the candle. The elders were talking about the war and the political situation. Lloyd George and Asquith, Asquith and Lloyd George. I remembered recently having switched on to Mr. Asquith at a private party where he had been drinking a lot. He was playing cards and when he came to cut the cards he tried to cut a large box of matches by mistake. On another occasion I had seen him putting his arm around a lady's shoulder in a Daimler motor car, and generally behaving towards her in a very friendly fashion. Strangely enough she said, "If you don't stop this nonsense immediately I'll order the chauffeur to stop and I'll get out." Mr. Asquith replied, "And pray, what reason will you give?" Well anyway it was my feeding time.

The guests arrived for my birthday. It was so sad, said one of the black widows, so sad about Wilfred Owen who was killed so late in the war, and she quoted from a poem of his:

> What passing-bells for these who die as cattle?
> Only the monstrous anger of the guns.

The children were squealing and toddling around. One was sick and another wet the floor and stood with his legs apart gaping at the puddle. All was mopped up. I banged my spoon on the table of my high chair.

> But I've a rendezvous with Death
> At midnight in some flaming town;
> When spring trips north again this year,
> And I to my pledged word am true,
> I shall not fail that rendezvous.

More parents and children arrived. One stout man who was warming his behind at the fire, said, "I always think those words of Asquith's after the armistice were so apt. . . . "

They brought the cake close to my high chair for me to see, with the candle shining and flickering above the pink icing. "A pity she never smiles."

"She'll smile in time," my mother said, obviously upset.

"What Asquith told the House of Commons just after the war," said that stout gentleman with his backside to the fire, "—so apt, what Asquith said. He said that the war has cleansed and purged the world, by God! I recall his actual words: 'All things have become new. In this great cleansing and purging it has been the privilege of our country to play her part. . . .'"

That did it. I broke into a decided smile and everyone noticed it, convinced that it was provoked by the fact that my brother had blown out the candle on the cake. "She smiled!" my mother exclaimed. And everyone was clucking away about how I was smiling. For good measure I crowed like a demented raven. "My baby's smiling," said my mother.

"It was the candle on her cake," they said.

The cake be damned. Since that time I have grown to smile quite naturally, like any other healthy and house-trained person, but when I really mean a smile, deeply felt from the core, then to all intents and purposes it comes in response to the words uttered in the House of Commons after the First World War by the distinguished, the immaculately dressed and the late Mr. Asquith.

GRACE PALEY
(1922–　)

Raised in the Bronx by Russian Jewish socialist immigrants, Paley, a lifelong activist on behalf of peace and justice, has lived true to her roots. Her belief that politics, morality, and religion cannot be separated calls to mind the Hebrew Bible's prophets as well as the savage indignation of Jonathan Swift; this moral vision lights up her short stories (*The Little Disturbances of Man* [1959], *Enormous Changes at the Last Minute* [1974], *Later the Same Day* [1985]) and her nonfiction (*Just As I Thought* [1998], from which "Traveling" is taken). "All over the world," writes Vivian Gornick, "in languages you never heard of, she is read as a master storyteller in the great tradition: people love life more because of her writing."

Samuel

Some boys are very tough. They're afraid of nothing. They are the ones who climb a wall and take a bow at the top. Not only are they brave on the roof, but they make a lot of noise in the darkest part of the cellar where even the super hates to go. They also jiggle and hop on the platform between the locked doors of the subway cars.

Four boys are jiggling on the swaying platform. Their names are Alfred, Calvin, Samuel, and Tom. The men and the women in the cars on either side watch them. They don't like them to jiggle or jump but don't want to interfere. Of course some of the men in the cars were once brave boys like these. One of them had ridden the tail of a speeding truck from New York to Rockaway Beach without getting off, without his sore fingers losing hold. Nothing happened to him then or later. He had made a compact with other boys who preferred to watch: Starting at Eighth Avenue and Fifteenth Street, he would get to some specified place, maybe Twenty-third and the river, by hopping the tops of the moving trucks. This was hard to do when one truck turned a corner in the wrong direction and the nearest truck was a couple of feet too high. He made three or four starts before succeeding. He had gotten this idea from a film at school called *The Romance of Logging*. He had finished high school, married a good friend, was in a responsible job and going to night school.

These two men and others looked at the four boys jumping and jiggling on the platform and thought, It must be fun to ride that way, especially now the weather is nice and we're out of the tunnel and way high over the Bronx. Then they thought, These kids do seem to be acting sort of stupid. They *are* little. Then they thought of some of the brave things they had done when they were boys and jiggling didn't seem so risky.

The ladies in the car became very angry when they looked at the four boys. Most of them brought their brows together and hoped the boys could see their extreme disapproval. One of the ladies wanted to get up and say, Be careful you dumb kids, get off that platform or I'll call a cop. But three of the boys were Negroes and the fourth was something else she couldn't tell for sure. She was afraid they'd be fresh and laugh at her and embarrass her. She wasn't afraid they'd hit her, but she was afraid of embarrassment. Another lady thought, Their mothers never know where they are. It wasn't true in this particular case. Their mothers all knew that they had gone to see the missile exhibit on Fourteenth Street.

Out on the platform, whenever the train accelerated, the boys would raise their hands and point them up to the sky to act like rockets going off, then they rat-tat-tatted the shatterproof glass pane like machine guns, although no machine guns had been exhibited.

For some reason known only to the motorman, the train began a sudden slow-down. The lady who was afraid of embarrassment saw the boys jerk forward and backward and grab the swinging guard chains. She had her own boy at home. She stood up with determination and went to the door. She slid it open and said, "You boys will be hurt. You'll be killed. I'm going to call the conductor if you don't just go into the next car and sit down and be quiet."

Two of the boys said, "Yes'm," and acted as though they were about to go. Two of them blinked their eyes a couple of times and pressed their lips together. The train resumed its speed. The door slid shut, parting the lady and the boys. She leaned against the side door because she had to get off at the next stop.

The boys opened their eyes wide at each other and laughed. The lady blushed. The boys looked at her and laughed harder. They began to pound each other's back. Samuel laughed the hardest and pounded Alfred's back until Alfred coughed and the tears came. Alfred held tight to the chain hook. Samuel pounded him even harder when he saw the tears. He said, "Why you bawling? You a baby, huh?" and laughed. One of the men whose boyhood had been more watchful than brave became angry. He stood up straight and looked at the boys for a couple of seconds. Then he walked in a citizenly way to the end of the car, where he pulled the emergency cord. Almost at once, with a terrible hiss, the pressure of air abandoned the brakes and the wheels were caught and held.

People standing in the most secure places fell forward, then backward. Samuel had let go of his hold on the chain so he could pound Tom as well as Alfred. All the passengers in the cars whipped back and forth, but he pitched only forward and fell head first to be crushed and killed between the cars.

The train had stopped hard, halfway into the station, and the conductor called at once for the trainmen who knew about this kind of death and how to take the body from the wheels and brakes. There was silence except for passengers from other cars who asked, What happened! What happened! The ladies waited around wondering if he might be an only child. The men recalled other afternoons with very bad endings. The little boys stayed close to each other, leaning and touching shoulders and arms and legs.

When the policeman knocked at the door and told her about it, Samuel's mother began to scream. She screamed all day and moaned all night, though the doctors tried to quiet her with pills.

Oh, oh, she hopelessly cried. She did not know how she could ever find another boy like that one. However, she was a young woman and she became pregnant. Then for a few months she was hopeful. The child born to her was a boy. They brought him to be seen and nursed. She smiled. But immediately she saw that this baby wasn't Samuel. She and her husband together have had other children, but never again will a boy exactly like Samuel be known.

Traveling

My mother and sister were traveling south. The year was 1927. They had begun their journey in New York. They were going to visit my brother, who was studying in the South Medical College of Virginia. Their bus was an express and had stopped only in Philadelphia, Wilmington, and now Washington. Here, the darker people who had gotten on in Philadelphia or New York rose from their seats, put their bags and boxes together, and moved to the back of the bus. People who boarded in Washington knew where to seat themselves. My mother had heard that something like this would happen. My sister had heard of it, too. They had not lived in it. This reorganization of passengers by color happened in silence. My mother and sister remained in their seats, which were about three-quarters of the way back.

When everyone was settled, the bus driver began to collect tickets. My sister saw him coming. She pinched my mother: Ma! Look! Of course, my mother saw him, too. What frightened my sister was the quietness. The white people in front, the black people in back—silent.

The driver sighed, said, You can't sit here, ma'am. It's for them, waving over his shoulder at the Negroes, among whom they were now sitting. Move, please.

My mother said, No.

He said, You don't understand, ma'am. It's against the law. You have to move to the front.

My mother said, No.

When I first tried to write this scene, I imagined my mother saying, That's all right, mister, we're comfortable. I can't change my seat every minute. I read this invention to my sister. She said it was nothing like that. My mother did not try to be friendly or pretend innocence. While my sister trembled in the silence, my mother said, for the third time, quietly, No.

Somehow finally, they were in Richmond. There was my brother in school among so many American boys. After hugs and my mother's anxious looks at her young son, my sister said, Vic, you know what Mama did?

My brother remembers thinking, What? Oh! She wouldn't move? He had a classmate, a Jewish boy like himself, but from Virginia, who had had a public confrontation with a Negro man. He had punched that man hard, knocked him down. My brother couldn't believe it. He was stunned. He couldn't imagine a Jewish boy wanting to knock anyone down. He had never wanted to. But he thought, looking back, that he had been set down to work and study in a nearly foreign place and had to get used to it. Then he told me about the Second World War, when the disgrace of black soldiers being forced to sit behind white German POWs shook him. Shamed him.

About fifteen years later, in 1943, in early summer, I rode the bus for about three days from New York to Miami Beach, where my husband in sweaty fatigues, along with hundreds of other boys, was trudging up and down the streets and beaches to prepare themselves for war.

By late afternoon of the second long day, we were well into the South, beyond Richmond, maybe South Carolina or Georgia. My excitement about travel in the wide world was damaged a little by a sudden fear that I might not recognize Jess or he, me. We hadn't seen each other for two months. I took a photograph out of my pocket; yes, I would know him.

I had been sleeping waking reading writing dozing waking. So many hours, the movement of the passengers was something like a tide that sometimes ebbed and now seemed to be noisily rising. I opened my eyes to the sound of new people brushing past my aisle seat. And looked up to see a colored woman holding a large sleeping baby, who, with the heaviness of sleep, his arms so tight around her neck, seemed to be pulling her head down. I looked around and noticed that I was in the last white row. The press of travelers had made it impossible for her to move farther back. She seemed so tired and I had been sitting and sitting for a day and a half at least. Not thinking, or maybe refusing to think, I offered her my seat.

She looked to the right and left as well as she could. Softly she said, Oh no. I became fully awake. A white man was standing right beside her, but on the other side of the invisible absolute racial border. Of course, she couldn't accept my seat. Her sleeping child hung mercilessly from her neck. She shifted a little to balance the burden. She whispered to herself, Oh, I just don't know. So I said, Well, at least give me the baby. First, she turned, barely looking at the man beside her. He made no move. So, to my surprise, but obviously out of sheer exhaustion, she disengaged the child from her body and placed him on my lap. He was deep in child-sleep. He stirred, but not enough to bother himself or me. I liked holding him, aligning him along my twenty-year-old young woman's shape. I thought ahead to that holding, that breathing together that would happen in my life if this war would ever end.

I was so comfortable under his nice weight. I closed my eyes for a couple of minutes, but suddenly opened them to look up into the face of a white man talking. In a loud voice he addressed me: Lady, I wouldn't of touched that thing with a meat hook.

I thought, Oh, this world will end in ice. I could do nothing but look straight into his eyes. I did not look away from him. Then I held that boy a little tighter, kissed his curly head, pressed him even closer so that he began to squirm. So sleepy, he reshaped himself inside my arms. His mother tried to narrow herself away from that dangerous border, too frightened at first to move at all. After a couple of minutes, she leaned forward a little, placed her hand on the baby's head, and held it there until the next stop. I couldn't look up into her mother face.

I write this remembrance more than fifty years later. I look back at that mother and child. How young she is. Her hand on his head is quite small, though she tries by spreading her fingers wide to hide him from the white man. But the child I'm holding, his little face as he turns toward me, is the brown face of my own grandson, my daughter's boy, the open mouth of the sleeper, the full lips, the thick little body of a child who runs wildly from one end of the yard to the other, leaps from dangerous heights with certain experienced caution, muscling his body, his mind, for coming realities.

Of course, when my mother and sister returned from Richmond, the family at home wanted to know: How was Vic doing in school among all those gentiles? Was the long bus ride hard, was the anti-Semitism really bad or just normal? What happened on the bus? I was probably present at that supper, the attentive listener and total forgetter of information that immediately started to form me.

Then last year, my sister, casting the net of old age (through which recent experience easily slips), brought up that old story. First I was angry. How come you never told me about your bus ride with Mama? I mean, really, so many years ago.

I don't know, she said, anyway you were only about four years old, and besides, maybe I did.

I asked my brother why we'd never talked about that day. He said he thought now that it had had a great effect on him; he had tried unraveling its meaning for years—then life family work happened. So I imagined him, a youngster really, a kid from the Bronx in Virginia in 1927; why, he was a stranger there himself.

In the next couple of weeks, we continued to talk about our mother, the way she was principled, adamant, and at the same time so shy. What else could we re-member . . . Well, I said, I have a story about those buses, too. Then I told it to them: How it happened on just such a journey, when I was still quite young, that I first knew my grandson, first held him close, but could protect him for only about twenty minutes fifty years ago.

MARIE PONSOT
(1922–   )

orn and raised in Queens in New York City, Marie Ponsot, at the age of
seventy-seven, won the National Book Critics Circle Award in Poetry for her
latest collection, *The Bird Catcher*. Questions were raised about why recognition
had taken so long to come her way. *True Minds*, the first of her four volumes of
poetry, had been published by City Lights Books in San Francisco in 1957, by her
friend Lawrence Ferlinghetti. What transpired between this debut and her next
book (*Admit Impediment*, 1981) were the births of her seven children, whom she
supported (she was divorced in 1970) as a teacher, a translator, and a writer of radio and television scripts (though she didn't have a TV). The central preoccupation of *The Bird Catcher*, from which the following poem is taken, is, in the
words of Irish poet Eavan Boland, "the life of feeling."

One Is One

Heart, you bully, you punk, I'm wrecked, I'm shocked
stiff. You? you still try to rule the world—though
I've got you: identified, starving, locked
in a cage you will not leave alive, no
matter how you hate it, pound its walls,
& thrill its corridors with messages.

Brute. Spy. I trusted you. Now you reel & brawl
in your cell but I'm deaf to your rages,
your greed to go solo, your eloquent
threats of worse things you (knowing me) could do.
You scare me, bragging you're a double agent

since jailers are prisoners' prisoners too.
Think! Reform! Make us one. Join the rest of us,
and joy may come, and make its test of us.

NADINE GORDIMER

(1923–   )

South African writer Nadine Gordimer is considered "certainly one of the half dozen best story writers in English today," according to *The Observer*. Set mostly in South Africa, her fiction represents an unsentimental dissection of the devastation caused by apartheid, the system that denied native Africans their civil and human rights. For their indictment of the moral failure inherent in this system, many of her books were banned in her native country. Respected there for the professional help she has given to black writers, Gordimer is a founding member of the Congress of South African Writers as well as a member of the African National Congress. She was awarded the Nobel Prize for Literature in 1991.

Something for the Time Being

He thought of it as discussing things with her, but the truth was that she did not help him out at all. She said nothing, while she ran her hand up the ridge of bone behind the rim of her child-sized yellow-brown ear, and raked her fingers tenderly into her hairline along the back of her neck as if feeling out some symptom in herself. Yet her listening was very demanding; when he stopped at the end of a supposition or a suggestion, her silence made the stop inconclusive. He had to take up again what he had said, carry it—where?

"Ve vant to give you a tsance, but you von't let us," he mimicked; and made a loud glottal click, half-angry, resentfully amused. He knew it wasn't because the Kalzin Brothers were Jews that he had lost his job at last, but just because he had lost it, Mr Solly's accent suddenly presented to him the irresistibly vulnerable. He had come out of prison nine days before, after spending three months as an awaiting-trial prisoner in a political case that had just been quashed—he was one of those who would not accept bail. He had been in prison three or four times since 1952; his wife Ella and the Kalzin Brothers were used to it. Until now, his employers had always given him his job back when he came out. They were importers of china and glass and he was head packer in a team of black men who ran the dispatch department. "Well, what the hell, I'll get something else," he said. "Hey?"

She stopped the self-absorbed examination of the surface of her skin for a slow moment and shrugged, looking at him.

He smiled.

Her gaze loosened hold like hands falling away from grasp. The ends of her nails pressed at small imperfections in the skin of her neck. He drank his tea and tore off pieces of bread to dip in it; then he noticed the tin of sardines she had opened and sopped up the pale matrix of oil in which ragged flecks of silver were suspended. She offered him more tea, without speaking.

They lived in one room of a decent, three-roomed house belonging to someone else; it was better for her that way, since he was often likely to have to be away for long stretches. She worked in a factory that made knitted socks; there was no one at home to look after their one child, a girl, and the child lived with a grandmother in a dusty, peaceful village a day's train-journey from the city.

He said, dismissing it as of no importance, "I wonder what chance they meant? You can imagine. I don't suppose they were going to give me an office with my name on it." He spoke as if she would appreciate the joke. She had known when she married him that he was a political man; she had been proud of him because he didn't merely want something for himself, like the other young men she knew, but everything, and for *the people*. It had excited her, under his influence, to change her awareness of herself as a young black girl to awareness of herself as belonging to the people. She knew that everything wasn't like something—a hand-out, a wangled privilege, a trinket you could hold. She would never get something from him.

Her hand went on searching over her skin as if it must come soon, come anxiously, to the flaw, the sickness, the evidence of what was wrong with her; for on this Saturday afternoon all these things that she knew had deserted her. She had lost her wits. All that she could understand was the one room, the child growing up far away in the mud house, and the fact that you couldn't keep a job if you kept being away from work for weeks at a time.

"I think I'd better look up Flora Donaldson," he said. Flora Donaldson was a white woman who had set up an office to help political prisoners. "Sooner the better. Perhaps she'll dig up something for me by Monday. It's the beginning of the month."

He got on all right with those people. Ella had met Flora Donaldson once; she was a pretty white woman who looked just like any white woman who would automatically send a black face round to the back door, but she didn't seem to know that she was white and you were black.

He pulled the curtain that hung across one corner of the room and took out his suit. It was a thin suit, of the kind associated with holidaymakers in American clothing advertisements, and when he was dressed in it, with a sharp-brimmed grey hat tilted slightly back on his small head, he looked a wiry, boyish figure, rather like one of those boy-men who sing and shake before a microphone, and whose clothes admirers try to touch as a talisman.

He kissed her good-bye, obliging her to put down, the lowering of a defence, the piece of sewing she held. She had cleared away the dishes from the table and set up the sewing-machine, and he saw that the shapes of cut material that lay on the table were the parts of a small girl's dress.

She spoke suddenly. "And when the next lot gets tired of you?"

"When that lot gets tired of me, I'll get another job again, that's all."

She nodded, very slowly, and her hand crept back to her neck.

"Who was that?" Madge Chadders asked.

Her husband had been out into the hall to answer the telephone.

"Flora Donaldson. I wish you'd explain to these people exactly what sort of factory I've got. It's so embarrassing. She's trying to find a job for some chap, he's a skilled packer. There's no skilled packing done in my workshop, no skilled jobs at all done by black men. What on earth can I offer the fellow? She says he's desperate and anything will do."

Madge had the broken pieces of a bowl on a newspaper spread on the Persian carpet. "Mind the glue, darling! There, just next to your foot. Well, anything is better than nothing. I suppose it's someone who was in the Soganiland sedition case. Three months awaiting trial taken out of their lives, and now they're chucked back to fend for themselves."

William Chadders had not had any black friends or mixed with coloured people on any but master-servant terms until he married Madge, but his views on the immorality and absurdity of the colour bar were sound; sounder, she often felt, than her own, for they were backed by the impersonal authority of a familiarity with the views of great thinkers, saints and philosophers, with history, political economy, sociology and anthropology. She knew only what she felt. And she always did something, at once, to express what she felt. She never measured the smallness of her personal protest against the establishment she opposed; she marched with Flora and eight hundred black women in a demonstration against African women being forced to carry passes; outside the university where she had once been a student, she stood between sandwich-boards bearing messages of mourning because a Bill had been passed closing the university, for the future, to all but white students; she had living in the house for three months a young African who wanted to write and hadn't the peace or space to get on with it in a location. She did not stop to consider the varying degree of usefulness of the things she did, and if others pointed this out to her and suggested that she might make up her mind to throw her weight on the side either of politics or philanthropy, she was not resentful but answered candidly that there was so little it was possible to do that she simply took any and every chance to get off her chest her disgust at the colour bar. When she had married William Chadders, her friends had thought that her protestant activities would stop; they underestimated not only Madge, but also William, who, although he was a wealthy businessman, subscribed to the view of absolute personal freedom as strictly as any bohemian. Besides he was not fool enough to want to change in any way the person who had enchanted him just as she was.

She reacted upon him, rather than he upon her; she, of course, would not hesitate to go ahead and change anybody. (But why not? she would have said, astonished. If it's to the good?) The attitude she sought to change would occur to her as something of independent existence, she would not see it as a cell in the organism of personality, whose whole structure would have to regroup itself round the change. She had the boldness of being unaware of these consequences.

William did not carry a banner in the streets, of course; he worked up there, among his first principles and historical precedents and economic necessities, but now they were translated from theory to practice of an anonymous, large-scale and behind-the-scenes sort—he was the brains and part of the money in a scheme to get Africans some economic power besides consumer power, through the setting up of an all-African trust company and investment corporation. A number of Madge's political friends, both white and black (like her activities, her friends were mixed, some political, some do-gooders), thought this was putting the middle-class cart before the proletarian horse, but most of the African leaders welcomed the attempt as an essential backing to popular movements on other levels—something to count on outside the unpredictability of mobs. Sometimes it amused Madge to think that William, making a point at a meeting in a boardroom, fifteen floors above life in the streets, might achieve in five minutes something of more value than she did in all her days of turning her hand to anything—from sorting old clothes to roneo-ing a manifesto or driving people during a bus boycott. Yet this did not knock the meaning out of her own life, for her; she knew that she had to see, touch and talk to people in order to care about them, that's all there was to it.

Before she and her husband dressed to go out that evening she finished sticking together the broken Chinese bowl and showed it to him with satisfaction. To her, it was whole again. But it was one of a set, that had belonged together, and whose unity had illustrated certain philosophical concepts. William had bought them long ago, in London; for him, the whole set was damaged for ever.

He said nothing to her, but he was thinking of the bowls when she said to him as they drove off, "Will you see that chap, on Monday, yourself?"

He changed gear deliberately, attempting to follow her out of his preoccupation. But she said, "The man Flora's sending. What was his name?"

He opened his hand on the steering wheel, indicating that the name escaped him.

"See him yourself?"

"I'll have to leave it to the works manager to find something for him to do," he said.

"Yes, I know. But see him yourself, too?"

Her anxious voice made him feel very fond of her. He turned and smiled at her suspiciously. "Why?"

She was embarrassed at his indulgent manner. She said, frank and wheedling, "Just to show him. You know. That you know about him and it's not much of a job."

"All right," he said. "I'll see him myself."

He met her in town straight from the office on Monday and they went to the opening of an exhibition of paintings and on to dinner and to see a play, with friends. He had not been home at all, until they returned after midnight. It was a summer night and they sat for a few minutes on their terrace, where it was still mild with the warmth of the day's sun coming from the walls in the darkness, and drank lime juice and water to quench the thirst that wine and the stuffy theatre had given them. Madge made gasps and groans of pleasure at the release from the pressures of company and noise. Then she lay quiet for a while, her voice lifting now and then in fragments of unrelated comment on the evening—the occasional chirp of a bird that has already put its head under its wing for the night.

By the time they went in, they were free of the evening. Her black dress, her earrings and her bracelets felt like fancy-dress; she shed the character and sat on the bedroom carpet, and, passing her, he said, "Oh—that chap of Flora's came today, but I don't think he'll last. I explained to him that I didn't have the sort of job he was looking for."

"Well, that's all right, then," she said enquiringly. "What more could you do?"

"Yes," he said, deprecating. "But I could see he didn't like the idea much. It's a cleaner's job; nothing for him. He's an intelligent chap. I didn't like having to offer it to him."

She was moving about her dressing-table, piling out upon it the contents of her handbag. "Then I'm sure he'll understand. It'll give him something for the time being, anyway, darling. You can't help it if you don't need the sort of work he does."

"Huh, he won't last. I could see that. He accepted it, but only with his head. He'll get fed up. Probably won't turn up tomorrow. I had to speak to him about his Congress button, too. The works manager came to me."

"What about his Congress button?" she said.

He was unbuttoning his shirt and his eyes were on the unread evening paper that lay folded on the bed. "He was wearing one," he said inattentively.

"I know, but what did you have to speak to him about it for?"

"He was wearing it in the workshop all day."

"Well, what about it?" She was sitting at her dressing-table, legs spread, as if she had sat heavily and suddenly. She was not looking at him, but at her own face.

He gave the paper a push and drew his pyjamas from under the pillow.

Vulnerable and naked, he said authoritatively, "You can't wear a button like that among the men in the workshop."

"Good heavens," she said, almost in relief, laughing, backing away from the edge of tension, chivvying him out of a piece of stuffiness. "And why can't you?"

"You can't have someone clearly representing a political organization like Congress."

"But he's not there *representing* anything, he's there as a workman?" Her mouth was still twitching with something between amusement and nerves.

"Exactly."

"Then why can't he wear a button that signifies his allegiance to an organization in his private life outside the workshop? There's no rule about not wearing tie-pins or club buttons or anything, in the workshop, is there?"

"No, there isn't, but that's not quite the same thing."

"My dear William," she said, "it is exactly the same. It's nothing to do with the works manager whether the man wears a Rotary button, or an Elvis Presley button, or an African National Congress button. It's damn all his business."

"No, Madge, I'm sorry," William said, patient, "but it's not the same. I can give the man a job because I feel sympathetic towards the struggle he's in, but I can't put him in the workshop as a Congress man. I mean that wouldn't be fair to Fowler. That I can't do to Fowler." He was smiling as he went towards the bathroom, but his profile, as he turned into the doorway, was incisive.

She sat on at her dressing-table, pulling a comb through her hair, dragging it down through knots. Then she rested her face on her palms, caught sight of herself and became aware, against her fingers, of the curving shelf of bone, like the lip of a strong shell, under each eye. Everyone has his own intimations of mortality. For her, the feel of the bone beneath the face, in any living creature, brought her the message of the skull. Once hollowed out of this, outside the world, too. For what it's worth. It's worth a lot, the world, she affirmed, as she always did, life rising at once in her as a fish opens its jaws to a fly. It's worth a lot; and she sighed and got up with the sigh.

She went into the bathroom and sat down on the edge of the bath. He was lying there in the water, his chin relaxed on his chest, and he smiled at her. She said, "You mean you don't want Fowler to know."

"Oh," he said, seeing where they were again. "What is it I don't want Fowler to know?"

"You don't want your partner to know that you slip black men with political ideas into your workshop. Cheeky kaffir agitators. Specially a man who's been in jail for getting people to defy the government! — What was his name; you never said?"

"Daniel something. I don't know. Mongoma or Ngoma. Something like that."

A line like a cut appeared between her eyebrows. "Why can't you remember his name?" Then she went on at once, "You don't want Fowler to know what you think, do you? That's it? You want to pretend you're like him, you don't mind the native in his place. You want to pretend that to please Fowler. You don't want Fowler to think you're cracked or Communist or whatever it is that good-natured, kind, jolly rich people like old Fowler think about people like us."

"I couldn't have less interest in what Fowler thinks outside our boardroom. And inside it, he never thinks about anything but how to sell more earth-moving gear."

"I don't mind the native in his place. You want him to think you go along with all that." She spoke aloud, but she seemed to be telling herself rather than him.

"Fowler and I run a factory. Our only common interest is the efficient running of that factory. Our *only* one. The factory depends on a stable, satisfied black labour-force, and that we've got. Right, you and I know that the whole black wage standard is too low, right, we know that they haven't a legal union to speak for them, right, we know that the conditions they live under make it impossible for them really to be stable. All that. But the fact is, so far as accepted standards go in this crazy country, they're a stable, satisfied labour-force with better working conditions than most. So long as I'm a partner in a business that lives by them, I can't officially admit an element that represents dissatisfaction with their lot."

"A green badge with a map of Africa on it," she said.

"If you make up your mind not to understand, you don't, and there it is," he said indulgently.

"You give him a job but you make him hide his Congress button."

He began to soap himself. She wanted everything to stop while she inquired into things, she could not go on while a remark was unexplained or a problem un-settled, but he represented a principle she subscribed to but found so hard to fol-low, that life must go on, trivially, commonplace, the trailing hem of the only power worth clinging to. She smoothed the film of her nightgown over the shape of her knees, over and over, and presently she said, in exactly the flat tone of state-ment that she had used before, the flat tone that was the height of belligerence in her, "He can say and do what he likes, he can call for strikes and boycotts and any-thing he likes, outside the factory, but he mustn't wear his Congress button at work."

He was standing up, washing his body that was full of scars; she knew them all, from the place on his left breast where a piece of shrapnel had gone in, all the way back to the place under his arm where he had torn himself on barbed wire as a child. "Yes, of course, anything he likes."

"Anything except his self-respect," she grumbled to herself. "Pretend, pretend. Pretend he doesn't belong to a political organization. Pretend he doesn't want to be a man. Pretend he hasn't been to prison for what he believes." Suddenly she spoke to her husband: "You'll let him have anything except the one thing worth giving."

They stood in uncomfortable proximity to each other, in the smallness of the bathroom. They were at once aware of each other as people who live in intimacy are only when hostility returns each to the confines of himself. He felt himself naked before her, where he had stepped out onto the towelling mat, and he took a towel and slowly covered himself, pushing the free end in round his waist. She felt herself an intrusion and, in silence, went out.

Her hands were tingling as if she were coming round from a faint. She walked up and down the bedroom floor like someone waiting to be summoned, called to account. I'll forget about it, she kept thinking, very fast, I'll forget about it again. Take a sip of water. Read another chapter. Don't call a halt. Let things flow, cover up, go on.

But when he came into the room with his wet hair combed and his stranger's face, and he said, "You're angry," it came from her lips, a black bird in the room, before she could understand what she had released—"I'm not angry. I'm beginning to get to know you."

Ella Mngoma knew he was going to a meeting that evening and didn't expect him home early. She put the paraffin lamp on the table so that she could see to finish the child's dress. It was done, buttons and all, by the time he came in at half past ten.

"Well, now we'll see what happens. I've got them to accept, *in principle*, that in future we won't take bail. You should have seen Ben Tsolo's face when I said that we lent the government our money interest-free when we paid bail. That really hit him. That was language he understood." He laughed, and did not seem to want to sit down, the heat of the meeting still upon him. "*In principle*. Yes, it's easy to accept in principle. We'll see."

She pumped the primus and set a pot of stew to warm up for him, "Ah, that's nice." He saw the dress. "Finished already?" And she nodded vociferously in pleasure; but at once she noticed his forefinger run lightly along the braid round the neck, and the traces of failure that were always at the bottom of her cup tasted on her tongue again. Probably he was not even aware of it, or perhaps his instinct for what was true—the plumb line, the coin with the right ring—led him absently to it, but the fact was that she had botched the neck.

She had an almost Oriental delicacy about not badgering him and she waited until he had washed and sat down to eat before she asked, "How did the job go?"

"Oh that," he said. "It went." He was eating quickly, moving his tongue strongly round his mouth to marshal the bits of meat that escaped his teeth. She was sitting with him, feeling, in spite of herself, the rest of satisfaction in her evening's work. "Didn't you get it?"

"It got *me*. But I got loose again, all right."

She watched his face to see what he meant. "They don't want you to come back tomorrow?"

He shook his head, no, no, no, to stem the irritation of her suppositions. He finished his mouthful and said, "Everything very nice. Boss takes me into his office, apologizes for the pay, he knows it's not the sort of job I should have and so forth. So I go off and clean up in the assembly shop. Then at lunchtime he calls me into the office again: they don't want me to wear my A.N.C. badge at work. Flora Donaldson's sympathetic white man, who's going to do me the great favour of paying me three pounds a week." He laughed. "Well, there you are."

She kept on looking at him. Her eyes widened and her mouth tightened; she was trying to prime herself to speak, or was trying not to cry. The idea of tears exasperated him and he held her with a firm, almost belligerently inquiring gaze. Her hand went up round the back of her neck under her collar, anxiously exploratory. "Don't do that!" he said. "You're like a monkey catching lice."

She took her hand down swiftly and broke into trembling, like a sweat. She began to breathe hysterically. "You couldn't put it in your pocket, for the day," she said wildly, grimacing at the bitterness of malice towards him.

He jumped up from the table. "Christ! I knew you'd say it! I've been waiting for you to say it. You've been wanting to say it for five years. Well, now it's out. Out with it. Spit it out!" She began to scream softly as if he were hitting her. The impulse to cruelty left him and he sat down before his dirty plate, where the battered spoon lay among bits of gristle and potato-eyes. Presently he spoke. "You come out and you think there's everybody waiting for you. The truth is, there isn't anybody. You think straight in prison because you've got nothing to lose. Nobody thinks straight, outside. They don't want to hear you. What are you all going to do with me, Ella? Send me back to prison as quickly as possible? Perhaps I'll get a banishment order next time. That'd do. That's what you've got for me. I must keep myself busy with that kind of thing."

He went over to her and said, in a kindly voice, kneading her shoulder with spread fingers, "Don't cry. Don't cry. You're just like any other woman."

DENISE LEVERTOV
(1923–97)

Born in England, the daughter of a Welsh mother and a Russian Jewish father who became an Anglican priest, Levertov was already a published poet (*The Double Image* [1946]) when she moved to the United States after World War II. There is a recurring evocation of a mystical presence in the world running through her many volumes of poetry—*With Eyes At the Back of Our Heads* (1960), *The Sorrow Dance* (1967), *The Freeing of the Dust* (1975), *Breathing the Water* (1987), and *The Door in the Hive* (1989). This spirit that enlivens and joins together all the forms of creation imposes, in her words, "the obligation of social conscience." In her own life she performed acts of resistance to war, nuclear arms, and injustice in Latin America. "The tragic and fearful character of our times is not something from which we can detach ourselves; we are in it, as fish are in the sea."

What Were They Like?

1) Did the people of Viet Nam
   use lanterns of stone?
2) Did they hold ceremonies
   to reverence the opening of buds?
3) Were they inclined to quiet laughter?
4) Did they use bone and ivory,
   jade and silver, for ornament?
5) Had they an epic poem?
6) Did they distinguish between speech and singing?

1) Sir, their light hearts turned to stone.
   It is not remembered whether in gardens
   stone lanterns illumined pleasant ways.
2) Perhaps they gathered once to delight in blossom,
   but after the children were killed
   there were no more buds.
3) Sir, laughter is bitter to the burned mouth.
4) A dream ago, perhaps. Ornament is for joy.
   All the bones were charred.

5) It is not remembered. Remember,
   most were peasants; their life
   was in rice and bamboo.
   When peaceful clouds were reflected in the paddies
   and the water buffalo stepped surely along terraces,
   maybe fathers told their sons old tales.
   When bombs smashed those mirrors
   there was time only to scream.
6) There is an echo yet of
   their speech which was like a song.
   It was reported their singing resembled
   the flight of moths in moonlight.
   Who can say? It is silent now.

Contraband

The tree of knowledge was the tree of reason.
That's why the taste of it
drove us from Eden. That fruit
was meant to be dried and milled to a fine powder
for use a pinch at a time, a condiment.
God had probably planned to tell us later
about this new pleasure.
                    We stuffed our mouths full of it,
gorged on *but* and *if* and *how* and again
but, knowing no better.
It's toxic in large quantities; fumes
swirled in our heads and around us
to form a dense cloud that hardened to steel,
a wall between us and God, Who was Paradise.
Not that God is unreasonable—but reason
in such excess was tyranny
and locked us into its own limits, a polished cell
reflecting our own faces. God lives
on the other side of that mirror,
but through the slit where the barrier doesn't
quite touch ground, manages still
to squeeze in—as filtered light,
splinters of fire, a strain of music heard
then lost, then heard again.

FLANNERY O'CONNOR
(1925–64)

A native Georgian whose paternal ancestors came from Tipperary in Ireland (and, like her father, a victim of a fatal lupus), Flannery O'Connor named her influences as "being a Catholic, and a Southerner, and a writer." The author of two novels (*Wise Blood* [1952] and *The Violent Bear It Away* [1960]) and three collections of short stories (*A Good Man Is Hard to Find* [1955], *Everything That Rises Must Converge* [1965], and the posthumously published *Collected Stories*, which won the National Book Award for fiction in 1971), she said she wrote "because I'm good at it." Her fiction casts a cold, comic, and original eye on the grotesque and eccentric characters who were her friends and neighbors in the Protestant Bible Belt.

A Late Encounter with the Enemy

General Sash was a hundred and four years old. He lived with his granddaughter, Sally Poker Sash, who was sixty-two years old and who prayed every night on her knees that he would live until her graduation from college. The General didn't give two slaps for her graduation but he never doubted he would live for it. Living had got to be such a habit with him that he couldn't conceive of any other condition. A graduation exercise was not exactly his idea of a good time, even if, as she said, he would be expected to sit on the stage in his uniform. She said there would be a long procession of teachers and students in their robes but that there wouldn't be anything to equal *him* in his uniform. He knew this well enough without her telling him, and as for the damn procession, it could march to hell and back and not cause him a quiver. He liked parades with floats full of Miss Americas and Miss Daytona Beaches and Miss Queen Cotton Products. He didn't have any use for processions and a procession full of schoolteachers was about as deadly as the River Styx to his way of thinking. However, he was willing to sit on the stage in his uniform so that they could see him.

Sally Poker was not as sure as he was that he would live until her graduation. There had not been any perceptible change in him for the last five years, but she had the sense that she might be cheated out of her triumph because she so often was. She had been going to summer school every year for the past twenty because when she started teaching, there were no such things as degrees. In those times, she said, everything was normal but nothing had been normal since she was sixteen, and for the past twenty summers, when she should have been resting, she

171

had had to take a trunk in the burning heat to the state teacher's college; and though when she returned in the fall, she always taught in the exact way she had been taught not to teach, this was a mild revenge that didn't satisfy her sense of justice. She wanted the General at her graduation because she wanted to show what she stood for, or, as she said, "what all was behind her," and was not behind them. This *them* was not anybody in particular. It was just all the upstarts who had turned the world on its head and unsettled the ways of decent living.

She meant to stand on that platform in August with the General sitting in his wheel chair on the stage behind her and she meant to hold her head very high as if she were saying, "See him! See him! My kin, all you upstarts! Glorious upright old man standing for the old traditions! Dignity! Honor! Courage! See him!" One night in her sleep she screamed, "See him! See him!" and turned her head and found him sitting in his wheel chair behind her with a terrible expression on his face and with all his clothes off except the general's hat and she had waked up and had not dared to go back to sleep again that night.

For his part, the General would not have consented even to attend her graduation if she had not promised to see to it that he sit on the stage. He liked to sit on any stage. He considered that he was still a very handsome man. When he had been able to stand up, he had measured five feet four inches of pure game cock. He had white hair that reached to his shoulders behind and he would not wear teeth because he thought his profile was more striking without them. When he put on his full-dress general's uniform, he knew well enough that there was nothing to match him anywhere.

This was not the same uniform he had worn in the War between the States. He had not actually been a general in that war. He had probably been a foot soldier; he didn't remember what he had been; in fact, he didn't remember that war at all. It was like his feet, which hung down now shriveled at the very end of him, without feeling, covered with a blue-gray afghan that Sally Poker had crocheted when she was a little girl. He didn't remember the Spanish-American War in which he had lost a son; he didn't even remember the son. He didn't have any use for history because he never expected to meet it again. To his mind, history was connected with processions and life with parades and he liked parades. People were always asking him if he remembered this or that—a dreary black procession of questions about the past. There was only one event in the past that had any significance for him and that he cared to talk about; that was twelve years ago when he had received the general's uniform and had been in the premiere.

"I was in that preemy they had in Atlanta," he would tell visitors sitting on his front porch. "Surrounded by beautiful guls. It wasn't a thing local about it. It was nothing local about it. Listen here. It was a nashnul event and they had me in it— up onto the stage. There was no bob-tails at it. Every person at it had paid ten dollars to get in and had to wear his tuxseeder. I was in this uniform. A beautiful gul presented me with it that afternoon in a hotel room."

"It was in a suite in the hotel and I was in it too, Papa," Sally Poker would say, winking at the visitors. "You weren't alone with any young lady in a hotel room."

"Was, I'd a known what to do," the old General would say with a sharp look and the visitors would scream with laughter. "This was a Hollywood, California, gul," he'd continue. "She was from Hollywood, California, and didn't have any part in the pitcher. Out there they have so many beautiful guls that they don't need that they call them a extra and they don't use them for nothing but presenting people with things and having their pitchers taken. They took my pitcher with her. No, it was two of them. One on either side and me in the middle with my arms around each of them's waist and their waist ain't any bigger than a half a dollar."

Sally Poker would interrupt again. "It was Mr. Govisky that gave you the uniform, Papa, and he gave me the most exquisite corsage. Really, I wish you could have seen it. It was made with gladiola petals taken off and painted gold and put back together to look like a rose. It was exquisite. I wish you could have seen it, it was . . ."

"It was as big as her head," the General would snarl. "I was tellin it. They gimme this soward and they say, 'Now General, we don't want you to start a war on us. All we want you to do is march right up on that stage when you're innerduced tonight and answer a few questions. Think you can do that?' 'Think I can do it!' I say. 'Listen here. I was doing things before you were born,' and they hollered."

"He was the hit of the show," Sally Poker would say, but she didn't much like to remember the premiere on account of what had happened to her feet at it. She had bought a new dress for the occasion—a long black crepe dinner dress with a rhinestone buckle and a bolero—and a pair of silver slippers to wear with it, because she was supposed to go up on the stage with him to keep him from falling. Everything was arranged for them. A real limousine came at ten minutes to eight and took them to the theater. It drew up under the marquee at exactly the right time, after the big stars and the director and the author and the governor and the mayor and some less important stars. The police kept traffic from jamming and there were ropes to keep the people off who wouldn't go. All the people who couldn't go watched them step out of the limousine into the lights. Then they walked down the red and gold foyer and an usherette in a Confederate cap and little short skirt conducted them to their special seats. The audience was already there and a group of UDC members began to clap when they saw the General in his uniform and that started everybody to clap. A few more celebrities came after them and then the doors closed and the lights went down.

A young man with blond wavy hair who said he represented the motion-picture industry came out and began to introduce everybody and each one who was introduced walked up on the stage and said how really happy he was to be here for this great event. The General and his granddaughter were introduced sixteenth on the program. He was introduced as General Tennessee Flintrock Sash of the Confederacy, though Sally Poker had told Mr. Govisky that his name was George Poker Sash and that he had only been a major. She helped him up from his seat but her heart was beating so fast she didn't know whether she'd make it herself.

The old man walked up the aisle slowly with his fierce white head high and his hat held over his heart. The orchestra began to play the Confederate Battle Hymn very softly and the UDC members rose as a group and did not sit down again until the General was on the stage. When he reached the center of the stage with Sally Poker just behind him guiding his elbow, the orchestra burst out in a loud rendition of the Battle Hymn and the old man, with real stage presence, gave a vigorous trembling salute and stood at attention until the last blast had died away. Two of the usherettes in Confederate caps and short skirts held a Confederate and a Union flag crossed behind them.

The General stood in the exact center of the spotlight and it caught a weird moon-shaped slice of Sally Poker—the corsage, the rhinestone buckle and one hand clenched around a white glove and handkerchief. The young man with the blond wavy hair inserted himself into the circle of light and said he was *really* happy to have here tonight for this great event, one, he said, who had fought and bled in the battles they would soon see daringly reenacted on the screen, and "Tell me, General," he asked, "how old are you?"

"Niiiiiinnttty-two!" the General screamed.

The young man looked as if this were just about the most impressive thing that had been said all evening. "Ladies and gentlemen," he said, "let's give the General the biggest hand we've got!" and there was applause immediately and the young man indicated to Sally Poker with a motion of his thumb that she could take the old man back to his seat now so that the next person could be introduced; but the General had not finished. He stood immovable in the exact center of the spotlight, his neck thrust forward, his mouth slightly open, and his voracious gray eyes drinking in the glare and the applause. He elbowed his granddaughter roughly away. "How I keep so young," he screeched, "I kiss all the pretty guls!"

This was met with a great din of spontaneous applause and it was at just that instant that Sally Poker looked down at her feet and discovered that in the excitement of getting ready she had forgotten to change her shoes: two brown Girl Scout oxfords protruded from the bottom of her dress. She gave the General a yank and almost ran with him off the stage. He was very angry that he had not got to say how glad he was to be here for this event and on the way back to his seat, he kept saying as loud as he could, "I'm glad to be here at this preemy with all these beautiful guls!" but there was another celebrity going up the other aisle and nobody paid any attention to him. He slept through the picture, muttering fiercely every now and then in his sleep.

Since then, his life had not been very interesting. His feet were completely dead now, his knees worked like old hinges, his kidneys functioned when they would, but his heart persisted doggedly to beat. The past and the future were the same thing to him, one forgotten and the other not remembered; he had no more notion of dying than a cat. Every year on Confederate Memorial Day, he was bundled up and lent to the Capital City Museum where he was displayed from one to four in a musty room full of old photographs, old uniforms, old artillery, and historic documents. All these were carefully preserved in glass cases so that children would not put their hands on them. He wore his general's uniform from the premiere and sat, with a fixed scowl, inside a small roped area. There was nothing about him to indicate that he was alive except an occasional movement in his milky gray eyes, but once when a bold child touched his sword, his arm shot forward and slapped the hand off in an instant. In the spring when the old homes were opened for pilgrimages, he was invited to wear his uniform and sit in some conspicuous spot and lend atmosphere to the scene. Some of these times he only snarled at the visitors but sometimes he told about the premiere and the beautiful girls.

If he had died before Sally Poker's graduation, she thought she would have died herself. At the beginning of the summer term, even before she knew if she would pass, she told the Dean that her grandfather, General Tennessee Flintrock Sash of the Confederacy, would attend her graduation and that he was a hundred and four years old and that his mind was still clear as a bell. Distinguished visitors were always welcome and could sit on the stage and be introduced. She made arrangements with her nephew, John Wesley Poker Sash, a Boy Scout, to come wheel the General's chair. She thought how sweet it would be to see the old man in his courageous gray and the young boy in his clean khaki—the old and the new, she thought appropriately—they would be behind her on the stage when she received her degree.

Everything went almost exactly as she had planned. In the summer while she was away at school, the General stayed with other relatives and they brought him and John Wesley, the Boy Scout, down to the graduation. A reporter came to the hotel where they stayed and took the General's picture with Sally Poker on one side of him and John Wesley on the other. The General, who had had his picture taken with beautiful girls, didn't think much of this. He had forgotten precisely what kind of event this was he was going to attend but he remembered that he was to wear his uniform and carry the sword.

On the morning of the graduation, Sally Poker had to line up in the academic procession with the B.S.'s in Elementary Education and she couldn't see to getting him on the stage herself—but John Wesley, a fat blond boy of ten with an executive expression, guaranteed to take care of everything. She came in her academic gown to the hotel and dressed the old man in his uniform. He was as frail as a dried spider. "Aren't you just thrilled, Papa?" she asked. "I'm just thrilled to death!"

"Put the sword across my lap, damm you," the old man said, "where it'll shine."

She put it there and then stood back looking at him. "You look just grand," she said.

"God damm it," the old man said in a slow monotonous certain tone as if he were saying it to the beating of his heart. "God damm every goddam thing to hell."

"Now, now," she said and left happily to join the procession.

The graduates were lined up behind the Science building and she found her place just as the line started to move. She had not slept much the night before and when she had, she had dreamed of the exercises, murmuring, "See him, see him?" in her sleep but waking up every time just before she turned her head to look at him behind her. The graduates had to walk three blocks in the hot sun in their black wool robes and as she plodded stolidly along she thought that if anyone considered this academic procession something impressive to behold, they need only wait until they saw that old General in his courageous gray and that clean young Boy Scout stoutly wheeling his chair across the stage with the sunlight catching the sword. She imagined that John Wesley had the old man ready now behind the stage.

The black procession wound its way up the two blocks and started on the main walk leading to the auditorium. The visitors stood on the grass, picking out their graduates. Men were pushing back their hats and wiping their foreheads and women were lifting their dresses slightly from the shoulders to keep them from sticking to their backs. The graduates in their heavy robes looked as if the last beads of ignorance were being sweated out of them. The sun blazed off the fenders of automobiles and beat from the columns of the buildings and pulled the eye from one spot of glare to another. It pulled Sally Poker's toward the big red Coca-Cola machine that had been set up by the side of the auditorium. Here she saw the General parked, scowling and hatless in his chair in the blazing sun while John Wesley, his blouse loose behind, his hip and cheek pressed to the red machine, was drinking a Coca-Cola. She broke from the line and galloped to them and snatched the bottle away. She shook the boy and thrust in his blouse and put the hat on the old man's head. "Now get him in there!" she said, pointing one rigid finger to the side door of the building.

For his part the General felt as if there were a little hole beginning to widen in the top of his head. The boy wheeled him rapidly down a walk and up a ramp and into a building and bumped him over the stage entrance and into position where he had been told and the General glared in front of him at heads that all seemed to flow together and eyes that moved from one face to another. Several figures in black robes came and picked up his hand and shook it. A black procession was flowing up each aisle and forming to stately music in a pool in front of him. The music seemed to be entering his head through the little hole and he thought for a second that the procession would try to enter it too.

He didn't know what procession this was but there was something familiar about it. It must be familiar to him since it had come to meet him, but he didn't like a black procession. Any procession that came to meet him, he thought irritably, ought to have floats with beautiful guls on them like the floats before the preemy. It must be something connected with history like they were always having. He had no use for any of it. What happened then wasn't anything to a man living now and he was living now.

When all the procession had flowed into the black pool, a black figure began orating in front of it. The figure was telling something about history and the General made up his mind he wouldn't listen, but the words kept seeping in through the little hole in his head. He heard his own name mentioned and his chair was shuttled forward roughly and the Boy Scout took a big bow. They called his name and the fat brat bowed. Goddam you, the old man tried to say, get out of my way, I can stand up!—but he was jerked back again before he could get up and take the bow. He supposed the noise they made was for him. If he was over, he didn't intend to listen to any more of it. If it hadn't been for the little hole in the top of his head, none of the words would have got to him. He thought of putting his finger up there into the hole to block them but the hole was a little wider than his finger and it felt as if it were getting deeper.

Another black robe had taken the place of the first one and was talking now and he heard his name mentioned again but they were not talking about him, they were still talking about history. "If we forget our past," the speaker was saying, "we won't remember our future and it will be as well for we won't have one." The General heard some of these words gradually. He had forgotten history and he didn't intend to remember it again. He had forgotten the name and face of his wife and the names and faces of his children or even if he had a wife and children, and he had forgotten the names of places and the places themselves and what had happened at them.

He was considerably irked by the hole in his head. He had not expected to have a hole in his head at this event. It was the slow black music that had put it there and though most of the music had stopped outside, there was still a little of it in the hole, going deeper and moving around in his thoughts, letting the words he heard into the dark places of his brain. He heard the words, Chickamauga, Shiloh, Johnston, Lee, and he knew he was inspiring all these words that meant nothing to him. He wondered if he had been a general at Chickamauga or at Lee. Then he tried to see himself and the horse mounted in the middle of a float full of beautiful girls, being driven slowly through downtown Atlanta. Instead, the old words began to stir in his head as if they were trying to wrench themselves out of place and come to life.

The speaker was through with that war and had gone on to the next one and now he was approaching another and all his words, like the black procession, were vaguely familiar and irritating. There was a long finger of music in the General's head, probing various spots that were words, letting in a little light on the words and helping them to live. The words began to come toward him and he said, Dammit! I ain't going to have it! and he started edging backwards to get out of the way. Then he saw the figure in the black robe sit down and there was a noise and the black pool in front of him began to rumble and to flow toward him from either side to the black slow music, and he said, Stop dammit! I can't do but one thing at a time! He couldn't protect himself from the words and attend to the procession too and the words were coming at him fast. He felt that he was running backwards and the words were coming at him like musket fire, just escaping him but getting nearer and nearer. He turned around and began to run as fast as he could but he found himself running toward the words. He was running into a regular volley of them and meeting them with quick curses. As the music swelled toward him, the entire past opened up on him out of nowhere and he felt his body riddled in a hundred places with sharp stabs of pain and he fell down, returning a curse for every hit. He saw his wife's narrow face looking at him critically through her round gold-rimmed glasses; he saw one of his squinting bald-headed sons; and his mother ran toward him with an anxious look; then a succession of places—Chickamauga, Shiloh, Marthasville—rushed at him as if the past were the only future now and he had to endure it. Then suddenly he saw that the black procession was almost on him. He recognized it, for it had been dogging all his days. He made such a desperate effort to see over it and find out what comes after the past that his hand clenched the sword until the blade touched the bone.

The graduates were crossing the stage in a long file to receive their scrolls and shake the president's hand. As Sally Poker, who was near the end, crossed, she glanced at the General and saw him sitting fixed and fierce, his eyes wide open, and she turned her head forward again and held it a perceptible degree higher and received her scroll. Once it was all over and she was out of the auditorium in the sun again, she located her kin and they waited together on a bench in the shade for John Wesley to wheel the old man out. That crafty scout had bumped him out the back way and rolled him at high speed down a flagstone path and was waiting now, with the corpse, in the long line at the Coca-Cola machine.

ANNE SEXTON
(1928–74)

A survivor of several mental breakdowns and hospitalizations, New Englander Anne Sexton began writing poetry on the advice of her psychiatrist. She found her lifeline, if only temporarily, as a poet. She made friends with the poet Sylvia Plath (see pages 222–23), her fellow student in a class taught by Robert Lowell at Boston University. The teacher and his two most famous students are now recognized as three of the most powerful "confessional poets" of the post-war period. Each tells the secrets of their personal history, showing where their private hells reverberate as public nightmare. Because she ignored the tradition of silence about women's sexuality, Sexton's many volumes of poetry were controversial. As her critics poured scorn, her admirers provided large audiences for her readings and awarded her many literary prizes. Obsessed for many years with the desire for self-destruction, Sexton committed suicide in 1974.

Housewife

Some women marry houses.
It's another kind of skin; it has a heart,
a mouth, a liver and bowel movements.
The walls are permanent and pink.
See how she sits on her knees all day,
faithfully washing herself down.
Men enter by force, drawn back like Jonah
into their fleshy mothers.
A woman *is* her mother.
That's the main thing.

MAYA ANGELOU
(1928–)

Born Marguerite Annie Johnson in St. Louis, Maya Angelou was sent at the age of three with her older brother, Bailey, to live with their beloved grandmother, Ann Henderson, in Stamps, Arkansas. Her first volume of autobiography, *I Know Why the Caged Bird Sings* (1970), recounts the four years in Stamps and then the move back to her mother's house in St. Louis, where she was raped by her mother's boyfriend. For the next five years, Maya Angelou was mute. But she listened intently, ultimately finding deliverance in language. "For a long time I would think of myself, of my whole body, as an ear. . . . Language. I loved it. I never did find a voice I didn't find wonderful and beautiful. Because I really like the way we talk. I find it wonderful." A prolific and joyful poet (and the first since Robert Frost to be invited to read her work—"On the Pulse of Morning"—at a presidential inauguration), she is best known for her autobiographies, which include *Gather Together in My Name* (1974), *Singin' & Swingin' & Gettin' Merry Like Christmas* (1976), *The Heart of a Woman* (1981), and *All God's Children Need Traveling Shoes* (1986).

---

from
Shades and Slashes of Light

" . . . We are a tongued folk. A race of singers. Our lips shape words and rhythms which elevate our spirits and quicken our blood. . . . I have spent over fifty years listening to my people."

. . . I write for the Black voice and any ear which can hear it. As a composer writes for musical instruments and a choreographer creates for the body, I search for sound, tempos, and rhythms to ride through the vocal cord over the tongue, and out of the lips of Black people. I love the shades and slashes of light. Its rumblings and passages of magical lyricism. I accept the glory of stridencies and purrings, trumpetings and sombre sonorities.

Having said that, I must now talk about content. I have noted most carefully for the past twenty years our speech patterns, the ambiguities, contradictions, the moans and laughter, and am even more enchanted at this time than I was when I began eavesdropping.

After, and during pestilential assaults of frustration, hate, demeanings, and murders, our language continues to expand and mature. Our lives, made inadequate and estranged by the experience of malice, loathing, and hostility, are enriched by the words we use to, and with, each other. By our intonations, our modulations, our shouts and hollers.

I write because I am a Black woman, listening attentively to her talking people.

When I turn my conscious mind to writing (my unconscious or subconscious is always busy recording images, phrases, sound, colors, and scents) I follow a fairly rigid habit. I rise early, around 5:30 or 6 A.M., wash, pray, put on coffee, and arrange my mind in writing order. That is, I tell myself how lucky I am that this morning is new, a day never seen before, that ideas will come to me which I have never consciously known. I have coffee and allow the work of the day before to flood my mind. The characters and situations take over the chambers of my existence until they are all I see and hear. Then I go to my writing room, most times a little cubicle I have rented in a cheap but clean hotel; rarely but sometimes it is a room in my own home.

I keep in my writing room a Bible, a dictionary, Roget's Thesaurus, a bottle of sherry, cigarettes, an ashtray, and three or four decks of playing cards. During the five hours I spend there I use every object, but I play solitaire more than I actually write. It seems to me that when my hands and small mind (a Southern Black phrase) are engaged in placing the reds on the blacks and blacks on the reds, my working mind arranges and rearranges the characters and the plot. Finally when they are in a plausible order, I simply have to write down where they are and what they say.

Later, after I have returned home or if I have worked at home, when I have left my writing room, I bathe and change clothes. This seems to signal my total mind that it may now stop working for the writer and begin to think for the woman, the wife, the friend, and the cook.

I begin thinking about dinner midafternoon. I love to cook and find it both creative and relaxing. After I have planned dinner and possibly begun a dish which demands long stewing, I take the morning's work to my dining room table and polish it, straighten out the grammar, clear up the syntax, and try to eliminate repetitions and contradictions. By dinnertime, I am ready to join my family or friends (although truthfully, when I'm working on a book I am never totally away from it). I know that they are aware that they and their concerns are not of great importance to me during the creative period (as long as a year, sometimes less), but we all pretend. The discipline I use to be in company stands me in good stead on the following morning when I must go alone into my small writing room and face a host of new ideas and headstrong characters, yet keep myself open so that they can interact, grow, and become real.

I also wear a hat or a very tightly pulled head tie when I write. I suppose I hope by doing that I will keep my brains from seeping out of my scalp and running in great gray blobs down my neck, into my ears, and over my face.

CYNTHIA OZICK
(1928–   )

Born and bred in the Bronx, which she has resurrected to vivid life in her novels, short stories, and essays—the collection *Art & Ardor* (1983) is excerpted here—Cynthia Ozick was described by William Abrahams as "one of the three greatest living American writers of short fiction" when her story "Rosa" won first prize in the 1984 O. Henry Prize Story Awards. (She has won four first prizes in the O. Henry Prize Stories competition.) Her artistic strength, according to novelist Edmund White, "derives from her moral energy, for Miss Ozick is not an aesthete. Judaism has given to her what Catholicism gave to Flannery O'Connor—authority, penetration, and indignation."

A Drugstore in Winter

This is about reading; a drugstore in winter; the gold leaf on the dome of the Boston State House; also loss, panic, and dread.

First, the gold leaf. (This part is a little like a turn-of-the-century pulp tale, though only a little. The ending is a surprise, but there is no plot.) Thirty years ago I burrowed in the Boston Public Library one whole afternoon, to find out—not out of curiosity—how the State House got its gold roof. The answer, like the answer to most Bostonian questions, was Paul Revere. So I put Paul Revere's gold dome into an "article," and took it (though I was just as scared by recklessness then as I am now) to the *Boston Globe*, on Washington Street. The Features Editor had a bare severe head, a closed parenthesis mouth, and silver Dickensian spectacles. He made me wait, standing, at the side of his desk while he read; there was no bone in me that did not rattle. Then he opened a drawer and handed me fifteen dollars. Ah, joy of Homer, joy of Milton! Grub Street bliss!

The very next Sunday, Paul Revere's gold dome saw print. Appetite for more led me to a top-floor chamber in Filene's department store: Window Dressing. But no one was in the least bit dressed—it was a dumbstruck nudist colony up there, a mob of naked frozen enigmatic manikins, tall enameled skinny ladies with bald breasts and skulls, and legs and wrists and necks that horribly unscrewed. Paul Revere's dome paled beside this gold mine! A sight—mute numb Walpurgisnacht—easily worth another fifteen dollars. I had a Master's degree (thesis topic: "Parable in the Later Novels of Henry James") and a job as an advertising copywriter (9 A.M. to 6 P.M. six days a week, forty dollars per week; if you were male and had no degree at all, sixty dollars). Filene's Sale Days—Crib

Bolsters! Lulla-Buys! Jonnie-Mops! Maternity Skirts with Expanding Invisible Trick Waist! And a company show; gold watches to mark the retirement of elderly Irish salesladies; for me the chance to write song lyrics (to the tune of "On Top of Old Smoky") honoring our Store. But "Mute Numb Walpurgisnacht in Secret Downtown Chamber" never reached the *Globe*. Melancholy and meaning business, the Advertising Director forbade it. Grub Street was bad form, and I had to promise never again to sink to another article. Thus ended my life in journalism.

Next: reading, and certain drugstore winter dusks. These come together. It is an aeon before Filene's, years and years before the Later Novels of Henry James. I am scrunched on my knees at a round glass table near a plate glass door on which is inscribed, in gold leaf Paul Revere never put there, letters that must be read backward: PARK VIEW PHARMACY There is an evening smell of late coffee from the fountain, and all the librarians are lined up in a row on the tall stools, sipping and chattering. They have just stepped in from the cold of the Traveling Library, and so have I. The Traveling Library is a big green truck that stops, once every two weeks, on the corner of Continental Avenue, just a little way in from Westchester Avenue, not far from a house that keeps a pig. Other houses fly pigeons from their roofs, other yards have chickens, and down on Mayflower there is even a goat. This is Pelham Bay, the Bronx, in the middle of the Depression, all cattails and weeds, such a lovely place and tender hour! Even though my mother takes me on the subway far, far downtown to buy my winter coat in the frenzy of Klein's on Fourteenth Street, and even though I can recognize the heavy power of a quarter, I don't know it's the Depression. On the trolley on the way to Westchester Square I see the children who live in the boxcar strangely set down in an empty lot some distance from Spy Oak (where a Revolutionary traitor was hanged—served him right for siding with redcoats); the lucky boxcar children dangle their stick-legs from their train-house maw and wave; how I envy them! I envy the orphans of the Gould Foundation, who have their own private swings and seesaws. Sometimes I imagine I am an orphan, and my father is an impostor pretending to be my father.

My father writes in his prescription book: *#59330 Dr. O'Flaherty Pow .60/ #59331 Dr. Mulligan Gtt .65/ #59332 Dr. Thron Tab .90*. Ninety cents! A terrifically expensive medicine; someone is really sick. When I deliver a prescription around the corner or down the block, I am offered a nickel tip. I always refuse, out of conscience; I am, after all, the Park View Pharmacy's own daughter, and it wouldn't be seemly. My father grinds and mixes powders, weighs them out in tiny snowy heaps on an apothecary scale, folds them into delicate translucent papers or meticulously drops them into gelatin capsules.

In the big front window of the Park View Pharmacy there is a startling display—goldfish bowls, balanced one on the other in amazing pyramids. A German lady enters, one of my father's cronies—his cronies are both women and men. My quiet father's eyes are water-color blue, he wears his small skeptical quiet smile and receives the neighborhood's life-secrets. My father is discreet and inscrutable. The German lady pokes a punchboard with a pin, pushes up a bit of rolled paper, and cries out—she has just won a goldfish bowl, with two swimming goldfish in it! Mr. Jaffe, the salesman from McKesson & Robbins, arrives, trailing two mists: winter steaminess and the animal fog of his cigar,* which melts into the coffee smell, the tarpaper smell, the eerie honeyed tangled drugstore smell. Mr. Jaffe and my mother and father are intimates by now, but because it is the 1930s, so long ago, and the old manners still survive, they address one another gravely as Mr. Jaffe, Mrs. Ozick, Mr. Ozick. My mother calls my father Mr. O, even at home, as in a Victorian novel. In the street my father tips his hat to ladies. In the winter his hat is a regular fedora; in the summer it is a straw boater with a black ribbon and a jot of blue feather.

What am I doing at this round glass table, both listening and not listening to my mother and father tell Mr. Jaffe about their struggle with "Tessie," the lion-eyed landlady who has just raised, threefold, in the middle of that Depression I have never heard of, the Park View Pharmacy's devouring rent? My mother, not yet forty, wears bandages on her ankles, covering oozing varicose veins; back and forth she strides, dashes, runs, climbing cellar stairs or ladders; she unpacks cartons, she toils behind drug counters and fountain counters. Like my father, she is on her feet until one in the morning, the Park View's closing hour. My mother and father are in trouble, and I don't know it. I am too happy. I feel the secret center of eternity, nothing will ever alter, no one will ever die. Through the window, past the lit goldfish, the gray oval sky deepens over our neighborhood wood, where all the dirt paths lead down to seagull-specked water. I am familiar with every frog-haunted monument: Pelham Bay Park is thronged with WPA art—statuary, fountains, immense rococo staircases cascading down a hillside, Bacchus-faced stelae—stone Roman glories afterward mysteriously razed by an avenging Robert Moses. One year—how distant it seems now, as if even the climate is past returning—the bay froze so hard that whole families, mine among them, crossed back and forth to City Island, strangers saluting and calling out in the ecstasy of the bright trudge over such a sudden wilderness of ice.

In the Park View Pharmacy, in the winter dusk, the heart in my body is revolving like the goldfish fleet-finned in their clear bowls. The librarians are still warming up over their coffee. They do not recognize me, though only half an hour ago I was scrabbling in the mud around the two heavy boxes from the Traveling Library—oafish crates tossed with a thump to the ground. One box contains magazines—*Boy's Life, The American Girl, Popular Mechanix*. But the other, the other!

---

*Mr. Matthew Bruccoli, another Bronx drugstore child, has written to say that he remembers with certainty that Mr. Jaffe did not smoke. In my memory the cigar is somehow there, so I leave it.

The other transforms me. It is tumbled with storybooks, with clandestine intimations and transfigurations. In school I am a luckless goosegirl, friendless and forlorn. In P.S. 71 I carry, weighty as a cloak, the ineradicable knowledge of my scandal—I am cross-eyed, dumb, an imbecile at arithmetic; in P.S. 71 I am publicly shamed in Assembly because I am caught not singing Christmas carols; in P.S. 71 I am repeatedly accused of deicide. But in the Park View Pharmacy, in the winter dusk, branches blackening in the park across the road, I am driving in rapture through the Violet Fairy Book and the Yellow Fairy Book, insubstantial chariots snatched from the box in the mud. I have never been *inside* the Traveling Library; only grownups are allowed. The boxes are for the children. No more than two books may be borrowed, so I have picked the fattest ones, to last. All the same, the Violet and the Yellow are melting away. Their pages dwindle. I sit at the round glass table, dreaming, dreaming. Mr. Jaffe is murmuring advice. He tells a joke about Wrong-Way Corrigan. The librarians are buttoning up their coats. A princess, captive of an ogre, receives a letter from her swain and hides it in her bosom. I can visualize her bosom exactly—she clutches it against her chest. It is a tall and shapely vase, with a hand-painted flower on it, like the vase on the secondhand piano at home.

I am incognito. No one knows who I truly am. The teachers in P.S. 71 don't know. Rabbi Meskin, my *cheder* teacher, doesn't know. Tessie the lion-eyed landlady doesn't know. Even Hymie the fountain clerk can't know—though he understands other things better than anyone: how to tighten roller skates with a skatekey, for instance, and how to ride a horse. On Friday afternoons, when the new issue is out, Hymie and my brother fight hard over who gets to see *Life* magazine first. My brother is older than I am, and doesn't like me; he builds radios in his bedroom, he is already W2LOM, and operates his transmitter (*da-di-da-dit, da-da-di-da*) so penetratingly on Sunday mornings that Mrs. Eva Brady, across the way, complains. Mrs. Eva Brady has a subscription to *The Writer*; I fill a closet with her old copies. How to Find a Plot. Narrative and Character, the Writer's Tools. Because my brother has his ham license, I say, "I have a license too." "What kind of license?" my brother asks, falling into the trap. "Poetic license," I reply; my brother hates me, but anyhow his birthday presents are transporting: one year *Alice in Wonderland, Pinocchio* the next, then *Tom Sawyer*. I go after Mark Twain, and find *Joan of Arc* and my first satire, *Christian Science*. My mother surprises me with *Pollyanna*, the admiration of her Lower East Side childhood, along with *The Lady of the Lake*. Mrs. Eva Brady's daughter Jeannie has outgrown her Nancy Drew and Judy Boltons, so on rainy afternoons I cross the street and borrow them, trying not to march away with too many—the child of immigrants, I worry that the Bradys, true and virtuous Americans, will judge me greedy or careless. I wrap the Nancy Drews in paper covers to protect them. Old Mrs. Brady, Jeannie's grandmother, invites me back for more. I am so timid I can hardly speak a word, but I love her dark parlor; I love its black bookcases. Old Mrs. Brady sees me off, embracing books under an umbrella; perhaps she divines who I truly am. My brother doesn't care. My father doesn't notice. I think my mother knows. My mother reads the *Saturday Evening Post* and the *Woman's Home Companion*; sometimes the *Ladies' Home Journal*, but never *Good Housekeeping*. I read all my mother's magazines. My father reads *Drug Topics* and *Der Tog*, the Yiddish daily. In Louie Davidowitz's house (waiting our turn for the rabbi's lesson, he teaches me chess in *cheder*) there is a piece of furniture I am in awe of: a shining circular table that is also a revolving bookshelf holding a complete set of Charles Dickens. I borrow *Oliver Twist*. My cousins turn up with *Gulliver's Travels, Just So Stories, Don Quixote*, Oscar Wilde's *Fairy Tales*, uncannily different from the usual kind. Blindfolded, I reach into a Thanksgiving grabbag and pull out *Mrs. Leicester's School*, Mary Lamb's desolate stories of rejected children. Books spill out of rumor, exchange, miracle. In the Park View Pharmacy's lending library I discover, among the nurse romances, a browning, brittle miracle: *Jane Eyre*. Uncle Morris comes to visit (*his* drugstore is on the other side of the Bronx) and leaves behind, just like that, a three-volume Shakespeare. Peggy and Betty Provan, Scottish sisters around the corner, lend me their *Swiss Family Robinson*. Norma Foti, a whole year older, transmits a rumor about Louisa May Alcott; afterward I read *Little Women* a thousand times. Ten thousand! I am no longer incognito, not even to myself. I am Jo in her "vortex"; not Jo exactly, but some Jo-of-the-future. I am under an enchantment: who I truly am must be deferred, waited for and waited for. My father, silently filling capsules, is grieving over his mother in Moscow. I write letters in Yiddish to my Moscow grandmother, whom I will never know. I will never know my Russian aunts, uncles, cousins. In Moscow there is suffering, deprivation, poverty. My mother, threadbare, goes without a new winter coat so that packages can be sent to Moscow. Her fiery justice-eyes are semaphores I cannot decipher.

Some day, when I am free of P.S. 71, I will write stories; meanwhile, in winter dusk, in the Park View, in the secret bliss of the Violet Fairy Book, I both see and do not see how these grains of life will stay forever, papa and mama will live forever, Hymie will always turn my skatekey.

Hymie, after Italy, after the Battle of the Bulge, comes back from the war with a present: *From Here to Eternity*. Then he dies, young. Mama reads *Pride and Prejudice* and every single word of Willa Cather. Papa reads, in Yiddish, all of Sholem Aleichem and Peretz. He reads Malamud's *The Assistant* when I ask him to.

Papa and mama, in Staten Island, are under the ground. Some other family sits transfixed in the sun parlor where I read *Jane Eyre* and *Little Women* and, long afterward, *Middlemarch*. The Park View Pharmacy is dismantled, turned into a Hallmark card shop. It doesn't matter! I close my eyes, or else only stare, and everything is in its place again, and everyone.

A writer is dreamed and transfigured into being by spells, wishes, goldfish, silhouettes of trees, boxes of fairy tales dropped in the mud, uncles' and cousins' books, tablets and capsules and powders, papa's Moscow ache, his drugstore jacket with his special fountain pen in the pocket, his beautiful Hebrew paragraphs, his Talmudist's rationalism, his Russian-Gymnasium Latin and German, mama's furnace-heart, her masses of memoirs, her paintings of autumn walks down to the sunny water, her braveries, her reveries, her old, old school hurts.

A writer is buffeted into being by school hurts—Orwell, Forster, Mann!—but after a while other ambushes begin: sorrows, deaths, disappointments, subtle diseases, delays, guilts, the spite of the private haters of the poetry side of life, the snubs of the glamorous, the bitterness of those for whom resentment is a daily gruel, and so on and so on; and then one day you find yourself leaning here, writing at that selfsame round glass table salvaged from the Park View Pharmacy—writing this, an impossibility, a summary of how you came to be where you are now, and where, God knows, is that? Your hair is whitening, you are a well of tears, what you meant to do (beauty and justice) you have not done, papa and mama are under the earth, you live in panic and dread, the future shrinks and darkens, stories are only vapor, your inmost craving is for nothing but an old scarred pen, and what, God knows, is that?

ADRIENNE RICH
(1929–   )

"Both the victimization and the anger experienced by women are real, and have real sources, everywhere in the environment, built into society, language, the structures of thought. They will go on being tapped and explored by poets, among others. We can neither deny them, nor will we rest there. A new generation of women poets is already working out of the psychic energy released when women begin to move out toward what the feminist philosopher Mary Daly has described as the 'new space' on the boundaries of patriarchy. Women are speaking to and of women in these poems, out of a newly released courage to name, to love each other, to share risk and grief and celebration." So concludes Adrienne Rich in "When We Dead Awaken: Writing as Re-Vision" (1971), an essay that has become a classic testament of literary feminism. In fifteen volumes of poetry and five of prose, her consistent focus has been the cultural oppression of women, in particular their erasure from the story of western civilization.

Snapshots of a Daughter-in-Law

1. You, once a belle in Shreveport,
   with henna-colored hair, skin like a peachbud,
   still have your dresses copied from that time,
   and play a Chopin prelude
   called by Corot: *"Delicious recollections*
   float like perfume through the memory."

   Your mind now, mouldering like wedding-cake,
   heavy with useless experience, rich
   with suspicion, rumor, fantasy,
   crumbling to pieces under the knife-edge
   of mere fact. In the prime of your life.

   Nervy, glowering, your daughter
   wipes the teaspoons, grows another way.

2. Banging the coffee-pot into the sink
   she hears the angels chiding, and looks out
   past the raked gardens to the sloppy sky.
   Only a week since They said: *Have no patience.*

The next time it was: *Be insatiable*.
Then: *Save yourself; others you cannot save*.
Sometimes she's let the tapstream scald her arm,
a match burn to her thumbnail,

or held her hand above the kettle's snout
right in the woolly steam. They are probably angels,
since nothing hurts her any more, except
each morning's grit blowing into her eyes.

3. A thinking woman sleeps with monsters.
   The beak that grips her, she becomes. And Nature,
   that sprung-lidded, still commodious
   steamer-trunk of *tempora* and *mores*
   gets stuffed with it all: the mildewed orange-flowers,
   the female pills, the terrible breasts
   of Boadicea beneath flat foxes' heads and orchids.

   Two handsome women, gripped in argument,
   each proud, acute, subtle, I hear scream
   across the cut glass and majolica
   like Furies cornered from their prey:
   The argument *ad feminem*, all the old knives
   that have rusted in my back, I drive in yours,
   ma semblable, ma soeur!

4. Knowing themselves too well in one another;
   their gifts no pure fruition, but a thorn,
   the prick filed sharp against a hint of scorn . . .
   Reading while waiting
   for the iron to heat,
   writing, *This is the gnat that mangles men*,
   in that Amherst pantry while the jellies boil and scum,
   or, more often,
   iron-eyed and beaked and purposed as a bird,
   dusting everything on the whatnot every day of life.

5. *Dulce ridentem, dulce loquentem*,*
   she shaves her legs until they gleam
   like petrified mammoth-tusk.

*"Sweetly laughing, sweetly singing"

6. When to her lute Corinna sings
   neither words nor music are her own;
   only the long hair dipping
   over her cheek, only the song
   of silk against her knees
   and these
   adjusted in reflections of an eye.

   Poised, trembling and unsatisfied, before
   an unlocked door, that cage of cages,
   tell us, you bird, you tragical machine—
   is this *fertilisante douleur?* Pinned down
   by love, for you the only natural action,
   are you edged more keen
   to prise the secrets of the vault? has Nature shown
   her household books to you, daughter-in-law,
   that her sons never saw?

7. *"To have in this uncertain world some stay*
   which cannot be undermined, is
   *of the utmost consequence."**
                         Thus wrote
   a woman, partly brave and partly good,
   who fought with what she partly understood.
   Few men about her would or could do more,
   hence she was labelled harpy, shrew and whore.

8. "You all die at fifteen," said Diderot,
   and turn part legend, part convention.
   Still, eyes inaccurately dream
   behind closed windows blankening with steam.
   Deliciously, all that we might have been,
   all that we were—fire, tears,
   wit, taste, martyred ambition—
   stirs like the memory of refused adultery
   the drained and flagging bosom of our middle years.

9. *Not that it is done well, but*
   that it is done at all? Yes, think
   of the odds! or shrug them off forever.

*The words of Mary Wollstonecraft (see pages 18–20)

This luxury of the precocious child,
Time's precious chronic invalid,—
would we, darlings, resign it if we could?
Our blight has been our sinecure:
mere talent was enough for us—
glitter in fragments and rough drafts.

Sigh no more, ladies.
                              Time is male
and in his cups drinks to the fair.
Bemused by gallantry, we hear
our mediocrities over-praised,
indolence read as abnegation,
slattern thought styled intuition,
every lapse forgiven, our crime
only to cast too bold a shadow
or smash the mould straight off.

For that, solitary confinement,
tear gas, attrition shelling.
Few applicants for that honor.

10.   Well,
     she's long about her coming, who must be
     more merciless to herself than history.
     Her mind full to the wind, I see her plunge
     breasted and glancing through the currents,
     taking the light upon her
     at least as beautiful as any boy
     or helicopter,
                         poised, still coming,
     her fine blades making the air wince

     but her cargo
     no promise then:
     delivered
     palpable
     ours.

TONI MORRISON

(1931–   )

Toni Morrison was born Chloe Anthony Wofford in Ohio, the setting of three of her novels: *The Bluest Eye* (1970), *Sula* (1973), and *Beloved* (1987). When, in 1993, she became the first African-American writer to be awarded the Nobel Prize for Literature—"for eloquently and imaginatively exploring African-American experience in her six novels"—Henry Louis Gates commented that the award would have been deserved had Morrison written only *Beloved*, which many consider her masterpiece. Morrison believes fiction "should be beautiful, and powerful, but it should also work. It should have something in it that enlightens; something in it that opens the door and points the way. Something in it that suggests what the conflicts are, what the problems are. But it need not solve those problems because it is not a case study—it is not a recipe." The great home of the soul, she says, is the open road.

Nobel Lecture, 7 December 1993

Members of the Swedish Academy, Ladies and Gentlemen:

Narrative has never been merely entertainment for me. It is, I believe, one of the principal ways in which we absorb knowledge. I hope you will understand, then, why I begin these remarks with the opening phrase of what must be the oldest sentence in the world, and the earliest one we remember from childhood: "Once upon a time . . ."

"Once upon a time there was an old woman. Blind but wise." Or was it an old man? A guru, perhaps. Or a *griot** soothing restless children. I have heard this story, or one exactly like it, in the lore of several cultures.

"Once upon a time there was an old woman. Blind. Wise."

In the version I know the woman is the daughter of slaves, black, American, and lives alone in a small house outside of town. Her reputation for wisdom is without peer and without question. Among her people she is both the law and its transgression. The honor she is paid and the awe in which she is held reach beyond her neighborhood to places far away; to the city where the intelligence of rural prophets is the source of much amusement.

One day the woman is visited by some young people who seem to be bent on disproving her clairvoyance and showing her up for the fraud they believe she is. Their plan is simple: they enter her house and ask the one question the answer to

*a storyteller in western Africa

192

which rides solely on her difference from them, a difference they regard as a profound disability: her blindness. They stand before her, and one of them says,

"Old woman, I hold in my hand a bird. Tell me whether it is living or dead."

She does not answer, and the question is repeated. "Is the bird I am holding living or dead?"

Still she does not answer. She is blind and cannot see her visitors, let alone what is in their hands. She does not know their color, gender, or homeland. She knows only their motive.

The old woman's silence is so long, the young people have trouble holding their laughter.

Finally she speaks, and her voice is soft but stern. "I don't know," she says. "I don't know whether the bird you are holding is dead or alive, but what I do know is that it is in your hands. It is in your hands."

Her answer can be taken to mean: if it is dead, you have either found it that way or you have killed it. If it is alive, you can still kill it. Whether it is to stay alive is your decision. Whatever the case, it is your responsibility.

For parading their power and her helplessness, the young visitors are reprimanded, told they are responsible not only for the act of mockery but also for the small bundle of life sacrificed to achieve its aims. The blind woman shifts attention away from assertions of power to the instrument through which that power is exercised.

Speculation on what (other than its own frail body) that bird in the hand might signify has always been attractive to me, but especially so now, thinking as I have been about the work I do that has brought me to this company. So I choose to read the bird as language and the woman as a practiced writer.

She is worried about how the language she dreams in, given to her at birth, is handled, put into service, even withheld from her for certain nefarious purposes. Being a writer, she thinks of language partly as a system, partly as a living thing over which one has control, but mostly as agency—as an act with consequences. So the question the children put to her, "Is it living or dead?," is not unreal, because she thinks of language as susceptible to death, erasure; certainly imperiled and salvageable only by an effort of the will. She believes that if the bird in the hands of her visitors is dead, the custodians are responsible for the corpse. For her a dead language is not only one no longer spoken or written, it is unyielding language content to admire its own paralysis. Like statist language, censored and censoring. Ruthless in its policing duties, it has no desire or purpose other than to maintain the free range of its own narcotic narcissism, its own exclusivity and dominance. However, moribund, it is not without effect, for it actively thwarts the intellect, stalls conscience, suppresses human potential. Unreceptive to interrogation, it cannot form or tolerate new ideas, shape other thoughts, tell another story, fill baffling silences. Official language smitheried to sanction ignorance and preserve privilege is a suit of armor, polished to shocking glitter, a husk from which the knight departed long ago. Yet there it is; dumb, predatory, sentimental. Exciting reverence in schoolchildren, providing shelter for despots, summoning false memories of stability, harmony among the public.

She is convinced that when language dies, out of carelessness, disuse, indifference, and absence of esteem, or killed by fiat, not only she herself but all users and makers are accountable for its demise. In her country children have bitten their tongues off and use bullets instead to iterate the void of speechlessness, of disabled and disabling language, of language adults have abandoned altogether as a device for grappling with meaning, providing guidance, or expressing love. But she knows tongue-suicide is not only the choice of children. It is common among the infantile heads of state and power merchants whose evacuated language leaves them with no access to what is left of their human instincts, for they speak only to those who obey, or in order to force obedience.

The systematic looting of language can be recognized by the tendency of its users to forgo its nuanced, complex, midwifery properties, replacing them with menace and subjugation. Oppressive language does more than represent violence; it is violence; does more than represent the limits of knowledge; it limits knowledge. Whether it is obscuring state language or the faux language of mindless media; whether it is the proud but calcified language of the academy or the commodity-driven language of science; whether it is the malign language of law-without-ethics, or language designed for the estrangement of minorities, hiding its racist plunder in its literary cheek—it must be rejected, altered, and exposed. It is the language that drinks blood, laps vulnerabilities, tucks its fascist boots under crinolines of respectability and patriotism as it moves relentlessly toward the bottom line and the bottomed-out mind. Sexist language, racist language, theistic language—all are typical of the policing languages of mastery, and cannot, do not, permit new knowledge or encourage the mutual exchange of ideas.

The old woman is keenly aware that no intellectual mercenary or insatiable dictator, no paid-for politician or demagogue, no counterfeit journalist would be persuaded by her thoughts. There is and will be rousing language to keep citizens armed and arming; slaughtered and slaughtering in the malls, courthouses, post offices, playgrounds, bedrooms, and boulevards; stirring, memorializing language to mask the pity and waste of needless death. There will be more diplomatic language to countenance rape, torture, assassination. There is and will be more seductive, mutant language designed to throttle women, to pack their throats like pâté-producing geese with their own unsayable, transgressive words; there will be more of the language of surveillance disguised as research; of politics and history calculated to render the suffering of millions mute; language glamorized to thrill the dissatisfied and bereft into assaulting their neighbors; arrogant pseudo-empirical language crafted to lock creative people into cages of inferiority and hopelessness.

Underneath the eloquence, the glamour, the scholarly associations, however stirring or seductive, the heart of such language is languishing, or perhaps not beating at all—if the bird is already dead.

She has thought about what could have been the intellectual history of any discipline if it had not insisted upon, or been forced into, the waste of time and life that rationalizations for and representations of dominance required—lethal discourses of exclusion blocking access to cognition for both the excluder and the excluded.

The conventional wisdom of the Tower of Babel story is that the collapse was a misfortune. That it was the distraction or the weight of many languages that precipitated the tower's failed architecture. That one monolithic language would have expedited the building, and heaven would have been reached. Whose heaven, she wonders? And what kind? Perhaps the achievement of Paradise was premature, a little hasty if no one could take the time to understand other languages, other views, other narratives. Had they, the heaven they imagined might have been found at their feet. Complicated, demanding, yes, but a view of heaven as life; not heaven as post-life.

She would not want to leave her young visitors with the impression that language should be forced to stay alive merely to be. The vitality of language lies in its ability to limn the actual, imagined, and possible lives of its speakers, readers, writers. Although its poise is sometimes in displacing experience, it is not a substitute for it. It arcs toward the place where meaning may lie. When a president of the United States thought about the graveyard his country had become, and said, "The world will little note nor long remember what we say here. But it will never forget what they did here," his simple words were exhilarating in their life-sustaining properties because they refused to encapsulate the reality of 600,000 dead men in a cataclysmic race war. Refusing to monumentalize, disdaining the "final word," the precise "summing up," acknowledging their "poor power to add or detract," his words signal deference to the uncapturability of the life it mourns. It is the deference that moves her, that recognition that language can never live up to life once and for all. Nor should it. Language can never "pin down" slavery, genocide, war. Nor should it yearn for the arrogance to be able to do so. Its force, its felicity, is in its reach toward the ineffable.

Be it grand or slender, burrowing, blasting or refusing to sanctify; whether it laughs out loud or is a cry without an alphabet, the choice word or the chosen silence, unmolested language surges toward knowledge, not its destruction. But who does not know of literature banned because it is interrogative; discredited because it is critical; erased because alternate? And how many are outraged by the thought of a self-ravaged tongue?

Word-work is sublime, she thinks, because it is generative; it makes meaning that secures our difference, our human difference—the way in which we are like no other life.

We die. That may be the meaning of life. But we *do* language. That may be the measure of our lives.

"Once upon a time . . ." Visitors ask an old woman a question. Who are they, these children? What did they make of that encounter? What did they hear in those final words: "The bird is in your hands"? A sentence that gestures toward possibility, or one that drops a latch? Perhaps what the children heard was, "It's not my problem. I am old, female, black, blind. What wisdom I have now is in knowing I cannot help you. The future of language is yours."

They stand there. Suppose nothing was in their hands. Suppose the visit was only a ruse, a trick to get to be spoken to, taken seriously as they have not been before. A chance to interrupt, to violate the adult world, its miasma of discourse about them. Urgent questions are at stake, including the one they have asked: "Is the bird we are holding living or dead?" Perhaps the question meant: "Could someone tell us what is life? What is death?" No trick at all; no silliness. A straightforward question worthy of the attention of a wise one. An old one. And if the old and wise who have lived life and faced death cannot describe either, who can?

But she does not; she keeps her secret, her good opinion of herself, her gnomic pronouncements, her art without commitment. She keeps her distance, enforces it and retreats into the singularity of isolation, in sophisticated, privileged space.

Nothing, no word follows her declaration of transfer. That silence is deep, deeper than the meaning available in the words she has spoken. It shivers, this silence, and the children, annoyed, fill it with language invented on the spot.

"Is there no speech," they ask her, "no words you can give us that help us break through your dossier of failures? through the education you have just given us that is no education at all because we are paying close attention to what you have done as well as to what you have said? to the barrier you have erected between generosity and wisdom?

"We have no bird in our hands, living or dead. We have only you and our important question. Is the nothing in our hands something you could not bear to contemplate, to even guess? Don't you remember being young, when language was magic without meaning? When what you could say, could not mean? When the invisible was what imagination strove to see? When questions and demands for answers burned so brightly you trembled with fury at not knowing?

"Do we have to begin consciousness with a battle heroes and heroines like you have already fought and lost, leaving us with nothing in our hands except what you have imagined is there? Your answer is artful, but its artfulness embarrasses us and ought to embarrass you. Your answer is indecent in its self-congratulation. A made-for-television script that makes no sense if there is nothing in our hands.

"Why didn't you reach out, touch us with your soft fingers, delay the sound bite, the lesson, until you knew who we were? Did you so despise our trick, our modus operandi, that you could not see that we were baffled about how to get your attention? We are young. Unripe. We have heard all our short lives that we have to be responsible. What could that possibly mean in the catastrophe this world has become; where, as a poet said, 'nothing needs to be exposed since it is already barefaced?' Our inheritance is an affront. You want us to have your old, blank eyes and see only cruelty and mediocrity. Do you think we are stupid enough to perjure ourselves again and again with the fiction of nationhood? How dare you talk to us of duty when we stand waist deep in the toxin of your past?

"You trivialize us and trivialize the bird that is not in our hands. Is there no context for our lives? No song, no literature, no poem full of vitamins, no history connected to experience that you can pass along to help us start strong? You are an adult. The old one, the wise one. Stop thinking about saving your face. Think of our lives and tell us your particularized world. Make up a story. Narrative is radical, creating us at the very moment it is being created. We will not blame you if your reach exceeds your grasp; if love so ignites your words that they go down in flames and nothing is left but their scald. Or if, with the reticence of a surgeon's hands, your words suture only the places where blood might flow. We know you can never do it properly—once and for all. Passion is never enough; neither is skill. But try. For our sake and yours forget your name in the street; tell us what the world has been to you in the dark places and in the light. Don't tell us what to believe, what to fear. Show us belief's wide skirt and the stitch that unravels fear's caul. You, old woman, blessed with blindness, can speak the language that tells us what only language can: how to see without pictures. Language alone protects us from the scariness of things with no names. Language alone is meditation.

"Tell us what it is to be a woman so that we may know what it is to be a man. What moves at the margin. What it is to have no home in this place. To be set adrift from the one you knew. What it is to live at the edge of towns that cannot bear your company.

"Tell us about ships turned away from shorelines at Easter, placenta in a field. Tell us about a wagonload of slaves, how they sang so softly their breath was indistinguishable from the falling snow. How they knew from the hunch of the nearest shoulder that the next stop would be their last. How, with hands prayered in their sex, they thought of heat, then sun. Lifting their faces as though it was there for the taking. Turning as though there for the taking. They stop at an inn. The driver and his mate go in with the lamp, leaving them humming in the dark. The horse's void steams into the snow beneath its hooves and the hiss and melt are the envy of the freezing slaves.

"The inn door opens: a girl and a boy step away from its light. They climb into the wagon bed. The boy will have a gun in three years, but now he carries a lamp and a jug of warm cider. They pass it from mouth to mouth. The girl offers bread, pieces of meat, and something more: a glance into the eyes of the one she serves. One helping for each man, two for each woman. And a look. They look back. The next stop will be their last. But not this one. This one is warmed."

It's quiet again when the children finish speaking, until the woman breaks into the silence.

"Finally," she says. "I trust you now. I trust you with the bird that is not in your hands because you have truly caught it. Look. How lovely it is, this thing we have done—together."

ALICE MUNRO

(1931-)

O n the basis of her eight volumes of short stories and one novel, the Cana- dian Alice Munro has been called one of the best short story writers in the English language, "our Chekhov," as Cynthia Ozick put it. A moralist who is never judgmental, Munro is always open to the ambiguity of every situation and choice. Her stories are rich in surprises. The collection *The Love of a Good Woman* (1998)—from which the following story comes—was described by one reviewer as amounting to "a portrait of a generation: a generation [of women] that came to adulthood with one set of rules and then found it could live with another."

The Children Stay

Thirty years ago, a family was spending a holiday together on the east coast of Vancouver Island. A young father and mother, their two small daughters, and an older couple, the husband's parents.

What perfect weather. Every morning, every morning it's like this, the first pure sunlight falling through the high branches, burning away the mist over the still water of Georgia Strait.

If it weren't for the tide, it would be hard to remember that this is the sea. You look across the water to the mountains on the mainland, the ranges that are the western wall of the continent of North America. These humps and peaks coming clear now through the mist are of interest to the grandfather and to his son, Brian. The two men are continually trying to decide which of these shapes are ac- tual continental mountains and which are improbable heights of the islands that ride in front of the shore.

There is a map, set up under glass, between the cottages and the beach. You can stand there looking at the map, then looking at what's in front of you and back at the map again, until you get things sorted out. The grandfather and Brian usually get into an argument—though you'd think there would not be much room for disagreement with the map right there.

Brian's mother won't look at the map. She says it boggles her mind. Her con- cern is always about whether anybody is hungry yet, or thirsty, whether the chil- dren have their sun hats on and have been rubbed with protective lotion. She makes her husband wear a floppy cotton hat and thinks that Brian should wear one, too—she reminds him of how sick he got from the sun that summer they went to the Okanagan, when he was a child. Sometimes Brian says to her, "Oh, dry up, Mother." His tone is mostly affectionate, but his father may ask him if that's the way he thinks he can talk to his mother nowadays.

"She doesn't mind," says Brian.

"How do you know?" says his father.

"Oh, for Pete's sake," says his mother.

Pauline, the young mother, slides out of bed as soon as she's awake every morning, slides out of reach of Brian's long, sleepily searching arms and legs. What wakes her is the first squeaks and mutters of the baby, Mara, in the children's room, then the creak of the crib as Mara—sixteen months old now, getting to the end of babyhood—pulls herself up to stand hanging on to the railing. She continues her soft amiable talk as Pauline lifts her out—Caitlin, nearly five, shifting about but not waking, in her nearby bed—and as she is carried into the kitchen to be changed, on the floor. Then she is settled into her stroller, with a biscuit and a bottle of apple juice, while Pauline gets into her sundress and sandals, goes to the bathroom, combs out her hair—all as quickly and quietly as possible. They leave the cottage and head for the bumpy unpaved road that runs behind the cottages, a mile or so north till it stops at the bank of the little river that runs into the sea. The road is still mostly in deep morning shadow, the floor of a tunnel under fir and cedar trees.

The grandfather, also an early riser, sees them from the porch of his cottage, and Pauline sees him. But all that is necessary is a wave. He and Pauline never have much to say to each other (though sometimes there's an affinity they feel, in the midst of some long-drawn-out antics of Brian's or some apologetic but insistent fuss made by the grandmother, there's an awareness of not looking at each other, lest their look reveal a bleakness that would discredit others).

On this holiday Pauline steals time to be by herself—being with Mara is still almost the same thing as being by herself. Early morning walks, the late morning hour when she washes and hangs out the diapers. She could have had another hour or so in the afternoons, while Mara is napping. But Brian has fixed up a shelter on the beach, and he carries the playpen down every day, so that Mara can nap there and Pauline won't have to absent herself. He says his parents might be offended if she's always sneaking off. He agrees, though, that she does need some time to go over her lines for the play she's going to be in, back in Victoria, this September.

Pauline is not an actress. This is an amateur production, and she didn't even try out for the role. She was asked if she would like to be in this play by a man she met at a barbecue, in June. The people there were mostly teachers, and their wives or husbands—it was held at the house of the principal of the high school where Brian taught. The woman who taught French was a widow—she had brought her grown son, who was staying for the summer with her and working as a night clerk in a downtown hotel. She told everybody that he had got a job teaching at a college in western Washington State and would be going there in the fall.

Jeffrey Toom was his name. "Without the 'b,'" he said, as if the staleness of the joke wounded him.

What was he going to teach?

"Dram-ah," he said, drawing the word out in a mocking way.

He spoke of his present job disparagingly as well.

"It's a pretty sordid place," he said. "Maybe you heard—a hooker was killed there last February. And then we get the usual losers checking in to O.D. or bump themselves off."

People did not quite know what to make of this way of talking and drifted away from him. Except for Pauline.

"I'm thinking about putting on a play," he said. He asked her if she had ever heard of "Eurydice."

Pauline said, "You mean Anouilh's?" and he was unflatteringly surprised. He immediately said he didn't know if it would ever work out. "I just thought it might be interesting to see if you could do something different here in the land of Noël Coward."

Pauline did not remember when there had been a play by Noël Coward put on in Victoria, though she supposed there had been several. She said, "We saw 'The Duchess of Malfi' last winter at the college."

"Yeah. Well," he said, flushing. She had thought he was older than she was, at least as old as Brian—who was thirty, though people were apt to say he didn't act it—but as soon as he started talking to her, in this offhand, dismissive way, never quite meeting her eyes, she suspected that he was younger than he'd like to appear. Now, with that flush, she was sure of it.

As it turned out, he was a year younger than she was. Twenty-five.

She said that she couldn't be Eurydice—she couldn't act. But Brian came over to see what the conversation was about and said at once that she must try it.

"She just needs a kick in the behind," Brian said to Jeffrey. "She's like a little mule—it's hard to get her started. No, seriously, she's too self-effacing. I tell her that all the time. She's very smart. She's actually a lot smarter than I am."

At that Jeffrey did look directly into Pauline's eyes—impertinently and searchingly—and she was the one who was flushing.

He had chosen her immediately as his Eurydice because of the way she looked. But it was not because she was beautiful. "I'd never put a beautiful girl in that part," he said. "I don't know if I'd ever put a beautiful girl onstage in anything. It's distracting."

So what did he mean about the way she looked? He said it was her hair, which was long and dark and rather bushy (not in style at that time), and her pale skin ("Stay out of the sun this summer") and, most of all, her eyebrows.

"I never liked them," said Pauline, not quite sincerely. Her eyebrows were level, dark, luxuriant. They dominated her face. Like her hair, they were not in style. But if she had really disliked them, wouldn't she have plucked them?

Jeffrey seemed not to have heard her. "They give you a sulky look and that's disturbing," he said. "Also your jaw's a little heavy and that's sort of Greek. It would be better in a movie, where I could get you close up. The routine thing for Eurydice would be a girl who looked ethereal. I don't want ethereal."

As she walked Mara along the road, Pauline did work at the lines. There was a long speech at the end that was giving her trouble. She bumped the stroller along and repeated to herself, "You are terrible, you know, you are terrible like the angels. You think everybody's going forward, as brave and bright as you are—oh, don't look at me, please, darling, don't look at me— Perhaps I'm not what you wish I was, but I'm here, and I'm warm, I'm kind, and I love you. I'll give you all the happiness I can. Don't look at me. Don't look. Let me live."

She had left something out. "Perhaps I'm not what you wish I was, but you feel me here, don't you? I'm warm and I'm kind—"

She had told Jeffrey that she thought the play was beautiful.

He said, "Really?" What she'd said didn't please or surprise him—he seemed to feel it was predictable, superfluous. He would never describe a play in that way. He spoke of it more as a hurdle to be got over. Also a challenge to be flung at various enemies. At the academic snots, as he called them, who had done "The Duchess of Malfi." And at the social twits, as he called them, in the little theatre. He saw himself as an outsider heaving his weight against these people, putting on his play—he called it his—in the teeth of their contempt and opposition. In the beginning Pauline thought that this must be all in his imagination. Then something would happen that could be, but might not be, a coincidence—repairs to be done on the church hall where the play was to be performed, making it unobtainable, an unexpected increase in the cost of printing advertising posters—and she found herself seeing it his way. If you were going to be around him much, you almost had to see it his way—arguing was dangerous and exhausting.

"Sons of bitches," said Jeffrey between his teeth, but with some satisfaction. "I'm not surprised. I'm going to get to the bottom of this."

The rehearsals were held upstairs in an old building on Fisgard Street. Sunday afternoon was the only time that everybody could get there, though there were fragmentary rehearsals during the week. Pauline had to depend on sometimes undependable high-school babysitters—for the first six weeks of the summer Brian was busy teaching summer school. And Jeffrey himself had to be at his hotel job by eight o'clock in the evening. But on Sunday afternoons they were all there, laboring in the dusty high-ceilinged room on Fisgard Street. The windows were rounded at the top as in some plain and dignified church, and propped open in the heat with whatever objects could be found—ledger books from the nineteen-twenties, belonging to the hat shop that had once operated downstairs, pieces of wood left over from the picture frames made by the artist whose canvases were now stacked against one wall and apparently abandoned. The glass was grimy, but outside the sunlight bounced off the sidewalks, the empty gravelled parking lots, the low stuccoed buildings, with what seemed a special Sunday brightness. Hardly anybody moved through these downtown streets. Nothing was open except the occasional hole-in-the-wall coffee shop or lackadaisical, flyspecked convenience store.

Pauline was the one who went out at the break to get soft drinks and coffee. She was the one who had the least to say about the play and the way it was going—even though she was the only one who had read it before—because she alone had never done any acting. So it seemed proper for her to volunteer. She enjoyed her short walk in the empty streets—she felt as if she had become an urban person, someone detached and solitary, who lived in the glare of an important dream. Sometimes she thought of Brian at home, working in the garden and keeping an eye on the children. Or perhaps he had taken them to Dallas Road—she recalled a promise—to sail boats on the pond. That life seemed ragged and tedious compared to what went on in the rehearsal room—the hours of effort, the concentration, the sharp exchanges, the sweating and tension. Even the taste of the coffee, its scalding bitterness, and the fact that it was chosen by nearly everybody in preference to a fresher-tasting and maybe more healthful drink out of the cooler, seemed satisfying to her.

When she said that she had to go away for the two-week holiday, Jeffrey looked thunderstruck, as if he had never imagined that things like holidays could come into her life. Then he turned grim and slightly satirical, as if this were just another blow that he might have expected. Pauline explained that she would miss only the one Sunday—the one in the middle of the two weeks—because she and Brian were driving up the Island on a Monday and coming back on a Sunday morning. She promised to get back in time for rehearsal. Privately she wondered how she would do this—it always took so much longer than you expected to pack up and get away. She wondered if she could possibly come back by herself, on the morning bus. That would probably be too much to ask for. She didn't mention it.

She couldn't ask him if it was only the play he was thinking about, only her absence from a rehearsal that caused the thunder-cloud. At the moment, it very likely was. When he spoke to her at rehearsals there was never any suggestion that he ever spoke to her in any other way. The only difference in his treatment of her was that perhaps he expected less of her, of her acting, than he did of the others.

And that would be understandable to anybody. She was the only one chosen out of the blue, for the way she looked—the others had all shown up at the audition he had advertised on signs put up in cafés and bookstores around town.

Yet she thought they all knew what was going on, in spite of Jeffrey's offhand and abrupt and none too civil ways. They knew that after every one of them had straggled off home he would walk across the room and bolt the staircase door. (At first Pauline had pretended to leave with the rest and had even got into her car and circled the block, but later such a trick had come to seem insulting, not just to herself and Jeffrey but to the others, whom she was sure would never betray her, bound as they all were under the temporary but potent spell of the play.)

Jeffrey crossed the room and bolted the door. Every time, this was like a new decision that he had to make. Until it was done, she wouldn't look at him. The sound of the bolt being pushed into place, the ominous or fatalistic sound of metal hitting metal, gave her a localized shock of capitulation. But she didn't make a move, she waited for him to come back to her with the whole story of the afternoon's labor draining out of his face, the expression of matter-of-fact and customary disappointment cleared away, replaced by the live energy she always found surprising.

"So. Tell us what this play of yours is about," Brian's father said. "Is it one of those ones where they take their clothes off on the stage?"

"Now, don't tease her," said Brian's mother.

Brian and Pauline had put the children to bed and walked over to his parents' cottage for an evening drink. The sunset was behind them, behind the forests of Vancouver Island, but the mountains in front of them, all clear now and hard cut against the sky, shone in its pink light. Some high inland mountains were capped with pink summer snow.

"The story of Orpheus and Eurydice is that Eurydice died," Pauline said. "And Orpheus goes down to the underworld to try to get her back. And his wish is granted, but only if he promises not to look at her. Not to look back at her. She's walking behind him—"

"Twelve paces," said Brian. "As is only right."

"It's a Greek story, but it's set in modern times," said Pauline. "At least this version is. More or less modern. Orpheus is a musician travelling around with his father—they're both musicians—and Eurydice is an actress. This is in France."

"Translated?" Brian's father said.

"No," said Brian. "But don't worry, it's not in French. It was written in Transylvanian."

"It's so hard to make sense of anything," Brian's mother said with a worried laugh. "It's so hard, with Brian around."

"It's in English," Pauline said.

"And you're what's-her-name?"

She said, "I'm Eurydice."

"He get you back O.K.?"

"No," she said. "He looks back at me and then I have to stay dead."

"Oh, an unhappy ending," Brian's mother said.

"You're so gorgeous?" said Brian's father skeptically. "He can't stop himself from looking back?"

"It's not that," said Pauline. But at this point she felt that something had been achieved by her father-in-law, he had done what he meant to do, which was the same thing that he nearly always meant to do, in any conversation she had with him. And that was to break through the careful structure of some explanation he had asked her for, and she had unwillingly but patiently given, and with a seemingly negligent kick knock it into rubble. He had been dangerous to her for a long time in this way, though he wasn't particularly so tonight.

But Brian did not know that. Brian was still figuring out how to come to her rescue.

"Pauline is gorgeous," Brian said.

"Yes indeed," said his mother.

"Maybe if she'd go to the hairdresser," his father said. But Pauline's long hair was such an old objection of his that it had become a family joke. Even Pauline laughed. She said, "I can't afford to till we get the veranda roof fixed." And Brian laughed boisterously, full of relief that she was able to take all this as a joke. It was what he had always told her to do.

"Just kid him back. It's the only way to handle him."

"Yeah, well, if you'd got yourselves a decent house," said his father. But this, like Pauline's hair, was such a familiar sore point that it couldn't rouse anybody. Brian and Pauline had bought a handsome house in bad repair on a street in Victoria where old mansions were being turned into ill-used apartment buildings. The house, the street, the messy old Garry oaks, the fact that no basement had been blasted out under the house, was all a horror to Brian's father. So what he said now about a decent house might be some kind of peace signal. Or could be taken so.

Brian was an only son. He was a math teacher. His father was a civil engineer, and part owner of a contracting company. If he had hoped that he would have a son who was an engineer and might come into the company, there was never any mention of it. Pauline had asked Brian whether he thought the carping about their house, and her hair, and the books she read, might be a cover for this larger disappointment, but Brian had said, "Nope. In our family we complain about just whatever we want to complain about. We ain't subtle, Ma'am."

Pauline still wondered, when she heard his mother talking about how teachers ought to be the most honored people in the world and they did not get half the credit they deserved and that she didn't know how Brian managed it, day after day. Then his father might say, "That's right," or "I sure wouldn't want to do it, I can tell you that. They couldn't pay me to do it."

And Brian would turn that into a joke, as he turned nearly everything into a joke.

"Don't worry, Dad. They don't pay you much."

Brian in his everyday life was a much more dramatic person than Jeffrey. He dominated his classes by keeping up a parade of jokes and antics, extending the role that he had always played, Pauline believed, with his mother and father. He acted dumb, he bounced back from pretended humiliations, he traded insults. He was a bully in a good cause—a chivying, cheerful, indestructible bully.

"Your boy has certainly made his mark with us," the principal said to Pauline. "He has not just survived, which is something in itself. He has made his mark."

Your boy.

He called his students boneheads. His tone was affectionate, fatalistic. He said that his father was the King of the Philistines, a pure and natural barbarian. And that his mother was a dishrag, good-natured and worn out. But however he dismissed such people, he could not be long without them. He took his students on camping trips. And he could not imagine a summer without this shared holiday. He was mortally afraid, every year, that Pauline would refuse to go along. Or that, having agreed to go, she was going to be miserable, take offense at something his father said, complain about how much time she had to spend with his mother, sulk because there was no way they could do anything by themselves. She might decide to spend all day in their own cottage, reading, and pretending to have a sunburn.

All those things had happened, on previous holidays. But this year she was easing up. He told her he could see that, and he was grateful to her.

"I know it's an effort," he said. "It's different for me. They're my parents and I'm used to not taking them seriously."

Pauline came from a family that took things so seriously that her parents had got a divorce. Her mother was now dead. She had a distant, though cordial, relationship with her father and her two much older sisters. She said that they had nothing in common. She knew Brian could not understand how that could be a reason. She saw what comfort it gave him, this year, to see things going so well. She had thought it was laziness or cowardice that kept him from breaking the arrangement, but now she saw that it was something far more positive. He needed to have his wife and his parents and his children bound together like this, he needed to involve Pauline in his life with his parents and to bring his parents to some recognition of her—though the recognition, from his father, would always be muffled and contrary, and from his mother too profuse, too easily come by, to mean much. Also he wanted Pauline to be connected—and the children, too—to his own childhood. He wanted these holidays to be linked to the holidays of his youth with their lucky or unlucky weather, car troubles, boating scares, bee stings, marathon Monopoly games, to all the things that he told his mother he was bored to death hearing about. He wanted pictures from this summer to be taken, and fitted into his mother's album, a continuation of all the other pictures that he groaned at the mention of.

The only time they could talk to each other was in bed, late at night. But they did talk then, more than was usual with them at home, where Brian was so tired that often he fell immediately asleep. And in ordinary daylight it was hard to talk to him because of his jokes. She could see the joke brightening his eyes. (His coloring was very like hers—dark hair and pale skin and gray eyes—but her eyes were cloudy and his were light, like clear water over stones.) She could see it pulling at the corners of his mouth as he foraged among your words to catch a pun or the start of a rhyme—anything that could take the conversation away, into absurdity. His whole body, tall and loosely joined together and still almost as skinny as a teenager's, twitched with comic propensity. Before she married him, Pauline had a friend named Gracie, a rather grumpy-looking girl, subversive about men. Brian had thought her a girl whose spirits needed a boost, and so he made even more than the usual effort. And Gracie said to Pauline, "How can you stand the non-stop show?"

"That's not the real Brian," Pauline had said. "He's different when we're alone." But, looking back, she wondered how true that had ever been. Had she said it simply to defend her choice, as you did when you had made up your mind to get married?

Even in the cottage, with the window open on the unfamiliar darkness and stillness of the night, he teased a little. He had to speak of Jeffrey as Monsieur le Directeur, which made the play, or the fact that it was a French play, slightly ridiculous. Or perhaps it was Jeffrey himself, Jeffrey's seriousness about the play, that had to be called into question.

Pauline didn't care. It was such a pleasure and a relief to her to mention Jeffrey's name.

Though most of the time she didn't mention him, she circled around that pleasure. She described all the others instead. The hairdresser and the harbor pilot and the busboy and the old man who claimed to have once acted on the radio. He played Orphée's father, and gave Jeffrey the most trouble, because he had the stubbornest notions of his own about acting.

The middle-aged impresario, M. Dulac, was played by a twenty-four-year-old travel agent. And Mathias, who was Eurydice's former boyfriend, presumably around her own age, was played by the manager of a shoe store, who was married and a father.

"Why didn't Monsieur le Directeur cast those two the other way round?" said Brian.

"That's the way he does things," Pauline said. "What he sees in us is something different from the obvious."

For instance, she said, the busboy was a difficult Orphée.

"He's only nineteen, he's terribly shy, but he's determined to be an actor. Even if it's like making love to his grandmother. Jeffrey has to keep at him. 'Keep your arms around her a little longer, stroke her a little—'"

"He might get to like it," Brian said. "Maybe I should come around and keep an eye on him."

At this Pauline snorted. When she had started to quote Jeffrey she had felt a giving-way in her womb or the bottom of her stomach, a shock that had travelled oddly upward and hit her vocal cords. She had to cover up this quaking by growling in a way that was supposed to be an imitation (though Jeffrey never growled or ranted or carried on in any theatrical way at all).

Stroke her a little.

"But there's a point about him being so innocent," she said hurriedly. "Being not so physical. Being awkward." She began to talk about Orphée in the play, not the busboy—Orphée's problems with love and reality. Orphée will not put up with anything less than perfection. He wants a love that is outside of ordinary life. He wants a perfect Eurydice.

"Eurydice is more realistic. She's carried on with Mathias and with M. Dulac. She's been around her mother and her mother's lover. She knows what people are like. But she loves Orphée. She loves him better, in a way, than he loves her. She loves him better because she's not such a fool. She loves him like a human person."

"She's slept with those other guys?"

"Well, with M. Dulac she had to, she couldn't get out of it. She didn't want to, but probably after a while she enjoyed it, because after a certain point she couldn't help enjoying it. Just because she's slept with those men doesn't mean she's corrupt," Pauline said. "She wasn't in love then. She hadn't met Orphée. There's one speech where he tells her that everything she's done is sticking to her, and it's disgusting. Lies she's told him. The other men. It's all sticking to her forever. And then of course M. Henri plays up to that. He tells Orphée that he'll be just as bad and that one day he'll walk down the street with Eurydice and he'll look like a man with a dog he's trying to lose."

Brian laughed. He said, "That could be true."

"But not inevitably," said Pauline. "That's what's silly. It's not inevitable at all."

So Orphée is at fault, Pauline said decidedly. He looks back at Eurydice on purpose to kill her and get rid of her because she isn't perfect. Because of him she has to die a second time.

Brian, on his back and with his eyes wide open (she knew that because of the tone of his voice), said, "But doesn't he die, too?"

"Yes. He chooses to."

"So then they're together?"

"Yes. Like Romeo and Juliet. Orphée is with Eurydice at last. That's what M. Henri says. That's the last line of the play. That's the end." Pauline rolled over onto her side and touched her cheek to Brian's shoulder—not to start anything but to emphasize what she said next. "It's a beautiful play in one way but in another it's so silly. And it isn't really like 'Romeo and Juliet,' because it isn't bad luck or circumstances. It's on purpose. So they don't have to go on with life and get married and have kids and buy an old house and fix it up and—"

"And have affairs," said Brian. "After all, they're French."

Then he said, "And be like my parents."

Pauline laughed. "Do they have affairs? I can't imagine."

"Oh, sure," said Brian. "I meant their life."

"Oh."

"Logically I can see killing yourself so you won't turn into your parents. I just don't believe anybody would do it."

They went on speculating, and comfortably arguing, in a way that was not usual, but not altogether unfamiliar to them. They had done this before, at long intervals in their married life—talked half the night about God or fear of death or how children should be educated or whether money was important. At last they admitted to being too tired to make sense any longer, and arranged themselves in a comradely cuddle and went to sleep.

Finally a rainy day. Brian and his parents were driving into Campbell River to get groceries, and gin, and to take Brian's father's car to a garage. Brian had to go along, with his car, just in case the other car had to be left in the garage overnight. Pauline said that she had to stay home because of Mara's nap.

She persuaded Caitlin to lie down, too—allowing her to take her music box to bed with her if she played it under the covers. Then Pauline spread the script on the kitchen table, and drank coffee and went over the scene in which Orphée says that it's intolerable, at last, to stay in two skins, two envelopes with their own blood and oxygen sealed up in their solitude, and Eurydice tells him to be quiet.

"Don't talk. Don't think. Just let your hand wander, let it be happy on its own."

Your hand is my happiness, says Eurydice. Accept that. Accept your happiness.

Of course he says he cannot.

Caitlin called out frequently to ask what time it was, and Pauline could hear the music box. She hurried to the bedroom door and hissed at her to turn it off, not to wake Mara.

"If you play it like that again I'll take it away from you. O.K.?"

But Mara was already rustling around in her crib and in the next few minutes there were sounds of soft, encouraging conversation from Caitlin, designed to get her sister wide awake. Then of Mara rattling the crib railing, pulling herself up, throwing her bottle out onto the floor, and starting the bird cries that would grow more and more desolate until they brought her mother.

"I didn't wake her," Caitlin said. "She was awake all by herself. It's not raining anymore. Can we go down to the beach?"

She was right. It wasn't raining. Pauline changed Mara, told Caitlin to get her bathing suit on and find her sand pail. She got into her own bathing suit and put on her shorts on top of it, in case the rest of the family arrived home while she was down there. ("Dad doesn't like the way some women just go right out of their cottages in their bathing suits," Brian's mother had said to her. "I guess he and I just grew up in other times.") She picked up the script to take it along, then laid it down. She was afraid that she would get too absorbed in it and take her eye off the children for a moment too long.

The thoughts that came to her, of Jeffrey, were not really thoughts at all—they were more like alterations in her body. This could happen when she was sitting on the beach (trying to stay in the half shade of a bush and so preserve her pallor, as Jeffrey had ordered). Or when she was wringing out diapers, or when she and Brian were visiting his parents. In the middle of Monopoly games, Scrabble games, card games. She went right on talking, listening, working, keeping track of the children, while some memory of her secret life disturbed her like a radiant explosion. Then a warm weight settled, reassurance filling up all her hollows. But it didn't last, this comfort leaked away, and she was like a miser whose windfall has vanished and who is convinced such luck can never strike again. Longing buckled her up and drove her to the discipline of counting days. Sometimes she even cut the days into fractions to figure out more exactly how much time had gone.

She thought of going in to Campbell River, making some excuse, so that she could get to a phone booth and call him. The cottages had no phones—the only public phone was in the hall of the Lodge, across from the entrance to the dining room. But she did not have the number of the hotel where Jeffrey worked. And, besides that, she could never get away to Campbell River in the evening. She was afraid that if she called him at home in the daytime his mother the French teacher might answer. He said she hardly ever left the house in the summer. Just once, she had taken the ferry to Vancouver for the day. Jeffrey had phoned Pauline to ask her to come over. Brian was teaching and Caitlin was at her play group.

Pauline said, "I can't. I have Mara."

"Couldn't you bring her along?" he asked.

She said no.

"Why not? Couldn't you bring some things for her to play with?"

No, said Pauline. "I couldn't," she said. "I just couldn't." It seemed too dangerous to her, to trundle her baby along on such a guilty expedition. To a house where cleaning fluids would not be bestowed on high shelves and all pills and cough syrups and cigarettes and buttons put safely out of reach. And even if she escaped poisoning or choking, Mara might be storing up time bombs—memories of a strange house where she was strangely disregarded, of a closed door, noises on the other side of it.

"I just wanted you," Jeffrey said. "I just wanted you in my bed."

She said again, weakly, "No."

Those words of his kept coming back to her. I wanted you in my bed. A half-joking urgency in his voice but also a determination, a practicality, as if "in my bed" meant something more, the bed he spoke of taking on larger, less material dimensions.

Had she made a great mistake, with that refusal? With that reminder of how fenced in she was, in what anybody would call her real life?

The beach was nearly empty—people had got used to its being a rainy day. The sand was too heavy for Caitlin to make a castle or dig an irrigation system—projects she would undertake only with her father, anyway, because she sensed that his interest in them was wholehearted, and Pauline's was not. She wandered a bit forlornly at the edge of the water, missing the presence of other children, the nameless instant friends and occasional stone-throwing, water-kicking enemies, the shrieking and splashing and falling about. A boy a little bigger than she was and apparently all by himself stood knee deep in the water farther down the beach. If these two could get together it might be all right, the whole beach experience might be retrieved. Pauline couldn't tell if Caitlin was now making those little splashy runs into the water for his benefit, or whether he was watching her with interest or scorn.

Mara didn't need company, at least for now. She stumbled toward the water, felt it touch her feet and changed her mind, stopped, looked around, and spotted Pauline. "Paw. Paw," she said, in happy recognition. "Paw" was what she said for "Pauline," instead of "Mother" or "Mommy." Looking around overbalanced her; she sat down half on the sand and half in the water, made a squawk of surprise which turned into an announcement, and then, by some determined ungraceful maneuvers that involved putting her weight on her hands, rose to her feet, wavering and triumphant. She had been walking for half a year, but getting around on the sand was still a challenge. Now she came back toward Pauline, making some reasonable casual remarks in her own language.

"Sand," said Pauline, holding up a clot of it. "Look. Mara. Sand."

Mara corrected her, calling it something else—it sounded like "whap." Her thick diaper under her plastic pants and her terrycloth playsuit gave her a fat bottom, and that, along with her plump cheeks and shoulders and her sidelong important expression, made her look like a roguish matron.

Pauline became aware of someone calling her name. It had been called two or three times, but because the voice was unfamiliar she had not recognized it. She stood up and waved. It was the woman who worked in the store at the Lodge. She was leaning over the porch rail and calling, "Mrs. Keating. Mrs. Keating? Telephone, Mrs. Keating."

Pauline hoisted Mara onto her hip and summoned Caitlin. She and the little boy were aware of each other now: they were both picking up stones from the bottom and flinging them out into the water. At first she didn't hear Pauline, or pretended not to hear.

"Store," called Pauline. "Caitlin. Store." When she was sure Caitlin would follow—it was the word "store" that had done it, the reminder of the tiny store in the Lodge where you could buy ice cream and candy—she began the trek across the sand and up the flight of wooden steps. Halfway up she stopped, said, "Mara, you weigh a ton," and shifted the baby to her other hip. Caitlin followed, banging a stick against the railing.

"Can I have a Fudgsicle? Mother? Can I?"

"We'll see."

The public phone was beside a bulletin board on the other side of the main hall and across from the door to the dining room. A bingo game had been set up in there, because of the rain.

"Hope he's still hanging on," the woman who worked in the store called out. She was unseen now behind her counter.

Pauline, still holding Mara, picked up the dangling receiver and said breathlessly, "Hello?" She was expecting to hear Brian telling her about some delay in Campbell River or asking her what it was she had wanted him to get at the drugstore. It was just the one thing—calamine lotion—so he had not written it down.

"Pauline," said Jeffrey. "It's me."

Mara was bumping and scrambling along Pauline's side, eager to get down. Caitlin came along the hall and went into the store, leaving wet sandy footprints. Pauline said, "Just a minute, just a minute." She let Mara slide down and hurried to close the door that led to the steps. She did not remember telling Jeffrey the name of this place, though she had told him roughly where it was. She heard the woman in the store speaking to Caitlin in a sharper voice than she would use to children whose parents were beside them.

"Did you forget to put your feet under the tap?"

"I'm here," said Jeffrey. "I didn't get along so well without you. I didn't get along at all."

Mara made for the dining room, as if the male voice calling out "Under the N" were a direct invitation to her.

"Here. Where?" said Pauline.

She read the signs that were tacked up on the bulletin board beside the phone:

No Person Under Fourteen Years of Age Not Accompanied
by Adult Allowed in Boats or Canoes.

Fishing Derby.

Bake and Craft Sale, St. Bartholomew's Church.

Your life is in your hands. Palms and Cards read.
Reasonable and Accurate. Call Claire.

"In a motel. In Campbell River."

Pauline knows where she is before she opens her eyes. Nothing surprises her. She has slept, but not deeply enough to let go of anything.

She had waited for Brian in the parking area of the Lodge, with the children in tow, and then she had asked for the keys. She told him in front of his parents that there was something else she needed, from Campbell River. He asked what was it? And did she have any money?

"Just something," she said, so he would think that it was tampons or birth-control supplies, something that she didn't want to mention.

"Sure. O.K., but you'll have to put some gas in," he said.

Later she had to speak to him on the phone. Jeffrey said she had to do it.

"Because he won't take it from me. He'll think I kidnapped you or something. He won't believe it."

But the strangest thing of all the things that day was that Brian did seem, immediately, to believe it. Standing where she had stood not so long before, in the public hallway of the Lodge—the bingo game over now, but people going past, she could hear them, people on their way out of the dining room after dinner—Brian had said, "Oh. Oh. Oh. O.K.," in a voice that would have to be quickly controlled but that seemed to draw on a supply of fatalism or foreknowledge that went far beyond that necessity.

"O.K.," he said. "What about the car?"

He said something else, something impossible, and then hung up, and she came out of the phone booth beside a row of gas pumps in Campbell River.

"That was quick," Jeffrey said. "Easier than you expected?"

Pauline said, "I don't know."

"He may have known it subconsciously. People do know."

She shook her head, to tell him not to say any more, and he said, "Sorry." They walked along the street not touching or talking.

Now, looking around at leisure—the first real leisure or freedom she's had since she came into that room—Pauline sees that there isn't much of anything in it. Just a junky dresser, the bed without a headboard, an armless upholstered chair. On the window a Venetian blind with a broken slat. Also a noisy air-conditioner—Jeffrey turned it off in the night and left the door open on the chain, since the window was sealed. The door is shut now. He must have got up in the night and shut it.

This is all she has. Her connection with the cottage where Brian lies now asleep or not asleep is broken. Also her connection with the house that has been an expression of her life with Brian, of the way they wanted to live. She has cut herself off from all the large solid acquisitions, like the washer and dryer and the oak table and the refinished wardrobe and the chandelier that is a copy of the one in a painting by Vermeer. And just as much from those things that were particularly hers—the pressed-glass tumblers that she had been collecting and the prayer rug that was probably not authentic, but beautiful. Especially from those things. The skirt and blouse and sandals she put on for the trip to Campbell River might as well be all she has now to her name. She would never go back to lay claim to anything. If Brian got in touch with her to ask what was to be done with things, she would tell him to do what he liked—throw everything into garbage bags and take it to the dump, if that was what he liked. (In fact she knows that he will probably pack up a trunk, which he does, sending on, scrupulously, not only her winter coat and boots but things like the waist cincher she wore at her wedding and never since, with the prayer rug draped on top of everything like a final statement of his generosity, either natural or calculated.)

She believes that she will never again care about what sort of rooms she lives in or what sort of clothes she puts on. She will not be looking for that sort of help to give anybody an idea of who she is, what she is like. Not even to give herself an idea. What she has done will be enough, it will be the whole thing.

What she has done will be what she has heard about and read about. It will be what Anna Karenina did and what Mme. Bovary wanted to do. And what a teacher at Brian's school did, with the school secretary. He ran off with her. That was what it was called. Running off with. Taking off with. It was spoken of disparagingly, humorously, enviously. It was adultery taken one step further. The people who did it had almost certainly been having an affair already, committing adultery for quite some time before they became desperate or courageous enough to take this step. Once in a long while a couple might claim their love was unconsummated and technically pure, but these people would be thought of—if anybody believed them—as being not only very serious and high-minded but almost devastatingly foolish, almost in a class with those who gave up everything to go and work in some poor and dangerous country.

The others, the adulterers, were seen as irresponsible, immature, selfish, or even cruel. Also lucky. They were lucky because the sex they had been having in parked cars or the long grass or in each other's sullied marriage beds or most likely in motels like this one must surely have been splendid. Otherwise they would never have got such a yearning for each other's company at all costs or such a faith that their shared future would be altogether better and different in kind from what they had in the past.

Different in kind. That is what Pauline must believe now—that there is this major difference in lives or in marriages or unions between people. That some of them have a necessity, a fatefulness about them, which others do not have. Of course she would have said the same thing a year ago. People did say that, they seemed to believe that, and to believe that their own cases were all of the first, the special kind, even when anybody could see that they were not.

It is too warm in the room. Jeffrey's body is too warm. Conviction and contentiousness seem to radiate from it, even in sleep. His torso is thicker than Brian's, he is pudgier around the waist. More flesh on the bones, yet not so slack to the touch. Not so good-looking in general—she is sure most people would say that. And not so fastidious. Brian in bed smells of nothing. Jeffrey's skin, every time she's been with him, has had a baked-in, slightly oily or nutty smell. He didn't wash last night—but, then, neither did she. There wasn't time. Did he even have a toothbrush with him? She didn't, but she had not known she was staying.

When she met Jeffrey here it was still in the back of her mind that she had to concoct some colossal lie to serve her when she got home. And she—they—had to hurry. When Jeffrey said to her that he had decided that they must stay together, that she would come with him to Washington State, that they would have to drop the play because things would be too difficult for them in Victoria, she had looked at him just in the blank way you'd look at somebody the moment that an earthquake started. She was ready to tell him all the reasons why this was not possible, she still thought she was going to tell him that, but her life was coming adrift in that moment. To go back would be like tying a sack over her head.

All she said was "Are you sure?"

He said, "Sure." He said sincerely, "I'll never leave you."

That did not seem the sort of thing that he would say. Then she realized he was quoting—maybe ironically—from the play. It was what Orphée says to Eurydice within a few moments of their first meeting in the station buffet.

So her life was falling forward, she was becoming one of those people who ran away. A woman who shockingly and incomprehensibly gave everything up. For love, observers would say wryly. Meaning, for sex. None of this would happen if it weren't for sex.

And yet what's the great difference there? It's not such a variable procedure, in spite of what you're told. Skins, motions, contact, results. Pauline isn't a woman from whom it's difficult to get results. Brian got them. Probably anybody would, who wasn't wildly inept or morally disgusting.

But nothing's the same, really. With Brian—especially with Brian, to whom she had dedicated a selfish sort of good will, with whom she's lived in married complicity—there can never be this stripping away, the inevitable flight, the feelings she doesn't have to strive for but only to give in to like breathing or dying. That she believes can only come when the skin is on Jeffrey, the motions made by Jeffrey, and the weight that bears down on her has Jeffrey's heart in it, also his habits, thoughts, peculiarities, his ambition and loneliness (that for all she knows may have mostly to do with his youth).

For all she knows. There's a lot she doesn't know. She hardly knows anything about what he likes to eat or what music he likes to listen to or what role his mother plays in his life (no doubt a mysterious but important one, like the role of Brian's parents). One thing she's pretty sure of: whatever preferences or prohibitions he has will be definite. Plates in his armor.

She slides out from under Jeffrey's hand and from under the top sheet, which has a harsh smell of bleach, slips down to the floor where the bedspread is lying and wraps herself quickly in that rag of greenish-yellow chenille. She doesn't want him to open his eyes and see her from behind and note the droop of her buttocks. He's seen her naked before, but generally in a more forgiving moment.

She rinses her mouth and washes herself, using the bar of soap that is about the size of two thin squares of chocolate and firm as stone. She's hard used between the legs, swollen and stinking. Urinating takes an effort and it seems she's constipated. Last night when they went out and got hamburgers she found she could not eat. Presumably she'll learn to do all these things again, they'll resume their natural importance in her life. At the moment it's as if she can't quite spare the attention.

She has some money in her purse. She has to go out and buy a toothbrush, toothpaste, deodorant, shampoo. Also vaginal jelly. Last night they used condoms the first two times but nothing the third time.

She didn't bring her watch and Jeffrey doesn't wear one. There's no clock in the room, of course. She thinks it's early—there's still an early look to the light in spite of the heat. The stores probably won't be open, but there'll be someplace where she can get coffee.

Jeffrey has turned onto his other side. She must have wakened him, just for a moment.

They'll have a bedroom. A kitchen, an address. He'll go to work. She'll go to the laundromat. Maybe she'll go to work, too. Selling things, waiting on tables, tutoring students. She knows French and Latin—do they teach French and Latin in American high schools? Can you get a job if you're not an American? Jeffrey isn't.

She leaves him the key. She'll have to wake him to get back in. There's nothing to write a note with, or on.

It is early. The motel is on the highway at the north end of town, beside the bridge. There's no traffic yet. She scuffs back and forth under the cottonwood trees at the edge of the lot for quite a while before a vehicle of any kind rumbles over the bridge—though the traffic on it shook their bed regularly late into the night.

Something is coming now. A truck. But not just a truck—there's a large bleak fact coming at her. And it has not arrived out of nowhere—it's been waiting, cruelly nudging at her ever since she woke up or even all night.

Caitlin and Mara.

Last night on the phone, after speaking in such a flat and controlled and almost agreeable voice—as if he prided himself on not being shocked, not objecting or pleading—Brian cracked open. He said with contempt and fury and no concern for whoever might hear him, "Well, then—what about the kids?"

The receiver began to shake against Pauline's ear.

She said, "We'll talk—" but he did not seem to hear her.

"The children," he said, in this same shivering and vindictive voice. Changing the word "kids" to "children" was like slamming a board down on her—a heavy, formal, righteous threat.

"The children stay," Brian said. "Pauline. Did you hear me?"

"No," said Pauline. "Yes. I heard you, but—"

"All right. You heard me. Remember. The children stay."

It was all he could do. To make her see what she was doing, what she was ending, and to punish her if she did so. Nobody would blame him. There might be finagling, there might be bargaining, there would certainly be humbling of herself, but there it was, like a round cold stone in her gullet, like a cannonball. And it would remain there unless she changed her mind entirely. The children stay.

Their car—hers and Brian's—is still sitting in the motel parking lot. Brian will have to ask his father or his mother to drive him up here today to get it. She has the keys in her purse. There are spare keys—he will surely bring them. She unlocks the car door and throws her keys on the seat, then locks the door from the inside and shuts it.

Now she can't go back. She can't get into the car and drive back and say that she'd been insane. If she did that he would forgive her but he'd never get over it and neither would she. They'd go on, though, as people did.

She walks out of the parking lot, she walks along the sidewalk, into town.

The weight of Mara on her hip yesterday. The sight of Caitlin's footprints on the floor.

Paw. Paw.

She doesn't need the keys to get back to them, she doesn't need the car. She could beg a ride on the highway. Give in, give in, get back to them any way at all—how can she not do that?

A sack over her head.

This is acute pain. It will become chronic. Chronic means that it will be permanent but perhaps not constant. It may also mean that you won't die of it. You won't get free of it but you won't die of it. You won't feel it every minute but you won't spend many days without it, either. And you'll learn some tricks to dull it or banish it or else you'll end up destroying what you've got. What you incurred this pain to get. It isn't his fault. He's still an innocent or a savage, who doesn't know there's a pain so durable in the world. Say to yourself, You lose them anyway. They grow up. For a mother there's always waiting this private, slightly ridiculous desolation. They'll forget this time, in one way or another they'll disown you. Or hang around till you don't know what to do about them, the way Brian has.

And, still, what pain. To carry along and get used to until it's only the past you're grieving for and no longer any possible present.

Her children have grown up. They don't hate her. For going away or staying away. They don't forgive her, either. Perhaps they wouldn't have forgiven her anyway, but it would have been about something different.

Caitlin remembers a little about the summer at the Lodge, Mara nothing. Caitlin calls it "that place Grandma and Grandpa stayed at."

"The place we were at when you went away," she says. "Only we didn't know you went away with the man who was Orphée."

Pauline has told them about the play.

Pauline says, "It wasn't Orphée."

"It wasn't Orphée? Oh, well. I thought it was."

"No."

"Who was it, then?"

"Just a man connected," says Pauline. "It wasn't him."

EDNA O'BRIEN
(1932–   )

"The most gifted woman now writing fiction in English," according to Philip Roth—with "the soul of Molly Bloom and the gifts of Virginia Woolf," according to another critic—O'Brien grew up on a farm in the West of Ireland but exiled herself to England in 1959, a year before the publication of her first novel, *The Country Girls*, which was banned in her native country as "a smear on Irish womanhood" in the words of the censor and burned by the parish priest on the grounds of her village church. ("Banning is only the tip of the iceberg," O'Brien has said. "Keeping our psyches closed is the real bogey.") In 1995 she was awarded the European Prize for Literature in recognition of her life's work: eighteen works of fiction. Her memoir, *Mother Ireland*—"Edna O'Brien at her best," to quote William Trevor—gives an indelible portrait of the country that's at the center of every story this Irish exile has ever written.

---

from
Mother Ireland

Escape to England

Leaving Ireland was no wrench at all. I took the mail boat, like most others, sat up all night, watched the drinking, the spilling, walked the deck, remembered how Mr Thackeray and Mr Heinrich Böll had come in by boat to write leisurely about it, remembered the myriad others, natives, who had gone out to forget. Euston Station was a jungle, grim and impersonal, the very pigeons looked factory-made, and when I saw the faces of the English I thought not of the long catalogue of blood-letting history, but of murder stories I had read in the Sunday papers and of that swarthy visiting English woman from long ago who brought corn caps and a powder puff stitched into her hanky.

This was to be home. It had nothing to recommend it. Unhealthy, unfriendly, mortarish and to my ignorant eye morbid because I kept seeing wreaths and did not know that there was such a thing in England as Remembrance Sunday.

But I had got away. That was my victory. The real quarrel with Ireland began to burgeon in me then; I had thought of how it had warped me, and those around me, and their parents before them, all stooped by a variety of fears—fear of church, fear of gombeenism, fear of phantoms, fear of ridicule, fear of hunger, fear of annihilation, and fear of their own deeply ingrained aggression that can only strike a blow at each other, not having the innate authority to strike at those who are higher. Pity arose too, pity for a land so often denuded, pity for a people reluctant to admit that there is anything wrong. That is why we leave. Because we beg to differ. Because we dread the psychological choke. But leaving is only conditional. The person you are, is anathema to the person you would like to be.

But time changes everything including our attitude to a place. There is no such thing as a perpetual hatred no more than there are unambiguous states of earthly love. Hour after hour I can think of Ireland, I can imagine without going far wrong what is happening in any one of the little towns by day or by night, can see the tillage and the walled garden, see the spilt porter foam along the counters, I can hear argument and ballads, hear the elevation bell and the prayers for the dead. I can almost tell what any one of my friends might be doing at any hour so steadfast is the rhythm of life there. I open a book, a school book maybe, or a book of superstition, or a book of place names, and I have only to see the names of Ballyhooly or Raheen* to be plunged into that world from which I have derived such a richness and an unquenchable grief. The tinkers at Rathkeale* will be driving back to their settlement by now I say, and the woman who tells fortunes in her caravan will be sending her child down for the tenth loaf of sliced bread, while a mile or two away in her domain Lady so-and-so will tell the groomsman how yet again she got her horse into a lather, and on some door in a town a little black crêpe scarf dangling from a knocker will have on it a handwritten black-edged card stating at what time the remains will be removed, while the hideous bald bungalows will be mushrooming along the main road-sides. The men will be trying as always to distance their fate either through drink, or dirty stories, and the older women will be filled with the knowledge of how crushing their burdens are, while young girls will be gabbling, to invent diversion for themselves.

It is true that a country encapsulates our childhood and those lanes, byres, fields, flowers, insects, suns, moons and stars are forever re-occurring and tantalizing me with a possibility of a golden key which would lead beyond birth to the roots of one's lineage. Irish? In truth I would not want to be anything else. It is a state of mind as well as an actual country. It is being at odds with other nationalities, having quite different philosophy about pleasure, about punishment, about life, and about death. At least it does not leave one pusillanimous.

Ireland for me is moments of its history, and its geography, a few people who embody its strange quality, the features of a face, a holler, a line from a Synge play, the whiff of night air, but Ireland insubstantial like the goddesses poets dream of, who lead them down into strange circles. I live out of Ireland because

*townlands in O'Brien's native County Clare in the west of Ireland

something in me warns me that I might stop if I lived there, that I might cease to feel what it has meant to have such a heritage, might grow placid when in fact I want yet again and for indefinable reasons to trace that same route, that trenchant childhood route, in the hope of finding some clue that will, or would, or could, make possible the leap that would restore one to one's original place and state of consciousness, to the radical innocence of the moment just before birth.

SYLVIA PLATH
(1932–63)

"I have this demon who wants me to run away screaming if I am going to be flawed, fallible. It wants me to think I'm so good I must be perfect. Or nothing . . . Not being perfect hurts. . . . Brief note: to self. Time to take myself in hand . . . to build into myself, to give myself backbone, however much I fail. . . . Salvation in work. What if my work is lousy?" These excerpts from Plath's diary provide a glimpse of an interior life in which demons of depression and perfectionism battled with her yearning to achieve "not perfection," "but an acceptance of myself as having a right to live on my own human, fallible terms." Eventually the demons triumphed. Overwhelmed by circumstances—a broken marriage, the responsibility of caring for two babies in the coldest London winter on record, and a history of mental illness—Plath committed suicide at the age of thirty. The posthumously published poems collected in *Ariel* (1965) established her reputation as one of the most important American poets of the twentieth century.

Kindness

Kindness glides about my house.
Dame Kindness, she is so nice!
The blue and red jewels of her rings smoke
In the windows, the mirrors
Are filling with smiles.

What is so real as the cry of a child?
A rabbit's cry may be wilder
But it has no soul.
Sugar can cure everything, so Kindness says.
Sugar is a necessary fluid,

Its crystals a little poultice.
O kindness, kindness
Sweetly picking up pieces!
My Japanese silks, desperate butterflies,
May be pinned any minute, anesthetized.

And here you come, with a cup of tea
Wreathed in steam.
The blood jet is poetry,
There is no stopping it.
You hand me two children, two roses.

The Moon and the Yew Tree

This is the light of the mind, cold and planetary.
The trees of the mind are black. The light is blue.
The grasses unload their griefs on my feet as if I were God,
Prickling my ankles and murmuring of their humility.
Fumy, spiritous mists inhabit this place
Separated from my house by a row of headstones.
I simply cannot see where there is to get to.

The moon is no door. It is a face in its own right,
White as a knuckle and terribly upset.
It drags the sea after it like a dark crime; it is quiet
With the O-gape of complete despair. I live here.
Twice on Sunday, the bells startle the sky—
Eight great tongues affirming the Resurrection.
At the end, they soberly bong out their names.

The yew tree points up. It has a Gothic shape.
The eyes lift after it and find the moon.
The moon is my mother. She is not sweet like Mary.
Her garments unloose small bats and owls.
How I would like to believe in tenderness—
The face of the effigy, gentled by candles,
Bending, on me in particular, its mild eyes.

I have fallen a long way. Clouds are flowering
Blue and mystical over the face of the stars.
Inside the church, the saints will be all blue,
Floating on their delicate feet over the cold pews,
Their hands and faces stiff with holiness.
The moon sees nothing of this. She is bald and wild.
And the message of the yew tree is blackness—
                              blackness and silence.

MARY OLIVER
(1935–)

The author of eight books of poetry—she won the Pulitzer Prize (for *American Primitive* in 1984) and a National Book Award (for *New and Selected Poems* in 1992)—and several of prose about the writing of poetry (*Blue Pastures* and *A Poetry Handbook*), Oliver considers poetry "a life-cherishing force. . . . Poems are not words, after all, but fires for the cold, ropes let down to the lost, something as necessary as bread in the pockets of the hungry." She started out in Cleveland, Ohio, then settled on Cape Cod after college at Vassar. The New England landscape and her attention to the natural world are at the heart of her celebratory and deeply religious poetry. "There is no complaint in Oliver's poetry," said one critic. "But neither is there the sense that life is in any way easy."

Wild Geese

You do not have to be good.
You do not have to walk on your knees
for a hundred miles through the desert, repenting.
You only have to let the soft animal of your body
    love what it loves.
Tell me about despair, yours, and I will tell you mine.
Meanwhile the world goes on.
Meanwhile the sun and the clear pebbles of the rain
are moving across the landscapes,
over the prairies and the deep trees,
the mountains and the rivers.
Meanwhile the wild geese, high in the clean blue air,
are heading home again.
Whoever you are, no matter how lonely,
the world offers itself to your imagination,
calls to you like the wild geese, harsh and exciting—
over and over announcing your place
in the family of things.

When Death Comes

When death comes
like the hungry bear in autumn;
when death comes and takes all the bright coins from his purse

to buy me, and snaps the purse shut;
when death comes
like the measle-pox;

when death comes
like an iceberg between the shoulder blades,

I want to step through the door full of curiosity, wondering:
what is it going to be like, that cottage of darkness?

And therefore I look upon everything
as a brotherhood and a sisterhood,
and I look upon time as no more than an idea,
and I consider eternity as another possibility,

and I think of each life as a flower, as common
as a field daisy, and as singular,

and each name a comfortable music in the mouth,
tending, as all music does, toward silence,

and each body a lion of courage, and something
precious to the earth.

When it's over, I want to say: all my life
I was a bride married to amazement.
I was the bridegroom, taking the world into my arms.

When it's over, I don't want to wonder
if I have made of my life something particular, and real.
I don't want to find myself sighing and frightened,
or full of argument.

I don't want to end up simply having visited this world.

JUNE JORDAN
(1936–2002)

As professor of African-American Studies and Women's Studies at Berkeley and an activist director of Berkeley's Poetry for the People project, Jordan bore witness to the power of language to redeem the world from ignorance and injustice, a vision articulated in more than twenty books of poetry and prose. A memoir, *Soldier: A Poet's Childhood* (2000), recounts her youth in Harlem, where she was born, and Bedford-Stuyvesant in Brooklyn, New York, where she grew up, the daughter of an abusive father and a mother who eventually committed suicide. Adrienne Rich calls Jordan "one of the most lyrically gifted poets of the late twentieth century." In the essay "Ruth and Naomi, David and Jonathan: One Love"*, Jordan wrote about the saving power of friendship in the lives of women.

In Memoriam: Poem for Mrs. Fannie Lou Hamer

You used to say, "June?
Honey when you come down here you
supposed to stay with me. Where
else?"
Meanin home
against the beer the shotguns and the
point of view of whitemen don'
never see Black anybodies without
some violent itch start up.
                              The ones who
said, "No Nigga's Votin in This Town . . .

less'n it be feet first to the booth"
Then jailed you
beat you brutal
bloody/battered/beat
you blue beyond the feeling
of the terrible
And failed to stop you.

*See *Wise Women*, ed. Susan Cahill

Only God could but He
wouldn't stop
you
fortress from self-
pity
Humble as a woman anywhere
I remember finding you inside the

   laundromat
in Ruleville
            lion spine relaxed/hell
            what's the point to courage
            when you washin clothes?

But that took courage

     just to sit there/target
     to the killers lookin
     for your singin face
     perspirey through the rinse
     and spin

and later
you stood mighty in the door on James Street
loud callin:

   "BULLETS OR NO BULLETS!
   THE FOOD IS COOKED
   AN' GETTIN COLD!"

We ate
A family tremulous but fortified
by turnips/okra/handpicked
like the lilies

filled to the very living
full
one solid gospel
        (*sanctified*)
   one gospel
        (*peace*)

one full Black lily
luminescent
in a homemade field

of love

MARGE PIERCY

(1936–)

A prolific writer—there are more than twelve volumes of poetry and six novels—Piercy found her inspiration as a poet and novelist in the sixties, when she worked in the anti–Vietnam War movement and the women's movement. Her work reflects her politics and her origins in a working-class Jewish family in Detroit, Michigan. The voice is at times harsh and darkly comic (her Barbie is a killer), at times visionary: A good daughter, in many poems she expresses a pragmatic love for her Mother Earth. The varieties of cultural oppression that she sees so acutely inspire her regular advocacy of cultural reinvention: "The myths we are living shape our choices; what we use we must remake."

Barbie doll

This girlchild was born as usual
and presented dolls that did pee-pee
and miniature GE stoves and irons
and wee lipsticks the color of cherry candy.
Then in the magic of puberty, a classmate said:
You have a great big nose and fat legs.

She was healthy, tested intelligent,
possessed strong arms and back,
abundant sexual drive and manual dexterity.
She went to and fro apologizing.
Everyone saw a fat nose on thick legs.

She was advised to play coy,
exhorted to come on hearty,
exercise, diet, smile and wheedle.
Her good nature wore out
like a fan belt.
So she cut off her nose and her legs
and offered them up.

In the casket displayed on satin she lay
with the undertaker's cosmetics painted on,

a turned-up putty nose,
dressed in a pink and white nightie.
Doesn't she look pretty? everyone said.
Consummation at last.
To every woman a happy ending.

JOYCE CAROL OATES

(1938–)

Oates grew up near Buffalo, New York, in an Irish-Catholic working-class family. A major contemporary writer—she's published more than seventy-five volumes of fiction, plays, poems, and essays—she has made the violence of families and the random and sexual aggression of teenagers a central theme of her fiction. Within this sinister and loveless culture, she plots the odyssey of the self: What she calls "the phantasmagoria of personality" trouble the lives of her characters, who are often the uncomprehending victims of unlucky circumstances. Though critics pay more attention to her novels than to her short stories, Oates won so many O. Henry awards for best short story of the year that the O. Henry Award committee gave her a special prize for continuing achievement.

Christmas Night 1962

Come on then! he said. Goddamn you I'll take you.

My mother was in the back bedroom crying. Christmas night, you wouldn't think it could still be the same day. She'd been crying seeing the raggedy doll thrown across the room. She'd been drinking too except with her, unlike the men, it made the freckles come out in her face, and the skin beneath like skim milk. It made her walk strange like the floor was tilted and laugh when nothing was funny and rub her knuckles into her eyes like she was trying to wake up and not succeeding. Her hair red-frizzed like mine except it was coarser than mine which was so fine I'd squirm and whimper when she ran the hairbrush through, then the steel comb. Frantic to get every last one of the snarls out she said, damn you hush! don't be a baby.

It started after we got home from Grandpa's. He was on the sofa watching the same TV football they'd had on at the other house then he said something making her laugh that sharp laugh like scraping your finger on a blackboard and that was the mistake. For always there was a mistake you could point to. First he slapped her with his open hand and she screamed and turned over the table where some of the presents were from that morning, and his beer, and somehow it happened the raggedy doll that was Grandma's present for me went flying across the room hitting the doorframe banging its head *crack!*

She'd tried to stop him but she'd run into his fist—more than his fist. When it happens it happens fast. Like the boxing he took us to in Port Oriskany, the men up in the ring in the lights coming at each other slow and wary so you think nothing's going to happen you could shut your eyes seeing something far away but suddenly people are yelling and it's happening faster than you can see so you have to invent what it was to account for one of the boxers down on the canvas, blood leaking from his mouth. Just like that, that fast, in the living room with the TV on high and the Christmas tree in the corner knocked now on its side and some of the glass bulbs shattered.

I cried, I wasn't to blame. I knew I would be blamed.

The red-swirled glass bulbs shaped like pears, that Grandma gave us, the ones that were so beautiful. And the frosted white ones with the glitter dust. Home by myself I'd drag the cardboard box of ornaments out of the closet just to look through them, touch them. The tinsel for looping over the tree branches, the colored lights in the shape of candles, the angel for the top of the tree with her pretty painted-on face and gold halo like the statue of the Blessed Virgin Mary in church. Where the tree was fallen over, the angel hung upside down like something in a cartoon.

Come on Honey, he said, wiping his mouth, squatting over where the raggedy doll was broken on the floor. You know you're okay.

If you'd stop that goddamn fucking crying, he said. His face going white like the blood was being squeezed out of it.

My mother came out of the back bedroom running with towels and a blanket and she screamed at him to get away, she was going to take me to Yewville to the hospital and he shoved at her saying she was too pissed to drive and she screamed *he* was too pissed, *he* was the crazy one, if he took me out of the house she'd call the police. He said, You call the police and I'll rip you apart, go for that phone to call anybody you'll wish you were never born, nor her either. She was trying to wrap the towel around my head where I was bleeding and they both pulled at me, *he* was going to take me he said, he guessed my leg might be broken, and my mother ran back into the bedroom then returned with the gun waving it at him, holding it in both hands waving it at him, You think I won't? You bastard, you think I won't?

This pistol he'd brought home last summer, he'd won playing poker. My mother was scared to have it in the house but later on, back in the woods, he'd target practice shooting bottles and got my mother to try it too, giggling and nervous and I'd crouch behind them pressing my hands against my ears as he held her with his right arm around her to steady her, helping her aim, pull the trigger, absorb the kick. And her hiding her face in his neck afterward, breathless from what she'd done.

Now my mother in a velour shirt the color of crushed strawberries ripped off the shoulder from where he'd grabbed her and her black slacks glistening with blood holding that pistol trembling in her hands. Screaming and waving it her eyes wild so he backed off on his haunches, Okay Anna, okay just don't pull that trigger, you're crazy enough to do it, and she said, That's right! I am! Just try me, mister, I *am*!

So she lifted me and wrapped me in the blanket holding him off with the gun. The blood soaked into the gray wool making it wet. I was crying, I couldn't stop, like hiccups when you can't stop. She was sobbing too saying, Don't fight me, Honey, you're going to be all right but it hurt so when she lifted me I had to scream.

That Christmas night. Snow blowing gritty as sand. She had to carry me, I couldn't walk where the bone was cracked. My left leg below the knee where I'd hit against the doorframe, and my forehead bleeding and swollen already to the size of a hen's egg. And my mouth, there was something wrong with my mouth Mommy was trying to hold the towel against slipping and sliding out to the car. Oh! oh! oh! our breaths were steaming, she'd grabbed her coat but hadn't time to put on boots. Saying, Honey don't cry Mommy has you safe now okay? trying to fit me in the front seat but I screamed with the pain so she had to put me in the back laying me out flat wrapped in the blanket. I screamed and held onto her not wanting to let go.

Christmas night, and the morning so long ago. Snowdrifts up to the windows, taller than a man by the garage, giant icicles glittering like knife blades hanging down from the roof's edge frozen solid in the minus-ten-degree-fahrenheit cold. That morning the windows were blinding with snow-light and now it was dark, snowflakes swirling in the car headlights like something you could stare and stare into and lose your way not remembering who you are.

I can't tell this. I don't have the words. I remember everything but I don't have the words. Even when I say them, the words are not the right ones.

The raggedy doll sewed by my grandmother, it was big enough for me to need both arms to carry it. A floppy head with shiny black button eyes and a button nose and a smile and orange-red pigtails braided out of yarn. Her top was cotton printed in tiny flowers and her bottom was cotton printed in bright yellow checks and her legs which had no bones were white wool stockings and she was stuffed with something soft like cotton batting. Every year for all the years I could re-member Grandma sewed me a Christmas doll, and things to wear.

I loved Grandma so much. She was his mother so she had to take his side. My other grandmother wasn't here they said and when I asked where was she they said with God in Heaven. But I knew what that was—buried in the cemetery that's just a hilly field behind the church.

That morning my mother dressed me for Christmas before she dressed herself. Only a few times a year we'd go to church and Christmas morning was one but *he* didn't go. Mommy brushed my hair wetting and shaping the curls into corkscrew-curls around her fingers then tickling blowing in my ear, Pretty girl! who's my pretty girl! Mommy loves you so. She pulled on over my head the new jumper Grandma had sewed for me for Christmas, soft velour to match

Mommy's shirt she'd sewed too with a big patch pocket green like a strawberry leaf. White woolly socks, black patent-leather shoes but the same old scuffed boots to fit over them.

A little velour bow too in my hair. A row of bobby pins, barrettes. Corkscrew curls to my shoulders so I'd turn my head and feel them moving, tickling. Before Mommy and I went to church he squatted down in front of me staring at me. Cupped my face in his hands looking at me for a long time his eyes like that kind of marble with a glaze to them so the colors inside look cracked. That way I knew he wasn't seeing me though he said, Merry Christmas, sweetheart! The big day's here, eh?

Mommy said in her careful voice, Don't scare her. You scare her looking at her like that.

Like what? he said. Now straightening up, and taking Mommy's chin in his hand, holding her so she had to look at him. Like this?

He used to be Daddy but says not to call him that anymore but sometimes I forget. But after Christmas night I won't forget.

It was at my grandparents' place the drinking started. The big old farmhouse, the long table for Christmas dinner. So much food at two in the afternoon, your stomach isn't ready for it. The men were playing poker and they were loud and laughing and my father was loud winning a hand but louder losing, red-faced and squinting up his eyes laughing like it was a joke only he got. Uncle Dwight who's married to Aunt Helen, Uncle Marcus who's married to Auntie Irene, Uncle Bud who used to be married but isn't now and you're not to ask why, you never ask *why* of adults. Grandpa and Uncle Dwight worked in the gypsum plant on the Jamestown Road where my father did except they were laid off through January. How long after that nobody knew. They'd been laid off, the factory gates chained shut, since before the first snow.

Who can you believe, they said. What any one of them tells you, or you read in the paper, if it's somebody in a suit and tie for sure he's lying to you because he makes his money off you. And if it's a politician he's already lied to get where he is. So fuck it.

Once when I was real little I said that word. My cousins whispered it in my ear and afterward when I said it some people laughed except not Grandma, and not Mommy. Mommy scolded saying that's not a nice word, nice little girls don't say that word. I giggled saying Yes they do! yes they do! and said the word again running around the table where she couldn't catch me. Except this time the way she looked at me I was sorry so I didn't say it ever again, that Mommy could hear.

My mother was driving our old 1957 Chevy along the Canal Road trying to keep the car's tires in the ruts in the snow made by other cars. The snow plow had come by in the morning and all day it had been snowing and now in the night the narrow road was drifting over and she was praying Holy Mary Mother of God! Holy Mary Mother of God! and in the back seat the limp sobbing raggedy doll. Leg cracked below the knee, bleeding from a swelling cut above her eye. And vomit, and the stink of vomit, on the gray blanket. No other cars were on the road. The headlights swung and lurched, snowflakes rushed at the windshield, the car's stops and starts and skids and jolts were stabs of pain Oh! oh! oh! At the steep ramp to the Yewville bridge the drifts are so high the car's front wheels get stuck. Back up, go forward, back up, go forward rocking the car until momentum carries it onto the ramp.

Honey, are you all right?—Honey?—your Mommy's going to take care of you. Don't cry! Don't cry!

Then scared and angry-sounding as the car moves slowly so slowly not five miles an hour across the high windblown shaky plank-floored bridge, Holy Mary Mother of God have mercy on us!

The water tower at the top of Church Street. The steep drop to Memorial Avenue, the ice-slick pavement where the car skids, begins to slide. The front tire jolting against the curb Oh! oh! Seneca Street, Ontario, Locust. The redbrick Episcopal Church with the high tower, the big stained-glass window. Bell Telephone Co. where my mother worked as an operator before she fell in love with and married the man who would be my father. Before she came to live in the country nine miles north of Yewville where I was born, where she became a woman who was a mother and where her life changed and could never return to what it was. And now at Locust near Main there are cars moving with painstaking slowness in the blizzard and my mother has no choice but to follow behind them sobbing Holy Mary help us! help us! God help us! like it was a curse.

At Providence Hospital on Locust and Van Buren there's a Christmas tree blinking red lights over the front entrance and the parking lot is two-thirds empty, drifted over in snow but my mother parks the car and carries me through the snow stinging gritty as sand in our faces and into the brightly lit reception area where there's only a single nurse behind the counter whose eyes swing onto us startled and disapproving. My mother begins to speak and the nurse cuts her off saying there's no emergency room in this hospital you'll have to go to Yewville General don't you know this isn't that kind of hospital, and my mother says, My little girl's hurt, she fell and hurt herself and I think her leg is broken, I think she's hurt her head bad, please can we see a doctor? please is there a doctor? I'll pay— and another nurse comes out and says in a loud voice like my mother might be hard of hearing, Ma'am? would you like us to call ahead to Yewville General? would you like us to call an ambulance to take you there? the two nurses staring at us, keeping their distance. My young mother with her windblown red-frizzed hair, her white skin splotched with freckles like tiny rust-stains, a purplish bruise swelling the right side of her face. Shivering, swaying with the weight of the child in her arms, a girl of about four years of age, wrapped in a blanket stained with blood and vomit. And my mother asks again for a doctor raising her voice and again the nurses raising their voices say you'll have to go to Yewville General, there's no doctor on duty here tonight and there are no emergency room facilities in this hospital and my mother says begging will you look at her, then? please help us will you please help us? coming forward so the nurses speak more sharply saying Sorry ma'am, sorry you'll have to go to Yewville General, we have no emergency room facilities in this hospital ma'am, and my mother begins to shout, Aren't you nurses? what the hell are you if you aren't nurses? my little girl's hurt, my little girl's in pain Goddamn you! and the older nurse says angrily, Ma'am, we'll have to ask you to leave these premises, picks up a telephone receiver threatening to call the police. So my mother backs off, sobbing and cursing carrying me back outside to the car where the headlights are on, the back door's wide open, the back seat already filling up with snow.

Driving then along Van Buren skidding through a red light then stuck behind a sanding truck moving at five miles an hour all the way to East Avenue where the big hospital Yewville General is. Where Auntie Irene was for her surgery and I was brought to visit one Sunday but we don't go to the front entrance, my mother drives around to the rear where the parking lot is filled with snow and almost empty of cars too and she parks at the curb and carries me half-staggering into another bright-lit reception area larger than the other but there's no one in the waiting room and just one woman at the desk saying Yes? What is it? How can we help you? and Mommy says, quick and scared like she knows she's going to be turned away, It's my little girl, she's hurt, I need to see a doctor!—coming forward past the desk toward the double swinging doors NO ADMITTANCE EMERGENCY and the woman calls out, Ma'am! Stop! and a young man in a white uniform appears to block her way and Mommy is saying, We need a doctor, please help us, my little girl is hurt bad, her head! her leg! I think her leg is broken please help us! her voice shrill and her eyes wild like she's been drinking. There's a nurse too saying, You'll have to check in at reception first, ma'am, ma'am?—you have to check in at reception first. My mother is pleading with the young man, Doctor? help us please, will you examine my little girl? she hit her head running, she fell down and I think her leg is broken, please Doctor? her voice rising as if to prevent the young man from interrupting saying he isn't a doctor, he isn't in charge.

Mommy is a thin woman, you wouldn't think she'd be strong enough to carry me, to hold me like this in her arms. The tight hard muscles tensing in her upper arms and shoulders like it's lifting from the bone.

And everybody in this bright-lit place staring at the limp raggedy doll, bleeding from a cut about the left eye. Wrapped in a filthy blanket. Frizzy red corkscrew curls messy as a rat's nest.

The strong smell pierces my nostrils like the dentist's office to make me gag. Mommy hugs me, whispering Honey it's all right, Honey you're safe now, but there's a woman's voice running on and on repeating no patients can be treated at Yewville General Hospital without first filling out the proper forms at reception, yes and you need insurance identification, this is hospital policy, this is New York State law. There's an artificial silver-tinsel Christmas tree, three feet high, on a table, glittery sequin-snow sprinkled onto the green cloth beneath. And brightly wrapped Christmas presents, the kind of presents that if you lift them are just empty boxes. At the reception desk there's a radio playing "Rudolph the Red-Nosed Reindeer." My mother is saying, pleading, I don't know about our insurance, I don't know the name of the insurance, I came out without my wallet and I.D. speaking fast so they can't interrupt, then angry, saying, You're going to take this child! this is a hurt child, an injured child, Goddamn you! And a nurse, an older woman with peach-colored hair and a little fringe of bangs says making her voice steely calm, Ma'am, this is a private hospital and we are not obliged to accept any patient not adequately covered by hospital and medical insurance so if you will please cooperate—, and my mother says screaming, I told you! I don't have my wallet! There isn't time! This is an emergency! Her arms are weakening and give way and she almost drops me on the floor carrying me to a couch in the waiting room, now the voices are louder, there are more of them and more disapproving and Mommy is saying, furious, You think we're trash, is that it, we're white trash is that it! We're poor, we're from the country, we don't count, we're shit on your shoes is that it! Now there's another, older man wearing a white coat, a doctor this time asking what's going on here, and the nurse tells him, and my mother interrupts, You're not going to let my daughter die, Goddamn you, you sons of bitches you're not going to let my daughter die, taking the pistol out of her coat pocket and waving it in their faces her hand trembling and her eyes wild and frightened as everybody goes Oh! oh! shrinking back in astonishment and the quick terror of animals you see in their eyes in a car's headlights at night but my mother lets the pistol fall, she's sobbing Goddamn you, Goddamn you, letting it fall clattering onto the floor and for a long moment there's no sound except over the radio the tinkly jingly "Rudolph the Red-Nosed Reindeer" coming to an end.

Then the older man, the doctor, stoops quickly to pick up the pistol. He hands it to the young man saying call the police, please.

And Mommy is standing there panting like she's been running, turning her head from side to side like she's trying to clear it, to wake up. And the doctor says, Yes, I will examine your little girl but you'll remain out here until the police arrive. Do you understand, ma'am?—you will remain out here. And Mommy says her lips moving slow, Yes Doctor.

There's a stretcher brought out to where I'm lying and they lift me onto it and

Mommy wants to help but they make her stand back. Staring at me seeing the ugly bruised cut on my forehead, the slack wet mouth and the bloody root of a missing front tooth, the blanket falls open showing the surprise of the strawberry-red velour jumper sewed by Grandma who loves me. White woolly socks and shiny patent-leather shoes and the skinny leg hanging limp, swelling below the knee like a giant bee had stung it.

On the radio, a woman's happy voice singing "Walking in a Winter Wonder-Land."

This woman who's my mother stands watching as I'm carried into the emergency room of Yewville General Hospital, Yewville, New York, 9:25 P.M. of Christmas night 1962. Standing clenching her fingers into fists her head slightly lowered as if to hide her own injuries and her lips moving and she begins to cry giving herself up to hoarse racking angry sobs, helpless sobs as if, now she's got what she has wanted, now she sees her child taken from her by strangers, now these strangers have yielded as if by magic to her desperate will, bearing me through the doors below NO ADMITTANCE EMERGENCY, she's surrendered me forever. It's over.

ANGELA CARTER
(1940–92)

Carter is British feminism's quickest wit. Reading her criticism, novels, and short stories (collected as *The Bloody Chamber*), you come to understand her point when she said, "Reading is just as creative an activity as writing, and most intellectual development depends upon new readings of old texts." Her criticism overturns old ideas, especially as they thwart a liberated sexual politics. Rick Moody called her "one of the most important thinkers of twentieth-century world literature and one of its most pungent voices." Grace Paley, commenting on the collection from which the following autobiographical piece is taken—*Shaking a Leg: Collected Writings*—remembers the company of "that real, intelligent tough writing woman."

Sugar Daddy

I would say my father did not prepare me well for patriarchy; himself confronted, on his marriage with my mother, with a mother-in-law who was the living embodiment of peasant matriarchy, he had no choice but to capitulate, and did so. Further, I was the child of his mid-forties, when he was just the age to be knocked sideways by the arrival of a baby daughter. He was putty in my hands throughout my childhood and still claims to be so, although now I am middle-aged myself while he, not though you'd notice, is somewhat older than the present century.

I was born in 1940, the week that Dunkirk fell. I think neither of my parents was immune to the symbolism of this, of bringing a little girl-child into the world at a time when the Nazi invasion of England seemed imminent, into the midst of death and approaching dark. Perhaps I seemed particularly vulnerable and precious and that helps to explain the overprotectiveness they felt about me, later on. Be that as it may, no child, however inauspicious the circumstances, could have been made more welcome. I did not get a birthday card from him a couple of years ago; when I querulously rang him up about it, he said: "I'd never forget the day you came ashore." (The card came in the second post.) His turn of phrase went straight to my heart, an organ which has inherited much of his Highland sentimentality.

He is a Highland man, the perhaps atypical product of an underdeveloped, colonialised country in the last years of Queen Victoria, of oat-cakes, tatties and the Church of Scotland, of four years' active service in the First World War, of the hurly-burly of Fleet Street in the 1920s. His siblings, who never left the native village, were weird beyond belief. To that native village he competently removed himself ten years ago.

He has done, I realise, what every Sicilian in New York, what every Cypriot in Camden Town wants to do, to complete the immigrant's journey, to accomplish the perfect symmetry, from A to B and back again. Just his luck, when he returned, that all was as it had been before and he could, in a manner of speaking, take up his life where it left off when he moved south seventy years ago. He went south; and made a career; and married an Englishwoman; and lived in London; and fathered children, in an enormous parenthesis of which he retains only sunny memories. He has "gone home," as immigrants do; he established, in his seventh decade, that "home" has an existential significance for him which is not part of the story of his children's independent lives. My father lives now in his granite house filled with the souvenirs of a long and, I think, happy life. (Some of them bizarre; that framed certificate from an American tramp, naming my father a "Knight of the Road," for example.)

He has a curious, quite unEnglish, ability to live life in, as it were, the *third person*, to see his life objectively, as a not unfortunate one, and to live up to that notion. Those granite townships on the edge of the steel-grey North Sea forge a flinty sense of self. Don't think, from all this, he isn't a volatile man. He laughs easily, cries easily, and to his example I attribute my conviction that tears, in a man, are a sign of inner strength.

He is still capable of surprising me. He recently prepared an electric bed for my boyfriend, which is the sort of thing a doting father in a Scots ballad might have done had the technology been available at the time. We knew he'd put us in separate rooms—my father is a Victorian, by birth—but not that he'd plug the metal base of Mark's bed into the electric-light fitment. Mark noticed how the bed throbbed when he put his hand on it and disconnected every plug in sight. We ate breakfast, next morning, as if nothing untoward had happened, and I should say, in the context of my father's house, it had not. He is an enthusiastic handyman, with a special fascination with electricity, whose work my mother once described as combining the theory of Heath Robinson with the practice of Mr Pooter.

All the same, the Freudian overtones are inescapable. However, unconsciously, as if *that* were an excuse, he'd prepared a potentially lethal bed for his daughter's lover. But let me not dot the i's and cross the t's. His final act of low, emotional cunning (another Highland characteristic) is to have lived so long; that everything is forgiven, even his habit of referring to the present incumbent by my first husband's name, enough to give anybody a temporary feeling.

He is a man of immense, nay, imposing physical presence, yet I tend to remember him in undignified circumstances.

One of my first memories is how I bust his nose. (I was, perhaps, three years old. Maybe four.) It was on a set of swings in a public park. He'd climbed up Pooterishly to adjust the chains from which the swings hung. I thought he was taking too long and set the swing on which I sat in motion. He wasn't badly hurt but there was a lot of blood. I was not punished for my part in this accident. They were a bit put out because I wanted to stay and play when they went home to wash off the blood.

They. That is my father and my mother. Impossible for me to summon one up out of the past without the other.

Shortly after this, he nearly drowned me, or so my mother claimed. He took me for a walk one autumn afternoon and stopped by the pond on Wandsworth Common and I played a game of throwing leaves into the water until I forgot to let go of one. He was in after me in a flash, in spite of the peril to his gents' natty suiting (ever the dandy, my old man) and wheeled me dripping in my pushchair home to the terrible but short-lived recriminations of my mother. Short-lived because both guilt and remorse are emotions alien to my father. Therefore the just apportioning of blame is not one of his specialities, and though my mother tried it on from time to time, he always thought he could buy us off with treats and so he could and that is why my brother and I don't sulk, much. Whereas she—

She has been dead for more than a decade, now, and I've had ample time to appreciate my father's individual flavour, which is a fine and gamy one, but, as parents, they were far more than the sum of their individual parts. I'm not sure they understood their instinctive solidarity against us, because my mother often tried to make us take sides. Us. As their child, the product of their parenting, I cannot dissociate myself from my brother, although we did not share a childhood for he is twelve years older than I and was sent off, with his gas mask, his packed lunch and his name tag, as an evacuee, a little hostage to fortune, at about the time they must have realised another one was on the way.

I can only think of my parents as a peculiarly complex unit in which neither bulks larger than the other, although they were very different kinds of people and I often used to wonder how they got on, since they seemed to have so little in common, until I realised that was *why* they got on, that not having much in common means you've always got something interesting to talk about. And their children, far from being the *raison d'être* of their marriage, of their ongoing argument, of that endless, quietly murmuring conversation I used to hear, at night, softly, dreamily, the other side of the bedroom wall, were, in some sense, a sideshow. Source of pleasure, source of grief; not the glue that held them together. And neither of us more important than the other, either.

Not that I suspected this when I was growing up. My transition from little girl to ravaged anorexic took them by surprise and I thought they wanted my blood. I didn't know what they wanted of me, nor did I know what I wanted for myself. In those years of ludicrously overprotected adolescence, I often had the feeling of being "pawns in their game" . . . in *their* game, note . . . and perhaps I indeed served an instrumental function, at that time, rather than being loved for myself.

All this is so much water under the bridge. Yet those were the only years I can remember when my mother would try to invoke my father's wrath against me, threaten me with his fury for coming home late and so on. Though, as far as the "and so on" was concerned, chance would have been a fine thing. My adolescent rebellion was considerably hampered by the fact that I could find nobody to rebel with. I now recall this period with intense embarrassment, because my parents' concern to protect me from predatory boys was only equalled by the enthusiasm with which the boys I did indeed occasionally meet protected themselves against me.

It was a difficult time, terminated, inevitably, by my early marriage as soon as I finally bumped into somebody who would go to Godard movies with me and on CND marches and even have sexual intercourse with me, although he insisted we should be engaged first. Neither of my parents were exactly overjoyed when I got married, although they grudgingly did all the necessary. My father was particularly pissed off because he'd marked me out for a career on Fleet Street. It took me twenty years more of living, and an involvement with the women's movement, to appreciate he was unusual in wanting this for his baby girl. Although he was a journalist himself, I don't think he was projecting his own ambitions on me, either, even if to be a child is to be, to some degree, the projective fantasy of its parents. No. I suspect that, if he ever had any projective fantasies about me, I sufficiently fulfilled them by being born. All he'd wanted for me was a steady, enjoyable job that, perhaps, guaranteed me sufficient income to ensure I wouldn't too hastily marry some nitwit (a favourite word of his) who would displace him altogether from my affections. So, since from a child I'd been good with words, he apprenticed me to a suburban weekly newspaper when I was eighteen, intending me to make my traditional way up from there. From all this, given my natural perversity, it must be obvious why I was so hell-bent on getting married—not, and both my parents were utterly adamant about this, that getting married meant I'd give up my job.

In fact, it *did* mean that because soon my new husband moved away from London. "I suppose you'll have to go with him," said my mother doubtfully. Anxious to end my status as their child, there was no other option and so I changed direction although, as it turns out, I *am* a journalist, at least some of the time.

As far as projective fantasies go, sometimes it seems the old man is only concerned that I don't end up in the workhouse. Apart from that, anything goes. My brother and I remain, I think, his most constant source of pleasure— always, perhaps, a more positive joy to our father than to our mother, who, a more introspective person, got less pure entertainment value from us, partly, like all mothers, for reasons within her own not untroubled soul. As for my father, few souls are less troubled. He can be simply pleased with us, pleased that we exist, and, from the vantage point of his wondrously serene and hale old age, he contemplates our lives almost as if they were books he can dip into whenever he wants.

As for the books I write myself, my "dirty books," he said the other day: "I was a wee bitty shocked, at first, but I soon got used to it." He introduces me in the third person. "This young woman . . . ." In his culture, it is, of course, a matter of principle to express pride in one's children. It occurs to me that this, too, is not a particularly English sentiment.

Himself, he is a rich source of anecdote. He has partitioned off a little room in the attic of his house, constructed the walls out of cardboard boxes, and there he lies, on a camp-bed, listening to the World Service on a portable radio with his cap on. When he lived in London, he used to wear a trilby to bed but, a formal man, he exchanged it for a cap as soon as he moved. There are two perfectly good bedrooms in his house, with electric blankets and everything, as I well know, but these bedrooms always used to belong to his siblings, now deceased. He moves downstairs into one of these when the temperature in the attic drops too low for even his iron constitution, but he always shifts back up again, to his own place, when the ice melts. He has a ferocious enthusiasm for his own private space. My mother attributed this to a youth spent in the trenches, where no privacy was to be had. His war was the war to end wars. He was too old for conscription in the one after that.

When he leaves this house for any length of time, he fixes up a whole lot of burglar traps, basins of water balanced on the tops of doors, tripwires, bags of flour suspended by strings, so that we worry in case he forgets where he's left what and ends up hoist with his own petard.

He has a special relationship with cats. He talks to them in a soft chirruping language they find irresistible. When we all lived in London and he worked on the night news desk of a press agency, he would come home on the last tube and walk, chirruping, down the street, accompanied by an ever-increasing procession of cats, to whom he would say good night at the front door. On those rare occasions, in my late teens, when I'd managed to persuade a man to walk me home, the arrival of my father and his cats always caused consternation, not least because my father was immensely tall and strong.

He is the stuff of which sitcoms are made.

His everyday discourse, which is conducted in the stately prose of a 1930s *Times* leader, is enlivened with a number of stock phrases of a slightly eccentric, period quality. For example. On a wild night: "Pity the troops on a night like this." On a cold day:

> Cold, bleak, gloomy and glum,
> Cold as the hairs on a polar bear's—

The last word of the couplet is supposed to be drowned by the cries of outrage. My mother always turned up trumps on this one, interposing: "Father!" on an ascending scale.

At random: "Thank God for the Navy, who guard our shores." On entering a room: "Enter the fairy, singing and dancing." Sometimes, in a particularly cheerful mood, he'll add to this formula: "Enter the fairy, singing and dancing and waving her wooden leg."

Infinitely endearing, infinitely irritating, irascible, comic, tough, sentimental, ribald old man, with his face of a borderline eagle and his bearing of a Scots guard, who, in my imagination as when I was a child, drips chocolate from his pockets as, a cat dancing in front of him, he strides down the road bowed down with gifts, crying: "Here comes the Marquess of Carrabus!" The very words, "my father," always make me smile.

But why, when he was so devilish handsome—oh, that photograph in battledress!—did he never marry until his middle thirties? Until he saw my mother, playing tennis with a girlfriend on Clapham Common, and that was it. The die was cast. He gave her his card, proof of his honourable intentions. She took him home to meet her mother. Then he must have felt as though he were going over the top, again.

In 1967 or 1968, forty years on, my mother wrote to me: "He really loves me (I think)." At that time, she was a semi-invalid and he tended her, with more dash than efficiency, and yet remorselessly, cooking, washing up, washing her smalls, hoovering, as if that is just what he'd retired from work to do, up to his elbows in soapsuds after a lifetime of telephones and anxiety. He'd bring her dinner on a tray with always a slightly soiled traycloth. She thought the dirty cloth spoiled the entire gesture. And yet, and yet . . . was she, after all those years, still keeping him on the hook? For herself, she always applauded his ability to spirit taxis up as from the air at crowded railway stations and also the dexterous way he'd kick his own backside, a feat he continued to perform until well into his eighties.

Now, very little of all this has to do with the stern, fearful face of the Father in patriarchy, although the Calvinist north is virtually synonymous with that ideology. Indeed, a short-tempered man, his rages were phenomenal; but they were over in the lightning flash they resembled, and then we all had ice-cream. And there was no fear. So that, now, for me, when fear steps in the door, then love and respect fly out of the window.

I do not think my father has ever asked awkward questions about life, or the world, or anything much, except when he was a boy reporter and asking awkward questions was part of the job. He would regard himself as a law-and-order man, a law-abiding man, a man with a due sense of respect for authority. So far, so in tune with his background and his sense of decorum. And yet somewhere behind all this lurks a strangely free, anarchic spirit. Doorknobs fall from doors the minute he puts his hand on them. Things fall apart. There is a sense that anything might happen. He is a law-and-order man helplessly tuned in to misrule.

And somewhere in all this must lie an ambivalent attitude to the authority to which he claims to defer. Now, my father is not, I repeat, an introspective man. Nor one prone to intellectual analysis; he's always got by on his wits so never felt the need of the latter. But he has his version of the famous story, about one of the Christmas truces during the First World War, which was *his* war, although, when he talks about it, I do not recognise Vera Brittain's war, or Siegfried Sassoon's war, or anything but a nightmarish adventure, for, as I say, he feels no fear. The soldiers, bored with fighting, remembering happier times, put up white flags, moved slowly forward, showed photographs, exchanged gifts—a packet of cigarettes for a little brown loaf . . . and then, he says, "Some fool of a first lieutenant fired a shot."

When he tells his story, he doesn't know what it *means*, he doesn't know what the story shows he really felt about the bloody officers, nor why I'm proud of him for feeling that; nor why I'm proud of him for giving the German private his cigarettes and remembering so warmly the little loaf of bread, and proud of him for his still undiminished anger at the nitwit of a boy whom they were all forced to obey just when the ranks were in a mood to pack it in and go home.

Of course, the old man thinks that, if the rank and file *had* packed it in and gone home in 1915, the Tsar would still rule Russia and the Kaiser Germany, and the sun would never have set on the British Empire. He is a man of grand simplicities. He still grieves over my mother's "leftish" views; indeed, he grieves over mine, though not enough to spoil his dinner. He seems, rather, to regard them as, in some way, genetically linked. I have inherited her nose, after all; so why not my mother's voting patterns?

She never forgave him for believing Chamberlain. She'd often bring it up, at moments of stress, as proof of his gullibility. "And what's more, you came home from the office and said: 'There ain't gonna be a war.'"

See how she has crept into the narrative, again. He wrote to me last year: "Your mammy was not only very beautiful but also very clever." (Always in dialect, always "mammy.") Not that she did anything with it. Another husband might have encouraged her to work, or study, although in the 1930s that would have been exceptional enough in this first-generation middle-class family to have projected us into another dimension of existence altogether. As it was, he, born a Victorian and a sentimentalist, was content to adore, and that, in itself, is sufficiently exceptional, dammit, although it was not good for her moral fibre. She, similarly, trapped by historic circumstances, did not even know, I think, that her own vague discontent, manifested by sick headaches and complicated later on by genuine ill-health, might have had something to do with being a "wife," a role for which she was in some respects ill suited, as my father's tribute ought to indicate, since beauty and cleverness are usually more valued in mistresses than they are in wives. For her sixtieth birthday, he gave her a huge bottle of Chanel No. 5.

For what it's worth, I've never been in the least attracted to older men—nor they to me, for that matter. Why is that? Possibly something in my manner hints I will expect, nay, demand, behaviour I deem appropriate to a father figure, that is, that he kicks his own backside from time to time, and brings me tea in bed, and weeps at the inevitability of loss; and these are usually young men's talents.

Don't think, from all this, it's been all roses. We've had our ups and downs, the old man and I, for he was born a Victorian. Though it occurs to me his unstated but self-evident idea that I should earn my own living, have a career, in fact, may have originated in his experience of the first wave of feminism, that hit in his teens and twenties, with some of whose products he worked, by one of whose products we were doctored. (Our family doctor, Helen Gray, was eighty when she retired twenty years ago, and must have been one of the first women doctors.)

Nevertheless, his Victorianness, for want of a better word, means he feels duty bound to come the heavy father, from time to time, always with a histrionic overemphasis: "You just watch out for yourself, that's all." "Watching out for yourself" has some obscure kind of sexual meaning, which he hesitates to spell out. If advice he gave me when I was a girl (I could paraphrase this advice as "Kneecap them"), if this advice would be more or less what I'd arm my own daughters with now, it ill accorded with the mood of the sixties. Nor was it much help in those days when almost the entire male sex seemed in a conspiracy to deprive me of the opportunity to get within sufficient distance. The old man dowered me with too much self-esteem.

But how can a girl have *too much* self-esteem?

Nevertheless, not all roses. He is, you see, a foreigner; what is more, a Highland man, who struck further into the heartland of England than Charles Edward Stuart's army ever did, and then buggered off, leaving his children behind to carve niches in the alien soil. Oh, he'd hotly deny this version of his life; it is my own romantic interpretation of his life, obviously. He's all for the Act of Union. He sees no difference at all between the English and the Scots, except, once my mother was gone, he saw no reason to remain among the English. And his always unacknowledged foreignness, the extroversion of his manners, the stateliness of his demeanour, his fearlessness, guiltlessness, his inability to feel embarrassment, the formality of his discourse, above all, his utter ignorance of and complete estrangement from the English system of social class, make him a being I puzzle over and wonder at.

It is that last thing—for, in England, he seemed genuinely classless—that may have helped me always feel a stranger, here, myself. He is of perfectly good petty-bourgeois stock; my grandfather owned a shoe shop although, in those days, that meant being able to make the things as well as sell them, and repair them, too, so my grandfather was either a shopkeeper or a cobbler, depending on how you looked at it. The distinction between entrepreneur and skilled artisan may have appeared less fine, in those days, in that town beside the North Sea which still looks as if it could provide a good turnout for a witchburning.

There are all manner of stories about my paternal grandfather, whom I never met; he was the village atheist, who left a fiver in his will to every minister in the place, just in case. I never met my Gaelic-speaking grandmother, either. (She died, as it happens of toothache, shortly before I was born.) From all these stories I know they both possessed in full measure that peculiar Highland ability, much perplexing to early tourists, which means that the meanest, grubbing crofter can, if necessary, draw himself up to his full height and welcome a visitor into his stinking hovel as if its miserable tenant were a prince inviting a foreign potentate into a palace. This is the courtly grace of the authentic savage. The women do it with especially sly elegance. Lowering a steaming bowl on to a filthy tablecloth, my father's sister used to say: "Now, take some delicious kale soup." And it was the water in which the cabbage had been boiled.

It's possible to suspect they're having you on, and so they may be; yet this formality always puts the visitor, no matter what his or her status, in the role of supplicant. Your humiliation is what spares you. When a Highlander grovels, then, oh, then is the time to keep your hand on your wallet. One learns to fear an apology most.

These are the strategies of underdevelopment and they are worlds away from those which my mother's family learned to use to contend with the savage urban class struggle in Battersea, in the 1900s. Some of my mother's family learned to manipulate cynically the English class system and helped me and my brother out. All of them knew, how can I put it, that a good table with clean linen meant self-respect and to love Shakespeare was a kind of class revenge. (Perhaps that is why those soiled tray-cloths upset my mother so; she had no quarrel with his taste in literature.) For my father, the grand gesture was the thing. He entered Harrods like a Jacobite army invading Manchester. He would arrive at my school "to sort things out" like the wrath of God.

This effortless sense of natural dignity, or his own unquestioned worth, is of his essence; there are noble savages in his heredity and I look at him, sometimes, to quote Mayakovsky, "like an Eskimo looking at a train."

For I know so little about him, although I know so much. Much of his life was conducted in my absence, on terms of which I am necessarily ignorant, for he was older than I am now when I was born, although his life has shaped my life. This is the curious abyss that divides the closest kin, that the tender curiosity appropriate to lovers is inappropriate, here, where the bond is involuntary, so that the most important things stay undiscovered. If I am short-tempered, volatile as he is, there is enough of my mother's troubled soul in me to render his very transparency, his psychic good health, endlessly mysterious. He is my father and I love him as Cordelia did, "according to my natural bond." What the nature of that "natural bond" might be, I do not know, and, besides, I have a theoretical objection to the notion of a "natural bond."

But, at the end of *King Lear*, one has a very fair notion of the strength of that bond, whatever it is, whether it is the construct of culture rather than nature, even if we might all be better off without it. And I do think my father gives me far more joy than Cordelia ever got from Lear.

SHARON OLDS

(1942–)

Born in San Francisco, Olds grew up in Berkeley, the daughter of an alcoholic father in a family that practiced, in her words, a "hellfire Episcopalianism." Her seven volumes of poetry have won many awards and sold well; her readings are SRO events. Founder of the poetry workshop at Goldwater Hospital for the severely disabled on Roosevelt Island in New York City, Olds believes: "Everybody is a poet. Or could be. A vein of art courses through all of us." She would put a poet in every elementary and high school, in every hospital and hospice, in every prison. "I think people don't imagine what others' lives are like. That's what the arts are for. We as a species seem to be in need of imagining each other." Other poets praise her work, noting how she "sacralizes," in the words of one, "the sexual and procreative body."

I Go Back to May 1937

I see them standing at the formal gates of their colleges,
I see my father strolling out
under the ochre sandstone arch, the
red tiles glinting like bent
plates of blood behind his head, I
see my mother with a few light books at her hip
standing at the pillar made of tiny bricks with the
wrought-iron gate still open behind her, its
sword-tips black in the May air,
they are about to graduate, they are about to get married,
they are kids, they are dumb, all they know is they are
innocent, they would never hurt anybody.
I want to go up to them and say Stop,
don't do it—she's the wrong woman,
he's the wrong man, you are going to do things
you cannot imagine you would ever do,
you are going to do bad things to children,
you are going to suffer in ways you never heard of,
you are going to want to die. I want to go
up to them there in the late May sunlight and say it,
her hungry pretty blank face turning to me,

her pitiful beautiful untouched body,
his arrogant handsome blind face turning to me,
his pitiful beautiful untouched body,
but I don't do it. I want to live. I
take them up like the male and female
paper dolls and bang them together
at the hips like chips of flint as if to
strike sparks from them, I say
Do what you are going to do, and I will tell about it.

Topography

After we flew across the country we
got in bed, laid our bodies
delicately together, like maps laid
face to face, East to West, my
San Francisco against your New York, your
Fire Island against my Sonoma, my
New Orleans deep in your Texas, your Idaho
bright on my Great Lakes, my Kansas
burning against your Kansas your Kansas
burning against my Kansas, your Eastern
Standard Time pressing into my
Pacific Time, my Mountain Time
beating against your Central Time, your
sun rising swiftly from the right my
sun rising swiftly from the left your
moon rising slowly from the left my
moon rising slowly from the right until
all four bodies of the sky
burn above us, sealing us together,
all our cities twin cities,
all our states united, one
nation, indivisible, with liberty and justice for all.

Bathing the New Born

I love with a fearful love to remember the
first baths I gave this boy—
my second child, so my hands knew what to do,

I laid the tiny torso along my
left forearm, nape of the noodle
neck in the crook of my elbow, hips
tiny as a bird's hips against my wrist, and the
thigh the thickness of a thick pencil held
loosely in the loop of my thumb and forefinger, the
sign that means perfect. I'd soap him slowly, the
long thin cold feet, the
scrotum tight and wrinkled as a rosy
shell so new it was flexible yet, the
miniature underweight athlete's chest, the
gummy furze of the scalp. If I got him too
soapy he'd get so slippery he'd
slide in my grip like an armful of white
buttered noodles, but I'd hold him not too tight,
I knew I was so good for him, and I'd
talk to him the whole time, I'd
tell him about his wonderful body
and the wonderful soap, the whole world made of love,
and he'd look up at me, one week old,
his eyes still wide and apprehensive of his
new life. I love that time
when you croon and croon to them, you can see the
calm slowly entering them, you can
feel it in your anchoring hand, the
small necklace of the spine against the
muscle of your forearm, you feel the fear
leaving their bodies, he lay in the blue
oval plastic baby tub and
looked at me in wonder and began to
move his silky limbs at will in the water.

ALICE WALKER
(1944–   )

In many volumes of poetry, of prizewinning fiction—*The Color Purple*—and of essays that have appeared since 1965, Alice Walker, who grew up in Georgia, the eighth child of sharecroppers, has probed the lives of southern African-American women. The piece that follows here has at its center an old woman, wrapped in silence, excluded from America's bounty (as she'd been from the canon of American literature) until the civil rights revolution led by Martin Luther King Jr. As a college student, Walker knew the movement. During the sixties, she worked on the campaign for voter registration in Georgia and for welfare rights in Mississippi.

The Civil Rights Movement: What Good Was It?

I wrote the following essay in the winter of 1966–67 while sharing one room above Washington Square Park in New York with a struggling young Jewish law student who became my husband It was my first published essay and won the three-hundred-dollar first prize in the annual *American Scholar* essay contest. The money was almost magically reassuring to us in those days of disaffected parents, outraged friends, and one-item meals, and kept us in tulips, peonies, daisies, and lamb chops for several months.

Someone said recently to an old black lady from Mississippi, whose legs had been badly mangled by local police who arrested her for "disturbing the peace," that the Civil Rights Movement was dead, and asked, since it was dead, what she thought about it. The old lady replied, hobbling out of his presence on her cane, that the Civil Rights Movement was like herself, "if it's dead, it shore ain't ready to lay down!"

This old lady is a legendary freedom fighter in her small town in the Delta. She has been severely mistreated for insisting on her rights as an American citizen. She has been beaten for singing Movement songs, placed in solitary confinement in prisons for talking about freedom, and placed on bread and water for praying aloud to God for her jailers' deliverance. For such a woman the Civil Rights Movement will never be over as long as her skin is black. It also will never be over for twenty million others with the same "affliction," for whom the Movement can never "lay down," no matter how it is killed by the press and made dead and buried by the white American public. As long as one black American survives, the struggle for equality with other Americans must also survive. This is a debt we owe to those blameless hostages we leave to the future, our children.

Still, white liberals and deserting Civil Rights sponsors are quick to justify their disaffection from the Movement by claiming that it is all over. "And since it is over," they will ask, "would someone kindly tell me what has been gained by it?" They then list statistics supposedly showing how much more advanced segregation is now than ten years ago—in schools, housing, jobs. They point to a gain in conservative politicians during the last few years. They speak of ghetto riots and of the survey that shows that most policemen are admittedly too anti-Negro to do their jobs in ghetto areas fairly and effectively. They speak of every area that has been touched by the Civil Rights Movement as somehow or other going to pieces.

They rarely talk, however, about human attitudes among Negroes that have undergone terrific changes just during the past seven to ten years (not to mention all those years when there was a Movement and only the Negroes knew about it). They seldom speak of changes in personal lives because of the influence of people in the Movement. They see general failure and few, if any, individual gains.

They do not understand what it is that keeps the Movement from "laying down" and Negroes from reverting to their former *silent* second-class status. They have apparently never stopped to wonder why it is always the white man— on his radio and in his newspaper and on his television—who says that the Movement is dead. If a Negro were audacious enough to make such a claim, his fellows might hanker to see him shot. The Movement is dead to the white man because it no longer interests him. And it no longer interests him because he can afford to be uninterested: he does not have to live by it, with it, or for it, as Negroes must. He can take a rest from the news of beatings, killings, and arrests that reach him from North and South—if his skin is white. Negroes cannot now and will never be able to take a rest from the injustices that plague them, for they—not the white man— are the target.

Perhaps it is naïve to be thankful that the Movement "saved" a large number of individuals and gave them something to live for, even if it did not provide them with everything they wanted. (Materially, it provided them with precious little that they wanted.) When a movement awakens people to the possibilities of life, it seems unfair to frustrate them by then denying what they had thought was of- fered. But what was offered? What was promised? What was it all about? What good did it do? Would it have been better, as some have suggested, to leave the Negro people as they were, unawakened, unallied with one another, unhopeful about what to expect for their children in some future world?

I do not think so. If knowledge of my condition is all the freedom I get from a "freedom movement," it is better than unawareness, forgottenness, and hope- lessness, the existence that is like the existence of a beast. Man only truly lives by knowing; otherwise he simply performs, copying the daily habits of others, but conceiving nothing of his creative possibilities as a man, and accepting someone else's superiority and his own misery.

When we are children, growing up in our parents' care, we await the spark from the outside world. Sometimes our parents provide it—if we are lucky— sometimes it comes from another source far from home. We sit, paralyzed, surrounded by our anxiety and dread, hoping we will not have to grow up into the narrow world and ways we see about us. We are hungry for a life that turns us on; we yearn for a knowledge of living that will save us from our innocuous lives that resemble death. We look for signs in every strange event; we search for heroes in every unknown face.

It was just six years ago that I began to be alive. I had, of course, been living before—for I am now twenty-three—but I did not really know it. And I did not know it because nobody told me that I—a pensive, yearning, typical high-school senior, but Negro—existed in the minds of others as I existed in my own. Until that time my mind was locked apart from the outer contours and complexion of my body as if it and the body were strangers. The mind possessed both thought and spirit—I wanted to be an author or a scientist—which the color of the body denied. I had never seen myself and existed as a statistic exists, or as a phantom. In the white world I walked, less real to them than a shadow; and being young and well hidden among the slums, among people who also did not exist—either in books or in films or in the government of their own lives—I waited to be called to life. And, by a miracle, I was called.

There was a commotion in our house that night in 1960. We had managed to buy our first television set. It was battered and overpriced, but my mother had gotten used to watching the afternoon soap operas at the house where she worked as maid, and nothing could satisfy her on days when she did not work but a continuation of her "stories." So she pinched pennies and bought a set.

I remained listless throughout her "stories," tales of pregnancy, abortion, hypocrisy, infidelity, and alcoholism. All these men and women were white and lived in houses with servants, long staircases that they floated down, patios where liquor was served four times a day to "relax" them. But my mother, with her swollen feet eased out of her shoes, her heavy body relaxed in our only comfortable chair, watched each movement of the smartly coiffed women, heard each word, pounced upon each innuendo and inflection, and for the duration of these "stories" she saw herself as one of them. She placed herself in every scene she saw, with her braided hair turned blond, her two hundred pounds compressed into a sleek size-seven dress, her rough dark skin smooth and *white*. Her husband became "dark and handsome," talented, witty, urbane, charming. And when she turned to look at my father sitting near her in his sweat shirt with his smelly feet raised on the bed to "air," there was always a tragic look of surprise on her face.

Then she would sigh and go out to the kitchen looking lost and unsure of herself. My mother, a truly great woman who raised eight children of her own and half a dozen of the neighbors' without a single complaint, was convinced that she did not exist compared to "them." She subordinated her soul to theirs and became a faithful and timid supporter of the "Beautiful White People." Once she asked me, in a moment of vicarious pride and despair, if I didn't think that "they" were "jest naturally smarter, prettier, better." My mother asked this: a woman who never got rid of any of her children, never cheated on my father, was never a hypocrite if she could help it, and never even tasted liquor. She could not even bring herself to blame "them" for making her believe what they wanted her to believe: that if she did not look like them, think like them, be sophisticated and corrupt-for-comfort's-sake like them, she was a nobody. Black was not a color on my mother; it was a shield that made her invisible.

Of course, the people who wrote the soap-opera scripts always made the Negro maids in them steadfast, trusty, and wise in a home-remedial sort of way; but my mother, a maid for nearly forty years, never once identified herself with the scarcely glimpsed black servant's face beneath the ruffled cap. Like everyone else, in her daydreams at least, she thought she was free.

Six years ago, after half-heartedly watching my mother's soap operas and wondering whether there wasn't something more to be asked of life, the Civil Rights Movement came into my life. Like a good omen for the future, the face of Dr. Martin Luther King, Jr., was the first black face I saw on our new television screen. And, as in a fairy tale, my soul was stirred by the meaning for me of his mission—at the time he was being rather ignominiously dumped into a police van for having led a protest march in Alabama—and I fell in love with the sober and determined face of the Movement. The singing of "We Shall Overcome"—that song betrayed by nonbelievers in it—rang for the first time in my ears. The influence that my mother's soap operas might have had on me became impossible. The life of Dr. King, seeming bigger and more miraculous than the man himself, because of all he had done and suffered, offered a pattern of strength and sincerity I felt I could trust. He had suffered much because of his simple belief in nonviolence, love, and brotherhood. Perhaps the majority of men could not be reached through these beliefs, but because Dr. King kept trying to reach them in spite of danger to himself and his family, I saw in him the hero for whom I had waited so long.

What Dr. King promised was not a ranch-style house and an acre of manicured lawn for every black man, but jail and finally freedom. He did not promise two cars for every family, but the courage one day for all families everywhere to walk without shame and unafraid on their own feet. He did not say that one day it will be us chasing prospective buyers out of our prosperous well-kept neighborhoods, or in other ways exhibiting our snobbery and ignorance as all other ethnic groups before us have done; what he said was that we had a right to live anywhere in this country we chose, and a right to a meaningful well-paying job to provide us with the upkeep of our homes. He did not say we had to become carbon copies of the white American middle class; but he did say we had the right to become whatever we wanted to become.

Because of the Movement, because of an awakened faith in the newness and imagination of the human spirit, because of "black and white together"—for the first time in our history in some human relationship on and off TV—because of the beatings, the arrests, the hell of battle during the past years, I have fought harder for my life and for a chance to be myself, to be something more than a shadow or a number, than I had ever done before in my life. Before, there had seemed to be no real reason for struggling beyond the effort for daily bread. Now there was a chance at that other that Jesus meant when He said we could not live by bread alone.

I have fought and kicked and fasted and prayed and cursed and cried myself to the point of existing. It has been like being born again, literally. Just "knowing" has meant everything to me. Knowing has pushed me out into the world, into college, into places, into people.

Part of what existence means to me is knowing the difference between what I am now and what I was then. It is being capable of looking after myself intellectually as well as financially. It is being able to tell when I am being wronged and by whom. It means being awake to protect myself and the ones I love. It means being a part of the world community, and being *alert* to which part it is that I have joined, and knowing how to change to another part if that part does not suit me. To know is to exist: to exist is to be involved, to move about, to see the world with my own eyes. This, at least, the Movement has given me.

The hippies and other nihilists would have me believe that it is all the same whether the people in Mississippi have a movement behind them or not. Once they have their rights, they say, they will run all over themselves trying to be just like everybody else. They will be well fed, complacent about things of the spirit, emotionless, and without that marvelous humanity and "soul" that the Movement has seen them practice time and time again. "What has the Movement done," they ask, "with the few people it has supposedly helped?" "Got them white-collar jobs, moved them into standardized ranch houses in white neighborhoods, given them nondescript gray flannel suits?" "What are these people now?" they ask. And then they answer themselves, "Nothings!"

I would find this reasoning—which I have heard many, many times from hippies and nonhippies alike—amusing if I did not also consider it serious. For I think it is a delusion, a cop-out, an excuse to disassociate themselves from a world in which they feel too little has been changed or gained. The real question, however, it appears to me, is not whether poor people will adopt the middle-class mentality once they are well fed; rather, it is whether they will ever be well fed enough to be able to choose whatever mentality they think will suit them. The lack of a movement did not keep my mother from *wishing* herself bourgeois in her daydreams.

There is widespread starvation in Mississippi. In my own state of Georgia there are more hungry families than Lester Maddox would like to admit—or even see fed. I went to school with children who ate red dirt. The Movement has prodded and pushed some liberal senators into pressuring the government for food so that the hungry may eat. Food stamps that were two dollars and out of the reach of many families not long ago have been reduced to fifty cents. The price is still out of the reach of some families, and the government, it seems to a lot of people, could spare enough free food to feed its own people. It angers people in the Movement that it does not; they point to the billions in wheat we send free each year to countries abroad. Their government's slowness while people are hungry, its unwillingness to believe that there are Americans starving, its stingy cutting of the price of food stamps, make many Civil Rights workers throw up their hands in disgust. But they do not give up. They do not withdraw into the world of psychedelia. They apply what pressure they can to make the government give away food to hungry people. They do not plan so far ahead in their disillusionment with society that they can see these starving families buying identical ranch-style houses and sending their snobbish children to Bryn Mawr and Yale. They take first things first and try to get them fed.

They do not consider it their business, in any case, to say what kind of life the people they help must lead. How one lives is, after all, one of the rights left to the individual—when and if he has opportunity to choose. It is not the prerogative of the middle class to determine what is worthy of aspiration. There is also every possibility that the middle-class people of tomorrow will turn out ever so much better than those of today. I even know some middle-class people of today who are not *all* bad.

I think there are so few Negro hippies because middle-class Negroes, although well fed, are not careless. They are required by the treacherous world they live in to be clearly aware of whoever or whatever might be trying to do them in. They are middle class in money and position, but they cannot afford to be middle class in complacency. They distrust the hippie movement because they know that it can do nothing for Negroes as a group but "love" them, which is what all paternalists claim to do. And since the only way Negroes can survive (which they cannot do, unfortunately, on love alone) is with the support of the group, they are wisely wary and stay away.

A white writer tried recently to explain that the reason for the relatively few Negro hippies is that Negroes have built up a "super-cool" that cracks under LSD and makes them have a "bad trip." What this writer doesn't guess at is that Negroes are needing drugs less than ever these days for any kind of trip. While the hippies are "tripping," Negroes are going after power, which is so much more important to their survival and their children's survival than LSD and pot.

Everyone would be surprised if the Israelis ignored the Arabs and took up "tripping" and pot smoking. In this country we are the Israelis. Everybody who can do so would like to forget this, of course. But for us to forget it for a minute would be fatal. "We Shall Overcome" is just a song to most Americans, *but we must do it*. Or die.

What good was the Civil Rights Movement? If it had just given this country Dr. King, a leader of conscience, for once in our lifetime, it would have been enough. If it had just taken black eyes off white television stories, it would have been enough. If it fed one starving child, it would have been enough.

If the Civil Rights Movement is "dead," and if it gave us nothing else, it gave us each other forever. It gave some of us bread, some of us shelter, some of us knowledge and pride, all of us comfort. It gave us our children, our husbands, our brothers, our fathers, as men reborn and with a purpose for living. It broke the pattern of black servitude in this country. It shattered the phony "promise" of white soap operas that sucked away so many pitiful lives. It gave us history and men far greater than Presidents. It gave us heroes, selfless men of courage and strength, for our little boys and girls to follow. It gave us hope for tomorrow. It called us to life.

Because we live, it can never die.

LESLIE MARMON SILKO

(1948–   )

B orn in Albuquerque, New Mexico, a child of Mexican, Laguna Pueblo, and white background, Silko grew up on the Laguna Pueblo Reservation. The stories and legends she heard about the Native American past from the women in her family seed the novels, poetry, and short stories that have made her reputation as, in the words of a *New York Times* reviewer, "without question the most accomplished Indian writer of her generation." It was her celebrated novel *Ceremony* (1977), the story of a Native American of mixed ancestry who is a veteran of World War II, that won her a large audience, and a few years later, a MacArthur "genius" Award.

Lullaby

The sun had gone down but the snow in the wind gave off its own light. It came in thick tufts like new wool—washed before the weaver spins it. Ayah reached out for it like her own babies had, and she smiled when she remembered how she had laughed at them. She was an old woman now, and her life had become memories. She sat down with her back against the wide cottonwood tree, feeling the rough bark on her back bones; she faced east and listened to the wind and snow sing a high-pitched Yeibechei song. Out of the wind she felt warmer, and she could watch the wide fluffy snow fill in her tracks, steadily, until the direction she had come from was gone. By the light of the snow she could see the dark outline of the big arroyo a few feet away. She was sitting on the edge of Cebolleta Creek, where in the springtime the thin cows would graze on grass already chewed flat to the ground. In the wide deep creek bed where only a trickle of water flowed in the summer, the skinny cows would wander, looking for new grass along winding paths splashed with manure.

Ayah pulled the old Army blanket over her head like a shawl. Jimmie's blanket—the one he had sent to her. That was a long time ago and the green wool was faded, and it was unraveling on the edges. She did not want to think about Jimmie. So she thought about the weaving and the way her mother had done it. On the tall wooden loom set into the sand under a tamarack tree for shade. She could see it clearly. She had been only a little girl when her grandma gave her the wooden combs to pull the twigs and burrs from the raw, freshly washed wool. And while she combed the wool, her grandma sat beside her, spinning a silvery strand of yarn around the smooth cedar spindle. Her mother worked at the loom with yarns dyed bright yellow and red and gold. She watched them dye the yarn in boiling black pots full of beeweed petals, juniper berries, and sage. The blankets her mother made were soft and woven so tight that rain rolled off them like birds' feathers. Ayah remembered sleeping warm on cold windy nights, wrapped in her mother's blankets on the hogan's sandy floor.

The snow drifted now, with the northwest wind hurling it in gusts. It drifted up around her black overshoes—old ones with little metal buckles. She smiled at the snow which was trying to cover her little by little. She could remember when they had no black rubber overshoes; only the high buckskin leggings that they wrapped over their elkhide moccasins. If the snow was dry or frozen, a person could walk all day and not get wet; and in the evenings the beams of the ceiling would hang with lengths of pale buckskin leggings, drying out slowly.

She felt peaceful remembering. She didn't feel cold anymore. Jimmie's blanket seemed warmer than it had ever been. And she could remember the morning he was born. She could remember whispering to her mother, who was sleeping on the other side of the hogan, to tell her it was time now. She did not want to wake the others. The second time she called to her, her mother stood up and pulled on her shoes; she knew. They walked to the old stone hogan together, Ayah walking a step behind her mother. She waited alone, learning the rhythms of the pains while her mother went to call the old woman to help them. The morning was already warm even before dawn and Ayah smelled the bee flowers blooming and the young willow growing at the springs. She could remember that so clearly, but his birth merged into the births of the other children and to her it became all the same birth. They named him for the summer morning and in English they called him Jimmie.

It wasn't like Jimmie died. He just never came back, and one day a dark blue sedan with white writing on its doors pulled up in front of the boxcar shack where the rancher let the Indians live. A man in a khaki uniform trimmed in gold gave them a yellow piece of paper and told them that Jimmie was dead. He said the Army would try to get the body back and then it would be shipped to them; but it wasn't likely because the helicopter had burned after it crashed. All of this was told to Chato because he could understand English. She stood inside the doorway holding the baby while Chato listened. Chato spoke English like a white man and he spoke Spanish too. He was taller than the white man and he stood straighter too. Chato didn't explain why; he just told the military man they could keep the body if they found it. The white man looked bewildered; he nodded his head and he left. Then Chato looked at her and shook his head, and then he told her, "Jimmie isn't coming home anymore," and when he spoke, he used the words to speak of the dead. She didn't cry then, but she hurt inside with anger. And she mourned him as the years passed, when a horse fell with Chato and broke his leg, and the white rancher told them he wouldn't pay Chato until he could work again. She mourned Jimmie because he would have worked for his father then; he would have saddled the big bag horse and ridden the fence lines each day, with wire cutters and heavy gloves, fixing the breaks in the barbed wire and putting the stray cattle back inside again.

She mourned him after the white doctors came to take Danny and Ella away. She was at the shack alone that day they came. It was back in the days before they hired Navajo women to go with them as interpreters. She recognized one of the doctors. She had seen him at the children's clinic at Cañoncito about a month ago. They were wearing khaki uniforms and they waved papers at her and a black ball-point pen, trying to make her understand their English words. She was frightened by the way they looked at the children, like the lizard watches the fly. Danny was swinging on the tire swing on the elm tree behind the rancher's house, and Ella was toddling around the front door, dragging the broomstick horse Chato made for her. Ayah could see they wanted her to sign the papers, and Chato had taught her to sign her name. It was something she was proud of. She only wanted them to go, and to take their eyes away from her children.

She took the pen from the man without looking at his face and she signed the papers in three different places he pointed to. She stared at the ground by their feet and waited for them to leave. But they stood there and began to point and gesture at the children. Danny stopped swinging. Ayah could see his fear. She moved suddenly and grabbed Ella into her arms; the child squirmed, trying to get back to her toys. Ayah ran with the baby toward Danny; she screamed for him to run and then she grabbed him around his chest and carried him too. She ran south into the foothills of juniper trees and black lava rock. Behind her she heard the doctors running, but they had been taken by surprise, and as the hills became steeper and the cholla cactus were thicker, they stopped. When she reached the top of the hill, she stopped to listen in case they were circling around her. But in a few minutes she heard a car engine start and they drove away. The children had been too surprised to cry while she ran with them. Danny was shaking and Ella's little fingers were gripping Ayah's blouse.

She stayed up in the hills for the rest of the day, sitting on a black lava boulder in the sunshine where she could see for miles all around her. The sky was light blue and cloudless, and it was warm for late April. The sun warmth relaxed her and took the fear and anger away. She lay back on the rock and watched the sky. It seemed to her that she could walk into the sky, stepping through clouds endlessly. Danny played with little pebbles and stones, pretending they were birds' eggs and then little rabbits. Ella sat at her feet and dropped fistfuls of dirt into the breeze, watching the dust and particles of sand intently. Ayah watched a hawk soar high above them, dark wings gliding; hunting or only watching, she did not know. The hawk was patient and he circled all afternoon before he disappeared around the high volcanic peak the Mexicans called Guadalupe.

Late in the afternoon, Ayah looked down at the gray boxcar shack with the paint all peeled from the wood; the stove pipe on the roof was rusted and crooked. The fire she had built that morning in the oil drum stove had burned out. Ella was asleep in her lap now and Danny sat close to her, complaining that he was hungry; he asked when they would go to the house. "We will stay up here until your father comes," she told him, "because those white men were chasing us." The boy remembered then and he nodded at her silently.

If Jimmie had been there he could have read those papers and explained to her what they said. Ayah would have known then, never to sign them. The doctors came back the next day and they brought a BIA policeman with them. They told Chato they had her signature and that was all they needed. Except for the kids. She listened to Chato sullenly; she hated him when he told her it was the old woman who died in the winter, spitting blood; it was her old grandma who had given the children this disease. "They don't spit blood," she said coldly. "The whites lie." She held Ella and Danny close to her, ready to run to the hills again. "I want a medicine man first," she said to Chato, not looking at him. He shook his head. "It's too late now. The policeman is with them. You signed the paper." His voice was gentle.

It was worse than if they had died: to lose the children and to know that somewhere, in a place called Colorado, in a place full of sick and dying strangers, her children were without her. There had been babies that died soon after they were born, and one that died before he could walk. She had carried them herself, up to the boulders and great pieces of the cliff that long ago crashed down from Long Mesa; she laid them in the crevices of sandstone and buried them in fine brown sand with round quartz pebbles that washed down the hills in the rain. She had endured it because they had been with her. But she could not bear this pain. She did not sleep for a long time after they took her children. She stayed on the hill where they had fled the first time, and she slept rolled up in the blanket Jimmie had sent her. She carried the pain in her belly and it was fed by everything she saw: the blue sky of their last day together and the dust and pebbles they played with; the swing in the elm tree and broomstick horse choked life from her. The pain filled her stomach and there was no room for food or for her lungs to fill with air. The air and the food would have been theirs.

She hated Chato, not because he let the policeman and doctors put the screaming children in the government car, but because he had taught her to sign her name. Because it was like the old ones always told her about learning their language or any of their ways: it endangered you. She slept alone on the hill until the middle of November when the first snows came. Then she made a bed for herself where the children had slept. She did not lie down beside Chato again until many years later, when he was sick and shivering and only her body could keep him warm. The illness came after the white rancher told Chato he was too old to work for him anymore, and Chato and his old woman should be out of the shack by the next afternoon because the rancher had hired new people to work there. That had satisfied her. To see how the white man repaid Chato's years of loyalty and work. All of Chato's fine-sounding English talk didn't change things.

It snowed steadily and the luminous light from the snow gradually diminished into the darkness. Somewhere in Cebolleta a dog barked and other village dogs joined with it. Ayah looked in the direction she had come, from the bar where Chato was buying the wine. Sometimes he told her to go on ahead and wait; and then he never came. And when she finally went back looking for him, she would find him passed out at the bottom of the wooden steps to Azzie's Bar. All the wine would be gone and most of the money too, from the pale blue check that came to them once a month in a government envelope. It was then that she would look at his face and his hands, scarred by ropes and the barbed wire of all those years, and she would think, this man is a stranger; for forty years she had smiled at him and cooked his food, but he remained a stranger. She stood up again, with the snow almost to her knees, and she walked back to find Chato.

It was hard to walk in the deep snow and she felt the air burn in her lungs. She stopped a short distance from the bar to rest and readjust the blanket. But this time he wasn't waiting for her on the bottom step with his old Stetson hat pulled down and his shoulders hunched up in his long wool overcoat.

She was careful not to slip on the wooden steps. When she pushed the door open, warm air and cigarette smoke hit her face. She looked around slowly and deliberately, in every corner, in every dark place that the old man might find to sleep. The bar owner didn't like Indians in there, especially Navajos, but he let Chato come in because he could talk Spanish like he was one of them. The men at the bar stared at her, and the bartender saw that she left the door open wide. Snowflakes were flying inside like moths and melting into a puddle on the oiled wood floor. He motioned to her to close the door, but she did not see him. She held herself straight and walked across the room slowly, searching the room with every step. The snow in her hair melted and she could feel it on her forehead. At the far corner of the room, she saw red flames at the mica window of the old stove door; she looked behind the stove just to make sure. The bar got quiet except for the Spanish polka music playing on the jukebox. She stood by the stove and shook the snow from her blanket and held it near the stove to dry. The wet wool smell reminded her of new-born goats in early March, brought inside to warm near the fire. She felt calm.

In past years they would have told her to get out. But her hair was white now and her face was wrinkled. They looked at her like she was a spider crawling slowly across the room. They were afraid; she could feel the fear. She looked at their faces steadily. They reminded her of the first time the white people brought her children back to her that winter. Danny had been shy and hid behind the thin white woman who brought them. And the baby had not known her until Ayah took her into her arms, and then Ella had nuzzled close to her as she had when she was nursing. The blonde woman was nervous and kept looking at a dainty gold watch on her wrist. She sat on the bench near the small window and watched the dark snow clouds gather around the mountains; she was worrying about the un-paved road. She was frightened by what she saw inside too: the strips of venison drying on a rope across the ceiling and the children jabbering excitedly in a lan-guage she did not know. So they stayed for only a few hours. Ayah watched the government car disappear down the road and she knew they were already being weaned from these lava hills and from this sky. The last time they came was in early June, and Ella stared at her the way the men in the bar were now staring. Ayah did not try to pick her up; she smiled at her instead and spoke cheerfully to Danny. When he tried to answer her, he could not seem to remember and he spoke English words with the Navajo. But he gave her a scrap of paper that he had found somewhere and carried in his pocket; it was folded in half, and he shyly looked up at her and said it was a bird. She asked Chato if they were home for good this time. He spoke to the white woman and she shook her head. "How much longer?" he asked, and she said she didn't know; but Chato saw how she stared at the boxcar shack. Ayah turned away then. She did not say good-bye.

She felt satisfied that the men in the bar feared her. Maybe it was her face and the way she held her mouth with teeth clenched tight, like there was nothing anyone could do to her now. She walked north down the road, searching for the old man. She did this because she had the blanket, and there would be no place for him ex-cept with her and the blanket in the old adobe barn near the arroyo. They always slept there when they came to Cebolleta. If the money and the wine were gone, she would be relieved because then they could go home again; back to the old hogan with a dirt roof and rock walls where she herself had been born. And the next day the old man could go back to the few sheep they still had, to follow along behind them, guiding them, into dry sandy arroyos where sparse grass grew. She knew he did not like walking behind old ewes when for so many years he rode big quarter horses and worked with cattle. But she wasn't sorry for him; he should have known all along what would happen.

There had not been enough rain for their garden in five years; and that was when Chato finally hitched a ride into the town and brought back brown boxes of rice and sugar and big tin cans of welfare peaches. After that, at the first of the month they went to Cebolleta to ask the postmaster for the check; and then Chato would go to the bar and cash it. They did this as they planted the garden every May, not because anything would survive the summer dust, but because it was time to do this. The journey passed the days that smelled silent and dry like the caves above the canyon with yellow painted buffaloes on their walls.

He was walking along the pavement when she found him. He did not stop or turn around when he heard her behind him. She walked beside him and she noticed how slowly he moved now. He smelled strong of woodsmoke and urine. Lately he had been forgetting. Sometimes he called her by his sister's name and she had been gone for a long time. Once she had found him wandering on the road to the white man's ranch, and she asked him why he was going that way; he laughed at her and said, "You know they can't run that ranch without me," and he walked on determined, limping on the leg that had been crushed many years before. Now he looked at her curiously, as if for the first time, but he kept shuffling along, moving slowly along the side of the highway. His gray hair had grown long and spread out on the shoulders of the long overcoat. He wore the old felt hat pulled down over his ears. His boots were worn out at the toes and he had stuffed pieces of an old red shirt in the holes. The rags made his feet look like little animals up to their ears in snow. She laughed at his feet; the snow muffled the sound of her laugh. He stopped and looked at her again. The wind had quit blowing and the snow was falling straight down; the southeast sky was beginning to clear and Ayah could see a star.

"Let's rest awhile," she said to him. They walked away from the road and up the slope to the giant boulders that had tumbled down from the red sandrock mesa throughout the centuries of rainstorms and earth tremors. In a place where the boulders shut out the wind, they sat down with their backs against the rock. She offered half of the blanket to him and they sat wrapped together.

The storm passed swiftly. The clouds moved east. They were massive and full, crowding together across the sky. She watched them with the feeling of horses—steely blue-gray horses startled across the sky. The powerful haunches pushed into the distances and the tail hairs streamed white mist behind them. The sky cleared. Ayah saw that there was nothing between her and the stars. The light was crystalline. There was no shimmer, no distortion through earth haze. She breathed the clarity of the night sky; she smelled the purity of the half moon and the stars. He was lying on his side with his knees pulled up near his belly for warmth. His eyes were closed now, and in the light from the stars and the moon, he looked young again.

She could see it descend out of the night sky: an icy stillness from the edge of the thin moon. She recognized the freezing. It came gradually, sinking snowflake by snowflake until the crust was heavy and deep. It had the strength of the stars in Orion, and its journey was endless. Ayah knew that with the wine he would sleep.

He would not feel it. She tucked the blanket around him, remembering how it was when Ella had been with her; and she felt the rush so big inside her heart for the babies. And she sang the only song she knew to sing for babies. She could not remember if she had ever sung it to her children, but she knew that her grandmother had sung it and her mother had sung it:

> The earth is your mother,
>   she holds you.
> The sky is your father,
>   he protects you.
> Sleep,
> sleep.
> Rainbow is your sister,
>   she loves you.
> The winds are your brothers,
>   they sing to you.
> Sleep,
> sleep.
> We are together always
> We are together always
> There never was a time
> when this
> was not so.

SANDRA CISNEROS

(1954–)

Cisneros was born in Chicago to a Mexican father and a Chicana mother, the only girl in a family of six boys. In her poetry, short stories—collected in *The House on Mango Street* (1984) and *Woman Hollering Creek* (1991)—and novel—*Carmelo* (2002)—her focus is the Latina community, especially the experience of Chicanas within a male-dominated culture. The title story of her second book of stories—which follows here—has been called "a story good enough to take its place in any anthology of American short stories." In the writer's words, "I write the kind of stories I didn't get growing up, stories about people I knew and loved, but never saw in the pages of the books I borrowed from the Chicago Public Library."

Woman Hollering Creek

The day Don Serafín gave Juan Pedro Martinez Sánchez permission to take Cleófilas Enriqueta DeLeón Hernández as his bride, across her father's threshold, over several miles of dirt road and several miles of paved, over one border and beyond to a town *en el otro lado*—on the other side—already did he divine the morning his daughter would raise her hand over her eyes, look south, and dream of returning to the chores that never ended, six good-for-nothing brothers, and one old man's complaints.

He had said, after all, in the hubbub of parting: I am your father, I will never abandon you. He *had* said that, hadn't he, when he hugged and then let her go. But at the moment Cleófilas was busy looking for Chela, her maid of honor, to fulfill their bouquet conspiracy. She would not remember her father's parting words until later. *I am your father, I will never abandon you.*

Only now as a mother did she remember. Now, when she and Juan Pedrito sat by the creek's edge. How when a man and a woman love each other, sometimes that love sours. But a parent's love for a child, a child's for its parents, is another thing entirely.

This is what Cleófilas thought evenings when Juan Pedro did not come home, and she lay on her side of the bed listening to the hollow roar of the interstate, a distant dog barking, the pecan trees rustling like ladies in stiff petticoats—*shh-shh-shh, shh-shh-shh*—soothing her to sleep.

In the town where she grew up, there isn't very much to do except accompany the aunts and godmothers to the house of one or the other to play cards. Or walk to

267

the cinema to see this week's film again, speckled and with one hair quivering annoyingly on the screen. Or to the center of town to order a milk shake that will appear in a day and a half as a pimple on her backside. Or to the girlfriend's house to watch the latest *telenovela* episode and try to copy the way the women comb their hair, wear their makeup.

But what Cleófilas has been waiting for, has been whispering and sighing and giggling for, has been anticipating since she was old enough to lean against the window displays of gauze and butterflies and lace, is passion. Not the kind on the cover of the *¡Alarma!* magazines, mind you, where the lover is photographed with the bloody fork she used to salvage her good name. But passion in its purest crystalline essence. The kind the books and songs and *telenovelas* describe when one finds, finally, the great love of one's life, and does whatever one can, must do, at whatever the cost.

Tú o Nadie. "You or No One." The title of the current favorite *telenovela*. The beautiful Lucía Méndez having to put up with all kinds of hardships of the heart, separation and betrayal, and loving, always loving no matter what, because *that* is the most important thing, and did you see Lucía Méndez on the Bayer aspirin commercials—wasn't she lovely? Does she dye her hair do you think? Cleófilas is going to go to the *farmacía* and buy a hair rinse; her girlfriend Chela will apply it—it's not that difficult at all.

Because you didn't watch last night's episode when Lucía confessed she loved him more than anyone in her life. In her life! And she sings the song "You or No One" in the beginning and end of the show. *Tú o Nadie.* Somehow one ought to live one's life like that, don't you think? You or no one. Because to suffer for love is good. The pain all sweet somehow. In the end.

Seguín. She had liked the sound of it. Far away and lovely. Not like *Monclova. Coahuia.* Ugly.

Seguín, Tejas. A nice sterling ring to it. The tinkle of money. She would get to wear outfits like the women on the *tele*, like Lucía Méndez. And have a lovely house, and wouldn't Chela be jealous.

And yes, they will drive all the way to Laredo to get her wedding dress. That's what they say. Because Juan Pedro wants to get married right away, without a long engagement since he can't take off too much time from work. He has a very important position in Seguín with, with . . . a beer company, I think. Or was it tires? Yes, he has to be back. So they will get married in the spring when he can take off work, and then they will drive off in his new pickup—did you see it?—to their new home in Seguín. Well, not exactly new, but they're going to repaint the house. You know newlyweds. New paint and new furniture. Why not? He can afford it. And later on add maybe a room or two for the children. May they be blessed with many.

Well, you'll see. Cleófilas has always been so good with her sewing machine. A little *rrrr, rrrr, rrrr* of the machine and *¡zas!* Miracles. She's always been so clever, that girl. Poor thing. And without even a mama to advise her on things like her wedding night. Well, may God help her. What with a father with a head like a burro, and those six clumsy brothers. Well, what do you think! Yes, I'm going to the wedding. Of course! The dress I want to wear just needs to be altered a teensy bit to bring it up to date. See, I saw a new style last night that I thought would suit me. Did you watch last night's episode of *The Rich Also Cry?* Well, did you notice the dress the mother was wearing?

La Gritona. Such a funny name for such a lovely *arroyo*. But that's what they called the creek that ran behind the house. Though no one could say whether the woman had hollered from anger or pain. The natives only knew the *arroyo* one crossed on the way to San Antonio, and then once again on the way back, was called Woman Hollering, a name no one from these parts questioned, little less understood. *Pues, allá de los indios, quién sabe*—who knows, the townspeople shrugged, because it was of no concern to their lives how this trickle of water received its curious name.

"What do you want to know for?" Trini the laundromat attendant asked in the same gruff Spanish she always used whenever she gave Cleófilas change or yelled at her for something. First for putting too much soap in the machines. Later, for sitting on a washer. And still later, after Juan Pedrito was born, for not understanding that in this country you cannot let your baby walk around with no diaper and his pee-pee hanging out, it wasn't nice, *¿entiendes? Pues.*

How could Cleófilas explain to a woman like this why the name Woman Hollering fascinated her. Well, there was no sense talking to Trini.

On the other hand there were the neighbor ladies, one on either side of the house they rented near the *arroyo*. The woman Soledad on the left, the woman Dolores on the right.

The neighbor lady Soledad liked to call herself a widow, though how she came to be one was a mystery. Her husband had either died, or run away with an ice-house floozie, or simply gone out for cigarettes one afternoon and never came back. It was hard to say which since Soledad, as a rule, didn't mention him.

In the other house lived *la señora* Dolores, kind and very sweet, but her house smelled too much of incense and candles from the altars that burned continuously in memory of two sons who had died in the last war and one husband who had died shortly after from grief. The neighbor lady Dolores divided her

time between the memory of these men and her garden, famous for its sun-
flowers—so tall they had to be supported with broom handles and old boards;
red red cockscombs, fringed and bleeding a thick menstrual color; and, especially, roses whose sad scent reminded Cleófilas of the dead. Each Sunday *la
señora* Dolores clipped the most beautiful of these flowers and arranged them
on three modest headstones at the Seguin cemetery.

The neighbor ladies, Soledad, Dolores, they might've known once the name of
the *arroyo* before it turned English but they did not know now. They were too
busy remembering the men who had left through either choice or circumstance
and would never come back.

Pain or rage, Cleófilas wondered when she drove over the bridge the first time
as a newlywed and Juan Pedro had pointed it out. *La Gritona*, he had said, and she
had laughed. Such a funny name for a creek so pretty and full of happily ever after.

The first time she had been so surprised she didn't cry out or try to defend herself.
She had always said she would strike back if a man, any man, were to strike her.

But when the moment came, and he slapped her once, and then again, and
again, until the lip split and bled an orchid of blood, she didn't fight back, she
didn't break into tears, she didn't run away as she imagined she might when she
saw such things in the *telenovelas*.

In her own home her parents had never raised a hand to each other or to their
children. Although she admitted she may have been brought up a little leniently
as an only daughter—*la consentida*, the princess—there were some things she
would never tolerate. Ever.

Instead, when it happened the first time, when they were barely man and wife,
she had been so stunned, it left her speechless, motionless, numb. She had done
nothing but reach up to the heat on her mouth and stare at the blood on her hand
as if even then she didn't understand.

She could think of nothing to say, said nothing. Just stroked the dark curls of
the man who wept and would weep like a child, his tears of repentance and
shame, this time and each.

The men at the ice house. From what she can tell, from the times during her
first year when still a newlywed she is invited and accompanies her husband,
sits mute beside their conversation, waits and sips a beer until it grows warm,
twists a paper napkin into a knot, then another into a fan, one into a rose, nods
her head, smiles, yawns, politely grins, laughs at the appropriate moments,
leans against her husband's sleeve, tugs at his elbow, and finally becomes good
at predicting where the talk will lead, from this Cleófilas concludes each is

nightly trying to find the truth lying at the bottom of the bottle like a gold dou-
bloon on the sea floor.

They want to tell each other what they want to tell themselves. But what is
bumping like a helium balloon at the ceiling of the brain never finds its way out.
It bubbles and rises, it gurgles in the throat, it rolls across the surface of the
tongue, and erupts from the lips—a belch.

If they are lucky, there are tears at the end of the long night. At any given moment, the fists try to speak. They are dogs chasing their own tails before lying
down to sleep, trying to find a way, a route, an out, and—finally—get some peace.

In the morning sometimes before he opens his eyes. Or after they have finished
loving. Or at times when he is simply across from her at the table putting pieces
of food into his mouth and chewing. Cleófilas thinks, This is the man I have
waited my whole life for.

Not that he isn't a good man. She has to remind herself why she loves him
when she changes the baby's Pampers, or when she mops the bathroom floor, or
tries to make the curtains for the doorways without doors, or whiten the linen.
Or wonder a little when he kicks the refrigerator and says he hates this shitty
house and is going out where he won't be bothered with the baby's howling and
her suspicious questions, and her requests to fix this and this and this because if
she had any brains in her head she'd realize he's been up before the rooster earning his living to pay for the food in her belly and the roof over her head and
would have to wake up again early the next day so why can't you just leave me in
peace, woman.

He is not very tall, no, and he doesn't look like the men on the *telenovelas*. His
face still scarred from acne. And he has a bit of a belly from all the beer he drinks.
Well, he's always been husky.

This man who farts and belches and snores as well as laughs and kisses and holds
her. Somehow this husband whose whiskers she finds each morning in the sink,
whose shoes she must air each evening on the porch, this husband who cuts his
fingernails in public, laughs loudly, curses like a man, and demands each course of
dinner be served on a separate plate like at his mother's, as soon as he gets home,
on time or late, and who doesn't care at all for music or *telenovelas* or romance or
roses or the moon floating pearly over the *arroyo*, or through the bedroom window
for that matter, shut the blinds and go back to sleep, this man, this father, this ri-
val, this keeper, this lord, this master, this husband till kingdom come.

A doubt. Slender as a hair. A washed cup set back on the shelf wrong-side-up. Her
lipstick, and body talc, and hairbrush all arranged in the bathroom a different way.

No. Her imagination. The house the same as always. Nothing.

Coming home from the hospital with her new son, her husband. Something comforting in discovering her house slippers beneath the bed, the faded house-coat where she left it on the bathroom hook. Her pillow. Their bed.

Sweet sweet homecoming. Sweet as the scent of face powder in the air, jasmine, sticky liquor.

Smudged fingerprint on the door. Crushed cigarette in a glass. Wrinkle in the brain crumpling to a crease.

Sometimes she thinks of her father's house. But how could she go back there? What a disgrace. What would the neighbors say? Coming home like that with one baby on her hip and one in the oven. Where's your husband?

The town of gossips. The town of dust and despair. Which she has traded for this town of gossips. This town of dust, despair. Houses farther apart perhaps, though no more privacy because of it. No leafy *zócalo* in the center of the town, though the murmur of talk is clear enough all the same. No huddled whispering on the church steps each Sunday. Because here the whispering begins at sunset at the ice house instead.

This town with its silly pride for a bronze pecan the size of a baby carriage in front of the city hall. TV repair shop, drugstore, hardware, dry cleaner's, chiropractor's, liquor store, bail bonds, empty storefront, and nothing, nothing, nothing of interest. Nothing one could walk to, at any rate. Because the towns here are built so that you have to depend on husbands. Or you stay home. Or you drive. If you're rich enough to own, allowed to drive, your own car.

There is no place to go. Unless one counts the neighbor ladies. Soledad on one side, Dolores on the other. Or the creek.

Don't go out there after dark, *mi'jita*. Stay near the house. *No es bueno para la salud. Mala suerte. Bad luck. Mal aire.* You'll get sick and the baby too. You'll catch a fright wandering about in the dark, and then you'll see how right we were.

The stream sometimes only a muddy puddle in the summer, though now in the springtime, because of the rains, a good-size alive thing, a thing with a voice all its own, all day and all night calling in its high, silver voice. Is it La Llorona, the weeping woman? La Llorona, who drowned her own children. Perhaps La Llorona is the one they named the creek after, she thinks, remembering all the stories she learned as a child.

La Llorona calling to her. She is sure of it. Cleófilas sets the baby's Donald Duck blanket on the grass. Listens. The day sky turning to night. The baby pulling up fistfuls of grass and laughing. La Llorona. Wonders if something as quiet as this drives a woman to the darkness under the trees.

* * *

What she needs is . . . and made a gesture as if to yank a woman's buttocks to his groin. Maximiliano, the foul-smelling fool from across the road, said this and set the men laughing, but Cleófilas just muttered, *Grosera*, and went on washing dishes.

She knew he said it not because it was true, but more because it was he who needed to sleep with a woman, instead of drinking each night at the ice house and stumbling home alone.

Maximiliano who was said to have killed his wife in an ice-house brawl when she came at him with a mop. I had to shoot, he had said—she was armed.

Their laughter outside the kitchen window. Her husband's, his friends'. Manolo, Beto, Efraín, el Perico. Maximiliano.

Was Cleófilas just exaggerating as her husband always said? It seemed the newspapers were full of such stories. This woman found on the side of the interstate. This one pushed from a moving car. This one's cadaver, this one unconscious, this one beaten blue. Her ex-husband, her husband, her lover, her father, her brother, her uncle, her friend, her co-worker. Always. The same grisly news in the pages of the dailies. She dunked a glass under the soapy water for a moment—shivered.

He had thrown a book. Hers. From across the room. A hot welt across the cheek. She could forgive that. But what stung more was the fact it was *her* book, a love story by Corín Tellado, what she loved most now that she lived in the U.S., without a television set, without the *telenovelas*.

Except now and again when her husband was away and she could manage it, the few episodes glimpsed at the neighbor lady Soledad's house because Dolores didn't care for that sort of thing, though Soledad was often kind enough to retell what had happened on what episode of *María de Nadie*, the poor Argentine country girl who had the ill fortune of falling in love with the beautiful son of the Arrocha family, the very family she worked for, whose roof she slept under and whose floors she vacuumed, while in that same house, with the dust brooms and floor cleaners as witnesses, the square-jawed Juan Carlos Arrocha had uttered words of love, I love you, María, listen to me, *mi querida*, but it was she who had to say No, no, we are not of the same class, and remind him it was not his place nor hers to fall in love, while all the while her heart was breaking, can you imagine.

Cleófilas thought her life would have to be like that, like a *telenovela*, only now the episodes got sadder and sadder. And there were no commercials in between for comic relief. And no happy ending in sight. She thought this when she sat with the baby out by the creek behind the house. Cleófilas de . . . ? But somehow she would have to change her name to Topazio, or Yesenia, Cristal, Adriana, Stefania, Andrea, something more poetic than Cleófilas. Everything happened to women with names like jewels. But what happened to a Cleófilas? Nothing. But a crack in the face.

Because the doctor has said so. She has to go. To make sure the new baby is all right, so there won't be any problems when he's born, and the appointment card says next Tuesday. Could he please take her. And that's all.

No, she won't mention it. She promises. If the doctor asks she can say she fell down the front steps or slipped when she was out in the backyard, slipped out back, she could tell him that. She has to go back next Tuesday, Juan Pedro, please, for the new baby. For their child.

She could write to her father and ask maybe for money, just a loan, for the new baby's medical expenses. Well then if he'd rather she didn't. All right, she won't. Please don't anymore. Please don't. She knows it's difficult saving money with all the bills they have, but how else are they going to get out of debt with the truck payments? And after the rent and the food and the electricity and the gas and the water and the who-knows-what, well, there's hardly anything left. But please, at least for the doctor visit. She won't ask for anything else. She has to. Why is she so anxious? Because.

Because she is going to make sure the baby is not turned around backward this time to split her down the center. Yes. Next Tuesday at five-thirty. I'll have Juan Pedrito dressed and ready. But those are the only shoes he has. I'll polish them, and we'll be ready. As soon as you come from work. We won't make you ashamed.

Felice? It's me, Graciela.

No, I can't talk louder. I'm at work.

Look, I need kind of a favor. There's a patient, a lady here who's got a problem.

Well, wait a minute. Are you listening to me or what?

I can't talk real loud 'cause her husband's in the next room.

Well, would you just listen?

I was going to do this sonogram on her—she's pregnant, right?—and she just starts crying on me. *Híjole*, Felice! This poor lady's got black-and-blue marks all over. I'm not kidding.

From her husband. Who else? Another one of those brides from across the border. And her family's all in Mexico.

Shit. You think they're going to help her? Give me a break. This lady doesn't even speak English. She hasn't been allowed to call home or write or nothing. That's why I'm calling you.

She needs a ride.

Not to Mexico, you goof. Just to the Greyhound. In San Anto.

No, just a ride. She's got her own money. All you'd have to do is drop her off in San Antonio on your way home. Come on, Felice. Please? If we don't help her, who will? I'd drive her myself, but she needs to be on that bus before her husband gets home from work. What do you say?

I don't know. Wait.

Right away, tomorrow even.

Well, if tomorrow's no good for you . . .

It's a date, Felice. Thursday. At the Cash N Carry off I-10. Noon. She'll be ready.

Oh, and her name's Cleófilas.

I don't know. One of those Mexican saints, I guess. A martyr or something. Cleófilas. C-L-E-O-F-I-L-A-S. Cle. O. Fi. Las. Write it down.

Thanks, Felice. When her kid's born she'll have to name her after us, right?

Yeah, you got it. A regular soap opera sometimes. *Qué vida, comadre. Bueno* bye.

All morning that flutter of half-fear, half-doubt. At any moment Juan Pedro might appear in the doorway. On the street. At the Cash N Carry. Like in the dreams she dreamed.

There was that to think about, yes, until the woman in the pickup drove up. Then there wasn't time to think about anything but the pickup pointed toward San Antonio. Put your bags in the back and get in.

But when they drove across the *arroyo*, the driver opened her mouth and let out a yell as loud as any mariachi. Which startled not only Cleófilas, but Juan Pedrito as well.

Pues, look how cute. I scared you two, right? Sorry. Should've warned you. Every time I cross that bridge I do that. Because of the name, you know. Woman Hollering. *Pues*, I holler. She said this in a Spanish pocked with English and laughed. Did you ever notice, Felice continued, how nothing around here is named after a woman? Really. Unless she's the Virgin. I guess you're only famous if you're a virgin. She was laughing again.

That's why I like the name of that *arroyo*. Makes you want to holler like Tarzan, right?

Everything about this woman, this Felice, amazed Cleófilas. The fact that she drove a pickup. A pickup, mind you, but when Cleófilas asked if it was her husband's, she said she didn't have a husband. The pickup was hers. She herself had chosen it. She herself was paying for it.

I used to have a Pontiac Sunbird. But those cars are for *viejas.* Pussy cars. Now this here is a *real* car.

What kind of talk was that coming from a woman? Cleófilas thought. But then again, Felice was like no woman she'd ever met. Can you imagine, when we crossed the *arroyo* she just started yelling like a crazy, she would say later to her father and brothers. Just like that. Who would've thought?

Who would've? Pain or rage, perhaps, but not a hoot like the one Felice had just let go. Makes you want to holler like Tarzan, Felice had said.

Then Felice began laughing again, but it wasn't Felice laughing. It was gurgling out of her own throat, a long ribbon of laughter, like water.

GISH JEN
(1956–　)

J en writes about the Chinese-American community and the efforts of the first
generation to assimilate; she looks, too, satirically and compassionately, at the
children of the immigrants, and the compromises and losses that both generations
suffer. A child of immigrants herself, she grew up on Long Island and in Scarsdale,
New York, went to Harvard, and now lives in Massachusetts. Her short stories,
which have won many prizes, and her novels, *Typical American* (1991) and *Mona
in the Promised Land* (1996), present the phenomenon of multiculturalism as a
funny and sometimes painful drama of contemporary American life.

Who's Irish?

In China, people say mixed children are supposed to be smart, and definitely my
granddaughter Sophie is smart. But Sophie is wild, Sophie is not like my daughter
Natalie, or like me. I am work hard my whole life, and fierce besides. My husband
always used to say he is afraid of me, and in our restaurant, busboys and cooks all
afraid of me too. Even the gang members come for protection money, they try to
talk to my husband. When I am there, they stay away. If they come by mistake,
they pretend they are come to eat. They hide behind the menu, they order a lot of
food. They talk about their mothers. Oh, my mother have some arthritis, need to
take herbal medicine, they say. Oh, my mother getting old, her hair all white now.

I say, Your mother's hair used to be white, but since she dye it, it become black
again. Why don't you go home once in a while and take a look? I tell them, Con-
fucius say a filial son knows what color his mother's hair is.

My daughter is fierce too, she is vice president in the bank now. Her new house
is big enough for everybody to have their own room, including me. But Sophie
take after Natalie's husband's family, their name is Shea. Irish. I always thought
Irish people are like Chinese people, work so hard on the railroad, but now I know
why the Chinese beat the Irish. Of course, not all Irish are like the Shea family, of
course not. My daughter tell me I should not say Irish this, Irish that.

How do you like it when people say the Chinese this, the Chinese that, she say.

You know, the British call the Irish heathen, just like they call the Chinese, she
say.

You think the Opium War was bad, how would you like to live right next door
to the British, she say.

And that is that. My daughter have a funny habit when she win an argument,

277

she take a sip of something and look away, so the other person is not embarrassed. So I am not embarrassed. I do not call anybody anything either. I just happen to mention about the Shea family, an interesting fact: four brothers in the family, and not one of them work. The mother, Bess, have a job before she got sick, she was executive secretary in a big company. She is handle everything for a big shot, you would be surprised how complicated her job is, not just type this, type that. Now she is a nice woman with a clean house. But her boys, every one of them is on welfare, or so-called severance pay, or so-called disability pay. Something. They say they cannot find work, this is not the economy of the fifties, but I say, Even the black people doing better these days, some of them live so fancy, you'd be surprised. Why the Shea family have so much trouble? They are white people, they speak English. When I come to this country, I have no money and do not speak English. But my husband and I own our restaurant before he die. Free and clear, no mortgage. Of course, I understand I am just lucky, come from a country where the food is popular all over the world. I understand it is not the Shea family's fault they come from a country where everything is boiled. Still, I say.

She's right, we should broaden our horizons, say one brother, Jim, at Thanksgiving. Forget about the car business. Think about egg rolls.

Pad thai, say another brother, Mike. I'm going to make my fortune in pad thai. It's going to be the new pizza.

I say, You people too picky about what you sell. Selling egg rolls not good enough for you, but at least my husband and I can say, We made it. What can you say? Tell me. What can you say?

Everybody chew their tough turkey.

I especially cannot understand my daughter's husband John, who has no job but cannot take care of Sophie either. Because he is a man, he say, and that's the end of the sentence.

Plain boiled food, plain boiled thinking. Even his name is plain boiled: John. Maybe because I grew up with black bean sauce and hoisin sauce and garlic sauce, I always feel something is missing when my son-in-law talk.

But, okay: so my son-in-law can be man, I am baby-sitter. Six hours a day, same as the old sitter, crazy Amy, who quit. This is not so easy, now that I am sixty-eight, Chinese age almost seventy. Still, I try. In China, daughter take care of mother. Here it is the other way around. Mother help daughter, mother ask, Anything else I can do? Otherwise daughter complain mother is not supportive. I tell daughter, We do not have this word in Chinese, *supportive*. But my daughter too busy to listen, she has to go to meeting, she has to write memo while her husband go to the gym to be a man. My daughter say otherwise he will be depressed. Seems like all his life he has this trouble, depression.

No one wants to hire someone who is depressed, she say. It is important for him to keep his spirits up.

Beautiful wife, beautiful daughter, beautiful house, oven can clean itself automatically. No money left over, because only one income, but lucky enough, got the baby-sitter for free. If John lived in China, he would be very happy. But he is not happy. Even at the gym things go wrong. One day, he pull a muscle. Another day, weight room too crowded. Always something.

Until finally, hooray, he has a job. Then he feel pressure.

I need to concentrate, he say. I need to focus.

He is going to work for insurance company. Salesman job. A paycheck, he say, and at least he will wear clothes instead of gym shorts. My daughter buy him some special candy bars from the health-food store. They say THINK! on them, and are supposed to help John think.

John is a good-looking boy, you have to say that, especially now that he shave so you can see his face.

I am an old man in a young man's game, say John.

I will need a new suit, say John.

This time I am not going to shoot myself in the foot, say John.

Good, I say.

She means to be supportive, my daughter say. Don't start the send her back to China thing, because we can't.

Sophie is three years old American age, but already I see her nice Chinese side swallowed up by her wild Shea side. She looks like mostly Chinese. Beautiful black hair, beautiful black eyes. Nose perfect size, not so flat looks like something fell down, not so large looks like some big deal got stuck in wrong face. Everything just right, only her skin is a brown surprise to John's family. So brown, they say. Even John say it. She never goes in the sun, still she is that color, he say. Brown. They say, Nothing the matter with brown. They are just surprised. So brown. Nattie is not that brown, they say. They say, It seems like Sophie should be a color in between Nattie and John. Seems funny, a girl named Sophie Shea be brown. But she is brown, maybe her name should be Sophie Brown. She never go in the sun, still she is that color, they say. Nothing the matter with brown. They are just surprised.

The Shea family talk is like this sometimes, going around and around like a Christmas-tree train.

Maybe John is not her father, I say one day, to stop the train. And sure enough, train wreck. None of the brothers ever say the word *brown* to me again.

Instead, John's mother, Bess, say, I hope you are not offended.

She say, I did my best on those boys. But raising four boys with no father is no picnic.

You have a beautiful family, I say.

I'm getting old, she say.

You deserve a rest, I say. Too many boys make you old.

I never had a daughter, she say. You have a daughter.

I have a daughter, I say. Chinese people don't think a daughter is so great, but you're right. I have a daughter.

I was never against the marriage, you know, she say. I never thought John was marrying down. I always thought Nattie was just as good as white.

I was never against the marriage either, I say. I just wonder if they look at the whole problem.

Of course you pointed out the problem, you are a mother, she say. And now we both have a granddaughter. A little brown granddaughter, she is so precious to me.

I laugh. A little brown granddaughter, I say. To tell you the truth, I don't know how she came out so brown.

We laugh some more. These days Bess need a walker to walk. She take so many pills, she need two glasses of water to get them all down. Her favorite TV show is about bloopers, and she love her bird feeder. All day long, she can watch that bird feeder, like a cat.

I can't wait for her to grow up, Bess say. I could use some female company.

Too many boys, I say.

Boys are fine, she say. But they do surround you after a while.

You should take a break, come live with us, I say. Lots of girls at our house.

Be careful what you offer, say Bess with a wink. Where I come from, people mean for you to move in when they say a thing like that.

Nothing the matter with Sophie's outside, that's the truth. It is inside that she is like not any Chinese girl I ever see. We go to the park, and this is what she does. She stand up in the stroller. She take off all her clothes and throw them in the fountain.

Sophie! I say. Stop!

But she just laugh like a crazy person. Before I take over as baby-sitter, Sophie has that crazy-person sitter, Amy the guitar player. My daughter thought this Amy very creative—another word we do not talk about in China. In China, we talk about whether we have difficulty or no difficulty. We talk about whether life is bitter or not bitter. In America, all day long, people talk about creative. Never mind that I cannot even look at this Amy, with her shirt so short that her belly button showing. This Amy think Sophie should love her body. So when Sophie take off her diaper, Amy laugh. When Sophie run around naked, Amy say she wouldn't want to wear a diaper either. When Sophie go *shu-shu* in her lap, Amy laugh and say there are no germs in pee. When Sophie take off her shoes, Amy say bare feet is best, even the pediatrician say so. That is why Sophie now walk around with no shoes like a beggar child. Also why Sophie love to take off her clothes.

Turn around! say the boys in the park. Let's see that ass!

Of course, Sophie does not understand. Sophie clap her hands, I am the only one to say, No! This is not a game.

It has nothing to do with John's family, my daughter say. Amy was too permissive, that's all.

But I think if Sophie was not wild inside, she would not take off her shoes and clothes to begin with.

You never take off your clothes when you were little, I say. All my Chinese friends had babies, I never saw one of them act wild like that.

Look, my daughter say. I have a big presentation tomorrow.

John and my daughter agree Sophie is a problem, but they don't know what to do.

You spank her, she'll stop, I say another day.

But they say, Oh no.

In America, parents not supposed to spank the child.

It gives them low self-esteem, my daughter say. And that leads to problems later, as I happen to know.

My daughter never have big presentation the next day when the subject of spanking come up.

I don't want you to touch Sophie, she say. No spanking, period.

Don't tell me what to do, I say.

I'm not telling you what to do, say my daughter. I'm telling you how I feel.

I am not your servant, I say. Don't you dare talk to me like that.

My daughter have another funny habit when she lose an argument. She spread out all her fingers and look at them, as if she like to make sure they are still there.

My daughter is fierce like me, but she and John think it is better to explain to Sophie that clothes are a good idea. This is not so hard in the cold weather. In the warm weather, it is very hard.

Use your words, my daughter say. That's what we tell Sophie. How about if you set a good example.

As if good example mean anything to Sophie. I am so fierce, the gang members who used to come to the restaurant all afraid of me, but Sophie is not afraid.

I say, Sophie, if you take off your clothes, no snack.

I say, Sophie, if you take off your clothes, no lunch.

I say, Sophie, if you take off your clothes, no park.

Pretty soon we are stay home all day, and by the end of six hours she still did not have one thing to eat. You never saw a child stubborn like that.

I'm hungry! she cry when my daughter come home.

What's the matter, doesn't your grandmother feed you? My daughter laugh.

No! Sophie say. She doesn't feed me anything!

My daughter laugh again. Here you go, she say.

She say to John, Sophie must be growing.

Growing like a weed, I say.

Still Sophie take off her clothes, until one day I spank her. Not too hard, but she cry and cry, and when I tell her if she doesn't put her clothes back on I'll spank her again, she put her clothes back on. Then I tell her she is good girl, and give her some food to eat. The next day we go to the park and, like a nice Chinese girl, she does not take off her clothes.

She stop taking off her clothes, I report. Finally!

How did you do it? my daughter ask.

After twenty-eight years experience with you, I guess I learn something, I say.

It must have been a phase, John say, and his voice is suddenly like an expert.

His voice is like an expert about everything these days, now that he carry a leather briefcase, and wear shiny shoes, and can go shopping for a new car. On the company, he say. The company will pay for it, but he will be able to drive it whenever he want.

A free car, he say. How do you like that.

It's good to see you in the saddle again, my daughter say. Some of your family patterns are scary.

At least I don't drink, he say. He say, And I'm not the only one with scary family patterns.

That's for sure, say my daughter.

Everyone is happy. Even I am happy, because there is more trouble with Sophie, but now I think I can help her Chinese side fight against her wild side. I teach her to eat food with fork or spoon or chopsticks, she cannot just grab into the middle of a bowl of noodles. I teach her not to play with garbage cans. Sometimes I spank her, but not too often, and not too hard.

Still, there are problems. Sophie like to climb everything. If there is a railing, she is never next to it. Always she is on top of it. Also, Sophie like to hit the mommies of her friends. She learn this from her playground best friend, Sinbad, who is four. Sinbad wear army clothes every day and like to ambush his mommy. He is the one who dug a big hole under the play structure, a foxhole he call it, all by himself. Very hardworking. Now he wait in the foxhole with a shovel full of wet sand. When his mommy come, he throw it right at her.

Oh, it's all right, his mommy say. You can't get rid of war games, it's part of their imaginative play. All the boys go through it.

Also, he like to kick his mommy, and one day he tell Sophie to kick his mommy too.

I wish this story is not true.

Kick her, kick her! Sinbad say.

Sophie kick her. A little kick, as if she just so happened was swinging her little leg and didn't realize that big mommy leg was in the way. Still I spank Sophie and make Sophie say sorry, and what does the mommy say?

Really, it's all right, she say. It didn't hurt.

After that, Sophie learn she can attack mommies in the playground, and some will say, Stop, but others will say, Oh, she didn't mean it, especially if they realize Sophie will be punished.

This is how, one day, bigger trouble come. The bigger trouble start when Sophie hide in the foxhole with that shovel full of sand. She wait, and when I come look for her, she throw it at me. All over my nice clean clothes.

Did you ever see a Chinese girl act this way?

Sophie! I say. Come out of there, say you're sorry.

But she does not come out. Instead, she laugh. Naaah, naah-na, naaa-naaa, she say.

I am not exaggerate: millions of children in China, not one act like this.

Sophie! I say. Now! Come out now!

But she know she is in big trouble. She know if she come out, what will happen next. So she does not come out. I am sixty-eight, Chinese age almost seventy, how can I crawl under there to catch her? Impossible. So I yell, yell, yell, and what happen? Nothing. A Chinese mother would help, but American mothers, they look at you, they shake their head, they go home. And, of course, a Chinese child would give up, but not Sophie.

I hate you! she yell. I hate you, Meanie!

Meanie is my new name these days.

Long time this goes on, long long time. The foxhole is deep, you cannot see too much, you don't know where is the bottom. You cannot hear too much either. If she does not yell, you cannot even know she is still there or not. After a while, getting cold out, getting dark out. No one left in the playground, only us.

Sophie, I say. How did you become stubborn like this? I am go home without you now.

I try to use a stick, chase her out of there, and once or twice I hit her, but still she does not come out. So finally I leave. I go outside the gate.

Bye-bye! I say. I'm go home now.

But still she does not come out and does not come out. Now it is dinnertime, the sky is black. I think I should maybe go get help, but how can I leave a little girl by herself in the playground? A bad man could come. A rat could come. I go back in to see what is happen to Sophie. What if she have a shovel and is making a tunnel to escape?

Sophie! I say.

No answer.

Sophie!

I don't know if she is alive. I don't know if she is fall asleep down there. If she is crying, I cannot hear her.

So I take the stick and poke.

Sophie! I say. I promise I no hit you. If you come out, I give you a lollipop.

No answer. By now I worried. What to do, what to do, what to do? I poke some more, even harder, so that I am poking and poking when my daughter and John suddenly appear.

What are you doing? What is going on? say my daughter.

Put down that stick! say my daughter.

You are crazy! say my daughter.

John wiggle under the structure, into the foxhole, to rescue Sophie.

She fell asleep, say John the expert. She's okay. That is one big hole.

Now Sophie is crying and crying.

Sophia, my daughter say, hugging her. Are you okay, peanut? Are you okay?

She's just scared, say John.

Are you okay? I say too. I don't know what happen, I say.

She's okay, say John. He is not like my daughter, full of questions. He is full of answers until we get home and can see by the lamplight.

Will you look at her? he yell then. What the hell happened?

Bruises all over her brown skin, and a swollen-up eye.

You are crazy! say my daughter. Look at what you did! You are crazy!

I try very hard, I say.

How could you use a stick? I told you to use your words!

She is hard to handle, I say.

She's three years old! You cannot use a stick! say my daughter.

She is not like any Chinese girl I ever saw, I say.

I brush some sand off my clothes. Sophie's clothes are dirty too, but at least she has her clothes on.

Has she done this before? ask my daughter. Has she hit you before?

She hits me all the time, Sophie say, eating ice cream.

Your family, say John.

Believe me, say my daughter.

A daughter I have, a beautiful daughter. I took care of her when she could not hold her head up. I took care of her before she could argue with me, when she was a little girl with two pigtails, one of them always crooked. I took care of her when we have to escape from China, I took care of her when suddenly we live in a country with cars everywhere, if you are not careful your little girl get run over. When my husband die, I promise him I will keep the family together, even though it was just two of us, hardly a family at all.

But now my daughter take me around to look at apartments. After all, I can cook, I can clean, there's no reason I cannot live by myself, all I need is a telephone. Of course, she is sorry. Sometimes she cry, I am the one to say everything will be okay. She say she have no choice, she doesn't want to end up divorced. I say divorce is terrible, I don't know who invented this terrible idea. Instead of live with a telephone, though, surprise, I come to live with Bess. Imagine that. Bess make an offer and, sure enough, where she come from, people mean for you to move in when they say things like that. A crazy idea, go to live with someone else's family, but she like to have some female company, not like my daughter, who does not believe in company. These days when my daughter visit, she does not bring Sophie. Bess say we should give Nattie time, we will see Sophie again soon. But seems like my daughter have more presentation than ever before, every time she come she have to leave.

I have a family to support, she say, and her voice is heavy, as if soaking wet. I have a young daughter and a depressed husband and no one to turn to.

When she say no one to turn to, she mean me.

These days my beautiful daughter is so tired she can just sit there in a chair and fall asleep. John lost his job again, already, but still they rather hire a baby-sitter than ask me to help, even they can't afford it. Of course, the new baby-sitter is much younger, can run around. I don't know if Sophie these days is wild or not wild. She call me Meanie, but she like to kiss me too, sometimes. I remember that every time I see a child on TV. Sophie like to grab my hair, a fistful in each hand, and then kiss me smack on the nose. I never see any other child kiss that way.

The satellite TV has so many channels, more channels than I can count, including a Chinese channel from the Mainland and a Chinese channel from Taiwan, but most of the time I watch bloopers with Bess. Also, I watch the bird feeder—so many, many kinds of birds come. The Shea sons hang around all the time, asking when will I go home, but Bess tell them, Get lost.

She's a permanent resident, say Bess. She isn't going anywhere.

Then she wink at me, and switch the channel with the remote control.

Of course, I shouldn't say Irish this, Irish that, especially now I am become honorary Irish myself, according to Bess. Me! Who's Irish? I say, and she laugh. All the same, if I could mention one thing about some of the Irish, not all of them of course, I like to mention this: Their talk just stick. I don't know how Bess Shea learn to use her words, but sometimes I hear what she say a long time later. *Permanent resident. Not going anywhere.* Over and over I hear it, the voice of Bess.

LORRIE MOORE
(1957–)

The humor that gives Moore's work such energy is part of her strategy: "People being funny with each other is also a kind of generosity between people," she has said. "And I'm interested in that, those little moments of generosity." The short story, according to Moore, "is one of the most beautiful, limber, and rewarding art forms there is . . . presenting the most emotionally enduring and dramatic aspects of a particular encounter or situation. [It's] a very emotional enterprise, like a song. It can be a single emotion pursued and interrogated, and in that way have a sustained intensity. Such a song within a novel would just be a strand, and would get lost. But as a story it is given its very own architecture." A native of Glens Falls, New York, she has published three short story collections — *Birds of America* (1998) was a National Book Award nominee — and two novels, *Anagrams* (1986) and *Who Will Run the Frog Hospital?* (1994).

You're Ugly, Too

You had to get out of them occasionally, those Illinois towns with the funny names: Paris, Oblong, Normal. Once, when the Dow-Jones dipped two hundred points, the Paris paper boasted a banner headline: NORMAL MAN MARRIES OBLONG WOMAN. They knew what was important. They did! But you had to get out once in a while, even if it was just across the border to Terre Haute, for a movie.

Outside of Paris, in the middle of a large field, was a scatter of brick buildings, a small liberal arts college with the improbable name of Hilldale-Versailles. Zoë Hendricks had been teaching American History there for three years. She taught "The Revolution and Beyond" to freshmen and sophomores, and every third semester she had the Senior Seminar for Majors, and although her student evaluations had been slipping in the last year and a half — *Professor Hendricks is often late for class and usually arrives with a cup of hot chocolate, which she offers the class sips of* — generally, the department of nine men was pleased to have her. They felt she added some needed feminine touch to the corridors — that faint trace of Obsession and sweat, the light, fast clicking of heels. Plus they had had a sex-discrimination suit, and the dean had said, well, it was time.

The situation was not easy for her, they knew. Once, at the start of last semester, she had skipped into her lecture hall singing "Getting to Know You" — both verses. At the request of the dean, the chairman had called her into his office, but did not ask her for an explanation, not really. He asked her how she was and then smiled in an avuncular way. She said, "Fine," and he studied the way she said it, her front teeth catching on the inside of her lower lip. She was almost pretty, but her face showed the strain and ambition of always having been close but not quite. There was too much effort with the eyeliner, and her earrings, worn no doubt for the drama her features lacked, were a little frightening, jutting out from the side of her head like antennae.

"I'm going out of my mind," said Zoë to her younger sister, Evan, in Manhattan. *Professor Hendricks seems to know the entire sound track to* The King and I. *Is this history?* Zoë phoned her every Tuesday.

"You always say that," said Evan, "but then you go on your trips and vacations and then you settle back into things and then you're quiet for a while and then you say you're fine, you're busy, and then after a while you say you're going crazy again, and you start all over." Evan was a part-time food designer for photo shoots. She cooked vegetables in green dye. She propped up beef stew with a bed of marbles and shopped for new kinds of silicone sprays and plastic ice cubes. She thought her life was "OK." She was living with her boyfriend of many years, who was independently wealthy and had an amusing little job in book publishing. They were five years out of college, and they lived in a luxury midtown high-rise with a balcony and access to a pool. "It's not the same as having your own pool," Evan was always sighing, as if to let Zoë know that, as with Zoë, there were still things she, Evan, had to do without.

"Illinois. It makes me sarcastic to be here," said Zoë on the phone. She used to insist it was irony, something gently layered and sophisticated, something alien to the Midwest, but her students kept calling it sarcasm, something they felt qualified to recognize, and now she had to agree. It wasn't irony. *What is your perfume?* a student once asked her. *Room freshener*, she said. She smiled, but he looked at her, unnerved.

Her students were by and large good Midwesterners, spacey with estrogen from large quantities of meat and cheese. They shared their parents' suburban values; their parents had given them things, things, things. They were complacent. They had been purchased. They were armed with a healthy vagueness about anything historical or geographic. They seemed actually to know very little about anything, but they were extremely good-natured about it. "All those states in the East are so tiny and jagged and bunched up," complained one of her undergraduates the week she was lecturing on "The Turning Point of Independence: The Battle at Saratoga." "Professor Hendricks, you're from Delaware originally, right?" the student asked her.

"Maryland," corrected Zoë.

"Aw," he said, waving his hand dismissively. "New England."

Her articles—chapters toward a book called *Hearing the One About: Uses of Humor in the American Presidency*—were generally well received, though they came slowly for her. She liked her pieces to have something from every time of day in them—she didn't trust things written in the morning only—so she reread and rewrote painstakingly. No part of a day, its moods, its light, was allowed to dominate. She hung on to a piece for over a year sometimes, revising at all hours, until the entirety of a day had registered there.

The job she'd had before the one at Hilldale-Versailles had been at a small college in New Geneva, Minnesota, Land of the Dying Shopping Mall. Everyone was so blond there that brunettes were often presumed to be from foreign countries. *Just because Professor Hendricks is from Spain doesn't give her the right to be so negative about our country.* There was a general emphasis on cheerfulness. In New Geneva you weren't supposed to be critical or complain. You weren't supposed to notice that the town had overextended and that its shopping malls were raggedy and going under. You were never to say you weren't fine thank you and yourself. You were supposed to be Heidi. You were supposed to lug goat milk up the hills and not think twice. Heidi did not complain. Heidi did not do things like stand in front of the new IBM photocopier, saying, "If this fucking Xerox machine breaks on me one more time, I'm going to slit my wrists."

But now, in her second job, in her fourth year of teaching in the Midwest, Zoë was discovering something she never suspected she had: a crusty edge, brittle and pointed. Once she had pampered her students, singing them songs, letting them call her at home, even, and ask personal questions. Now she was losing sympathy. They were beginning to seem different. They were beginning to seem demanding and spoiled.

"You act," said one of her Senior Seminar students at a scheduled conference, "like your opinion is worth more than everybody else's in the class."

Zoë's eyes widened. "I *am* the teacher," she said. "I *do* get paid to act like that." She narrowed her gaze at the student, who was wearing a big leather bow in her hair, like a cowgirl in a TV ranch show. "I mean, otherwise *everybody* in the class would have little offices and office hours." *Sometimes Professor Hendricks will take up the class's time just talking about movies she's seen.* She stared at the student some more, then added, "I bet you'd like that."

"Maybe I sound whiny to you," said the girl, "but I simply want my history major to mean something."

"Well, there's your problem," said Zoë, and with a smile, she showed the student to the door. "I like your bow," she added.

Zoë lived for the mail, for the postman, that handsome blue jay, and when she got a real letter, with a real full-price stamp, from someplace else, she took it to bed with her and read it over and over. She also watched television until all hours and had her set in the bedroom, a bad sign. *Professor Hendricks has said critical things about Fawn Hall, the Catholic religion, and the whole state of Illinois. It is unbelievable.* At Christmastime she gave twenty-dollar tips to the mailman and to

Jerry, the only cabbie in town, whom she had gotten to know from all her rides to and from the Terre Haute airport, and who, since he realized such rides were an extravagance, often gave her cut rates.

"I'm flying in to visit you this weekend," announced Zoë.

"I was hoping you would," said Evan. "Charlie and I are having a party for Halloween. It'll be fun."

"I have a costume already. It's a bonehead. It's this thing that looks like a giant bone going through your head."

"Great," said Evan.

"It is, it's great."

"Alls I have is my moon mask from last year and the year before. I'll probably end up getting married in it."

"Are you and Charlie getting *married*?" Foreboding filled her voice.

"Hmmmmmmnnno, not immediately."

"Don't get married."

"Why?"

"Just not yet. You're too young."

"You're only saying that because you're five years older than I am and *you're* not married."

"*I'm* not married? Oh, my God," said Zoë. "I forgot to get married."

Zoë had been out with three men since she'd come to Hilldale-Versailles. One of them was a man in the Paris municipal bureaucracy who had fixed a parking ticket she'd brought in to protest and who then asked her to coffee. At first she thought he was amazing—at last, someone who did not want Heidi! But soon she came to realize that all men, deep down, wanted Heidi. Heidi with cleavage. Heidi with outfits. The parking ticket bureaucrat soon became tired and intermittent. One cool fall day, in his snazzy, impractical convertible, when she asked him what was wrong, he said, "You would not be ill-served by new clothes, you know." She wore a lot of gray-green corduroy. She had been under the impression that it brought out her eyes, those shy stars. She flicked an ant from her sleeve.

"Did you have to brush that off in the car?" he said, driving. He glanced down at his own pectorals, giving first the left, then the right, a quick survey. He was wearing a tight shirt.

"Excuse me?"

He slowed down at a yellow light and frowned. "Couldn't you have picked it up and thrown it outside?"

"The ant? It might have bitten me. I mean, what difference does it make?"

"It might have bitten you! Ha! How ridiculous! Now it's going to lay eggs in my car!"

The second guy was sweeter, lunkier, though not insensitive to certain paintings and songs, but too often, too, things he'd do or say would startle her. Once, in a restaurant, he stole the garnishes off her dinner plate and waited for her to notice. When she didn't, he finally thrust his fist across the table and said, "Look," and when he opened it, there was her parsley sprig and her orange slice, crumpled to a wad. Another time he described to her his recent trip to the Louvre. "And there I was in front of Géricault's *Raft of the Medusa*, and everyone else had wandered off, so I had my own private audience with it, all those painted, drowning bodies splayed in every direction, and there's this motion in that painting that starts at the bottom left, swirling and building, and building, and building, and going up to the right-hand corner, where there's this guy waving a flag, and on the horizon in the distance you could see this teeny tiny boat. . . . " He was breathless in the telling. She found this touching and smiled in encouragement. "A painting like that," he said, shaking his head. "It just makes you shit."

"I have to ask you something," said Evan. "I know every woman complains about not meeting men, but really, on my shoots, I meet a lot of men. And they're not all gay, either." She paused. "Not anymore."

"What are you asking?"

The third guy was a political science professor named Murray Peterson, who liked to go out on double dates with colleagues whose wives he was attracted to. Usually the wives would consent to flirt with him. Under the table sometimes there was footsie, and once there was even kneesie. Zoë and the husband would be left to their food, staring into their water glasses, chewing like goats. "Oh, Murray," said one wife, who had never finished her master's in physical therapy and wore great clothes. "You know, I know everything about you: your birthday, your license plate number. I have everything memorized. But then that's the kind of mind I have. Once at a dinner party I amazed the host by getting up and saying good-bye to every single person there, first *and* last names."

"I knew a dog who could do that," said Zoë, with her mouth full. Murray and the wife looked at her with vexed and rebuking expressions, but the husband seemed suddenly twinkling and amused. Zoë swallowed. "It was a Talking Lab, and after about ten minutes of listening to the dinner conversation this dog knew everyone's name. You could say, 'Bring this knife to Murray Peterson,' and it would."

"Really," said the wife, frowning, and Murray Peterson never called again.

"Are you seeing anyone?" said Evan. "I'm asking for a particular reason, I'm not just being like mom."

"I'm seeing my house. I'm tending to it when it wets, when it cries, when it throws up." Zoë had bought a mint-green ranch house near campus, though now she was thinking that maybe she shouldn't have. It was hard to live in a house. She kept wandering in and out of the rooms, wondering where she had put things. She went downstairs into the basement for no reason at all except that it amused her to own a basement. It also amused her to own a tree. The day she moved in, she had tacked to her tree a small paper sign that said *Zoë's Tree*.

Her parents, in Maryland, had been very pleased that one of their children had at last been able to afford real estate, and when she closed on the house they sent her flowers with a Congratulations card. Her mother had even UPS'd a box of old decorating magazines saved over the years, photographs of beautiful rooms her mother used to moon over, since there never had been any money to redecorate. It was like getting her mother's pornography, that box, inheriting her drooled-upon fantasies, the endless wish and tease that had been her life. But to her mother it was a rite of passage that pleased her. "Maybe you will get some ideas from these," she had written. And when Zoë looked at the photographs, at the bold and beautiful living rooms, she was filled with longing. Ideas and ideas of longing.

Right now Zoë's house was rather empty. The previous owner had wallpapered around the furniture, leaving strange gaps and silhouettes on the walls, and Zoë hadn't done much about that yet. She had bought furniture, then taken it back, furnishing and unfurnishing, preparing and shedding, like a womb. She had bought several plain pine chests to use as love seats or boot boxes, but they came to look to her more and more like children's coffins, so she returned them. And she had recently bought an Oriental rug for the living room, with Chinese symbols on it she didn't understand. The salesgirl had kept saying she was sure they meant *Peace* and *Eternal Life*, but when Zoë got the rug home, she worried. What if they didn't mean *Peace* and *Eternal Life*? What if they meant, say, *Bruce Springsteen*. And the more she thought about it, the more she became convinced she had a rug that said *Bruce Springsteen*, and so she returned that, too.

She had also bought a little baroque mirror for the front entryway, which she had been told, by Murray Peterson, would keep away evil spirits. The mirror, however, tended to frighten *her*, startling her with an image of a woman she never recognized. Sometimes she looked puffier and plainer than she remembered. Sometimes shifty and dark. Most times she just looked vague. *You look like someone I know*, she had been told twice in the last year by strangers in restaurants in Terre Haute. In fact, sometimes she seemed not to have a look of her own, or any look whatsoever, and it began to amaze her that her students and colleagues were able to recognize her at all. How did they know? When she walked into a room, how did she look so that they knew it was her? Like this? Did she look like this? And so she returned the mirror.

"The reason I'm asking is that I know a man I think you should meet," said Evan. "He's fun. He's straight. He's single. That's all I'm going to say."

"I think I'm too old for fun," said Zoë. She had a dark bristly hair in her chin, and she could feel it now with her finger. Perhaps when you had been without the opposite sex for too long, you began to resemble them. In an act of desperate invention, you began to grow your own. "I just want to come, wear my bone-head, visit with Charlie's tropical fish, ask you about your food shoots."

She thought about all the papers on "Our Constitution: How It Affects Us" she was going to have to correct. She thought about how she was going in for ul-trasound tests on Friday, because, according to her doctor and her doctor's assis-tant, she had a large, mysterious growth in her abdomen. Gallbladder, they kept saying. Or ovaries or colon. "You guys practice medicine?" asked Zoë, aloud, af-ter they had left the room. Once, as a girl, she brought her dog to a vet, who had told her, "Well, either your dog has worms or cancer or else it was hit by a car."

She was looking forward to New York.

"Well, whatever. We'll just play it cool. I can't wait to see you, hon. Don't for-get your bonehead," said Evan.

"A bonehead you don't forget," said Zoë.

"I suppose," said Evan.

The ultrasound Zoë was keeping a secret, even from Evan. "I feel like I'm dy-ing," Zoë had hinted just once on the phone.

"You're not dying," said Evan. "You're just annoyed."

"Ultrasound," Zoë now said jokingly to the technician who put the cold jelly on her bare stomach. "Does that sound like a really great stereo system, or what?" She had not had anyone make this much fuss over her bare stomach since her boyfriend in graduate school, who had hovered over her whenever she felt ill, waved his arms, pressed his hands upon her navel, and drawled evangelically, "Heal! Heal for thy Baby Jesus' sake!" Zoë would laugh and they would make love, both secretly hoping she would get pregnant. Later they would worry to-gether, and he would sink a cheek to her belly and ask whether she was late, was she late, was she sure, she might be late, and when after two years she had not gotten pregnant, they took to quarreling and drifted apart.

"OK," said the technician absently.

The monitor was in place, and Zoë's insides came on the screen in all their gray and ribbony hollowness. They were marbled in the finest gradations of black and white, like stone in an old church or a picture of the moon. "Do you suppose," she babbled at the technician, "that the rise in infertility among so many couples in this country is due to completely different species trying to reproduce?" The technician moved the scanner around and took more pictures. On one view in particular, on Zoë's right side, the technician became suddenly alert, the machine he was operating clicking away.

Zoë stared at the screen. "That must be the growth you found there," sug-gested Zoë.

"I can't tell you anything," said the technician rigidly. "Your doctor will get the radiologist's report this afternoon and will phone you then."

"I'll be out of town," said Zoë.

"I'm sorry," said the technician.

Driving home, Zoë looked in the rearview mirror and decided she looked— well, how would one describe it? A little wan. She thought of the joke about the guy who visits his doctor and the doctor says, "Well, I'm sorry to say you've got six weeks to live."

"I want a second opinion," says the guy. *You act like your opinion is worth more than everyone else's in the class.*

"You want a second opinion? OK," says the doctor. "You're ugly, too." She liked that joke. She thought it was terribly, terribly funny.

She took a cab to the airport, Jerry the cabbie happy to see her.

"Have fun in New York," he said, getting her bag out of the trunk. He liked her, or at least he always acted as if he did. She called him "Jare."

"Thanks, Jare."

"You know, I'll tell you a secret: I've never been to New York. I'll tell you two secrets: I've never been on a plane." And he waved at her sadly as she pushed her way in through the terminal door. "Or an escalator!" he shouted.

The trick to flying safe, Zoë always said, was never to buy a discount ticket and to tell yourself you had nothing to live for anyway, so that when the plane crashed it was no big deal. Then, when it didn't crash, when you had succeeded in keeping it aloft with your own worthlessness, all you had to do was stagger off, locate your luggage, and, by the time a cab arrived, come up with a persuasive reason to go on living.

"You're here!" shrieked Evan over the doorbell, before she even opened the door. Then she opened it wide. Zoë set her bags on the hall floor and hugged Evan hard. When she was little, Evan had always been affectionate and devoted. Zoë had always taken care of her, advising, reassuring, until recently, when it seemed Evan had started advising and reassuring *her*. It startled Zoë. She suspected it had something to do with Zoë's being alone. It made people uncomfortable. "How *are* you?"

"I threw up on on the plane. Besides that, I'm OK."

"Can I get you something? Here, let me take your suitcase. Sick on the plane. Eeeyew."

"It was into one of those sickness bags," said Zoë, just in case Evan thought she'd lost it in the aisle. "I was very quiet."

The apartment was spacious and bright, with a view all the way downtown along the East Side. There was a balcony and sliding glass doors. "I keep forgetting how nice this apartment is. Twentieth floor, doorman . . . " Zoë could work her whole life and never have an apartment like this. So could Evan. It was Charlie's apartment. He and Evan lived in it like two kids in a dorm, beer cans and clothes strewn around. Evan put Zoë's bag away from the mess, over by the fish tank. "I'm so glad you're here," she said. "Now what can I get you?"

Evan made them a snack—soup from a can, and saltines.

"I don't know about Charlie," she said, after they had finished. "I feel like we've gone all sexless and middle-aged already."

"Hmmm," said Zoë. She leaned back into Evan's sofa and stared out the window at the dark tops of the buildings. It seemed a little unnatural to live up in the sky like this, like birds that out of some wrongheaded derring-do had nested too high. She nodded toward the lighted fish tanks and giggled. "I feel like a bird," she said, "with my own personal supply of fish."

Evan sighed. "He comes home and just sacks out on the sofa, watching fuzzy football. He's wearing the psychic cold cream and curlers, if you know what I mean."

Zoë sat up, readjusted the sofa cushions. "What's fuzzy football?"

"We haven't gotten cable yet. Everything comes in fuzzy. Charlie just watches it that way."

"Hmmm, yeah, that's a little depressing," Zoë said. She looked at her hands. "Especially the part about not having cable."

"This is how he gets into bed at night." Evan stood up to demonstrate. "He whips all his clothes off, and when he gets to his underwear, he lets it drop to one ankle. Then he kicks up his leg and flips the underwear in the air and catches it. I, of course, watch from the bed. There's nothing else. There's just that."

"Maybe you should just get it over with and get married."

"Really?"

"Yeah. I mean, you guys probably think living together like this is the best of both worlds, but . . . " Zoë tried to sound like an older sister; an older sister was supposed to be the parent you could never have, the hip, cool mom. " . . . I've always found that as soon as you think you've got the best of both worlds"—she thought now of herself, alone in her house; of the toad-faced cicadas that flew around like little caped men at night, landing on her screens, staring; of the size fourteen shoes she placed at the doorstep, to scare off intruders; of the ridiculous inflatable blow-up doll someone had told her to keep propped up at the breakfast table—"it can suddenly twist and become the worst of both worlds."

"Really?" Evan was beaming. "Oh, Zoë. I have something to tell you. Charlie and I *are* getting married."

"Really." Zoë felt confused.

"I didn't know how to tell you."

"Yes, well, I guess the part about fuzzy football misled me a little."

"I was hoping you'd be my maid of honor," said Evan, waiting. "Aren't you happy for me?"

"Yes," said Zoë, and she began to tell Evan a story about an award-winning violinist at Hilldale-Versailles, how the violinist had come home from a competition in Europe and taken up with a local man, who made her go to all his summer softball games, made her cheer for him from the stands, with the wives, until she later killed herself. But when she got halfway through, to the part about cheering at the softball games, Zoë stopped.

"What?" said Evan. "So what happened?"

"Actually, nothing," said Zoë lightly. "She just really got into softball. I mean, really. You should have seen her."

Zoë decided to go to a late-afternoon movie, leaving Evan to chores she needed to do before the party—*I have to do them alone*, she'd said, a little tense after the violinist story. Zoë thought about going to an art museum, but women alone in art museums had to look good. They always did. Chic and serious, moving languidly, with a great handbag. Instead, she walked over and down through Kips Bay, past an earring boutique called Stick It in Your Ear, past a beauty salon called Dorian Gray's. That was the funny thing about *beauty*, thought Zoë. Look it up in the yellow pages, and you found a hundred entries, hostile with wit, cutesy with warning. But look up *truth*—ha! There was nothing at all.

Zoë thought about Evan getting married. Would Evan turn into Peter Pumpkin Eater's wife? Mrs. Eater? At the wedding would she make Zoë wear some flouncy lavender dress, identical with the other maids'? Zoë hated uniforms, had even, in the first grade, refused to join Elf Girls, because she didn't want to wear the same dress as everyone else. Now she might have to. But maybe she could distinguish it. Hitch it up on one side with a clothespin. Wear surgical gauze at the waist. Clip to her bodice one of those pins that said in loud letters, SHIT HAPPENS.

At the movie—*Death by Number*—she bought strands of red licorice to tug and chew. She took a seat off to one side in the theater. She felt strangely self-conscious sitting alone and hoped for the place to darken fast. When it did, and the coming attractions came on, she reached inside her purse for her glasses. They were in a Baggie. Her Kleenex was also in a Baggie. So were her pen and her aspirin and her mints. Everything was in Baggies. This was what she'd become: *a woman alone at the movies with everything in a Baggie.*

At the Halloween party, there were about two dozen people. There were people with ape heads and large hairy hands. There was someone dressed as a leprechaun. There was someone dressed as a frozen dinner. Some man had brought his two small daughters: a ballerina and a ballerina's sister, also dressed as a ballerina. There was a gaggle of sexy witches—women dressed entirely in black, beautifully made up and jeweled. "I hate those sexy witches. It's not in the spirit of

Halloween," said Evan. Evan had abandoned the moon mask and dolled herself up as a hausfrau, in curlers and an apron, a decision she now regretted. Charlie, because he liked fish, because he owned fish, collected fish, had decided to go as a fish. He had fins and eyes on the side of his head. "Zoë! How are you! I'm sorry I wasn't here when you first arrived!" He spent the rest of his time chatting up the sexy witches.

"Isn't there something I can help you with here?" Zoë asked her sister. "You've been running yourself ragged." She rubbed her sister's arm, gently, as if she wished they were alone.

"Oh, God, not at all," said Evan, arranging stuffed mushrooms on a plate. The timer went off, and she pulled another sheetful out of the oven. "Actually, you know what you can do?"

"What?" Zoë put on her bonehead.

"Meet Earl. He's the guy I had in mind for you. When he gets here, just talk to him a little. He's nice. He's fun. He's going through a divorce."

"I'll try." Zoë groaned. "OK? I'll try." She looked at her watch.

When Earl arrived, he was dressed as a naked woman, steel wool glued strategically to a body stocking, and large rubber breasts protruding like hams.

"Zoë, this is Earl," said Evan.

"Good to meet you," said Earl, circling Evan to shake Zoë's hand. He stared at the top of Zoë's head. "Great bone."

Zoë nodded. "Great tits," she said. She looked past him, out the window at the city thrown glitteringly up against the sky; people were saying the usual things: how it looked like jewels, like bracelets and necklaces unstrung. You could see Grand Central station, the clock of the Con Ed building, the red-and-gold-capped Empire State, the Chrysler like a rocket ship dreamed up in a depression. Far west you could glimpse the Astor Plaza, its flying white roof like a nun's habit. "There's beer out on the balcony, Earl—can I get you one?" Zoë asked.

"Sure, uh, I'll come along. Hey, Charlie, how's it going?"

Charlie grinned and whistled. People turned to look. "Hey, Earl," someone called, from across the room. "Va-va-va-voom."

They squeezed their way past the other guests, past the apes and the sexy witches. The suction of the sliding door gave way in a whoosh, and Zoë and Earl stepped out onto the balcony, a bonehead and a naked woman, the night air roaring and smoky cool. Another couple was out here, too, murmuring privately. They were not wearing costumes. They smiled at Zoë and Earl. "Hi," said Zoë. She found the plastic-foam cooler, dug into it, and retrieved two beers.

"Thanks," said Earl. His rubber breasts folded inward, dimpled and dented, as he twisted open the bottle.

"Well," sighed Zoë anxiously. She had to learn not to be afraid of a man, the way, in your childhood, you learned not to be afraid of an earthworm or a bug.

Often, when she spoke to men at parties, she rushed things in her mind. As the man politely blathered on, she would fall in love, marry, then find herself in a bitter custody battle with him for the kids and hoping for a reconciliation, so that despite all his betrayals she might no longer despise him, and in the few minutes remaining, learn, perhaps, what his last name was and what he did for a living, though probably there was already too much history between them. She would nod, blush, turn away.

"Evan tells me you're a professor. Where do you teach?"

"Just over the Indiana border into Illinois."

He looked a little shocked. "I guess Evan didn't tell me that part."

"She didn't?"

"No."

"Well, that's Evan for you. When we were kids we both had speech impediments."

"That can be tough," said Earl. One of his breasts was hidden behind his drinking arm, but the other shone low and pink, full as a strawberry moon.

"Yes, well, it wasn't a total loss. We used to go to what we called peach pearapy. For about ten years of my life I had to map out every sentence in my mind, way ahead, before I said it. That was the only way I could get a coherent sentence out."

Earl drank from his beer. "How did you do that? I mean, how did you get through?"

"I told a lot of jokes. Jokes you know the lines to already—you can just say them. I love jokes. Jokes and songs."

Earl smiled. He had on lipstick, a deep shade of red, but it was wearing off from the beer. "What's your favorite joke?"

"Uh, my favorite joke is probably . . . OK, all right. This guy goes into a doctor's office and—"

"I think I know this one," interrupted Earl, eagerly. He wanted to tell it himself. "A guy goes into a doctor's office, and the doctor tells him he's got some good news and some bad news—that one, right?"

"I'm not sure," said Zoë. "This might be a different version."

"So the guy says, 'Give me the bad news first,' and the doctor says, 'OK. You've got three weeks to live.' And the guy cries, 'Three weeks to live! Doctor, what is the good news?' And the doctor says, 'Did you see that secretary out front? I finally fucked her.'"

Zoë frowned.

"That's not the one you were thinking of?"

"No." There was accusation in her voice. "Mine was different."

"Oh," said Earl. He looked away and then back again. "You teach history, right? What kind of history do you teach?"

"I teach American, mostly—eighteenth and nineteenth century." In graduate school, at bars, the pickup line was always: "So what's your century?"

"Occasionally I teach a special theme course," she added, "say, 'Humor and Personality in the White House.' That's what my book's on." She thought of something someone once told her about bowerbirds, how they build elaborate structures before mating.

"Your book's on *humor?*"

"Yeah, and, well, when I teach a theme course like that, I do all the centuries." *So what's your century?*

"All three of them."

"Pardon?" The breeze glistened her eyes. Traffic revved beneath them. She felt high and puny, like someone lifted into heaven by mistake and then spurned.

"Three. There's only three."

"Well, four, really." She was thinking of Jamestown, and of the Pilgrims coming here with buckles and witch hats to say their prayers.

"I'm a photographer," said Earl. His face was starting to gleam, his rouge smearing in a sunset beneath his eyes.

"Do you like that?"

"Well, actually I'm starting to feel it's a little dangerous."

"Really?"

"Spending all your time in a darkroom with that red light and all those chemicals. There's links with Parkinson's, you know."

"No, I didn't."

"I suppose I should wear rubber gloves, but I don't like to. Unless I'm touching it directly, I don't think of it as real."

"Hmmm," said Zoë. Alarm buzzed through her, mildly, like a tea.

"Sometimes, when I have a cut or something, I feel the sting and think, *Shit.* I wash constantly and just hope. I don't like rubber over the skin like that."

"Really."

"I mean, the physical contact. That's what you want, or why bother?"

"I guess," said Zoë. She wished she could think of a joke, something slow and deliberate, with the end in sight. She thought of gorillas, how when they had been kept too long alone in cages, they would smack each other in the head instead of mating.

"Are you . . . in a relationship?" Earl suddenly blurted.

"Now? As we speak?"

"Well, I mean, I'm sure you have a relationship to your *work.*" A smile, a weird one, nestled in his mouth like an egg. She thought of zoos in parks, how when cities were under siege, during world wars, people ate the animals. "But I mean, with a *man.*"

"No, I'm not in a relationship with a *man.*" She rubbed her chin with her hand

and could feel the one bristly hair there. "But my last relationship was with a very sweet man," she said. She made something up. "From Switzerland. He was a botanist—a weed expert. His name was Jerry. I called him 'Jare.' He was so funny. You'd go to the movies with him and all he would notice were the plants. He would never pay attention to the plot. Once, in a jungle movie, he started rattling off all these Latin names, out loud. It was very exciting for him." She paused, caught her breath. "Eventually he went back to Europe to, uh, study the edelweiss." She looked at Earl. "Are you involved in a relationship? With a *woman?*"

Earl shifted his weight, and the creases in his body stocking changed, splintering outward like something broken. His pubic hair slid over to one hip, like a corsage on a saloon girl. "No," he said, clearing his throat. The steel wool in his underarms was inching toward his biceps. "I've just gotten out of a marriage that was full of bad dialogue, like 'You want more *space?* I'll give you more space!' *Clonk.* Your basic Three Stooges."

Zoë looked at him sympathetically. "I suppose it's hard for love to recover after that."

His eyes lit up. He wanted to talk about love. "But *I* keep thinking love should be like a tree. You look at trees and they've got bumps and scars from tumors, infestations, what have you, but they're still growing. Despite the bumps and bruises, they're . . . straight."

"Yeah, well," said Zoë, "where I'm from, they're all married or gay. Did you see that movie *Death by Number?*"

Earl looked at her, a little lost. She was getting away from him. "No," he said.

One of his breasts had slipped under his arm, tucked there like a baguette. She kept thinking of trees, of gorillas and parks, of people in wartime eating the zebras: She felt a stabbing pain in her abdomen.

"Want some hors d'oeuvres?" Evan came pushing through the sliding door. She was smiling, though her curlers were coming out, hanging bedraggled at the ends of her hair like Christmas decorations, like food put out for the birds. She thrust forward a plate of stuffed mushrooms.

"Are you asking for donations or giving them away," said Earl, wittily. He liked Evan, and he put his arm around her.

"You know, I'll be right back," said Zoë.

"Oh," said Evan, looking concerned.

"Right back. I promise."

Zoë hurried inside, across the living room, into the bedroom, to the adjoining bath. It was empty; most of the guests were using the half bath near the kitchen. She flicked on the light and closed the door. The pain had stopped and she didn't really have to go to the bathroom, but she stayed there anyway, resting. In the mirror above the sink she looked haggard beneath her bonehead, violet grays showing under the skin like a plucked and pocky bird. She leaned closer, raising her chin a little to find the bristly hair. It was there, at the end of the jaw, sharp and dark as a wire. She opened the medicine cabinet, pawed through it until she found some tweezers. She lifted her head again and poked at her face with the metal tips, grasping and pinching and missing. Outside the door she could hear two people talking low. They had come into the bedroom and were discussing something. They were sitting on the bed. One of them giggled in a false way. She stabbed again at her chin, and it started to bleed a little. She pulled the skin tight along the jawbone, gripped the tweezers hard around what she hoped was the hair, and tugged. A tiny square of skin came away with it, but the hair remained, blood bright at the root of it. Zoë clenched her teeth. "Come on," she whispered. The couple outside in the bedroom were now telling stories, softly, and laughing. There was a bounce and squeak of mattress, and the sound of a chair being moved out of the way. Zoë aimed the tweezers carefully, pinched, then pulled gently away, and this time the hair came, too, with a slight twinge of pain and then a great flood of relief. "Yeah!" breathed Zoë. She grabbed some toilet paper and dabbed at her chin. It came away spotted with blood, and so she tore off some more and pressed hard until it stopped. Then she turned off the light and opened the door, to return to the party. "Excuse me," she said to the couple in the bedroom. They were the couple from the balcony, and they looked at her, a bit surprised. They had their arms around each other, and they were eating candy bars.

Earl was still out on the balcony, alone, and Zoë rejoined him there.

"Hi," she said. He turned around and smiled. He had straightened his costume out a bit, though all the secondary sex characteristics seemed slightly doomed, destined to shift and flip and zip around again any moment.

"Are you OK?" he asked. He had opened another beer and was chugging.

"Oh, yeah. I just had to go to the bathroom." She paused. "Actually I have been going to a lot of doctors recently."

"What's wrong?" asked Earl.

"Oh, probably nothing. But they're putting me through tests." She sighed. "I've had sonograms. I've had mammograms. Next week I'm going in for a candygram." He looked at her worriedly. "I've had too many gram words," she said.

"Here, I saved you these." He held out a napkin with two stuffed mushroom caps. They were cold and leaving oil marks on the napkin.

"Thanks," said Zoë, and pushed them both in her mouth. "Watch," she said, with her mouth full. "With my luck, it'll be a gallbladder operation."

Earl made a face. "So your sister's getting married," he said, changing the subject. "Tell me, really, what you think about love."

"*Love?*" Hadn't they done this already? "I don't know." She chewed thoughtfully and swallowed. "All right. I'll tell you what I think about love. Here is a love story. This friend of mine—"

"You've got something on your chin," said Earl, and he reached over to touch it.

"*What?*" said Zoë, stepping back. She turned her face away and grabbed at her chin. A piece of toilet paper peeled off it, like tape. "It's nothing," she said. "It's just—it's nothing."

Earl stared at her.

"At any rate," she continued, "this friend of mine was this award-winning violinist. She traveled all over Europe and won competitions; she made records, she gave concerts, she got famous. But she had no social life. So one day she threw herself at the feet of this conductor she had a terrible crush on. He picked her up, scolded her gently, and sent her back to her hotel room. After that she came home from Europe. She went back to her old hometown, stopped playing the violin, and took up with a local boy. This was in Illinois. He took her to some Big Ten bar every night to drink with his buddies from the team. He used to say things like 'Katrina here likes to play the violin,' and then he'd pinch her cheek. When she once suggested that they go home, he said, 'What, you think you're too famous for a place like this? Well, let me tell you something. You may think you're famous, but you're not *famous* famous.' Two famouses. 'No one here's ever heard of you.' Then he went up and bought a round of drinks for everyone but her. She got her coat, went home, and shot a gun through her head."

Earl was silent.

"That's the end of my love story," said Zoë.

"You're not at all like your sister," said Earl.

"Ho, really," said Zoë. The air had gotten colder, the wind singing minor and thick as a dirge.

"No." He didn't want to talk about love anymore. "You know, you should wear a lot of blue—blue and white—around your face. It would bring out your coloring." He reached an arm out to show her how the blue bracelet he was wearing might look against her skin, but she swatted it away.

"Tell me, Earl. Does the word *fag* mean anything to you?"

He stepped back, away from her. He shook his head in disbelief. "You know, I just shouldn't try to go out with career women. You're all stricken. A guy can really tell what life has done to you. I do better with women who have part-time jobs."

"Oh, yes?" said Zoë. She had once read an article entitled "Professional Women and the Demographics of Grief." Or no, it was a poem: *If there were a lake, the moonlight would dance across it in conniptions.* She remembered that line. But perhaps the title was "The Empty House: Aesthetics of Barrenness." Or maybe "Space Gypsies: Girls in Academe." She had forgotten.

Earl turned and leaned on the railing of the balcony. It was getting late. Inside, the party guests were beginning to leave. The sexy witches were already gone. "Live and learn," Earl murmured.

"Live and get dumb," replied Zoë. Beneath them on Lexington there were no cars, just the gold rush of an occasional cab. He leaned hard on his elbows, brooding.

"Look at those few people down there," he said. "They look like bugs. You know how bugs are kept under control? They're sprayed with bug hormones, female bug hormones. The male bugs get so crazy in the presence of this hormone, they're screwing everything in sight: trees, rocks—everything but female bugs. Population control. That's what's happening in this country," he said drunkenly. "Hormones sprayed around, and now men are screwing rocks. Rocks!"

In the back the Magic Marker line of his buttocks spread wide, a sketchy black on pink like a funnies page. Zoë came up, slow, from behind and gave him a shove. His arms slipped forward, off the railing, out over the city below. Beer spilled out of his bottle, raining twenty stories down to the street.

"Hey, what are you doing?!" he said, whipping around. He stood straight and readied and moved away from the railing, sidestepping Zoë. "What the *hell* are you doing?"

"Just kidding," she said. "I was just kidding." But he gazed at her, appalled and frightened, his Magic Marker buttocks turned away now toward all of downtown, a naked pseudo-woman with a blue bracelet at the wrist, trapped out on a balcony with—with *what? "Really, I was just kidding!"* Zoë shouted. The wind lifted the hair up off her head, skyward in spines behind the bone. If there were a lake, the moonlight would dance across it in conniptions. She smiled at him, and wondered how she looked.

ANDREA LEE

(1960–)

Lee grew up in suburban Philadelphia, her father a Baptist minister and civil rights activist, her mother a schoolteacher. She received her bachelor's and master's degrees from Harvard, worked at *The New Yorker*, and has published *Russian Journal* (1981), an account of her year in the Soviet Union—nominated for a National Book Award—and an autobiographical novel, *Sarah Phillips* (1984). *Interesting Women* (2002)—from which the following story comes—has been called "irresistible," *Sex and the City* for the international set, a collection of profound insight into the underlying struggles of gender, race and class that shape relationships worldwide: "Lee writes like a dream." She told an interviewer that it was Katherine Mansfield's "The Garden Party" (see pages 94–105) that first showed her the intensity of the short story form. "It can offer a sharp concentrated insight like a stiletto thrust." She lives in Turin, Italy, with her husband and two children.

Brothers and Sisters Around the World

"I took them around the point toward Dzamandzar," Michel tells me. "Those two little whores. Just ten minutes. They asked me for a ride when I was down on the beach bailing out the Zodiac. It was rough and I went too fast on purpose. You should have seen their titties bounce!"

He tells me this in French, but with a carefree lewdness that could be Roman. He is, in fact, half Italian, product of the officially French no man's land where the Ligurian Alps touch the Massif Central. In love, like so many of his Mediterranean compatriots, with boats, with hot blue seas, with dusky women, with the steamy belt of tropics that girdles the earth. We live above Cannes, in Mougins, where it is always sunny, but on vacation we travel the world to get hotter and wilder. Islands are what Michel prefers: in Asia, Oceania, Africa, the Caribbean, it doesn't matter. Any place where the people are the color of different grades of coffee, and mangoes plop in mushy heaps on the ground, and the reef fish are brilliant as a box of new crayons. On vacation Michel sheds his manicured ad-man image and with innocent glee sets about turning himself into a Eurotrash version of Tarzan. Bronzed muscles well in evidence, shark's tooth on a leather thong, fishing knife stuck into the waist of a threadbare pareu, and a wispy sun-streaked ponytail that he tends painstakingly along with a chin crop of Hollywood stubble.

He loves me for a number of wrong reasons connected with his dreams of hot islands. It makes no difference to him that I grew up in Massachusetts, wearing L. L. Bean boots more often than sandals; after eight years of marriage, he doesn't seem to see that what gives strength to the spine of an American black woman, however exotic she appears, is a steely Protestant core. A core that in its absolutism is curiously cold and Nordic. The fact is that I'm not crazy about the tropics, but Michel doesn't want to acknowledge that. Mysteriously, we continue to get along. In fact, our marriage is surprisingly robust, though at the time of our wedding, my mother, my sister, and my girlfriends all gave it a year. I some-times think the secret is that we don't know each other and never will. Both of us are lazy by nature, and that makes it convenient to hang on to the fantasies we conjured up back when we met in Milan: mine of the French gentleman-adventurer, and his of a pliant black goddess whose feelings accord with his. It's no surprise to me when Michel tries to share the ribald thoughts that run through the labyrinth of his Roman Catholic mind. He doubtless thought that I would get a kick out of hearing about his boat ride with a pair of African sluts.

Those girls have been sitting around watching us from under the mango tree since the day we rolled up from the airport to spend August in the house we bor-rowed from our friend Jean-Claude. Michel was driving Jean-Claude's car, a Cit-roën so rump-sprung from the unpaved roads that it moves like a tractor. Our four-year-old son, Lele, can drag his sneakers in red dust through the holes in the floor. The car smells of failure, like the house, which is built on an island off the northern coast of Madagascar, on a beach where a wide scalloped bay spreads like two blue wings, melting into the sky and the wild archipelago of lemur islands beyond. Behind the garden stretch fields of sugarcane and groves of silvery, arthritic-looking ylang-ylang trees, whose flowers lend a tang of Africa to French perfume.

The house is low and long around a grandiose veranda, and was once white-washed into an emblem of colonial vainglory; now the walls are the indetermi-nate color of damp, and the thinning palm thatch on the roof swarms with mice and geckos. It has a queenly housekeeper named Hadijah, whose perfect *pommes frites* and plates of crudités, like the dead bidet and dried-up tubes of Bain de Soleil in the bathroom, are monuments to Jean-Claude's ex-wife, who went back to Toulon after seeing a series of projects—a frozen-fish plant, a perfume com-pany, a small luxury hotel—swallowed up in the calm fireworks of the sunsets. Madagascar is the perfect place for a white fool to lose his money, Michel says. He and I enjoy the scent of dissolution in our borrowed house, fuck inventively in the big mildewed ironwood bed, sit in happiness in the sad, bottomed-out can-vas chairs on the veranda after a day of spearfishing, watching our son race in and out of herds of humpbacked zebu cattle on the beach.

The only problem for me has been those girls. They're not really whores, just local girls who dance at Bar Kariboo on Thursday nights and hang around the few French and Italian tourists, hoping to trade sex for a T-shirt, a hair clip. They don't know to want Ray-Bans yet; this is not the Caribbean.

I'm used to the women from the Comoros Islands who crowd onto the beach near the house, dressed up in gold bangles and earrings and their best lace-trimmed blouses. They clap and sing in circles for hours, jumping up to dance in pairs, wagging their backsides in tiny precise jerks, laughing and flashing gold teeth. They wrap themselves up in their good time in a way that intimidates me. And I've come to an understanding with the older women of the village, who come by to bring us our morning ration of zebu milk (we drink it boiled in coffee) or to barter with *rideaux Richelieu*, the beautiful muslin cutwork curtains that they embroider. They are intensely curious about me, *l'Américaine*, who looks not unlike one of them, but who dresses and speaks and acts like a foreign madame, and is clearly married to the white man, not just a casual concubine. They ask me for medicine, and if I weren't careful they would clean out my supply of Advil and Bimaxin. They go crazy over Lele, whom they call *bébé métis*—the mixed baby. I want to know all about them, their still eyes, their faces of varying colors that show both African and Indonesian blood, as I want to know everything about this primeval chunk of Africa floating in the Indian Ocean, with its bottle-shaped baobabs and strange tinkling music, the *sega*, which is said to carry traces of tunes from Irish sailors.

But the girls squatting under the mango tree stare hard at me whenever I sit out on the beach or walk down to the water to swim. Then they make loud comments in Malagasy, and burst out laughing. It's juvenile behavior, and I can't help sinking right down to their level and getting provoked. They're probably about eighteen years old, both good-looking; one with a flat brown face and the long straight shining hair that makes some Madagascar women resemble Polynesians; the other darker, with the tiny features that belong to the coastal people called Merina, and a pile of kinky hair tinted reddish. Both are big-titted, as Michel pointed out, the merchandise spilling out of a pair of Nouvelles Frontières T-shirts that they must have got from a tour-group leader. Some days they have designs painted on their faces in yellow sulfur clay. They stare at me, and guffaw and stretch and give their breasts a competitive shake. Sometimes they hoot softly or whistle when I appear.

My policy has been to ignore them, but today they've taken a step ahead, got a rise, however ironic, out of my man. It's a little triumph. I didn't see the Zodiac ride, but through the bathroom window I saw them come back. I was shaving my legs—waxing never lasts long enough in the tropics. Squealing and laughing, they floundered out of the rubber dinghy, patting their hair, settling their T-shirts, re-tying the cloth around their waists. One of them blew her nose through her fingers into the shallow water. The other said something to Michel, and he laughed and patted her on the backside. Then, arrogantly as two Cleopatras, they strode across the hot sand and took up their crouch under the mango tree. A pair of brown *netsuke*. Waiting for my move.

So, finally, I act. Michel comes sauntering inside to tell me, and after he tells me I make a scene. He's completely taken aback; he's gotten spoiled since we've been married, used to my American cool, which can seem even cooler than French nonchalance. He thought I was going to react the way I used to when I was still modeling and he used to flirt with some of the girls I was working with, some of the bimbos who weren't serious about their careers. That is, that I was going to chuckle, display complicity, even excitement. Instead I yell, say he's damaged my prestige among the locals, say that things are different here. The words seem to be flowing up into my mouth from the ground beneath my feet. He's so surprised that he just stands there with his blue eyes round and his mouth a small *o* in the midst of that Indiana Jones stubble.

Then I hitch up my Soleiado bikini, and march outside to the mango tree. *"Va-t'en!"* I hiss to Red Hair, who seems to be top girl of the duo. "Go away! *Ne parle plus avec mon homme!"*

The two of them scramble to their feet, but they don't seem to be going anywhere, so I slap the one with the straight hair. Except for once, when I was about ten, in a fight with my cousin Brenda, I don't believe I've ever seriously slapped anyone. This, on the scale of slaps, is half-assed, not hard. In that second of contact I feel the strange smoothness of her cheek and an instantaneous awareness that my hand is just as smooth. An electric current seems to connect them. A red light flickers in the depths of the girl's dark eyes, like a computer blinking on, and then, without saying anything to me, both girls scuttle off down the beach, talking loudly to each other, and occasionally looking back at me. I make motions as if I'm shooing chickens. *"Allez-vous-en!"* I screech. Far off down the beach, they disappear into the palms.

Then I go and stretch out in the water, which is like stretching out in blue air. I take off my bikini top and let the equatorial sun print my shadow on the white sand below, where small white fish graze. I feel suddenly calm, but at the same time my mind is working very fast. "My dear, who invited you to come halfway across the world and slap somebody?" I ask myself in the ultra-reasonable tones of my mother, the school guidance counselor. Suddenly I remember another summer on yet another island. This was in Indonesia, a few years ago, when we were exploring the back roads of one of the Moluccas. The driver was a local kid who didn't speak any language we spoke, and was clearly gay. A great-looking kid with light brown skin pitted with a few acne scars, and neat dreadlocks that would have looked stylish in Manhattan. A Princess Di T-shirt, and peeling red nail polish. When we stopped at a waterfall, and Michel the Adventurer went off to climb the lava cliffs, I sat down on a flat rock with the driver, whipped out my beauty case, and painted his nails shocking pink. He jumped when I first grabbed his hand, but when he saw what I was up to he gave me a huge ecstatic grin, and then closed his eyes. And there it was: paradise. The waterfall, the jungle, and that beautiful kid with his long fingers lying in my hand. It was Michel who made a fuss that time, jealous of something he couldn't even define. But I had the same feeling I do now, of acting on instinct and on target. The right act. At the right moment.

"Mama, what did you do?" Lele comes running up to me from where he has been squatting naked on the beach, playing with two small boys from the village. His legs and backside and little penis are covered with sand. I see the boys staring after him, one holding a toy they've been squabbling over: a rough wooden model of a truck, without wheels, tied with a piece of string to a stick. "Ismail says you hit a lady."

Word has already spread along the beach, which is like a stage where a different variety show goes on every hour of the day. The set acts are the tides, which determine the movements of fishing boats, pirogues, Zodiacs, and sailboats. There is always action on the sand: women walk up and down with bundles on their heads; bands of ragged children dig clams at low tide, or launch themselves into the waves at high tide to surf with a piece of old timber; yellow dogs chase chickens and fight over shrimp shells; palm branches crash down on corrugated-iron roofs; girls with lacy dresses and bare sandy shanks parade to Mass; the little mosque opens and shuts its creaky doors; boys play soccer, kicking a plastic water bottle; babies howl; sunburnt tourist couples argue and reconcile. Gossip flashes up and down with electronic swiftness.

I sit up in the water and grab Lele, and kiss him all over while he splashes and struggles to get away. "Yes, that's right," I tell him. It's the firm, didactic voice I use when we've turned off the Tele-tubbies videos and I am playing the ideal parent. "I did hit a lady," I say. "She needed hitting." I, the mother who instructs her cross-cultural child in tolerance and nonviolence. Lele has a picture book called *Brothers and Sisters Around the World*, full of illustrations of cookie-cutter figures of various colors, holding hands across continents. All people belong to one family, it teaches. All oceans are the same ocean.

Michel, who has watched the whole scene, comes and tells me that in all his past visits to the island he's never seen anything like it. He's worried. The women fight among themselves, or they fight with their men for sleeping with the tourists, he says. But no foreign woman has ever got mixed up with them. He talks like an anthropologist about loss of face and vendetta. "We might get run out of here," he says nervously.

I tell him to relax, that absolutely nothing will happen. Where do I get this knowledge? It has sifted into me from the water, the air. So, as we planned, we go off spearfishing over by Nosy Komba, where the coral grows in big pastel poufs like furniture in a Hollywood bedroom of the fifties. We find a den of rock lobster and shoot two, and take them back to Jean-Claude's house for Hadijah to cook. Waiting for the lobster, we eat about fifty small oysters the size of mussels and shine flashlights over the beach in front of the veranda, which is crawling with crabs. Inside, Lele is snoring adenoidally under a mosquito net. The black sky above is alive with falling stars. Michel keeps looking at me and shaking his head.

Hadijah comes out bearing the lobster magnificently broiled with vanilla sauce. To say she has presence is an understatement. She got married when she was thirteen, and is now, after eight children, an important personage, the matriarch of a vast and prosperous island clan. She and I have got along fine ever since she realized that I wasn't going to horn in on her despotic rule over Jean-Claude's house, or say anything about the percentage she skims off the marketing money. She has a closely braided head and is as short and solid as a boulder—on the spectrum of Madagascar skin colors well toward the darkest. This evening she is showing off her wealth by wearing over her pareu a venerable Guns N' Roses T-shirt. She puts down the lobster, sets her hands on her hips, and looks at me, and my heart suddenly skips a beat. Hers, I realize, is the only opinion I care about. "Oh, Madame," she says, flashing me a wide smile and shaking her finger indulgently, as if I'm a child who has been up to mischief. I begin breathing again. "Oh, Madame!"

"Madame has a quick temper," Michel says in a placating voice, and Hadijah throws her head back and laughs till the Guns N' Roses logo shimmies.

"She is right!" she exclaims. *"Madame a raison!* She's a good wife!"

Next morning our neighbor PierLuigi pulls up to the house in his dust-covered Renault pickup. PierLuigi is Italian, and back in Italy has a title and a castle. Here he lives in a bamboo hut when he is not away leading a shark-hunting safari to one of the wild islands a day's sail to the north. He is the real version of what Michel pretends to be: a walking, talking character from a boys' adventure tale, with a corrugated scar low down on one side where a hammerhead once snatched a mouthful. The islanders respect him, and bring their children to him for a worm cure he's devised from crushed papaya seeds. He can bargain down the tough Indian merchants in the market, and he sleeps with pretty tourists and island girls impartially. Nobody knows how many kids he has fathered on the island.

"I hear your wife is mixing in local politics," he calls from the truck to Michel, while looking me over with those shameless eyes that have got so many women in trouble. PierLuigi is sixty years old and has streaks of white in his hair, but he is still six feet four and the best-looking man I have ever seen in my life. "Brava," he says to me. "Good for you, my dear. The local young ladies very often need things put in perspective, but very few of our lovely visitors know how to do it on their own terms."

After he drives off, Michel looks at me with new respect. "I can't say you don't have guts," he says later. Then, "You really must be in love with me."

In the afternoon after our siesta, when I emerge onto the veranda from Jean-Claude's shuttered bedroom, massaging Phyto Plage into my hair, smelling on my skin the pleasant odor of sex, I see—as I somehow expected—that the two girls are back under the mango tree. I walk out onto the burning sand, squinting against the glare that makes every distant object a flat black silhouette, and approach them for the second time. I don't think that we're in for another round, yet I feel my knees take on a wary pugilistic springiness. But as I get close, the straight-haired girl says, *"Bonjour, Madame."*

The formal greeting conveys an odd intimacy. It is clear that we are breathing the same air, now, that we have taken each other's measure. Both girls look straight at me, no longer bridling. All three of us know perfectly well that the man—my European husband—was just an excuse, a playing field for our curiosity. The curiosity of sisters separated before birth and flung by the caprice of history half a world away from each other. Now in this troublesome way our connection has been established, and between my guilt and my dawning affection I suspect that I'll never get rid of these two. Already in my mind is forming an exasperating vision of the gifts I know I'll have to give them: lace underpants; Tampax; music cassettes; body lotion—all of them extracted from me with the tender ruthlessness of family members anywhere. And then what? What, after all these years, will there be to say? Well, the first thing to do is answer. *"Bonjour, Mesdemoiselles,"* I reply, in my politest voice.

And because I can't think of anything else, I smile and nod at them and walk into the water, which as always in the tropics is as warm as blood. The whole time I swim, the girls are silent, and they don't take their eyes off me.

"Christmas Night 1962" copyright © The Ontario Review Inc. Reprinted by permission of John Hawkins & Associates, Inc.

"Sugar Daddy" copyright © Angela Carter 1983. Reproduced by permission of the Estate of Angela Carter c/o Rogers, Coleridge & White Ltd., 10 Powis Mews, London W11 1JN.

"I Go Back to May 1937" and "Topography" from *The Gold Cell* by Sharon Olds, copyright © 1987 by Sharon Olds. Used by permission of Alfred A. Knopf, a division of Random House, Inc.

"Bathing the New Born" from *The Wellspring* by Sharon Olds, copyright © 1996 by Sharon Olds. Used by permission of Alfred A. Knopf, a division of Random House, Inc.

"The Civil Rights Movement: What Good Was It?" from *In Search of Our Mothers' Gardens: Womanist Prose*, copyright © 1967 by Alice Walker, reprinted by permission of Harcourt, Inc.

Copyright © 1981 by Leslie Marmon Silko. "Lullaby" reprinted from *Storyteller* by Leslie Marmon Silko, published by Seaver Books, New York, New York.

From *Woman Hollering Creek*. Copyright © 1991 by Sandra Cisneros. Published by Vintage Books, a division of Random House, Inc., New York and originally in hardcover by Random House, Inc. Reprinted by permission of Susan Bergholz Literary Services, New York. All rights reserved.

Copyright © 1998 by Gish Jen, from the collection *Who's Irish? Stories* published by Alfred A. Knopf in 1999. First published in *The New Yorker*. Reprinted by permission of the author.

"You're Ugly, Too" from *Like Life* by Lorrie Moore, copyright © 1990 by Lorrie Moore. Used by permission of Alfred A. Knopf, a division of Random House, Inc.

"Brothers and Sisters Around the World" from *Interesting Women* by Andrea N. Lee, copyright © 2002 by Andrea N. Lee. Used by permission of Random House, Inc.